This volume, richly illustrated with clinical examples, explores the curative power of the intersubjective analytic encounter from the vertex of post-Bionian field theory. In so doing, it offers psychoanalysts of all levels of experience a pragmatic, clinical metapsychology of psychic process and the analytic encounter and demonstrates the centrality of transformations in dreaming and the value of the oneiric model of the mind.

— **Howard B. Levine, MD,** Editor-in-Chief, The Routledge
Wilfred Bion Studies Book Series

Antonino Ferro, one of the most brilliant psychoanalytic thinkers of his time brings us directly into the heart of the psychoanalytic encounter, this time accompanied by a stellar list of contributors. Theoretically astute and clinically inspiring, *Psychoanalytic Practice* offers the reader a vivid and clear understanding of innovative Italian Psychoanalysis inspired by the later work of Bion on dreaming, reverie, and affect. This joins the ranks of Ferro's most important contributions.

— **Galit Atlas, Ph.D,** NYU Postdoctoral program for Psychotherapy
and Psychoanalysis, Author of *The Enigma of Desire:
Sex, Longing and Belonging in Psychoanalysis*

Psychoanalytic Practice Today

Psychoanalytic Practice Today offers the reader a good understanding of the school of thought inspired by the late work of Wilfred R. Bion. The contributors share a belief in the curative power of the analytic encounter and in the capacity of the human mind to develop from the encounter with a mind capable of reverie, dreaming and thinking. The multitude of vignettes presented emphasise the necessity of the emotional involvement of the analyst with his or her patients for improvement to take place.

The book is divided in two parts: 'Psychopathology' and 'Emotions and Feelings'. The first part adapts a more classic description of psychiatric disorders by diagnostic criteria, from neuroses to psychoses and including depression and borderline states. The second part of the book takes a closer look at specific clinical manifestations of basic emotions such as anger, surprise, sadness and more complex ones such as jealousy, abandonment and betrayal. The common thread is represented by the central place of dreaming in the psychoanalytic field as a tool to understand these clinical manifestations, and to allow for their psychic representation as an emotional experience.

The contributions together offer a varied introduction to current ideas that are growing increasingly interesting to English speaking readers, with a sufficient character of originality, irreverence and creativity that bears witness to the maturity of Italian psychoanalysis. *Psychoanalytic Practice Today* will offer new ideas to the practicing psychoanalyst and psychodynamic psychotherapist.

Antonino Ferro is a training analyst in the Italian Psychoanalytic Society, the American Psychoanalytic Association and the International Psychoanalytical Association. He is the current president of Pavia's Psychoanalytic Centre. He received the Sigourney Award in 2007.

Psychoanalytic Practice Today

A Post-Bionian Introduction to Psychopathology, Affect and Emotions

Edited by Antonino Ferro

Routledge
Taylor & Francis Group

LONDON AND NEW YORK

First published 2020
by Routledge
2 Park Square, Milton Park, Abingdon, Oxon OX14 4RN

and by Routledge
52 Vanderbilt Avenue, New York, NY 10017

Routledge is an imprint of the Taylor & Francis Group, an informa business

This book is a translation of a work previously published in Italian by
Carocci Editore as *La clinica psicanalitica oggi* (2016).

All chapters translated by Adam Elgar except chapter 10 translated by
Giuseppe Civitarese and chapter 13 translated by Gina Atkinson.

Trademark notice: Product or corporate names may be trademarks
or registered trademarks, and are used only for identification and
explanation without intent to infringe.

British Library Cataloguing-in-Publication Data
A catalogue record for this book is available from the British Library

Library of Congress Cataloging-in-Publication Data
Names: Ferro, Antonino, 1947– editor.
Title: Psychoanalytic practice today : a post-Bionian introduction to
    psychopathology, affect and emotions / edited by Antonino Ferro.
    Other titles: Clinica psicanalitica oggi. English.
Description: Abingdon, Oxon ; New York, NY : Routledge, 2019. |
    Includes bibliographical references and index.
Identifiers: LCCN 2019011793 (print) | LCCN 2019013015 (ebook) |
    ISBN 9780429288616 (Master) | ISBN 9781000021998 (Adobe) |
    ISBN 9781000022223 (Mobipocket) | ISBN 9781000022452 (ePub) |
    ISBN 9780367137083 (hardback : alk. paper) | ISBN 9780367137090
    (pbk. : alk. paper) | ISBN 9780429288616 (ebk)
Subjects: | MESH: Bion, Wilfred R. (Wilfred Ruprecht), 1897–1979. |
    Psychoanalytic Therapy | Mental Disorders—therapy | Affective
    Symptoms—therapy | Psychoanalytic Theory
Classification: LCC RC454.4 (ebook) | LCC RC454.4 (print) |
    NLM WM 460.6 | DDC 616.89—dc23
LC record available at https://lccn.loc.gov/2019011793

ISBN: 978-0-367-13708-3 (hbk)
ISBN: 978-0-367-13709-0 (pbk)
ISBN: 978-0-429-28861-6 (ebk)

Typeset in Times New Roman
by Apex CoVantage, LLC

MIX
Paper from
responsible sources
FSC™ C013985

Printed in the United Kingdom
by Henry Ling Limited

Contents

Emotions and feelings   161

8 **Abandonment**   163
   ANTONINO FERRO

9 **On the feeling of exclusion**   168
   MAURIZIO COLLOVÀ

   9.1 We are a crossroads of emotions and feelings 168
   9.2 What are we being excluded from? 169
        9.2.1 Sara and the recovery of a retro-perspective 170
        9.2.2 From missing crib syndrome to the "ripped-off" crib 171
   9.3 At the origin of the bi-personal 173
   9.4 The experience of exclusion in vivo 174
        9.4.1 The feeling of exclusion in a session 174
   9.5 Opposite declensions of exclusion 176
        9.5.1 The Family 177
        9.5.2 Fanny and Alexander 178
   9.6 The disappearance of the mind 179
        9.6.1 Conversation with the mother 179
   *9.7 Ogden's napkin. Exclusion as a "collapse of the
         dialectic of experience" 180*
   9.8 Conclusions 182

10 **Rage and shame**   185
    GIUSEPPE CIVITARESE

    10.1 Characters who express rage 186
         10.1.1 The lipless 187
         10.1.2 The time of the decision 188
         10.1.3 Green with rage 189
         10.1.4 The sense of justice 189
         10.1.5 The self-feeding effect 190
         10.1.6 Full moon 192
         10.1.7 Impotence 193
         10.1.8 Shame 194
         10.1.9 Slow rage and the art of exaggeration 197
    10.2 Shame as the photo-like negative of rage 198
    10.3 Curing rage 201

Contributors

Giuseppe Civitarese is a training and supervising analyst in the Italian Psycho-analytic Society and the International Psychoanalytical Association. He is a member of the American Psychoanalytic Association and a past Editor of the *Rivista di Psicoanalisi*.

Maurizio Collovà is a full member of the Italian Psychoanalytic Society and the International Psychoanalytical Association. He is the Scientific Secretary of the Pavia Psychoanalytic Centre.

Antonino Ferro is a training and supervising analyst in the Italian Psychoana-lytic Society, the American psychoanalytic Association and the International Psychoanalytic Association. He received the Sigourney Award in 2007 and is a former President of the Italian Psychoanalytic Society. He is the President of the Pavia Psychoanalytic Centre.

Giovanni Foresti is a training and supervising analyst in the Italian Psychoana-lytic Society and the International Psychoanalytical Association. He is a mem-ber of the Scientific Committee for the NODO Group (Torino) and for OPUS (London).

Mauro Manica, psychiatrist and psychoanalyst, is a full member of the Italian Psychoanalytic Society and the International Psychoanalytic Association. He was the recipient of the Tycho Award.

Fulvio Mazzacane is a training and supervising analyst in the Italian Psychoana-lytic Society and full member of the International Psychoanalytic Association.

Elena Molinari is a psychoanalyst of the Italian Psychoanalytic Society and an International Psychoanalytic Association member. She began her profes-sional life working as a pediatrician. Since 2000, she has been in private analytic practice, treating both adults and children. She also teaches child neuropsychiatry for the undergraduate course in art therapy at the Academy of Fine Arts of Brera, Milan. She is a past Editor of the SPI journal *Rivista di Psicoanalisi*.

Luca Nicoli, psychologist and psychoanalyst, is a member of the Italian Society of Psychoanalysis and International Psychoanalytic Association. He is co-author of the book *The New Analyst's Guide to the Galaxy.*

Violet Pietrantonio is a clinical psychologist and member of the Italian Psychoanalytic Society and International Psychoanalytic Association.

Acknowledgements

The editor wishes to thank the contributors for their thoughtful and creative contributions, Adam Elgar for his sensitive translation, and Gillian Jarvis for her excellent work on this project.

Part I

Psychopathologies

Chapter 1

Anorexias and dyschronias

Antonino Ferro

We know that there are a variety of defence mechanisms against very primitive anxieties.

For purely illustrative purposes, we can list the following:

1   Modes of elimination:

    a   repression;
    b   splitting;
    c   evacuations.

The last of these can occur

- in the body: psychosomatic illnesses;
- by inverting the functioning of sense organs: hallucinations;
- in the body social: transformations in hallucinosis, characteropathies, and criminal behaviour.

2   Modes of "staunching and management" without large-scale evacuation (immediately perceptible):

    a   Hibernation: that mode in which the field is put to sleep, sedated: by boredom, for example. It is like a circus in which the lion-tamers and animals, especially the fierce ones, have been put to sleep. This comes about through particular communicative strategies: for example, a discourse based on a predominance of coordinate clauses (which form a kind of open plain that tends to grow misty in the absence of any alternation with the landscape of subordinate clauses) or through hypnagogic projective identifications. In these modes, emotions end up in hibernation.

    b   Bonsaification: this consists in the miniaturising of emotions, transforming them into mini-emotions with no force; it would be like turning an oak tree into a series of bonsai oaks. In this way, worlds of micro-emotions are created which find narrative voice in worn-out, cut-price stories where everything is made saccharine, free from conflict, and free from any kind of passion.

c   Computerisation: this mode is not very different. Violent emotions are turned into computer games and role plays. It is not unlike the technique used by Quentin Tarantino in *Kill Bill*: whenever the emotions at work are too violent, the scenes with actors are turned into animated cartoons, losing their overwhelming, bloody violence.

d   Glaciation: this is a mode in which freezing or petrification are used to extinguish emotions that are feared because of their indigestibility. When the bulls are running in Pamplona, if we lower the temperature to many tens of degrees below zero, or if the bulls are turned into statues, the problem of the uncontainability of these emotions is (apparently) solved.

3   Predominantly spatial modes:

a   quashing;
b   two-dimensionalising;
c   linearisation.

These modes bring into play the defence mechanisms associated with the autistic spectrum, including those of Asperger's syndrome. One example is Chekhov's extraordinary story *The Exclamation Mark*. The story tells of an employee who has spent years writing or transcribing dossiers, always carrying out his work conscientiously. One day, at a social event, he is taxed with the inadequacy of his academic qualifications, given that all he does is edit or copy documents. On his return home, he cannot sleep because all the thousands, or tens of thousands, of immaculately written documents are running through his mind, and he remembers all the possible rules for commas, full stops, semicolons, even question marks.

But his tossing and turning stops dead when he is confronted by the exclamation mark.

He has no recollection of ever having used it. How does it work? He wakes his wife, who went all the way through college, and she proudly tells him she knows the whole grammar book by heart, explaining that the exclamation mark is used when you want to emphasise something or indicate an emotion: anger, joy, good fortune; any emotion, in short.

It seems clear enough to him how it should be used in a letter, but how would you do so in an official document? Once again he runs through the thousands of documents he's written with not one exclamation mark in any of them, he's sure of it.

The story highlights how a routine, factual existence is possible with everything just as it should be, with every i dotted and every t crossed, without ever feeling any emotion; anger, joy, jealousy, or anything else.

At this point, after his sleepless night, the story's protagonist decides to see his head of department, and when he comes to sign the admissions book, after writing his name, Yefim Perekladin, he adds three exclamation marks. As Chekhov concludes, "as he wrote those three marks, he felt delight and indignation, he was joyful and he seethed with rage. 'Take that, take that!' he muttered, pressing down hard on the pen."

Sometimes, if they become firmly established in the long term, these defence mechanisms (and sometimes others) take the form of a thorough-going pathology. In this connection, I would like to address the subject of anorexia and the difficulty of taking on the ephemeral nature of our existence: in other words, the difficulty or impossibility of accepting the linearity of time, thereby putting an incredible multiplicity of defences into play: atempo-ralities or dyschronias.

I put these two modes together because one predominantly concerns space, the other time.

1.1 Anorexias

Anorexia is often considered in terms of misperception: patients see themselves as fat, swollen, overweight, not the way they really are: thin, underweight, emaciated.

I think we should reverse the viewpoint and accept that the anorexic uses ultrasound to view her or himself. That is, they see gigantic emotions which they try to compress, attempting to starve them so as not to feel overwhelmed by them.

There is no end to the possible metaphors: it is as if they looked like chihuahuas and instead saw an enormous pit-bull lurking behind them with its fangs at the ready. In other words, they know they are dealing with a tangle of emotions which they are afraid will savage them and tear them apart.

The illusion is that by denying the pit-bull food, they can "dachshundify" or "chihuahuaise" it; that it might be possible to make violent passions containable and manageable.

An anorexic girl dreamed that, by taking some bricks out of a wall, she arrived at the start of the French Revolution just as the Bastille was being stormed.

She smelled burning and felt a sense of guilt. A seemingly good girl, on the other side of the wall she had access to this revolutionary world full of fire where everything was burning to ashes, which made her feel guilty.

Then she saw a "terrible dragon" in a Rorschach blot.

So here is the pit-bull I was talking about: the problem is how to alphabetise this mass of undifferentiated proto-emotions and transform them into their com-ponents so that the "proto-emotional lava" can become tolerable emotions.

The "dragon", this magmatic proto-emotional nucleus, would have to find other ways of being managed.

But let's go back to anorexia, where the strategy in operation was described by another patient who expressed her hatred for hot places like Naples and her love of cold places like Germany where every one queues obediently, maybe because the cold makes them calmer: there is also the idea that a gla-ciation of Vesuvian emotions could be helpful to those who are hungrier than

Figure 1.1 Distortion of an internal gaze

the inmates of a concentration camp, the idea of a dream where "violent and explosive young people" were interned and made obedient, giving them just enough food for them to survive while having no strength left to express their own violence.

Perhaps Figure 1.1 expresses this way of conceiving of anorexia: the subject perceives, "sees" the giant mass of proto-emotions which usually escapes every gaze that doesn't use ultrasound. It shows how ultrasound vision enables one to see what generally escapes normal sight.

Obviously bulimic behaviour is simply the other side of the coin: it would be like placating the Hound of the Baskervilles by stuffing it with food and putting it to sleep. Let's remember Polyphemus, who falls deeply asleep after eating and drinking too much. So, if in anorexia there is the illusion of "taking away the energy" of emotions, in bulimia it is one of putting otherwise unmanageable emotions into hibernation.

The analyst's task will be, with the patient, to dream the "fiery dragon" which is terrorising her and has no other way of being managed.

In many of his drawings, Fellini vividly portrays excessive emotions overflowing inadequate containers which have been left flattened by them (Figure 1.2).

Or else he shows the claustro-hypercontaining solution for emotions that would otherwise overflow.

We'll look now at some examples using fragments from clinical histories; what can be managed by the anorexic mechanism (the "chihuahuaisation" of the pitbull) can alternatively be managed by "computerisation" (or "bonsaification" if we prefer).

Ermanno is seriously school-phobic and dependent on his computer. We are faced with two scenarios or sets of over-intense emotions we are afraid of and want to avoid: not going to the place where emotions are activated – school – or emotions miniaturised into very low voltages (micro-voltages of information technology):

School 20,000 volts – Computer 0.25 volts

Figure 1.2 Drawing by Federico Fellini

ERMANNO AND HIS VIRTUAL STRUGGLE

Ermanno is unable to go to school because for him it's Pamplona or the Plaza de Toros, where he is persecuted by rampant emotions. Instead he plays "video war games" in which he can miniaturise all violence.

Computerised miniaturisation is, like anorexia, an attempt to de-terrorise Pamplona by not giving any more food to the bulls/emotions by which one is afraid of being overwhelmed.

Ermanno either has phobias or he plays with his computer: he is a patient who alternates two kinds of functioning.

After a few months of analysis, he brings the following dream: he wakes up in bed . . . full of anxiety . . . he bursts into flames . . . his arms melt . . . a dream which seems to be a good description of how he "catches fire". The igniting of anger and jealousy, of passions which he will need to learn to contain and metabolise.

Some time later he has another dream in which the zoo is short of keepers, and so the animals will have to be put to sleep with tranquillisers, and during this period the sessions start to be full of boredom which is evoked by calm speech full of parentheses and asides, and asides within asides, a narrative mode with no bridges or traffic lights, nothing but coordinate clauses, one inside another.

Hibernation is induced less by the contents than by the mode; it is a foggy plain without hills, rivers or mountains. But when the fog lifts, the "fierce animals" become clearly visible.

VALERIA AND THE FEAR OF "ALIENS"

Valeria has been self-harming, an act in which it is not hard to see the attempt/ desire to eliminate alien aspects of herself: that Alien which it is impossible to eliminate or split off is, thus, by means of an illusion, transformed from an uncontainable pit-bull into a chihuahua which no longer frightens her.

Obviously the bulimic strategy is simply the mirror image of this: giving the mastiff so much to eat that it becomes stupefied and inert. It hardly matters what proto-emotions the mastiff is made of.

Before the explosion of anorexic symptomatology, Valeria had tried to "hide" her knot of proto-emotions by keeping busy with dance, music, and schoolwork. She begins therapy where she shows herself extremely eager to please her analyst in the sessions, and then sends him surprising text messages saying "You're a bastard" or "I'd rather be ill."

During therapy she will say, "I can't look at myself," "I can't wash myself," "I feel sick if I put on weight," "I really want to lose weight," and later she will even be able to say "I'm afraid of the emotions I feel": her symptoms become evidence of the dialectic between truth and lies, according to which of her identities is predominant at that moment.

CLAUDIA AND THE LIGHT OF ANALYSIS

Claudia is also an anorexic girl who sees herself as fat and ugly, and so has been subjecting herself to a starvation diet for a long time.

After a long period of analysis, she brings this dream: she is with two friends, a girl and a boy, and the boy suddenly turns into a terrible creature, a werewolf; in the second part of the dream, the girl lights a match and its light and smoke act as a cure, a sort of antidote which can neutralise even a ravening beast.

The light and smoke of analysis seem to exorcise the aspects that are feared as diabolical. After a few months Claudia dreams she is in a meadow, and has got better at riding her pony, which takes her to an open-air concert in the country. The ferocious beast has been transformed into a pony, and something disastrous and devouring into something vital which takes her to a concert, an emotional music she has never experienced before.

1.2 Atemporalities (dyschronias)

Before I can attempt to disentangle them, I would like to put together all those situations in which it is impossible to accept the passing of time with all that entails.

The prototype could be what Elliott Jaques brilliantly described as "midlife crisis", a crisis which few of us escape and which is located in the third decade of life. A classic example could be the incipit of the *Divine Comedy*: "In the middle of our life's journey, I found myself in a dark wood, where the right path was lost" and it will take dozens of cantos "to see the stars again", in the double sense, I would say, of leaving the infernal tunnel of depression and being able to come back to life and bear pain.

Now, with the lengthening of middle age, I prefer to speak of a "crisis of the zip years" which unfolds every ten years and, after a certain age, as often as every five years.

We can see a possible series of mechanisms for avoiding these crises and, above all, the depressive component and the mourning which they entail.

Some of the antidepressant mechanisms used are the familiar ones:

- mania,
- negation,
- denial,
- excitation,
- eroticisation,
- compulsive buying,
- compulsive gambling, and
- bulimia.

A lady who has reached the age of 45 devotes every weekend to what she calls "my little celebrations": tranquillising herself with binge-drinking and junk food which seem to challenge and stifle the idea of mourning the passage of time. In the film *Song for Marion* by Paul Andrew Williams, when Marion receives the diagnosis of a terminal and incurable tumour, her doctor tells her without cynicism, but with tact and extremely good sense, to go home and "eat chips and ice cream, as much as you want." Maybe chips and ice cream should be capable all our lives of dosing us into accepting the linearity of time. We see an especially apt example in the film *The Blue Angel*, or better still in Heinrich Mann's book *Professor Unrat*, such a frequent phenomenon that it should be given the name "Unrat's syndrome". A teacher at the local grammar school in a small German town is hopelessly in love with a cheeky young showgirl who gives him the illusion of rediscovering his youth, the emotions and vivid colour of youth compared to the gloom of depression tied to his sense of time's passing. This will bring Professor Unrat to ruin after the doses of stimulant are increased until they resemble an orgiastic organisation as an antidote to the pain of mourning which he was incapable of facing.

On reaching the age of fifty, Mario, an extraordinarily talented architect, with no warning to himself or to others, leaves his wife and teenage children, and launches into a series of relationships with transvestites.

If the weight of depression is too great, all kinds of lifeguards/analgesics are employed to avoid plunging into catastrophic grief. It is just that, as in Aesop's fable of the "Ass and the Salt", we need to know what kind of load is being carried: if it's salt, this will dissolve as we cross the river of the crisis; if it's sponges, the absorption of water will inevitably increase the burden.

This theme, one that is quintessential to our sense of ourselves as Westerners, has been exorcised in many ways, addressed by Goethe in *Faust*, by Mozart in

Don Giovanni, and fundamentally by religions which promise that real life is the afterlife.

If we need painkillers, they will work as long as we take the emotional cost into account and understand what affective and metaphorical stores are being drawn on.

This is different from what happens to Professor Richard Wanley in Fritz Lang's film, *The Woman in the Window*. The protagonist goes to his club for his usual drink. We see him get up from his armchair, leave the club – it's now very late – and pause to admire a portrait of a very beautiful woman. Suddenly he hears a woman's voice asking him for a light; he turns and sees the woman from the portrait, perhaps the model who had posed for it. This leads to an intense passion which comes to dominate Wanley's life, causing him to slip further and further into a story of disruptive emotions made of sexuality, betrayal, and revenge, which leads to his being accused of murder and seemingly bound for prison.

It is only at this point that the viewer realises he has been watching a dream, after which Wanley wakes, gets up from his armchair, and leaves the club. Then we see him admire the painting again, which really is on display in the window of an antique shop, and the woman in the portrait appears alongside him asking for a light; at which our hero flees in terror at the thought of what would follow. It is interesting that two well-known psychoanalysts have taken opposite points of view about this: one took the side of the hero as someone able to dream his "midlife crisis" with all its possible consequences, but without acting them out; the other emphasised the protagonist's emotional "cowardice" as he retreats from the strong emotions knocking on his door and thus prevents an existential turning point, one which might not necessarily have been negative.

What happens to Dr Isak Borg in Ingmar Bergman's *Wild Strawberries* is different again. Here the protagonist is an old physician who has to go and receive a medal for long service in his profession after a night in which he dreams of a clock with no hands and then of his own funeral. He takes a sort of trip down memory lane, finding significant places from his life and accepting the finiteness of the human journey and human existence.

Another way to present a dyschronia may be by trying to play a board game going backwards through as many squares as possible; we have many ways of doing this, from plastic surgery to the most varied use of prostheses, going far beyond the antidepressant modes mentioned earlier: from eroticisation to compulsive play, to various kinds of "excitatory little celebrations", extreme sports, to every possible strongly adrenalinising situation.

It is not uncommon for us to witness these withdrawals in relation to specific existential turning points: a typical example is a man falling in love with a much younger woman shortly before his marriage, so as to avoid a significant existential turning point; or the less frequent situation in which someone confesses, the day before the graduation ceremony, to having taken no exams.

Every existential transition is a fault line which may start to vibrate, creating emotional earthquakes that we must simply watch as they play out, which may lead to our rediscovering the passage of time, a "reculer pour mieux sauter", as the French say, or else staying as long as possible trapped in an atemporal bubble which not infrequently, as we see all too often in the news, leads to truly ridiculous and sometimes tragic outcomes.

In any case, the topic of temporality and the move from a circular temporality to a linear one is a hot topic in every analysis, and I would say in every human life.

So, those who work with the emotions (analysts, psychotherapists) are especially exposed to this type of pathology, as also are people who work in show business and any who invest in eternal youth.

Let's not forget the rich literature on this subject, from *Faust*, already mentioned, to *The Picture of Dorian Gray*, and so on.

As far as the therapists are concerned, Gabriele Junkers, a German colleague of rare sensitivity, has addressed the subject in depth. In her exquisite article on the ephemeral, she underlines how for analysts too there is a necessary oscillation between defence against and acknowledgement of time. She also emphasises how difficult this "work of aging" is for analysts because of certain conditions connected with what we could call the empty couch syndrome, which is when we say "no" to a new analysis because of our age. This topic is developed in Junkers' book *The Empty Couch* (2013).

I am keen to re-emphasise how the midlife crisis is chopped up these days and occurs well beyond the classic cruxes of leaving childhood, adolescent, aging. It makes itself felt from time to time and demands a payment, at least in instalments, of mental pain.

A patient of mine from whom I had had no news for years and who had lived a normally happy life, surprised me with a letter; here are some extracts:

> It's appalling to reach the age of 64 . . . soon 65 and 66 (a diabolical age) and then 70. . . . You're close to death, only 6 years off an age with no hope, 70, in other words you're heading for a catastrophic turning point. Pain pain dismay terror are so intense that you'd rather burn down the theatre than let the show go on. . . . I want my schooldays back . . . I want my youth . . . I want to be 26 . . . I beg you, whoever you might be, I'll sell my soul, just to stop time. . . . I can't accept the idea of death, of my death . . . old age, the end of youth. . . . I'm so afraid, rescue me dreams, fantasies, desires. . . . I dreamed I went to the Centre for an aperitif, but the bar turned out to be the "Cremation Centre" . . . death awaits me, I'm terrified, disoriented, ill-equipped, I'm a coward . . . help me, ancestors, in the end I'll do what you did . . . and what a lot of stupid things they did! Will I be more stupid than the stupid? Dignity . . . let's exorcize excitation, let's face pain and death, but as I was writing this, dear Doctor, I heard my son arriving with my three grandchildren . . . I can hear laughter . . . they're calling me . . . maybe I should go and be grandad. . . . I'm sorry about this outburst of melancholy, but as you see, my analysis is still working and I'll start swimming again!

Just as the violence of the emotions which tear us was doped or starved by anorexia, here the fangs of our finiteness are exorcised with every possible dilatory manoeuvre.

The best antidote might be to accept our own, real location in time, allowing ourselves an innocent ride on the merry-go-round every now and then. We could quote Freud and say that the reality principle must have the upper hand over the pleasure principle (leaving the latter some room to continue existing), or we could quote Bion and say that the reality of time must also be dreamt and become manageable and digestible psychic material, even if a few very brief flights into transformation in hallucinosis might be permitted rights of citizenship.

It would be hard to think of something more unlike Pirandello's story *The Train Whistled*.

We can't avoid giving a general glance at phobias.

Faced with a phobia, we can go and consult our manual and look up what we already know, or we can put the known aside as an "encyclopaedia of basic notions" and open ourselves up to the fantasies which a given situation ignites in it.

If someone has a phobia about lifts or confined spaces, apart from all the usual things – fear of falling, fear of dependency, fear of trusting – why not think that the lift with room in it for Mario has no room for his split-off "gorilla", which would find itself in a *claustrum*, in a structure that's too small and rigid compared to the hoist it really needs? So what are we going to do with the gorilla? Why and how has it come to mind? Are we dealing with split-off modes of functioning that will be oxygen-deprived if we put them in the cage of the lift? Or with modes of functioning sent up into orbit, leaving only a residual trace in the phobia?

For example, if someone is afraid of knives, how could we not think of Georg Wilhelm Pabst's film *Secrets of a Soul* starring Werner Krauss, in which the protagonist, Professor Mathias, develops such a phobia for knives that he has to be fed by his mother when he learns that a young, good-looking cousin will be a guest in his house and his beautiful young wife is highly involved with the new arrival. Is this a case of jealousy? Or is it rather a fear of his own most passionate aspects (the cousin), whose entry on the scene is not tolerated and must be eliminated because they are too intense? Or if we start instead from the narreme of the knives, what story will we construct?

If someone has a phobia of his or her own emotions, which might be so savage as to terrify him or her, they could develop a phobia of emotional truths and take refuge in the lie. The liar constantly finds him or herself between two fires, that of his or her own Superego and that of the explosive emotions which emotional contact might set off. The liar's strategy is to deconstruct facts and replace them with the inventiveness of lying. Fundamentally, the lie is a way of over-dressing the naked truth in clothes that can't make the truth more tolerable but simply mask it excessively. The lie is to transformations in hallucinosis as the truth is to transformations in dream.

If someone has a phobia about her or his own emotions and alternates bulimic and anorexic behaviours, and tells us about being afraid that a neighbour's dog will bite her or him, we could try to see which direction these biting emotions are heading in, and if the fear of being torn apart is being put to sleep with a lot of food or weakened by lack of nourishment.

If someone has a phobia about death and insists on talking about his or her own "jealousy", why not look at the fear of being "congealed" as fear of death and consider the overwhelming whirlwind of emotions he or she is living in as the most effective anti-coagulant he or she can find in the bookshelves of his or her mind.

Finally, we could quote Ogden and say that phobias tell us in words of one syllable about bits of the mind that it has been impossible to dream and thus integrate into our emotional DNA.

Naturally we could go on ad infinitum, from the phobia about dirt to the phobia of animals: but there is one phobia, the one most widely shared by all analysts, which is the phobia of the unknown, and we often tie it onto the trellis of the known rather than setting off to explore the world beyond what has already been mapped.

Reference

Junkers, G. (2013). *The Empty Couch: The Taboo of Ageing and Retirement in Psychoanalysis*. Edited by Gabriele Junkers. Routledge, Hove.

Chapter 2

Phobia

Maurizio Collovà

2.1 Presuppositions for a different nosography

> How and why is it that the general processes which account for the forma-
> tion of neurosis (e.g. the defensive conflict) assume specific shape in neurotic
> organisations so diverse that a nosography can be established?
>
> (Laplanche and Pontalis, 1967, p. 69)

To speak about phobic neuroses or any other nosographic formulation of the psychic disturbances requires that we also accept a certain type of theorisation further
"upstream". We know that there are many different psychoanalytic theorisations
about the functioning of the mind and its disturbances; some have been abandoned
(Freud, 1897), while others have evolved over time and others have marked a
profound break with the past, as in *The Psycho-Analytic Study of Thinking* (Bion,
1962b). Hence, the nosographies deriving from them may also be very varied.
By its nature, psychoanalysis has never had much sympathy for the grouping of
pathological behaviours into nosographic classes, since these tend to cause the
disappearance of the elements of subjectivity and uniqueness of the history, written and yet to be written, of every human being. Psychoanalysis is concerned with
the person, more precisely with "that" person and his or her specific functioning.
Once we enter the specific encounter between analyst and patient, psychoanalysis
concerns itself with the functioning of the field in which they are immersed and
how that functions.

As for the relationship which a classification may have with the theory which stands
behind it, we see how Winnicott's (1965, p. 135) contribution about "environmental
distortion" leads him to claim that "If it be true that the disorders which come under
the wide heading of psychosis (and which comprise the various types of schizophrenia) are produced by environmental deficiency at a stage of maximal or double
dependence, then the classification has to be adapted in order to meet this idea."

Naturally it is outside the scope of this chapter to address all the theorisations
which have given rise to the various ways of understanding nosography. Nevertheless, I am interested in pointing out some paths by which we will be able to
propose a psychoanalytic nosography with its own objectivity, alongside another

that is rooted in a strong subjectivity of patient and therapist, which in the session becomes the subjectivity of the psychoanalytic field. So I will consider psycho-analytic nosography from a viewpoint inside the session, in that it is determined by the meteorology of the field in a specific space-time.

Psychoanalysis has reflected on the construction of a psychoanalytic nosog-raphy from the start, when Freud propounded the doctrine of specific infantile sexual trauma. In the first Freudian system, the reference points for building a classification were the three areas in which Freud was interested up until 1910: 1. behaviour and the patient's relationship with reality, 2. symptom formation, and 3. the developmental process.

In 1910, Freud developed his structural conception of the personality. The study of the Ego's processes and its defences, and the history of pre-genital instinctual development introduce the conception by which the nature of the neu-roses depends on when the psychic conflict responsible for the neurosis itself were experienced. Here we are witnessing the elaboration of the concept of regression to the point of fixation, which leads us to consider these and the Ego's defences as original points of reference for the corresponding nosological forms. At the centre of all this is castration anxiety, the overcoming of the oedipal complex.

Once the anxiety has become unbearable, the organisation of defences is its necessary consequence, but these limit the progress of instinctual development. The disturbances which derive from this are the psycho-neuroses.[1]

But it was the case of Little Hans (1909) which enabled Freud to understand the specific nature of the phobic neurosis. The phobias were initially included in the obsessional neurosis or anxiety neurosis. Freud later reached the conclusion that the shift onto a phobic object is subsequent to the arising of a free anxiety which does not undergo conversion and is not tied to an object. The phobic neurosis is born out of a constant effort to tie the free anxiety down again.

We are given another example of nosographic variability by the work of Mela-nie Klein who influenced psychiatric classification by highlighting two types of depression. The first is linked to the capacity for feeling a sense of guilt, while the other results from a failure in affective development which begins at an early stage during the establishment of the depressive position.

Lastly, I fully share Winnicott's (1965) conviction when he says that the psy-choanalyst has a very different perspective on mental disturbance from that of the psychiatrist; the latter makes a very close examination of a patient at a certain moment in his or her clinical history, as for example when there has been a break-down or a hospitalisation. For Winnicott it is possible to follow a disturbance from childhood through adolescence into adult life, and to observe the way in which there has been a continual transformation from one type of disturbance to another. In this way he endows his diagnosis with a dynamic quality. But in their clinical practice, psychoanalysts experience the dynamic character of their nosography not only in connection with childhood, adolescence, and adult life. They know very well how in any session the field in which the pair are immersed can function in a paranoid, obsessional, or phobic way without being at that moment specifically adolescent, infantile, or adult, or any of these in alternation or combination.

In order to understand the viewpoint I want to express, I find it helpful to cite an amusing story by Italo Calvino called *The Contemplation of the Stars* in which Mr Palomar, the book's eponymous character, spends an entire night undergoing the taxing experience of having to switch his gaze back and forth between fixed systems like star maps on paper, without which he would not know what he is observing (in the case of the psychoanalyst, diagnostic manuals, DSM, etc.) to a system which seems to him to be in perennial movement like the vault of heaven (the emotional field of the session). "In other words, to locate a star involves the checking of various maps against the vault of the sky, with all the related actions: putting on and taking off of eyeglasses, turning the flashlight on and off, unfolding and folding the large chart, losing and finding again the reference points. Since the last time Mr Palomar looked at the stars weeks or months have gone by; the sky is all changed" (Calvino, 1983, p. 40). And I think that the psychoanalyst's sky has also changed since the inspired and indispensable kick-start it was given by Freud; and it goes on changing, just as the sky of every session is changeable.

The field of which we are a part, together with the patient, is necessarily a dynamic, progressively configured field where emotions are in constant movement and where a simple photo tells us little unless it is placed in a sequence with others which show its evolutions and revolutions, including its changes of direction. But above all, as Calvino also tells us,

> In identifying a constellation the decisive proof is to see how it answers when you call it. More convincing than the matching of distances and configurations with those marked on the chart [which would be like exclaiming at a certain point in the session, "Look, this is the primal scene, we've found it!"] is the reply that the luminous dot gives to the name by which it has been called, its promptness in responding to that sound, becoming one with it.

For Ogden (2008) every symptom, every psychopathological expression is linked to the failure of the individual's ability to dream his or her own emotional experience. But even in Ogden (1989, p. 46) we find variations on this definition, as when he claims that psychopathology can be thought of in terms of the collapse of the richness and articulation of experience generated between the contiguous-autistic, paranoid-schizoid, and depressive polarities. The consequence, which may be an inability to dream or the collapse of the articulations between different polarities of experience, is the obligatory choice of the symptomatological path in its various defensive articulations until the alpha function is in a position to digest, metabolise, and construct the first unconscious images, and reopen the way to dreaming. A classification based on these theoretical presuppositions must necessarily take into consideration the state of the "dreaming ensemble" (Grotstein, 2007) of that apparatus for thinking which permits access to the oneiric.

2.2   Post-Bionian developments

The change which occurs with Bion (1962a) and post-Bionian developments
(Ferro, 2005; Ogden, 2005, 2008; Grotstein, 2007, 2009; Civitarese, 2012;
Ferro et al., 2008, 2011, 2017; Ferro, Basile, *The Analytic Field*, Karnac, 2009)
have introduced a psychoanalysis of the functions which tells us (in a different
way from, while not replacing, the Freudian analysis of contents) what happens
upstream of the thematic choices which testify to our mind's need to find and
build narratives. In the same way, we can claim that Freud too, albeit from different theoretical presuppositions, considers that something exists upstream which
determines the pathological response. "However great the differences may be
between the various modalities of the defensive process in hysteria, obsessional
neurosis, paranoia, etc. . . . the two poles of the conflict are invariably the ego
and the instinct: it is against an internal threat that the ego seeks to defend itself"
(Laplanche and Pontalis, 1967, p. 105).

Ferro and Vender (2010, pp. 67–8), referring to post-Bionian developments,
see the question of the symptomatological choices as depending solely on the
quantity of proto-emotions to be managed. For them, there are different things
going on upstream of the pathologies that can be depicted: i.e. those in which
there is no pictogram of the proto-emotions against which the mind is defend-
ing itself through its functioning, and those evacuative pathologies such as
the personality disorders (today among those listed in the International Classification of Diseases ICD-10), psychosomatic pathology, and hallucinatory
pathology.

I have therefore considered two nosographies: one downstream, narrative
in kind and characterised by a strong subjectivity of the field; and the other
upstream and functional, which refers to dysfunctions of the first and second
levels of the thinking apparatus described by Bion (1962a),[2] and also described
by Ferro (2005). Using Bionian parameters, Ferro hints at a nosographic theory
to be considered in more detail later, identifying a series of clinical characteristics both from the diagnostic perspective of the analysand's prevailing disposition, and from a micrometric perspective as transitory configurations which
the couple adopts in the session. He recognises the following: 1. patients with
a deficient alpha function (the function which enables the mind to transform
sensory impressions and emotions); 2. pathologies of the second level: inadequate development of the $♀/♂$ mechanism; an inadequate container, killer
content, excessive pressure on the container, explosion of the container (a
porous or deforming container); inadequate or undeveloped oscillation of the
ps/d mechanism (paranoid-schizoid position/ depressive position), or of the
nc/sf oscillation (between negative capability and the selected fact). Alpha elements are formed but the apparatuses for working with them are inadequate;
and 3. traumatic situations in which beta elements (untransformed sensorial
impressions and emotions) start to dominate the alpha function both quantitatively and qualitatively.

Ferro specifies that each patient is a chimera of three situations.

We must naturally hypothesise the existence of mixed situations with infinite shades of expression.

Put briefly, we can speak of the following types of nosography.

a   Functional nosography, relating to

- pathologies of the alpha function;
- pathologies of the inadequacy of the container;
- pathologies of an excess of emotional facts (hyper-contents).

b   Narrative nosography, referring to themes whose content can be:

- obsessional (cleaning, the toothpaste tube, excessive punctuality, etc.);
- phobic (fear of lifts, of flying, of snakes, etc.);
- paranoid (my neighbours are spying on me, the Russians are going to invade, I'm fated to die, etc.).

Each of these can have its own narrative thread occasioned by, on the one hand, the level of anxiety to be managed and, on the other, by the variety of pictograms available in order to dream the free anxiety while waiting for an adequate narrative to accept and contain it and produce meaning. We will see this aspect in a clinical example.

2.3   The weight of thinking thoughts

Bion (1962a, p. 57) advances the hypothesis "that thinking is something forced on an apparatus, not suited for the purpose, by the demands of reality, and is contemporary with, as Freud said, the dominance of the reality principle." He is claiming in other words that our mind is not yet sufficiently equipped and that our apparatus for thinking has undergone, and must further undergo, various changes in order to be able to face a relationship with emotions that arise from inside and outside our body. This means that our mind will seek shelter when faced with this pressure, "it will certainly seek refuge in unreasonableness, in sexualisation, in acting out, and in various degrees of torpor" (Bion, 1973, p. 170) and, I will add, in the myriad possible defences, including the phobic, with the aim of avoiding or managing mental pain.

These statements would be enough to establish the one true reason why someone seeks help from psychotherapies and psychoanalysis. This is how we can understand the omnipresent ambivalence of the patients which we encounter in almost all analyses. On the one hand, psychoanalysis is asked to provide the tools with which to learn to think our own thoughts, while on the other hand we are terrified by their impact in their crude form and try to avoid the encounter. During the course of analytic treatments it is thus possible to see in concrete form the variety and degrees of avoidance of thought through various mechanisms that are neurotic or psychotic in nature, and by contrast the transformations which, through the acquisition of the tools for feeling, thinking, and dreaming, which permit access to their thinkability. From this hypothesis about the origins of pathologies in general, such as phobias, it would follow that, independently of the choice of phobic content, of the thought which at that moment is the representative of a phobic functioning, the psychoanalytic treatment will nevertheless be directed towards acquiring, repairing or developing functions of the apparatus for thinking thoughts.[3] Having made such an acquisition, we may have less recourse to "thermal shields" (Ferro, 1999): for example, the dislocation of space and time, along with displacement, negation, lying as a filter when faced with a blinding light of truth; and indeed less recourse to delusion as a substitute narrative which attempts to maintain a sense of cohesion and to hallucination as a liberating projection, "indistinguishable from freedom" (Bion, 1970, p. 17), with the aim of avoiding the frustration and pain entailed by the inability to alphabetise and organise one's own emotions and render them publishable to consciousness.

This preface is intended to support the hypothesis that the origin of a phobic functioning, a sort of proto-phobia, like the other choices of defence, can be the terror of having to think one's own thoughts, just as the terror of leaving the house and facing an absence of walls (agoraphobia) can find its forerunner, its proto-thought, in the caesura of birth.

2.4   Avoidance: a very wide-spread practice

Every day, all of us make emotional compromises which are often not conscious and are irrelevant in the extent to which they limit our quality of life. Instead they produce a constant alleviation of emotional tensions and conflicts as banal as they are familiar; but if they assume greater depth and a broader perspective they cause the avoidance of a growth and maturation that are felt as risky and a source of anxiety. We do this by resorting to a range of behaviours which, if persisted in, can become the way we manage our lives, configuring itself as a specific way of functioning. Examples are the telephone call we decide not to make, forgetfulness, taking refuge in stupidity, recourse to various degrees of lying, letting ourselves be hypnotically enslaved by the use of a TV which deactivates mental functions by offering us programmes or fictions of absolutely irrelevant interest, the pre-emptive use of tranquillisers or substances which filter our relationship with a difficult reality, the choice of friends who never make us feel inferior. Even the choice of life-partners can turn out to be strategic, aimed at not creating internal turbulences in territories that we have made an effort to exclude from our thoughts because they cause bodily emotional fluxes against which we insufficiently equipped.

So, before arriving at what can be properly called a phobia, there exist a number of behaviours whose purpose is avoidance and which I would simply call proto-phobias; a sort of extremely widespread basic phobic level with the function of withdrawing our mind from the task of having to think our thoughts. I am reminded of an example which an experienced colleague often used to tell: "When I have to begin writing a new paper and I am ready with my blank sheet of paper in front of me, up jumps something very important or urgent, imposing itself in the way of my potential thoughts and becoming pre-eminent: I've got to water the plants."

I think that today's sociological sciences can tell us a lot about the most banal and widespread level of this human state of mind. The culture of avoidance becomes a sort of social organiser which is set in motion through the quality of entertainment and information in the media; the creation of a pill for every pain and the destructive pressure towards attainments of little intellectual value.

Directing our attention to the accumulation of material goods, of status symbols falsely considered as important attributes of an identity which demonstrates our success, strongly contributes to bringing the functions of our apparatus for thinking to a standstill, rendering them somnolent, or even switching them off. The range of anaesthetic on offer is undoubtedly enormous, like a cafeteria open to all.

As we shall see, from the wide diffusion of this basic level, the need to manage internal territories that, because of periodic emotional upheavals, are not very amenable to domestication can produce more specialised levels of management that impose truly limiting compromises which result in the construction of symptoms such as the phobias with their infinite permutations, where avoidance nevertheless remains the fundamental mechanism. In this connection Ogden (2008, p. 32) claims that "The neurotic symptom marks the point at which the individual ceases to be able to do unconscious psychological work, and in the place of such work a static psychological construction/symptom is generated."

2.5   In search of a narrative

Fortunately for us, alongside the mechanisms described earlier, there are others which can counterbalance the possible evacuative, projective, and symptomatological outcomes which the mind uses to defend itself against emotional pressures it finds unbearable. The unconscious, claims Grotstein (2007, pp. 65–73, 299–303), brings with it an innate tendency to narrative and to the search for narratives which might convert incoming events, whether from the internal or external worlds, into personal experiences. These stories, myths, or novels have the function of binding the anxieties of uncertainty and the chaos left in the shadow of "O", which cuts across the subject's emotional frontier (Figure 2.1).[4]

How can we see this dynamic in practice, using some clinical material which shows a phobic mode of functioning?

A colleague in supervision tells me about Antonio, a six-year-old boy who is too frightened to play near a second door inside the therapist's consulting room, and so this door has to stay shut. Antonio is therefore compelled to create a buffer, we could call it a ditch, between himself and the door if he wants to preserve the possibility of going on playing. My colleague, referring to something imagined behind the door, says to the boy, "Maybe there's a treasure being kept safe there." A few sessions later Antonio starts slipping his drawings under the door, saying "This is

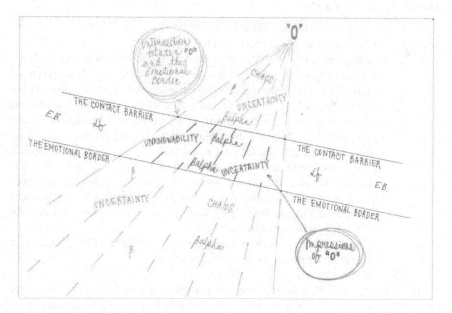

Figure 2.1 Representation of the emotional frontier

my treasure chest!" Beyond the dynamics which have permitted this development, we can see from the sequence that the anxieties linked to unknowability (what will be hidden behind that door?) have been accepted into a jointly constructed narrative with a different character. This has enabled the boy to deconstruct an area of limited and phobic functioning, to expand his area for play, transforming his fantasies into characters narrating a functioning that is capable of evoking protective feelings about his own creativity. It should not be forgotten that play is an important way of developing one's capacity for thinking – and it applies both to children and adults – through which to have experiences and to transform their contents, but at the same a development of one's own tools for thought.

We can speculate that in the absence of that alternative narrative, the little patient could have established defensive constructions, one of which might have been phobic: for example, establishing a phobia about closed doors, at the cost of limiting his capacity for exploration and the sacrifice of horizons of experience.

2.5.1 A providential narrative

A patient in the textile business, at a very constructive point in her analysis, which marks the departure from a claustrophobic functioning and the birth of a closer and freer relationship with the analysis, tells me about an event which certainly changed her life from the moment she was born.

The importance of a story

Patient: Have I ever told you about my birth?

Analyst: I don't at the moment recall you having done so.

Patient: It came back to me because yesterday my father came out with his familiar story about my birth; it crops up every now and then. You need to know that I'm from that generation who were born at home with a midwife, especially if you lived in a little village as I did. The story is that things started speeding up all of a sudden, and I was coming out of the womb so fast that there was a risk that the midwife would be caught unprepared. My father's intervention – he was always present, at my sisters' births too – was providential, yelling "Catch it, catch it!" Naturally I was completely unaware of what was going on, but ever since I first heard that story, I've felt that something very important had happened to me. What if my father hadn't been there? My destiny might have been very different.

Analyst: I imagine you were welcomed by two arms, instead of by a hard floor. Sometimes being alert can change your life.

In any case, this narrative acquired by the patient as a narrative experience after the event – whether or not it is true – has certainly had the job of placing itself in that caesura of birth which Bion (1977) speaks about, assuring her – like an image in her photo album – of some sense of continuity and containment. The narratives handed down to us by our parents are important, and sometimes take on the character of an experience. If things had gone differently, or if the event had stayed, as I like to say, at narrative zero, I wonder whether the patient would have built herself a fear of heights or an obsessional syndrome dedicated to meticulous control of the reliability of her workmates or the very common fear of air travel.

Naturally it occurs to me to think about the significance of the level on which re-dreaming takes place at a turning point in the analysis, but this is not part of my present concern.

I wanted to introduce the story I have just told at this point in order to illustrate the value of stories which come to form part of family myths. In this way I am anticipating the importance I want to give in this chapter to the containing and transformative aspect of a story which might remain relevant to the emotional field, but seemed inadequately developed from a starting point further upstream.

2.5.2   A faulty roundabout: only one exit – to "phobias"

From what I have set out so far we can hypothesise that phobic functioning is also the result of a limited capacity for narrative, immobilised in some way, which assumes a permanent character in our minds. Using the model of the "round-about",[5] we will find ourselves in a roundabout with only one signpost (Figure 2.3) which indicates a single exit, a single narrative choice, and, worse still, a

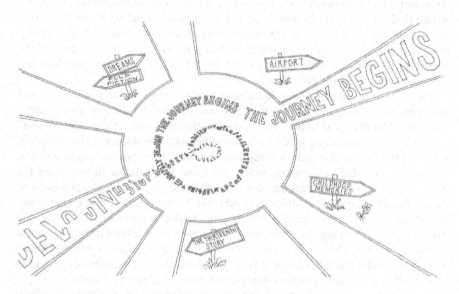

Figure 2.2 Functioning roundabout

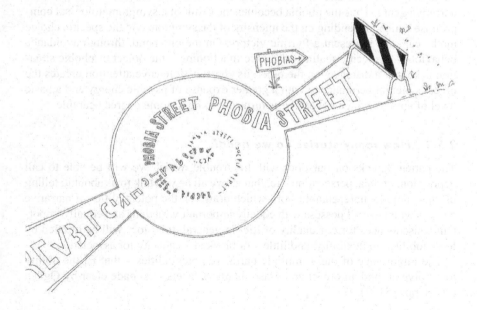

Figure 2.3 Dysfunctional roundabout

dead-end with no development. Translating the question in theoretical terms, we would find ourselves dealing with an alpha function struggling to get the bricks of thought out of the kiln and a single derived narrative that is impoverished and repetitive since it is prevented from being lifted to the second level of the apparatus for thinking which brings about the oscillations between container and contained (PS□↔D and NC□↔sf).

There is no doubt that the specific nature of an event – if it is a one-off and not instead a toxic microclimate, invisible but long breathed – can give a narrative "there" to the construction, but I consider that the cause of the real "trauma" is located upstream of the fact which is at odds with our apparatus for thinking; when, at that moment in our development and under the present environmental and emotional-relational contingencies, our mind is incapable of accepting the proto-emotions which are asking to be alphabetised and to give development to dream-thought and the narratives derived from it. The proof of this is that many people could respond in quite different ways to the same event – let's say the loss of a job – spanning the entire arc from suicide to a developmental response involving growth. Briefly, it is our mind (its level of efficiency) which decides what is traumatic and what is not; it is our mind which takes account of the degree of limitation which the symptomatological/defensive choice will entail.

In the case of the phobic choice, the alpha function has its own capacity, albeit limited, for producing pictograms for dream-thought, but the derived narrative remains stifled, circumscribed in a mono-construction which has the task of containing anxieties and distresses with the distinctive character of a personal narrative genre. Thus the phobia becomes the result of a symptomatological compromise which, depending on the intensity of the symptom and the specific choice made, can also represent a Pyrrhic victory. On the one hand, through avoidance behaviour – a specific feature of phobic functioning – the object or phobic situation is kept at a distance; on the other, its constant defensive attention creates the object's mental permanence with a greater expense of psychic energy and a basic level of anxiety which nevertheless turns out to be to some degree bearable.

2.5.3   How many stories do we need?

The patient knocks on our door with his trouble, which we will be able to call depression, phobia, persecution, etc.: but above all he will talk to us about it, telling us "his" unique, unrepeatable story which draws on the potentialities of narrative choices which we all possess with equally important variations and equally important consequences for our quality of life. In general, this story will be typified by low mobility, no flexibility, and little – or blocked – capacity for association.

The importance of these multiple narrative potentialities – that is, the ability to revolve around an object and grasp its many facets – is made clear by Ogden (2008, pp. 151–2):

> Sanity involves a capacity for generating and maintaining a multiplicity of perspectives. . . . For example, a medical student in a state of relative

psychological health may be able simultaneously to experience the cadaver that he is dissecting as the body of a once-living human being; a non-human object constructed for the purpose of teaching anatomy; terrifying, inescapable evidence of the reality of death (his own death, the death of those he loves, the death of the patients he will treat); a reflection of the generosity of the person who granted permission for the use of his or her remains for purposes of medical education. . . . Thinking, so conceived, is a process in which ideas and feelings live in continual conversation with one another, a conversation in which thoughts are forever in the process of being transformed (de-integrated) and formed anew as a consequence of shifting organisations of meaning.

This takes place in a mind that is sufficiently functional and therefore capable of tolerating death, its own impotence, separation, our fundamentally animal nature, the human feelings capable of making oneself a gift to a future in which we won't be there. Each of these is a candidate for the production of a story; a mind capable of many readings will have more possibility of accepting and transforming anxieties and distresses of varying degrees and kinds.

I am thinking about a patient with whom I had shared the metaphor of the roundabout and who, having freed himself of his symptom said, "Doctor, that roundabout isn't there anymore. Now we're at the international terminal of an airport." By this, he wanted to represent the multiplication of narrative options which were now making themselves present in his mind, the regaining of a flexibility and ability to make connections with places in the internal and external world which had previously been inaccessible.

2.6 On the subject of multiple storylines: The Best Offer[6]

"In every falsehood there is a hidden element of truth!" This is the thread which runs through the film from beginning to end.

I found this film interesting because the storyline and its intricacies give us a way of analysing the co-presence in the field of characters with multiple phobic, criminal, and mendacious ways of functioning which, as they interact, structure the story in such a way as to disorient its spectators, making us oscillate between truth and falsehood until at the end, in a *coup de théâtre*, the thread of the deception is revealed: triple in nature – perpetrated against the work, friendships, and love life of Virgil Oldman, incomparable auctioneer and infallible connoisseur of fine art, as well as being highly skilled at spotting that detail which the forger always leaves in his fakes, perhaps because he cannot bring himself to make a renunciation of his narcissism.

Virgil will suffer devastating mental consequences, being deprived of all his psychic defences and exposed, unarmed, to all his fragility. From that kernel of hidden truth, after long suffering, Virgil will try to put his mind back together again.

Mr Oldman is afflicted with a serious phobia about contact, which compels him to wear gloves; in fact, he has little inclination for human contact, which he reduces to the strictly necessary occasions of his work. This aspect is reflected in an obsession for collecting portraits of female faces, jealously preserved in a sort of vault built into his luxurious house. Every now and then he spends some time in solitude exchanging glances with the women in the portraits, with whom he can uniquely live in a protected relationship, safe from the emotional contaminations he finds unbearable. A long-standing friendship exists between the main protagonist and Billy, a painter of little worth, which is coupled with a fraudulent complicity in the acquisition of works of art. To this end, Billy takes part in the auctions conducted by Virgil, purchasing portraits for him, under his direction and at low prices, to be added to his collection. Despite this strong bond, Virgil misses no opportunity to belittle his friend's artistic talents, as a result of which, Billy starts to nurse a deep and insidious bitterness towards him. Out of this wound will grow the feelings of hatred and revenge which will motivate the con to be perpetrated against Virgil, whose life seems to proceed solidly and successfully under the protection of a rigid and long-practised defensive organisation until, after much resistance, he accepts a commission from Claire to value the many pieces of furniture and objects of value which adorn her house, and to auction them off. After a series of appointments cancelled by Claire for reasons which so annoy Virgil that he almost turns the job down, the first meeting takes place, although it astonishes him. In fact, because of a serious agoraphobia and an equally serious phobia of showing herself to the eyes of others, Claire receives Virgil in a large drawing room protected from sight by the door which leads to another wing of the house. The set-up of this scene already contains the emotional trap which will snare Virgil and direct his behaviour. This is the "truth" offered to the viewer which will establish a climate of great curiosity about possible developments.

The film has a highly complex plot which suggests more reflections of a psychoanalytic kind than can find space in this chapter. One example, which lies outside the subject of this chapter, is the central importance of maintaining a careful and rigorous internal setting, and the need for constant management of the analyst's mind in the face of the emotions which may strike him. So I will use only a few elements that are most closely connected to the context of this study.

What we understand immediately is that the protagonist is starting to be attracted less to the value of the furniture than to the presence on the other side of the wall, through which he can detect her footsteps and her persuasive voice.

To Virgil the obsessive collector, the face of Claire hidden by the wall is in fact equivalent to a painting not available for auction, and reverses the image of the vault so that he himself is now the one being shut out: out of Claire's secret rooms. The reason for his curiosity is better understood later on when the viewer can start to wonder, "Who is looking after whom?" In fact, following the overcoming of Claire's pathology so that she is able to leave that room and live with him, we note corresponding changes in Virgil, though these remain more in the background: he starts to do without his gloves and begins to live happily with the gift that life is offering him, even seeming almost extravert.

Another interesting aspect of the film, besides the mise-en-scène of two pairs of phobic functioning – the phobia of contact and of people, and that of being exposed to the other's gaze and a consequent agoraphobia – is the way these are interwoven with other forms of functioning such as criminality and mendacity: the phobia as a symptom and the lying phobia as a key for entering and plundering the other's mind (and not only that) – in this case Virgil's.

In caring for the other's phobia, whether it be false or true, the protagonist finds he is starting to care for himself, once again experiencing feelings he had sterilised in the flat images of the portraits with which he secretly entertains himself. Now he has not only a face in front of him, colours on a canvas, but a fascinating, living woman, and his contact with the emotions which flow from this is experienced without filters or avoidance.

The mechanism which enables Virgil to start looking after himself is a shifting of his diseased functioning onto Claire. Virgil exerts himself as a carer sustained by an overwhelming curiosity and a burning desire for possession, and in this way he unconsciously brings himself closer to the feared emotions which are produced by falling in love with Claire and which he starts to experience. Obviously it doesn't matter which phobias are involved, and which permutations each runs through according to his or her own subjectivity: was does matter is the modification of the functioning which occurs upstream. The gradual way in which Virgil brings Claire closer to her feared emotions is a process which he is experiencing himself in the background. A sort of unconscious mirroring thereby emerges between the two and modifies the immobility of the field, activating new emotional experiences. The symmetry constructed between them, as I have said, gives rise to the question, "Who is caring for whom?", a question which it often makes sense to ask in analysis, accepting that the patient also produces a certain change in us, immerses us in a mental state which reconnects us to moments from our own life and analysis, fostering a new dream to our mutual advantage.

2.7   Collaborative or necessary illnesses of the field? Dario and the magnetic bike

Dario has been in analysis for several years. At one point he reveals his passion for his bicycle. He has had various different models of "city" bikes. Now he would like to take a step up, make a change that would give him the experience of the "Dolomite passes" and many others, further prompted by the insistence of his friends who are already equipped for this kind of undertaking. He comes to a session upset and disconsolate. He's gone around shop after shop looking for a racing bike, and when he finds one, the assistant invites him to try it, providing him with magnetised shoes and explaining how they work. Dario jumps onto the bike but is struck by a great anxiety. He really can't stand having those magnetic pedals under his feet. He tries and tries again, but cannot even start pedalling, afraid that if he needed to stop he wouldn't be able to detach his foot and keep himself from falling. Dario experiences his limitation as an insuperable obstacle, and feels really stupid because he can detect both the banality of the problem and the state of paralysis which has seized him and is causing him great discouragement. He feels he won't be able to share his friends' new experiences.

As he is telling me for the umpteenth time about the overwhelming terror which immobilises him so that he can't move a centimetre on a wonderful bike, I try to adopt some other viewpoints, thinking about the "magic filter" mentioned by Ferro (2015), but in an explicit and partly inverted way. I say to Dario, "But wait a minute, if we consider this situation, just for a moment, as if it were a dream that you've been telling me in session after session, what would we think of it? It would certainly be a very upsetting dream, especially when it recurs so often!"

For my part, I feel quite spontaneous thinking about the difficulty of separating oneself and taking one's own path, undertaking one's own enterprises, scaling the Dolomites of one's own "myths" and "pains",[7] as well as meeting one's friends; changes which analysis has already produced in his life. I had already said these things in various ways to Dario, but they had had no effect, allowing the phobic object – because this is what it had now become – to grow and make itself ever more set in stone. In addition to which, as a specific instance of this functioning, shame was now being added, and with it the avoidance of the bicycle, with the resulting loss of any desire to purchase one in case there should be a repeat of the embarrassing scene in front of the shop assistant.

While I am thinking all this, Dario can only respond with a wry "Doctor, what can I say? . . . I really don't know . . . that's how it is!" and in his silence the image comes to me of my father's hand holding onto the saddle of my little bicycle, and then as if in the foreground the image of that same open hand letting go after giving me a push. A sequence full of meaning: the push, the open hand, the letting go. For a moment there was a certain sadness coupled with the awareness that in order to separate ourselves serenely, there need to be two of us and we need to be able to have faith in ourselves. I realised how difficult it was for me to leave that patient who had given me so many satisfactions. Dario was equipping himself to address self-analytic undertakings, but I was keeping him magnetically attached to me, perhaps without informing him sufficiently about the mechanisms for detaching oneself from analysis, which he felt as my saying "You're not ready yet!" and not valuing or heeding a request from him which it was time for me take into consideration.

In this connection, I remember a boy with whom I had worked for four years, who dreamed he was given a Ferrari as a present but couldn't find how to get out of the car. He was helped by my frequently allowing him to attend parties he was invited to, tolerating the cancellation of sessions: a sort of slippage in the direction of the real world, to which he was giving back the time he had spent in analysis.

Returning to Dario, I told him that perhaps if the shop assistant had given him a push he would have coped with it. After a few months, the topic of "the end of the analysis" started to have more concrete connotations, until we decided the month and day on which we would say goodbye. I knew nothing more about the bicycle since it disappeared from the analytic discourse.

In these situations it can be difficult to divine how far the field has been made ill by the maintenance of a phobic functioning opposed to any change, or by contrast how much it has been influenced by my difficulties in tolerating separation, which had found an easy pretext in the couplings of shoe-pedal and analyst-patient. There is no doubt that the intervention of a different narrative brought movement to the field, allowing us to take new "steps".

2.8 Agoraphobia in the session. "But which piazza were you telling me about?"

Every time I hear colleagues wondering about the place of reality in the session, I think that it means respect for the patient's emotional reality. If a young patient says he knows his parents are separating or tells me about the unexpected loss of his grandfather, I think that the only response can be a participation which takes the reality of the facts into consideration. But I have no doubt that a second later I will think of what he has said as a story also inherent in the facts of the session. In relation to this, I have always been struck by a little story of Cesare Musatti's (1987). I know it by heart, and it is the reply I generally give my colleagues.

After a long silence from the analyst, a patient tells him about a big piazza in his home town where a watermill stood, a huge one which him feel very small and alone every time he found himself having to walk through the square until his anxiety became so great that he contrived the strategy of walking along the walls of the house before reaching the shop on the other side of the square.

Some years after the conclusion of the analysis, Musatti found himself passing through that town and, recalling the patient and that session, was prompted by curiosity to find the piazza. He asked around for information, and finally an old man told him, "But this is it, look, there's the mill, closed now, and this is the chemist that's been here for years and years!" Musatti couldn't believe his eyes. Everything fitted, except for the enormous piazza: it was so small that it hardly deserved to be called a piazza, extremely narrow, hardly a town square at all.

So, what piazza was his patient talking about? I don't think this is the place to try supervising the celebrated psychoanalyst. We can only play, as if for practice, with the small amount of material we have available. The patient's story could be understood as a negative expansion of the container, which loses adherence and contact with the patient's emotional requirements. The absence of vocal dykes provided by the analyst, being left with only the vibrations of one's own voice, revives an agoraphobic anxiety in the patient's story which marks the analyst's emotional distance/absence.

Moral: as Dr Luciana Nissim Momigliano said in a paper given at the Milan Centre of Psychoanalysis during a seminar on the sexual perversions, "We don't need to go to the public toilets to understand and know about our patients' perversions, but just stay in our consulting rooms and listen to them." I would add that the only reality that counts for us is the emotional one which comes to life in the encounter with our patient. Once again it is the way in to a functioning – deficient or overtly pathological – within the field which gives us the opportunity, after getting "lost" with the patient, of re-emerging in a transformative way.

2.9   A phobia about birds? Certainly the result of a sexual trauma!

> MAN[8] That is an example of your obsession with the past. . . . You wear the Past as if it were a decoration. It has no importance, though its debris can still be seen and felt impinging on the present.
>
> Bion (1975, p. 393)

Eugenia contacts me by telephone, asking for an appointment because she is seriously troubled by a phobia about birds. Her youthful, jaunty voice with a lilt which I experience as anything but foreign, and the specific nature of the disturbance provoke a pleasant curiosity in me.

I don't ask her anything else over the phone and she adds nothing further.

At our first meeting, I realise after a few exchanges that Eugenia is a substantial character, physically but above all intellectually, although something in her – how consciously, I don't know – tends to diminish, if not to conceal, this quality.

Very succinctly, but with great precision and choosing her words carefully, she tells me how she has been afraid of birds, especially pigeons, for as long as she can remember, and to such an extent that merely thinking that one might be nearby is enough to make her quite anxious. I ask Eugenia why it is only now that she has decided to seek help. She replies that it is the first time she has felt a sense of urgency and the need for a response. Spontaneously she comes up with some questions and asks me, "Do you think there might have been some incident of abuse? – though I have to tell you I have no memory of it, and there's no story in the family to make me think it. Could I have repressed it?" I have never had much sympathy for premature, pre-packaged solutions, and in this case I feel that the question is an attempt to close down discussion. I wonder what she is trying to avoid by presenting this ready-made trauma, and what function repression might now have. I try to distance myself from the temptation to make an appropriate reply and instead I choose the path of narrative, saying that pigeons are also great travellers, as well as being carriers of messages. I am struck by the immediacy of Eugenia's reply and by its somewhat persecutory tone, which makes me aware that I have caused a rise in the emotional temperature. "When I think of them I see their wings spreading over my head. . . . It's as if they were going to black everything out!" As I prompt her further, Eugenia shuts her eyes, constructing a "phobic defensive barrier" (Ferro, 2015, p. 121) on her mental screen so that it seems no longer possible to project any image onto it. For my part, I associate "as if they were going to black everything out!" to the darkness my grandfather used to talk about when telling us about the German bombing of Palermo, and how the population was ordered to black out their windows so as not to be seen, and all the city's lights were turned off. I wonder, entirely speculatively, what Eugenia needs to black out from her and my sight. Understanding that I had come close to an area of greater conflict in her emotional life, I look for more tangential narratives, not least to avoid a subsequent session being "blacked out".

So Eugenia starts to tell me that she too is from Palermo, a teacher of philosophy but now about to retire. She was unsure for a long time, and to some extent still is, about where to live – whether to go back to Palermo or to stay in Pavia, since she enjoys good friendships in both cities. A discussion starts up about the fear of putting down roots and about the worry that doing so might be like shutting oneself in a cage, cancelling every other possibility.

I tell her that, in the end, uncertainty leaves many doors open, doors which she is perhaps not yet ready to close; furthermore, the concrete fact of approaching retirement sharpens this conflict, making it more urgent to have a response to the fear that the theatre may come to the end of its season and go dark.

"I remember that when I was little, whenever I made a promise my father would tell me with a smile that humiliated me, '*Ma zittuti, c'affari tu!*' [Palermitano dialect: 'Be quiet, what can you do?'], suggesting I would be incapable of anything, making me a kind of nullity."

On the basis of this statement, which seems to catch the most painful emotional matter, and after taking stock of the situation, we decide to start an analysis; it is a point of take-off in a flight towards the choice of struggling against the blackout.

Now the question arises: how to transform persecutory wings which cause a blackout into wings which enable flight; how to free oneself from a heavy emotional dimension (a weight) which leaves us earthbound, and find or build future narratives which may encourage the realisation of narcissistic impulses that have been humiliated and made fragile, even if never soothed. What journey to undertake and what messages, letters written and never sent, to bring to their destination? Even if the content of the answer remains unknown for a long time, the important thing is to re-activate a narrative function, understood as greater efficacy of the alpha function capable of multiple viewpoints: a reopening of those exits on the roundabout which had been defensively blocked, and the opening of new exits for destinations never thought of before.

2.10   Conclusions

I wanted to conclude with reference to a poem by Alda Merini (1885) because it reprises the initial theme of my chapter. From the start, I have wanted to construct a defence against diagnostic standardisations which I do not feel are in the founding spirit of psychoanalysis. Such standardisation, as in Merini's poem, deletes a history, smooths over identities freighted with pain and reparations: in the poet's words, the identities of "lover", "prostitute", one who lusts for blood", "hypo-crite", and "hysteric". The poem "Alda Merini" is part of a collection entitled *Empty of Love*, in which the writer has set aside space for some compositions whose titles are the names of people and/or characters she has encountered, either having met them in person or knowing about them for some reason. So, giving the poem her own name as a title, she means to say that this is what she is, someone who is capable of loving, of having secrets, of acting against herself, of selling herself, idealising herself, hating and lying. Anyone who gives this life a name merely kills it.

This is why I would rather give the chapter about phobias a different title, maybe one like this: *Giovanni, Ada, Antonio, voices of people and characters from a certain room*. But the party line is that I must adapt myself to influences from psychiatry, even though Winnicott (1965, p. 132) claimed that "The analyst gets a view of mental disorder which is very different from that of the psychiatrist who makes a very careful examination of a patient at a certain moment in the history of the case, as for instance when there has been a breakdown or when hospitalization has occurred" and, I would add, in that "certain moment" the psychiatrist takes a photo which he immobilises definitively with a name, ruling out any perception of the dynamic qualities, the oscillation of functions and ways of experiencing internal and external reality.

"Somewhere in the analytic situation, buried in masses of neuroses, psychoses and so on, there is a person struggling to be born," says Bion (1994, p. 45). This is what analytic work offers to do: removing the encrustations and stratifications of names that make us "howl with the wolves" (Gaburri and Ambrosiano, 2003) so as to make contact with "O" and give it the possibility of becoming personal, to write our own story, our own futures. These are the thoughts which have made me imagine that someone might be able to write their own narrative diagnosis in their preferred language and genre, without suffering losses and accepting imposed names that may be scientifically useful but are emotionally and affec-tively mute.

At the *Espace Dalì* in Montmartre a sculpture is on display (Figure 2.4) por-traying Newton with a hole in his head and another in his chest and abdomen, through which we can see emptiness. The caption beside the sculpture reads as follows:

> According to Dalì, Isaac Newton the man has become just a scientific name, stripped of his personality and individuality. In order to give a form to this transformation, Dalì has perforated the sculpture with two large holes: one represents Newton's lack of vital organs, while the other represents the absence of his soul. What remains is solely a symbolic representation.
>
> (1969)

I would like it if nobody was ever again forced to say, "and I was just a scientific name!"

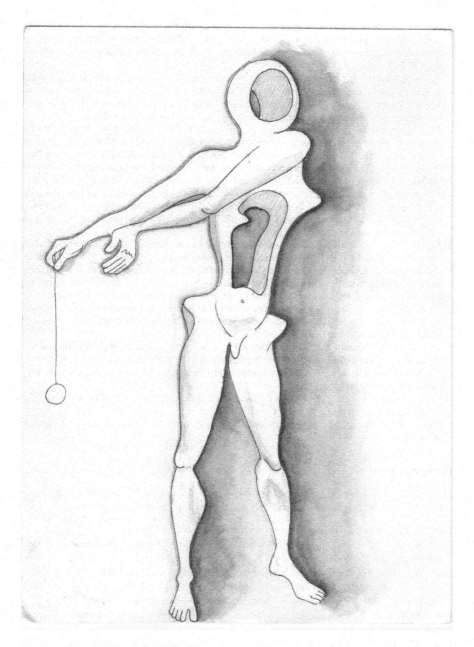

Figure 2.4 Homage to Newton

Notes

1 A term used by Freud to characterise, by contrast with the actual neuroses, the illnesses whose symptoms are the symbolic expression of the infantile conflicts: that is, the translation (or transference) of neuroses and the narcissistic neuroses (Laplanche and Pontalis, 1967, p. 200).
2 According to the Bionian model, the first level of the thinking apparatus is understood to be that part which includes the work of the alpha function on the proto-emotions or beta elements, as well as the construction and continual repair of the contact barrier until pictograms and the alpha sequence for waking dream-thought are produced.
3 This assertion in itself presupposes the hypothesis of the existence that there are unthought thoughts, thoughts in search of a thinker, as theorised by Bion (1970, p. 117).
4 I have imagined "O" as a comet in whose "tail", as Grotstein (2007) states, "we find clouds of uncertainty, chaos, balpha elements, beta elements, or 'a myriad of unknowabilities'." This structure, which waits and looks for realisation – that is, to become a personal "O" – can come into contact with our emotional frontier, consisting of: the contact barrier which separates consciousness from the unconscious; our alpha function's degree of efficiency; the emotional charge still to be disposed of in that moment; or even a condition of absolute receptivity.
5 Figure 2.2 shows a model of a functioning mind where incoming beta elements find an adequate alpha function which produces pictograms, and a second level of the apparatus for thinking capable of developing adequate narratives both in terms of variety and their individual degree of development. By contrast, in Figure 2.3, we see how the incoming beta elements can have only one outcome: there is a lack of narrative multiplicity and a single offer which provides for no development, as is indicated instead by the "Airport" sign in Figure 2.2, which suggests other journeys or further elaborations or episodes (drawings by the author).
6 *The Best Offer*, title of a 2013 film directed by Giuseppe Tornatore, with Geoffrey Rush in the part of Virgil Oldman, impeccable auctioneer; Sylvia Hoeks in the part of Claire, fascinating owner of an old stately home; and Donald Sutherland in the part of Billy Whistler, painter and long-time friend of Virgil.
7 [Translator's note: the author plays on the name "Dolomites" as a blend of *dolori* (pains, griefs) and *miti* (myths).]
8 "Man" is an imaginary character invented by Bion, belonging to his trilogy *Memoir of the Future*.

References

Note: S.E. = *The Standard Edition of the Complete Psychological Works of Sigmund Freud.* Trans. J. Strachey. London: Hogarth Press and the Institute of Psychoanalysis.

Bion, W.R. (1962a). *Learning From Experience*. London: Heinemann.
Bion, W.R. (1962b). The Psychoanalytic Study of Thinking. *International Journal of Psychoanalysis* 43: 306–10.
Bion, W.R. (1970). *Attention and Interpretation*. London: Tavistock Publications.
Bion, W.R. (1973). *Brazilian Lectures*. London: Karnac Books, 1980.
Bion, W.R. (1975). *A Memoir of the Future*. London: Karnac Books, 1991, p. 271.
Bion, W.R. (1977). Caesure. In *Two Papers: The Grid and Caesura*. London: Karnac Books, 1989, pp. 35–56.
Bion, W.R. (1994). *Clinical Seminars and Other Works*. London: Karnac Books.
Calvino, I. (1983). Contemplation of the Stars. In *Mr Palomar*. New York: Random House, 2010, p. 40.

Civitarese, G. (2012). *The Violence of Emotions: Bion and Post-Bionian Psychoanalysis.* London: Routledge.

Ferro, A. (1999). *The Bipersonal Field: Experiences in Child Analysis.* London and New York: Routledge.

Ferro, A. (2005). *Seeds of Illness Seeds of Recovery.* London: New Library/Routledge.

Ferro, A. (2015). *Torments of the Soul.* London: New Library/Routledge.

Ferro, A., and Basile, R. (Eds.). (2009). *The Analytic Field: A Clinical Concept.* London: Karnac Books.

Ferro, A., and Vender, S. (2010). *La terra di nessuno fra psichiatria e psicoterapia.* Torino: Bollati Boringhieri.

Ferro, A. et al. (2008). *Sognare l'analisi. Sviluppi clinici del pensiero di Wilfred R. Bion.* Torino: Bollati Boringhieri.

Ferro, A. et al. (2011). *Psicoanalisi in giallo. L'analista come detective.* Milano: Cortina.

Ferro, A. et al. (2017). *Contemporary Bionian Theory and Technique in Psychoanalysis.* Edited by Antonino Ferro. London: Routledge.

Freud, S. (1897). *The Complete Letters of Sigmund Freud to Wilheim Fleiss 1887–1904.* Translated and edited by Jeffrey Moussaieff Masson. Cambridge, MA/London: The Belknap Press of Harvard University Press 1986.

Freud, S. (1909). Analysis of a Phobia in a Five-Year-Old Boy. In *SE* 10: 3–149.

Gaburri, E., and Ambrosiano, L. (2003). *Ululare con i lupi. Conformismo e rêverie (Howling With Wolves: Conformism and Rêverie).* Torino: Bollati Boringhieri.

Grotstein, J.S. (2007). *A Beam of Intense Darkness: Wilfred Bion's Legacy to Psychoanalysis.* London: Karnac Books.

Grotstein, J.S. (2009). *But at the Same Time and on Another Level: Psychoanalytic Theory and Technique in the Kleinian/Bionian Mode.* New York: Routledge, 2018.

Laplanche, J., and Pontalis, J.B. (1967). *The Language of Psychoanalysis.* Trans. D. Nicholson-Smith. New York: W.W. Norton; London: The Hogarth Press, 1973.

Merini, A. (1885). *Love Lessons: Selected Poems of Alda Merini.* Trans. Susan Stewart. Princeton, NJ: Princeton University Press, 2009, p. 1.

Musatti, C. (1987). Psicoanalista e scenografo. In *Chi ha paura del lupo cattivo?* Roma: Editori Riuniti.

Ogden, T.H. (1989). *The Primitive Edge of Experience.* Northvale, NJ: Jason Aronson.

Ogden, T.H. (2005). *This Art of Psychoanalysis: Dreaming Undreamt Dreams and Interrupted Cries.* London: Routledge.

Ogden, T.H. (2008). *Rediscovering Psychoanalysis: Thinking and Dreaming, Learning and Forgetting.* London: Routledge.

Winnicott, D.W. (1965). *The Maturational Processes and the Facilitating Environment; Studies in the Theory of Emotional Development.* New York: International Universities Press.

Chapter 3

Obsessionality. Algorithms, compulsions, rituals, and obsessions

Giovanni Foresti and Mauro Manica

It is well known that Freud (1894, 1909, 1922, 1924) was extremely interested in obsessional neurosis and regarded its treatment as difficult but necessary if progress was to be made in the study and understanding of psychic functioning (Freud, 1924, p. 262). In their classic reconstruction, Laplanche and Pontalis (Laplanche and Pontalis, 1973) recall that it was Freud himself who identified obsessional neurosis as an autonomous nosological entity. Borrowing the term *Zwangsvorstellung* ("compulsive idea or representation") from a work by Krafft-Ebing of 1867 (Löwenfeld, 1904), Freud had characterised obsessional disturbance as a neurosis in which

> the psychical conflict is expressed through symptoms which are described as compulsive-obsessive ideas, compulsions towards undesirable acts, struggles against these thoughts and tendencies, exorcistic rituals, etc. – and through a mode of thinking which is characterised in particular by rumination, doubt and scruples, and which leads to inhibitions of thought and action.
> (Laplanche and Pontalis, 1973, p. 281)

In the early phase of this theorising, Freud's interpretative effort had been concentrated on comprehending the structure of the drives which characterised the libidinal economy of the obsessional subject. And so, in 1907, he had postulated that obsessional individuals had, in their early childhood, developed a particular fixation on that constellation of physiological stimuli and early relational anxieties (the "control" of the object) which constitute the anal phase (Foresti and Rossi Monti, 2010).

In the later phase of his work, when the structure of the psychic apparatus had been rethought in the light of the second topography, Freud did not substantially modify these first hypotheses, but integrated them into a more detailed representation of the relationships in play between the various psychic agencies. In the case of obsessional neurosis, he then proposed the presence of especially dramatic conflictual tensions between a Superego with a markedly demanding structure and an insufficiently developed Ego that is not yet solid enough.

Almost seventy years later in the Italian psychoanalytic tradition (drawing on Cesare Musatti's *Trattato di psicoanalisi* [Treatise on psychoanalysis] published by Einaudi in 1948) the continuities and conceptual innovations on the theme of obsessionality converged in the composition of a new *Trattato di psicoanalisi* (1988–89) edited by Alberto Semi.

In this rich double volume, if we set ourselves the aim of representing the subjective experience (and the metapsychological algorithms) of the person afflicted with obsessive-compulsive manifestations, it is still interesting to retrace the reference to numerous "psychopathological models", psychoanalytic ideas which reconsider post-Freudian studies from various schools and try to integrate them with the traditional conception.

In this regard, there are exemplary pages dedicated to the question of subjectivity (Spaçal, 1989) where an in-depth examination of the defence mechanisms is preceded by a description – drawing on the study of psychopathology and phenomenology – of the inner life of a person who suffers from an obsessive-compulsive disorder (OCD).

Of course, this is yesterday's news. So what are we to say about obsessionality today? How are we to think about its algorithms, compulsions, and rituals from a vertex that faces towards the future?

Perhaps two more present-day readers might enable us to articulate the clinical content of the obsessional experience with a method (a "container") which permits us to attribute a meaning to them that is as much intrapsychic as it is inter- and trans-personal.

From a perspective inspired by the Bionian model of container/contained ($♀↔♂$), the first reading concerns the theoretical container and the method used ($♀$). We are referring to a reflection by Luis Kancyper in a collection of writings by South American authors entitled *Truth, Reality and the Psychoanalyst* (Lewkowicz and Flechner, 2005). In this book, characterised by a very interesting polyphonic structure (one too rarely replicated: an essay by a South American psychoanalyst is followed by a comment/counterpoint by one from Europe or North America), Kancyper's contribution is one of the essays devoted to field theory and proposes a general hypothesis which seems as simple as it is convincing.

In the present day, the various conceptualisations of this theory could provoke a number of reservations, or, in Kancyper's words, "awaken much resistance among analysts" (ibid., p. 78.). In fact, what they seem to have in common is a radical suspension of judgement on what distinguishes the perceived object from the perceiving subject: an apparently obvious operation which nevertheless requires substantial work of rethinking the psychoanalytic tradition in the light of the interpretations proposed by Civitarese (2014), Ferro (2013), and Ogden (2008) for example.

The extended clinical *epoché* which results from this can in fact pose ethical, theoretical, and technical problems to the therapist which greatly enlarge the mound of professional responsibilities. Kancyper writes that the hypothesis of the bi-personal clinical field

> inflicts a new wound on the analyst's narcissism and power. . . . The analyst can no longer claim that his position is that of a passive observer. . . . Through his own psychic functioning, conditioned by the complementary series of his own internal factors, the analyst plays a significant, though asymmetrical, part in the development of the relationship and in its eutrophic or destructive outcomes.

The other reading, which could help us to think about contents (♂), is one of Glen Gabbard's many writings on the symptomatology of the psychopathologies, reformulated in a psychoanalytic key: in particular, the continuum of obsessive-compulsive symptoms which we have decided to summarise around the concept of obsessionality (Gabbard, 2000).

But what is obsessionality? Is it a syndrome? Is it a symptom? Is it the character a life takes on when it becomes hard, or even impossible, to live?

An essay which might perhaps help us to initiate a study of obsessionality is available in a volume of *Psychoanalytic Inquiry* entirely devoted to what the DSB-IV calls obsessive-compulsive personality disorders (OCPD) and obsessive-compulsive disorders (OCD).

Gabbard's contribution concentrates on the latter which, unlike the former (for which analytic treatment remains the therapy of choice in his opinion), have been the subject of studies which have demonstrated the efficacy of interventions using cognitive-behavioural techniques and pharmacological therapies (Gabbard, 2001). Even when the importance of biological factors and their role in the genesis of the disturbance has been documented, there seems to be incontestable evidence that careful observation of the familial, psychotherapeutic, and institutional relational fields helps us to understand the emotional meaning of the symptomatology and enables us to claim that "The symptoms of OCD almost always have interpersonal meanings that must be addressed" (ibid., p. 218). Therefore, even if the heterogeneity of the clinical picture counsels against categorical claims and hasty generalisations, the manifestations which belong to the obsessive-compulsive spectrum are a psychopathological problem which, concludes, "demonstrate the value of an integrated approach to the treatment of major psychiatric disorders" (ibid., p. 219).

Referring back to the epigraphs (which describe mankind's continual efforts to control the uncontrollable, claiming to be able to stop time and divide it ad infinitum into sequences of repetitive acts) and encouraged by a brilliant hypothesis by Eugenio Gabburi (2005), which suggests considering obsessional defences as a barrier against intolerable death-anxieties, the thesis which might guide a reflection on obsessionality would, put briefly, be a spectrum with many distinct aspects and open to a wide range of interpretations.

Although the importance of research into the obsessive-compulsive spectrum has been stressed since the dawn of psychoanalysis, it is not possible to eliminate interference from the demands of clarity, theoretical coherence, and conceptual order (demands which we could therefore regard as obsessional), which have made it difficult to keep the description of clinical phenomena that are especially resistant to diagnostic portrayal (perhaps obsessionality is the most trans-nosological of all psychopathologies) together with research into the processes of transformation which makes its treatment possible (a treatment universally noted for its difficulty and the slowness with which therapeutic effects become apparent).

So we could proceed towards an attempt to demonstrate how a discussion of the problems posed by the comprehension and treatment of obsessive disturbances – when it is combined with a detailed theory of the clinical field – can contribute to giving conceptual substance and clarity of meaning to otherwise generic definitions like "integrated treatment" and "psychoanalytically informed approach".

3.1   Towards a(n obsessive?) definition of obsessionality

Paradoxically, it seems inevitable that we start with a problem of definitions and classifications, with the hope that we won't let ourselves be imprisoned by the demon (obsession, anancasm) which emanates from the nature of the problem under discussion.

What do we mean, what can we be referring to, when we talk about obsessionality?

As we know, the etymology of the terms which designate the problem of OCD is obvious and unambiguous. Obsession derives from the verb *obsidēre*, to besiege, while compulsion derives from *compellere* and can be translated as "constrain", "oblige".

Following a different semantic route, a dialectical (and phenomenological) psychiatrist has restored the Greek derivation from αναγκασμός in order to define obsessional phenomena as anankastic, an adjective which draws its set of meanings from the Greek term which means "constraint" and becomes "anancasm": "constriction", "violence".

So is there a "violence" infusing the varied manifestations of obsessionality? – that "violence" which Freud (1894, 1907) and Abraham (1911, 1924) had intuited and perhaps (obsessively) rigidified in the description of the "anal character"?

Let's start to orient ourselves clinically by referring to a first clinical case.

CAMILLA'S ENCHANTMENT

As soon as she had crossed the threshold into adolescence, Camilla had started an analysis because she was apparently compelled to put life on hold by an obsessive ritual which seemed to want to keep her sealed within the four walls of her family home. If her hair was not clean and perfectly tidy, if her skin was not immaculately washed, if her clothes were not in absolute harmony with the latest fashions – even her underwear had to be impeccable, despite the fact that any intimate contact had been ruled out – there was no possibility of her emerging into the world. She had left school, where all social relations had been reduced; although brilliantly gifted intellectually, she could now only "dream" of fulfilling herself in activities involving the treatment and aesthetics of the person. So, in the early phases of the analysis, she had dedicated herself to employment which was in tune with her desires, until she found herself a permanent position as a sales assistant at a leading upmarket company in the clothing industry. Always punctual and impeccable in actions governed by a "principle of duty", she seemed disorganised and at a loss in all aspects of existence that would be guided by a "principle of duty". Every act had to be undertaken in correspondence with other people's demands, and only in this way, having been subjected to rigid preparatory rituals, could it be brought to a conclusion. So she was punctual and precise in her work, assiduous and loyal in her friendships, though at the cost of sacrificing her own desires and personal plans (for example, breaking off a romantic relationship because of the narcissistic needs and demands of a homosexual friend who wanted an exclusive bond with her). On the other hand, when desires and needs of her own arose, her anancasms forced her into interminable cosmetic preparations in front of the bathroom mirror, after which she would take refuge in bed exhausted, plunging into the darkness of a dreamless sleep. In this way she signed up pointlessly to gyms or English lessons or technology courses which she was never able to attend, and analysis likewise suffered from the impossibility of Camilla devoting herself to the task of becoming free of herself. She regularly missed sessions: once intoxicated by her preparatory rituals, she was gripped by a soporific torpor which seemed to rob her all vital energy.

Her apparently worried parents seemed to urge her into activity, but in fact there was something about her not going out that appeared to tranquillise them. Her father, a thorough and meticulous employee, divided his time between working and looking after his mother, who had been widowed early and whom he attended solicitously right up to the end of her life. Camilla's mother seemed to have more vitality but found it hard to tolerate any change. When, as a result of the analytic work, Camilla became able to think about reorganising her "little room", moving some objects which had been considered untouchable till then, bringing order to the chaos of accumulating items that were previously considered incapable of being disentangled, she encountered a "strange" and implacable opposition from her mother.

The traumatic constellation, the *proton pseudos* of Camilla's obsessionality, seemed to have derived its first impulse in her childhood experience from the birth of a sister when she was two years old. Jealousy, sibling rivalry, hatred, anal sadism, badly managed by the poor care given by two parents with difficulties, seemed to confirm in full Freud's thesis of *Zwangsneurosen*: it seemed that Camilla had to set aside, isolate, and retrospectively cancel the affects of a primary aggressive conflict. Ambivalent and fixated at the anal stage, she might have seemed imprisoned by an internalised sadomasochistic relationship in the form of a scarcely bearable tension between the Ego and a particularly cruel Superego.

In the analytic field, however, it gradually became possible that Camilla might be able to present herself "as she was": little by little, she had started to come to the session with her hair not perfectly combed, not dressed as if she had to appear on a catwalk, sometimes even wearing dungarees, no makeup, her hair still wet as if she'd rushed out of the house. In the analyst's mind there had been reveries taking shape which painted Camilla as the victim of an original violence, a fierce and pitiless enchantment: Sleeping Beauty, Rapunzel, Snow White, Beauty and the Beast.

What fairy tale, what fiction was the analytic field composing? What other violence could the anancasms of Camilla's obsessionality be speaking about? And to what extent might the obsessionality of the analytic device, with the necessary rituals of the setting, reiterate her original enchantment? Was it becoming possible to think that the missed sessions were not only the symptomatic expressions of a resistance, but the desperate communication of a need for freedom and mirroring?

After having been transferred by the company she worked for to a shop/studio in a different region for a month, Camilla had come back to analysis surprised, even amazed. Outside the four walls of her house, far from home (and perhaps also far from the analytic rituals), she had felt transformed: light, full of energy, able to get up in the morning without being compelled to perform the liturgies and purification rites of the bathroom and the mirror. She went out among people without being afraid that she'd disgust them, worked without feeling compelled to check her every move, and spent happy evenings with her colleagues.

However, after returning home she had plunged back into the enchantment, into the constriction of an apparent disease of idealisation. The analyst's response was a reflex, oneiric, and spontaneous: "I thought it would be better to go on with our analysis like this: come to a session when you want to. You're under no obligation to these four walls. I'm here and you'll come when you can."

The meaning of the enchantment to which Camilla was subject became evident only gradually, as is often the case with obsessive patients: the sense of a transgenerational illusion of being able to control the uncontrollable; the promise that by not being separated, not being differentiated, refusing change, replacing the unpredictable movement of life with ritualism, we can emancipate ourselves from death and enter the eternity of an unchanging existence, though with the irrefutable condition that we renounce any form of passion and ecstasy.

So, is obsessionality just a state of mind characterised by an established (or frozen/paralysed) internal conflict which can be imagined and comprehended thanks to the metaphor of the siege? Can it just be attributed to an oppressive internal stalemate in which thoughts that are acknowledged as one's own (though disagreeable and intrusive) parasitise psychic life, so that the subject tries to flee them by obeying the orders of another internal authority which dictates the content of his or her thoughts and/or the directions for his or her behaviour? Or is it a question of something not worked through or impossible to work through, which spans the generations?

Perhaps we need to take a step back and consider how the efforts at classification have developed from the initial intuitive nucleus.

Unlike other forms of psychic distress, of which we find precise descriptions going back to antiquity, obsessionality is a disturbance that we do not find in literature until the fourteenth and fifteenth centuries. The authors of the texts which address it belonged to religious orders of various confessional traditions and used the past participle of the verb *obsidēre* as a noun in the passive voice to designate the one besieged (*ossessus*, possessed, persecuted), or in the active voice to refer to the role of the besieging force (the devil, the evil and malignly influencing spirit). Rather an eloquent example of what has always been intuited – and at the same time denied: the intersubjective genealogy of psychic phenomena.

In the most famous treatise on witchcraft, the *Malleus maleficarum* by Jacob Sprenger and Institor Kramer published 1487, the obsessed are a class of demons which can easily be driven out by minor exorcisms, vanquished for example by resorting to the cult of relics (Sanavio, 2014). However, in the work of the German exorcist, Johann Joseph Gassner (1727–79), the classification of illnesses due to malign influences is based on a three-part scheme which distinguishes the clinical scenarios caused by witchcraft and called *obsessio*, from those in which the disturbances are attributable to diabolical forces which simulate a natural illness (*circumsessio*), and others in which the symptomatology would have been caused by diabolical possession: *possessio* (Ellenberger, 1970; Mangini, 2005).

At the present time, the World Health Organisation defines obsessive thoughts as "ideas, images or impulses which repeatedly enter the mind of the subject in a stereotyped way" (International Statistical Classification of Diseases and Related Health Problems (ICD-10, WHO Version for 2016). The symptoms are described as "almost invariably painful (because they are violent, obscene or simply meaningless)" and, though acknowledged by the patient as his or her own, they seem to be characterised by the struggle which "the subject generally tries without success to resist them" (ibid.). Similarly, "compulsive actions or rituals are stereotyped behaviours which are continually repeated," even though "they are not in themselves pleasant, nor result in the achievement of tasks of any use in themselves," and are characterised by the fact "the patient sees them as a way to ward off some objectively unpleasant event" which he or she imagines may happen (ibid.).

With regard to the tradition which has always distinguished between "ego-dystonic symptoms" and "ego-syntonic disturbances", in the tenth edition of the *International Classification of Diseases* (ICD-10) obsessive-compulsive scenarios are classified in two long diagnostic chapters:

1   Neurotic syndromes (F40–F48) – where the manifestations of obsessionality are called "F42 obsessive-compulsive syndrome" in order to emphasise their still uncertain and not clearly definable nosological status.
2   Adult personality and behavioural disorders (F60–F69), the manifestations of which appear in category "F60.5 Anankastic personality disorders".

The most ambitious and, in its time, innovative diagnostic tool available for those working in the field of mental health, the *Diagnostic Statistical Manual* (DSM) of the American Psychiatric Association, had divided the topic of obsessionality under two headings (OCD and OCPD, as we saw earlier). In recent years, this manual has undergone a series of conceptual transformations which are worth analysing with some care, but at arm's length (that is, without losing our way in the minutiae: resisting the temptation, which this tool makes all too easy, to concentrate "obsessively" on details).

Despite the long tradition of the study of psychopathology (which maintained that obsessional neurosis was nosologically autonomous from other forms of neurosis), both DSM-III and DSM-IV locate OCD among the anxiety disturbances, since – as Gabbard (1994, p. 252, 1991) writes, trying to justify the choice – the primary function of an obsession or a ritual seems to be that of regulating anxiety.

The most significant innovations in the DSM's system were the diagnostic criteria and decision-making algorithms, which permit diagnostic definitions to be put into practice and improve the percentages of agreement (inter-rater reliability) with which a disturbance is noted by the clinical practice which makes use of the manual. Using this logic, both the third and fourth editions of the DSM championed the need to classify the patient's functioning on the basis of a plurality of viewpoints called "axes": disturbances of the clinical type as traditionally understood (axis i), personality disorders (axis ii), pre-existent and intercurrent somatic diseases (axis iii), life events and stressful psychosocial factors (axis iv), and the level of relational functioning observed during the previous year (axis v).

As in the WHO definition of health, in DSM-III, IV, and 5, an obsessive-compulsive disorder noted on axis i could thus be combined with a obsessive-compulsive personality disorder on axis ii. The latter is diagnosed when at least four of the following eight psychopathological factors are noted:

1   excessive attention to details, rules, lists, and order to the point that the main aim of the activity is lost;
2   perfectionism which interferes with the fulfilment of tasks;
3   excessive dedication to work and productivity, to the detriment of recreational activities and friendships;
4   conscientiousness, scrupulosity, and inflexibility in ethics and values;
5   inability to throw away used objects of little value;
6   reluctance to delegate one's own tasks to others unless they adhere exactly to one's own way of doing them;
7   lack of generosity to oneself and others;
8   rigidity of thought and obstinacy of character.

In 2014, however, the status of obsessiveness in psychiatric diagnosis changed radically. As if responding to one of the most critical contributions of the previously cited *Psychoanalytic Inquiry* (a paper by Chessick challengingly entitled "Acronyms Do Not Make a Disease", *Psychoanal. Inq.*, 21(2): 183–207, 2001)

DSM-5 threw over the nosological approach of the previous editions, did away with the logic of the multi-axial classifications, and detached obsessive-compulsive disorder from the collection of anxiety disorders to which it had previously been related (APA, 2013). After being lumped together with heterogeneous psychic disturbances, and having a highly dubious nosological status endowed with a diagnostic value equal to that of ODC (compulsive collecting, trichotillomania, picking at the skin) obsessionality has become a heading in its own right, losing all its correlations with other state-trait psychopathological manifestations which make it so elusive (in this field, anyone who daily crosses the threshold between the normal and the pathological), but thus also helpful and relevant on the clinical level.

Blurring its uncertain boundaries with normality on the one hand and with the category of personality disorders on the other, DSM-5's new OCD attests to the persistence of a biological and pharmacocentric drift which exacerbates the consequences of its own most debatable assumptions, provoking heated polemics and much justifiable perplexity (Frances, 2013). In fact, what disappears with this choice of classification is the most delicate problem in the diagnoses of obsessional disturbances, which is the need to recognise, behind the more immediate symptomatology, the characteristics of the overall psychic functioning of the subject in whom the symptomatology has been organised.

But what is disavowed above all is the failure of the freely oneiric and creatively poetic dimension interwoven into all human suffering and every dimension of psychopathology (Manica, 2007), that failure which Arrigo Lucchin (1983, p. 13) has succeeded in transforming into memorable, heartrending, indispensable poetry:

> Mario L. (Obsessional neurosis. Voluntary hospitalisation.) Anxious; ruminates obsessively over contradictory ideas. Feels distant from people, no meaning to the actions he tries to perform. Always stops himself half way through.
>
> My thought is a crazed ball struck by an unknown stick runs after itself often breaks muddles its path confuses the beginning and the end straight lines and junctions walks hugging the kerbs sticks to the sides of the table clutches leans against the corners never points towards the centre carefully checks distances evades flees the courtyard the heart of the castle is scared of smashing itself by crashing into the skittle backtracks plunges into the hole.

Maybe that's exactly how it is. On the other side of all their efforts to create a system, the F42s and F60.5s, the fighter-bombers of obsessionality in apparent pursuit of perfection and an order that would enable them to control the world, lose punctuation: commas, full stops, semi-colons. Any suspension, any waiting or break that tells of the other's (the object's) presence/absence seems to situate itself in the obsessive circle which has an essentially traumatic character. The *nothing* of the breast's absence looks out, with no possibility of intermediation, onto *nothing*: onto the void, that precipice of death which, instead of following life, seems to precede any possibility of it (Gabburi, 2005; Manica, 2014).

3.2 The psychoanalytic tradition

The questions that no clinician can evade, because they give rise to the possibilities of development, prognostic hypotheses, and therapeutic choices, could perhaps be articulated along these lines: what is the psychopathological structure of each specific individual subject's obsessional disturbances? Does obsessionality have evolved and neurotic variants of its own? Or are we in the presence of more primitive, borderline, or psychotic manifestations? Are we dealing with clinical scenarios with a good prognosis which will respond well to analytic treatment or with nosographic areas which the psychopathologists of the past suggested should be characterised as pseudo-neurotic?

A clinical case of a kind encountered quite frequently and with a favourable prognosis might perhaps help us to clarify the discussion.

MARTINA'S OBSESSIONS

Martina is a woman aged twenty-seven who has just given birth to her second child. Like her first, now aged five, Carlo is a boy with a robust constitution who nevertheless presents with symptoms of a chronic respiratory illness. If the manifestations of the disease turn out to be mild, as everything indicates, no special therapeutic measures will be necessary. Otherwise, the medical treatments will be quite protracted, laborious, and burdensome.

Martina asks for a consultation because she is suffering from sudden, troubling thoughts, which have been provisionally diagnosed as "obsessive-compulsive manifestations". The idea she finds intolerable usually appears towards evening and is a murderous fantasy: for a moment, the idea passes through her mind that she could harm her son with one of the kitchen knives that her husband gave her a while ago.

Within a few weeks, the fear of not being able to control the compulsion, and the obsessive measures she has taken to avoid/control the situation in which she might enact it have developed into a highly incapacitating symptomatology.

Despite usually being uninterested in diagnostic questions, the psychoanalytic literature has been very attentive to the differentiation of clinical scenarios in the case of obsessional neurosis, perhaps because the cases of the "Wolf Man" (Freud, 1914) and the "Rat Man" (Freud, 1909) have increasingly required psychoanalysts to ask themselves questions about the difficulties encountered in treating these types of patient (Manica and Oldoini, 2014).

Both the chapter on obsessionality in the *Trattato di psicoanalisi* (Spaçal, 1989; Semi, 1989), and a detailed monograph in the *Rivista di psicoanalisi* (Mangini, 2005) devote much space to the distinction between acute and chronic versions of OCD, as they also do when describing obsessive personalities and examining their diagnostic and prognostic characteristics (see in particular Speziale Bagliacca, 2004; Gabbard, 1994).

The scheme for assessment proposed by Nancy McWilliams (2011) in her *Psychoanalytic Diagnosis* is well known and justly much cited, having been used in preparing the second edition of the *Psychodynamic Diagnostic Manual (PDM-2)* (Lingiardi, V and McWilliams, N eds. New York, The Guildford Press, 2017).

Indeed, McWilliams proposes that the diagnosis of obsessive-compulsive personalities should only be made after a careful differential diagnosis which isolates them from narcissistic and schizoid personalities and, last but not least, from psycho-organic conditions. When the clinical picture of obsessionality has been clearly recognised, McWilliams suggests paying close attention to what she calls the "developmental aspect" of the disturbance: that is, the intrapsychic and relational organisation achieved by the subject, which permits the neurotic level of obsessionality to be differentiated from the borderline and the psychotic.

So we can understand how Martina's case may belong to the group of acute obsessive manifestations which emerge in personalities that have attained and established a highly developed level of functioning. Indeed, the treatment lasted only a few months and passed through two phases. The first was characterised by a brief period of preliminary clarification which occupied only a few meetings. The second phase of treatment lasted three months in all and developed with one meeting a week. Although the patient regularly used the couch (saying that it helped her feel freer to speak if she didn't have to meet her therapist's gaze), the treatment was not a psychoanalytic psychotherapy in the strict sense (assuming that there is a precise definition of this type of intervention), but rather an intervention/interaction in a crisis.

Being able to benefit from containment in a non-specific setting sui generis, and internally equipped to make spontaneous use of the mind's psychoanalytic function (Bion, 1962; Ogden, 2008), Martina "only" needed an interlocutor who would help her to un-dramatise the scandal provoked in her by the disturbances and to establish the missing nexus between the emergence of the compulsive ideas and the state of mind into which her second pregnancy had precipitated her. When no longer faced with the assailing/controlling siege of obsessive strategies, the compulsive ideas can be transformed, sometimes very quickly. The subject herself, having becoming the effective de-constructor of her constructions, can without too much difficulty undertake the psychic work that is necessary for working through the contents of her thought and the consequent development of her emotional-cognitive integration.

In Martina's case, a dream described in one of the first meetings and then often returned to and discussed, formed the guiding thread in the work of re-elaboration. Thanks to Winnicott's pages on physiological hate of the child in the mother-infant relationship, the therapist is able to help the patient to trace her scandalous compulsions back to the emotions stirred up in her by the problems of motherhood in general and by the birth of her second child in particular. Even a much-loved child is a factor causing dramatic reorganisation of psychic and social life which concerns both parents, but especially the mother. Dreams like the one described below help us to recognise the multi-functional nature of psychic life and to tolerate emotions which can be understood and un-dramatised, once we have rethought the social and existential context in which they are being manifested.

MARTINA'S PRIVATE FABLE

Martina says she dreamed of waking abruptly from a particularly deep sleep and deciding to go to the kitchen in the dark so as not to wake anyone else. She was hungry and thirsty. As she groped her way forwards, she seemed to feel irregularities under her feet, as if the children had left their toys on the floor. Suddenly, something occurred to her: she switched on the light and saw that what she'd been treading on was gnomes and Smurfs which move around her house at night. Her distress at damaging the Smurfs woke her up, but her state of mind quickly changed from distress to relief. "Luckily it was only a dream!"

In her dream, Marina returns to the themes which torment her and transforms them into a private fable (the mysterious nocturnal invasion, the urgent presence of her neglected primary needs, the accidental and grotesque un-dramatised deaths detectable only by turning on the light). Magical and imaginary figures are paying the price for her anxieties, while her children, fortunately, are safe in their beds.

Naturally, cases like this are by no means prototypical of OCD. However, they do represent one extreme of the diagnostic continuum: that in which the symptomatology is of recent inception (i.e. it has never appeared before), is acute (in the reactions it provokes in the subject and those around her) and lacks any correlation with the structure of the subject's personality (who has no specific co-morbidity in the psychic dimensions which characterise her mental disposition).

The observation of the processes of elaboration in these cases is as fleeting as the flow of representative transformations is rapid, and in particular the translation of the micro-transformations which are observed in the clinical dialogue into macro-transformations which stably reorganise psychic life.

Let's move on to the opposite extreme: the varieties of obsessiveness which are found on the more "chronic" and decidedly psychotic side of the continuum.

PAOLO'S BACKWARDS STEPS

Paolo is a forty-two year-old man, the second of numerous siblings. He is referred by the psychologist caring for him in the therapeutic community which has been housing him for some months. Paolo was diagnosed with OCD when he was aged about fifteen. Supported by his family, he had been able at the time to undertake psychotherapy which had enabled him to make improvements on the behavioural level (compulsive and highly disabling cleaning rituals) and to complete, though with delays, a diploma in accountancy.

When he was twenty, Paolo lost his father in a road accident. His father had been a barman and worked late into the night: but the patient is afraid of the dark, keeps as many lights on as he can, and even compels his room-mate to reverse the rhythm of sleeping and waking.

After the accident, the family's life changes radically. This is when Paolo's relationship with the public services begins, and his clinical situation stops improving. The community centre staff know that he made two other experiments in residential settings before coming to live with them. The first of these was in a community in Liguria: a small set-up near an inland village but within sight of the sea. Here Paolo starts to improve. He establishes lasting relationships with workers and fellow inmates, takes care of himself without excessive hygiene, and moves freely in the limited geographical context available to him. However, the community is low on funds and has to be expanded. Paolo is transferred to another residential service for better functioning patients: personality disorders and eating disorders. The second experience quickly becomes a disaster. In a few weeks Paolo loses what he had gained over the previous years, and continues to deteriorate over the next five years. When his case managers decide to transfer him again, Paolo is no longer in the grip of the cleaning rituals which characterised him in the past. He is now a sort of vagrant: he doesn't wash of his own accord or cut his beard and hair, alternating a supine submission to the injunctions of the care team with outbursts of apparently unmotivated anger.

The critical factor which brought about the change is not hard to intuit. Needing, as he does, to exercise an absolute control over his objects, Paolo does not move flexibly in the triangle of emotional positions between which we oscillate as we organise our emotional experience (the autistic-contiguous position, the paranoid-schizoid, and the depressive). He prefers the material and tangible kind which are immobile and can be handled to those that are human and relational, which in his experience are unstable and hard to predict. Out of the fusional and autistic-contiguous position (Ogden, 1989), which confers a relative stability on being-in-the-world, we usually emerge accepting the alternation of illusions and disappointments: in other words, reconciling ourselves to a certain degree of omnipotence and impotence following on from each other, which gives way to the alternation between paranoid-schizoid and depressive positions.

Paolo agreed to leave home and be placed in a community which should have been therapeutic, and so he ran the risk of letting someone enter the sphere of his existential concerns. But things did not go as hoped and he probably felt abandoned by the very people with whom he had lived up until then. When the world around him changed, Paolo (like the protagonist of *The Pointsman*, a Dutch film of 1986) was not able to reorganise himself and gave up the struggle. Instead of insisting on looking after himself by controlling his internal world with rituals and obsessive algorithms, he gave in to destructive compulsions which manifested themselves in attacks on his external appearance and in apparently incomprehensible and exasperated protests. "Look, now he's furious because the coffee is never good enough for him," says a worker at the community. "His father worked in a bar: he really did know how to make coffee!"

Using the McWilliams scale, this case can be understood as a type of OCD characterised by a level of psychic and relational functioning which has steadily deteriorated. On an emotional level probably characterised by difficulties in separation/individuation, in maintaining object constancy and thus stabilising the relationship, Paolo has taken a number of steps back over the years. Traumatised by the losses which short-circuited his relationship with his father, he tends to shut himself away in a withdrawal from the human context, which is probably founded on the recourse to ever more primitive psychic defences: denial, Ego-splitting, primitive idealisation and self-denigration, and dissociation.

Between these two extremes are the cases which come to the psychoanalyst's consulting room, usually entailing prolonged treatments which sometimes obtain partial and debatable clinical results and sometimes are highly satisfactory.

CARLO AND THE LONG PROCESS OF "CLIMBING BACK UP"

A wealthy family's only heir, Carlo graduated in chemistry like his father, who died when he was an adolescent. When I meet him for the first time, he is a little over thirty, and is accompanied by the impressive and dominating figure of his mother who is terrified by her son's distress and unable to make any headway against the obsessive ideas which constantly occupy his thoughts.

I am being consulted about the second major crisis which Carlo has experienced.

The first had been a hypochondriacal crisis originating in a compulsive idea (the fear that he had contracted mad cow disease). This time the disturbances initially concerned his girlfriend, because it is Marta's demands (or rather, the demands which these have set in motion inside him) which constitute the true novelty of his life. His obsessive thinking is an interminable rumination about his girlfriend's body, which he judges to be different from the idea to which he aspired, and inadequate to function as a narcissistic complement to his own. Nevertheless, Carlo has a vigorous sex life with Marta. His experience of this aspect of life is a heterogeneous mélange which combines old onanistic practices (anal masturbation, organised on the basis of his mother's habit of regulating his sphincter activity with glycerine suppositories) with frenetic genital activity: the Dionysiac hypersexuality of which Meltzer writes.

The analysis of four sessions a week lasts for six years, and its management clinically and theoretically benefits from the conceptual model of original mourning (Racamier, 1992; Sassolas, 1999). Various processes develop in parallel during the treatment. Inside the consulting room, Carlo seems to be looking for a father figure to help him mourn his highly tenacious fusional aspects, to which his mother continues to give very strong and concrete support. Outside the consulting room, he at first confines himself to action (he buys a racing motorbike, for example, and then starts attending large sporting events, racing in the amateur category), but later, a little at a time, he begins to reflect on the meaning of his intense motoric activity.

The interpretative line followed in order to encourage reflection on his ruminations about his girlfriend's body makes reference to the model of narcissistic object relations: the female figure is fantasied as an ideal which can never be given up, since only if it is perfect can the subject hope to reconstruct with her an analogue of primitive relational fusion.

While the work proceeds on this level, the patient's own body is discussed: its speed and sporting activity. On various occasions, I tell him that he seems to be using motoric activity to strengthen his growing autonomy from the female universe. His mother's and girlfriend's opposition to his use of the motorbike facilitates the analyst's work, which has to show both a reasonable (maternal) anxiety about the consequences of a mobility manically powered by mechanical prostheses, and a (paternal) understanding of the developmental reasons for this aspect of his psychic functioning.

Each new cycle of the analytic process, each new phase in the laborious freeing of Carlo from the primal fantasy, is accompanied by a reorganisation of his relationship, first with cars and motorbikes and then with the analyst, and finally with the body and with mobility.

When he finally begins to be afraid of excessive speed and tells me that this makes him feel like a coward, I tell him that his fear of cowardice is an interesting theme with which to confront his paternal figure and that, in fact, fear is the beginning of wisdom. It is not difficult to make him observe that the absence of anxiety about the risks incurred by his activities reflects a presumption of immortality and constitutes one of the omnipotent fantasies which have sustained his relationship with his mother.

The following year – the fourth year of analysis – Carlo gets married.

One day, as he was leaving work, a colleague makes a joke about his cars, which strikes him forcibly. "Nice ride!" he says, commenting on the Mercedes in which Carlo has come to work. "You've only got all this because of your mother's money."

We talk about this a lot for several sessions. The colleague's joke is taken on board by the patient as a pertinent and largely "accurate" comment, although cruel and maybe envious. It's not long after that, however, that Carlo starts to get rid of his motor vehicles and begins to ride a bicycle, goes jogging, and loses weight.

The analysis ends during the following year.

3.3   Orienting oneself: obsessionality and the bi-personal clinical field

After an initial delineation (psychopathological and psychoanalytic) of anankastic experiences and having reviewed their complex diagnostic articulations, we can now try to put together a reflection on the observational and interactive (inter-subjective, inter-psychic, and trans-psychic) functions which are implied by the demands of treatment.

As in any psychopathological sphere, including the obsessional, we have the possibility of thinking about the constitution of a field (intersubjective, inter-psychic, dual) and, equally, we can hypothesise the existence of an experience which may remain outside the field (group, trans-personal, social). So, in clinical assessment and in taking on therapeutic responsibilities, what are the specific and aspecific factors to be taken into account? What functions may the diagnosis in the field and/or outside the field come to assume? And, given that the field is bi-personal from the outset, how far can diagnosis, being essentially and deeply uni-personal, have anything to do with it?

In the first instance, we could say that diagnosis has nothing whatever to do with the field. In the end, the field is loyal to Freud: the patient's illness must be the illness – the transference neurosis – of the field. But perhaps, viewed from a different vertex, the diagnosis could be worked out as a piece of sensitive, trans-personal information from outside the field, capable on the one hand of facilitating the importing into the field of a greater number of clinical factors and, on the other hand, the exporting to the institutional and social third of what has been created in the field (as is done, for example, when working in a multidisciplinary setting).

We believe that, in order to navigate these uncertain paths, the psychopatho-logical meaning of diagnosis must first of all be recovered: that is, diagnosis as a description and knowledge of the world and of a particular relationship of the other with reality and with him or herself. We cannot conceal from ourselves the fact that as clinicians (as psychoanalysts in clinical practice) we constantly oscil-late in the course of our work between two states with radically different natures. A constant oscillation between "being-with-someone" and "having-something-in-front-of-us" (Cargnello, 1980), because even the facts of psychoanalysis, as Mod-ell (1984) observed, can be situated within two different categories depending on the relationship which the observer maintains with the "thing" observed: the suffering other and the modes of his or her suffering. In the end, the state of objec-tivation is an inescapable part of any cognitive operation (Rossi Monti, 2008).

In the case of obsessional disturbances, we cannot fail to take into account the fact that, in order to work effectively, every clinician needs to pass back and forth through the stage of reduction and diagnostic summarising. Just as we clearly cannot stop at diagnosis, since the psychoanalytic focus, Freud's *Fixierung*, can-not be adopted as a model or tool for diagnostic fixity, nor can it be understood as the expression of a rigid mechanism in the libido's developmental stages. It must instead be recovered as a possible way to represent the traumatic events which can intervene more or less early on in life to distort, arrest or divert the development (perhaps even the birth) of the mind and its capacities for thinking and symbolis-ing: for giving sense to life and for comprehending its beauty.

So, from a psychoanalytic perspective, a diagnosis, any diagnosis, immediately flips over into the necessity for reflection on the indicators that there may be for organising the setting (pharmaco-psychiatric support, involvement of the nuclear family, social mediators, etc.) and on the limits of analysability. In the latter case, we believe that the criterion for what is and is not analysable consists above all in the analyst questioning him or herself without prejudice about his or her abil-ity to take on the responsibility for maintaining a setting with this specific patient (Manica, 2010). This responsibility must be understood first of all in its etymo-logical sense as a capacity for responding to the needs of that patient, and a setting which must be thought of more in terms of a disposition within the analyst than as a formal framework, even though a framework is absolutely indispensable.

Compared to the classical "psychopathological diagnosis" – which acquires substance as a form of knowledge achieved through the patient, or passes through the patient (-K) – the "psychoanalytic diagnosis" is a form of knowledge (K→O) achieved "in between": that is to say, in what happens between patient and analyst in that fabric of projective identifications which weave the bi-personal field of their relationship.

Overall then, it is necessary for the analyst to be aware of his or her own readiness to pass beyond the Pillars of Hercules of an exotic human experience, and to have available a personal and professional novel which will enable him to face what for him or her may be a never-before-thought-unknown, without ceasing to be him or herself.

As Bleger (1967, p. 88) wrote:

> Exaggerating slightly, I could say that the analysis of these patients does not reside fundamentally . . . in analysing the patients, but in the analyst being able to analyse what the patient is continually making of the analyst, with the aim of playing only the role of depository without becoming fused with what is deposited, *thereby preserving the analyst's personality or identity.*
>
> [My italics]

Movement, going to meet, opening oneself up, accepting are dimensions which the anankastic world seems unable to accommodate. It is too assailed, too constrained, too obliged, too inhabited by an original violence to be able to make itself permeable to the encounter with the object and with the other.

Diagnostic definitions try to shore up a mystery about differentiating oneself, the search to be oneself over the abyss which distinguishes the true Self from the false Self and over the abyss which situates the individual Self within the group Self. In its rigorous and apparently efficacious search for order, obsessionality disorientates us.

Perhaps a metaphor and an extra-clinical observation can come to our aid.

3.3.1 The metaphor

In baseball – as in clinical practice – the ball thrown by the pitcher (patient?), with the most unpredictable trajectories, can be hit right out of the park by the batter (analyst?), thereby achieving what is called in the sporting jargon a home run.

In this case, do we have a success or a failure (disaster)?

In the basic economy of baseball as a sport, it is undoubtedly a success for the batter and a defeat for the pitcher and his team.

In baseball as a metaphor for the analytic encounter, on the other hand, a diagnosis "hit" by the analyst in a merciless, reifying way (even if only in his or her own mind) objectifies the patient and risks forcing him or her into hyperbole (Bion, 1965): not only the ball/diagnosis, but the patient him or herself (or his or her essential parts) can be hit out of the park. In fact, as Bion (1970, p. 150) astutely observed, a patient who is forced into "acting out the analysis is 'in' a situation of which the boundaries are unknown."

And the never-thought-unknown – the exotic – frightens the patient as much as it does the analyst. Maybe there is a β and an O in obsessionality which disorientates us. The diagnosis tries to create order in disorder, and disorder pushes against the definition of any possible order.

Perhaps we should go back to Bion (ibid., p. 121):

> Actions that appear to be compulsive are in reality *beta-elements* confined to the domain of action and thus *insulated*[1] against thoughts, which are confined to the domain of thought – which includes psycho-analysis. Similarly, thoughts are within the domain of thought and cannot be influenced by *beta-elements* confined within the domain of action.
>
> [My italics]

Resorting to the jargon of Bion's Grid (see Chapter 7), we can perhaps think that in obsessionality, swarms of beta elements shoot into A6 or slip into F1 (into column 6/action or into row F/concept of the Grid) without the possibility of passing through column 2 and row C, without having been able to encounter the rêverie of that maternal/paternal unconscious which might transform them into dreamthoughts, myths or dreams (see Table 3.1).

Table 3.1 Bion's Grid

	Definitory Hypothesis 1	Ψ 2	Notation 3	Attention 4	Inquiry 5	Action 6	...n
A β-elements	A1	A2				A6	
B α-elements	B1	B2	B3	B4	B5	B6	...Bn
C Dreams Thoughts, Dream Myths	C1	C2	C3	C4	C5	C6	...Cn
D Pre-conception	D1	D2	D3	D4	D5	D6	...Dn
E Conception	E1	E2	E3	E4	E5	E6	...En
F Concept	F1	F2	F3	F4	F5	F6	...Fn
G Scientific Deductive System		G2					
H Algebraic Calculus							

From a more current psychoanalytic perspective, we could perhaps think of the Grid as a periodic table of the emotional elements which compose the relational field, as an organogram which decodes the interactions of the infant's mind with those of the object, the mother/environment, in the same way that it could allow us to decode the communications between patient and analyst.

But if the Grid is a sort of map of the analytic field, how can we orient ourselves outside the field? What Pole Star could show us the way in a (Bionian) "situation of which the boundaries are unknown?"

3.4   The ♀/♂ dialectic and the dimensions of the field

The field is created, exists, lives inside the analytic consulting room. Hence, it has extension in space and time, but this does not stop it being constantly assailed ("obsessed") by the world outside the field: a pathogenic constellation in the family, a dogmatic institution, a fundamentalist group, or a structure organised on basic assumptions can absorb and neutralise the field's creative derivatives and transform the diagnosis, for example, into stigma. Thus, knowledge gained through the vitality of the analytic encounter can be induced to stop being diaphanous, transparent: lightness and light become opacity and heaviness. The psychoanalysis of obsessionality risks becoming a psychoanalytic obsession which, instead of generating development, is forced to uproot itself from its own generative matrix of meanings. The trans-personal (and always potentially traumatic) world outside the field can then suffocate the bi-personal field. In extreme cases, the group reacts to the new, to the messianic idea (Bion, 1970), which an individual mystic would like to visualise, and envelops it in the reiteration of an ideology that is always exposed to anankastic temptation. Indeed, obsessionality tends towards groups and claims to tame any thought that is "wandering" or "wild" by nature (Bion, 1977). And this tendency could confirm the fact that every improvement achieved by an obsessional patient in analysis comes up against the resistance of those around him or her. Just as it confirms the fact that every new psychoanalytic idea clashes with the establishment's "Bible".

So, what kind of obsessionality does "anankastic politics" tell us about? The obsessionality of the field or the world outside the field? The analyst's politics or the patient's?

Obsessionality robs the lambs of silence:[2] if the patient isn't "dirty", the analyst is, or vice versa. It seems essential to "wash one's hands" ad infinitum, to suspend time and diffuse space because any change could incur the danger of "dirtying oneself" again, of acknowledging that no form of life is immune to death. Thus, the world outside the field is intolerant of the new that is generated in the field. But except in illusion, no anankastic group constellation generates life but, on the contrary becomes – to borrow Morton Schatzman's (1973) classic definition – a "family that kills".

Here we encounter the difficulty of multidisciplinary treatments and psychoanalytically informed approaches. Here the analyst must be able to trust the *epoché* of his or her theories and must succeed in overturning the world outside the field in suspending every prejudice and every pre-constituted ideology. Obsessionality is the disease of prejudice and for this reason it is intimately related to delusion, with that "morbid error of judgement" which the psychopathology of Jaspers (Jaspers, 1913) proposed as the essential formal definition of delusional experience. So, any possibility of treatment is played out not in the transferring of comprehension (*verstehen*) of the field to the necessity of explaining (*erklären*) the world outside the field, but perhaps comes about in their intersection. Knowledge (*gnosis*) makes itself diagnostic: it must pass through the symptom and break up by means of the symptom, where the mind intersects with the body and where the individual intersects with the group.

To clarify this last, indispensable aspect of our discussion, we will make use of a final clinical case.

PLAYING WITH FEDERICO

When, by means of analysis, Federico dilutes the ritual behaviour which makes his life a prison, his fibromyalgic and chronically depressed mother seems to go mad: she claims that Federico is celebrating her suffering and is responsible for the incurability of her illness. His father explodes into a boundless fury.

The hyper-contained (♂) has, as it were, burst out of its isolation, the safety belt flimsily yet rigidly created by a succession of inadequate containers (♀):

To stop the haemorrhage, the analyst decides to arrange a session with Federico and his parents: a micro-version of mother (or parent/s)-child therapy where the analyst plays with the child in order to allow the parents to take part in the game and create a playing ensemble. The aim will then become not only that of transmitting "digestible" meanings (♂), but also the method – the transformation in play (Ferro, 2019 – which enables them to be generated.

And in the relationship between the field and what is outside the field, between "dyadic" and "group", two intuitions extrapolated from the thinking of Francesco Corrao (1983, 1993) seem rich in new possibilities.

The first intuition, not in chronological order, concerns the observation (Corrao, 1993, p. 177) that "it is not possible . . . to use group models in the radical sense to explain the phenomena which are experienced in dyadic situations; conversely, it is not possible to use the situations experienced in the dyadic field in order to give an exhaustive explanation of group situations." More specifically, it would not be correct from a theoretical (or clinical) viewpoint to extrapolate directly from the field to the world outside the field or vice versa.

The second theoretical elaboration would refer to the distinction proposed by Corrao (1983) between β elements and weak β elements. If it is the latter which burst into the group, we have the possibility on the one hand, of transforming them into micro-hallucinations and, on the other, of working on them by means of a specific group function which, in an analogy with individual α function, could be called a γ function.

And yet we have the feeling that (trans-personal) γ function is more delicate and less powerful than (personal) α function: thus, when the individual psychic destructurings with their disorganising character come to produce strong β elements, as in the case of anankastic disturbances, not only do they produce violent projective identifications, but also bring exposure to the risk of explosive micro-hallucinatory expulsions.

Corrao writes (ibid., p. 51):

> Furthermore, strong beta elements can probably be conveyed into the structuring of basic assumptions, conferring on them an impetus which strengthens their translation into acting-out, but above all, endowing them with the primitive characteristics of proto-mental activity, previously split off from the processes of symbolisation, and moreover capable of provoking chaotic turbulence or *freezing solid in the group*.
>
> [My italics]

What saves the patient from becoming psychotic is isolation from the turbulence of their affects, the "freezing solid", control, as much in dyadic situations as in groups: the content, a hyper-content ♂ is surrounded and "besieged" by a corona of hyper-evolved containers ♀ incapable of assimilating it:

$$
\begin{array}{ccc}
 & ♀ & \\
♀ & & ♀ \\
♀ & ♂ & ♀ \\
♀ & & ♀ \\
 & ♀ & \\
\end{array}
$$

From Corrao's perspective, the only transformative possibility is given by the propensity of the analyst: of his whole personality (and not only of his Ego), to take on an operational disposition – both in group and dyadic situations – which leads him to become a "simulator" of the patient's experiences; unquestionably not a simulator in a social sense, but in the sense that he is able to construct within himself an apparatus of simulation similar to that by which a certain event is simulated on the computer.

The obsessiveness of (group) diagnosis or that of the (dyadic) analytic device can also then become part of a fiction which as a certain similarity to the world of the theatre, in which the whole experience of simulation comes into play. And a good actor has to be able to activate a system of simulation relevant to the character he or she is "performing". Corrao also writes (1993, p. 181):

> The theatrical situation is interesting in the degree to which there is a meta-phorical representation of the mind as "theatrical" . . . but the Freudian model is, in fact, impregnated with the theatrical dimension which, to the degree to which it has provided us with a dimension of the personality as plural, multiple, has populated our mind with "theatrical" images and characters, or at least characters in that kind of relationship to each other, to be configured into a situation which is unquestionably dramaturgic. The theatrical dimension, incidentally, is present in all the descriptions which Melanie Klein has given us of the object world. The theatrical dimension is relevant to the group situation: we need only take a step in the direction of Moreno's (1953) model of taking on roles to encounter the psychodrama of the group.

Only by means of fiction, the simulation of dream, the activation of a dreaming ensemble (Grotstein, 2007), and a dream-playing can one withdraw from the siege which obsessionality organises in the dyadic field; and perhaps also through the recovery of a poetic dream-function of diagnosis can one preserve the analytic field from the assault and temptation of the world outside the field.

3.5   Concluding observations

Poets say all this in their own way, and that is with greater concision and some-times also more clearly. In order to challenge the predominance of thinking that is too slow, too precise and obsessive, which in the end only has "ornamental" value, what is needed – as Mariangela Gualtieri claims in *Bestia di gioia* – is to understand the function which is implicit in weeping: that is, the importance of an emotion which has become strong because it is nourished by a "bold grief".

It is better not to imitate "marble", men. Better not to deceive ourselves into thinking we can always control, order, and triumph over the uncertain. Better something that takes the fictional form (+obsessiveness, positive obsessiveness) of an analysis, a negative capability, β-without-too-much-persecution, rather than "marble" (obsessiveness, negative obsessiveness) of Freudian and almost delu-sional "monuments of memory".

Better to know that the facts of life will make us experience emptiness, absence, and pain: the experience of a no-thing which, having been accepted and worked through, will avoid our having to cope with despair and the nothing: with the nothing of *Hilflosigkeit*, when it presents itself in the extreme form of a being (radically) without help (Haynal, 1976).

Notes

1 "Insulated" refers to isolation, one of the essential defence mechanisms postulated by Freud in the genesis of obsessional disturbances.
2 The associative reference is to the film version of *The Silence of the Lambs*.

References

Note: S.E. = *Standard Edition of the Complete Psychological Works of Sigmund Freud*. Trans. J. Strachy. London: Hogarth Press and the Institute of Psychoanalysis.

Abraham, K. (1911). Notes on the Psychoanalytic Investigation and Treatment of Manic-Depressive Insanity and Allied Conditions. In *Selected Papers on Psychoanalysis*. London: Hogarth Press, 1927, pp. 137–56.

Abraham, K. (1924). A Short Study of the Development of the Ego. In *Selected Papers on Psychoanalysis*. London: Hogarth Press, 1927, pp. 418–501.

American Psychiatric Association (APA). (2013). *Diagnostic and Statistical Manual of Mental Disorders, Fifth Edition (DSM-5)*. Washington, DC: APA.

Bion, W.R. (1962). The Psycho-Analytic Study of Thinking. *International Journal of Psychoanalysis*, 43, pp. 306–10.

Bion, W.R. (1965). *Transformations: Change from Learning to Growth*. London: Tavistock.

Bion, W.R. (1970). *Attention and Interpretation*. London: Tavistock Publications.

Bion, W.R. (1977). Emotional Turbulence. In *Borderline Personality Disorders*. London: Karnac Books, 1994.

Bleger, J. (1967). *Symbiosis and Ambiguity: A Psychoanalytic Study*. London: Routledge, 2013, p. 88.

Cargnello, D. (1980). Ambiguità della psichiatria. *Comprendre*, 9, pp. 7–48.

Chessick, R.D. (2001). OCD, OCPD: Acronyms Do Not Make a Disease. *Psychoanalytic Inquiry*, 21(2), pp. 183–207.

Civitarese, G. (2014). Bion and the Sublime: The Origins of an Aesthetic Paradigm. *International Journal of Psychoanalysis*, 95, pp. 1059–86.

Corrao, F. (1983). Il gruppo esperienziale: fondamenti epistemologici. In *Orme II*, Milano: Cortina, 1998.

Corrao, F. (1993). Duale-Gruppale. In *Orme II*, Milano: Cortina, 1998.

Ellenberger, H.E. (1970). *Discovery of the Unconscious: The History and Evolution of Dynamic Psychiatry*. New York: Basic Books, Inc., 1970.

Ferro, A. (2019). *Psychoanalysis and Dreams: Bion, the Field and the Viscera of the Mind*. Abingdon, Oxon: Routledge.

Ferro, A. et al. (2013). *Contemporary Bionian Theory and Technique in Psychoanalysis*. London: Taylor and Francis Ltd, 2017.

Foresti, G., and Rossi Monti, M. (2010). *Esercizi di visioning, psicanalisi, psichiatria, istituzioni*. Roma: Borla.

Frances, A. (2013). *Essentials of Psychiatric Diagnosis: Responding to the Challenge of DSM-5*. New York: Guilford.

Freud, S. (1894). Obsessions and phobias. In *SE*, 3.

Freud, S. (1907). Obsessive Actions and Religious Practice. In *SE*, 9.

Freud, S. (1909). Notes Upon a Case of Obsessional Neurosis (Rat Man Case) Notes Upon a Case of Obsessional Neurosis. In *SE*, 10, pp. 151–318.

Freud, S. (1914). From the History of an Infantile Neurosis (Wolf Man Case). In *SE*, 17, pp. 1–122.

Freud, S. (1922). The Ego and the Id. In *SE*, 19, pp. 1–66.

Freud, S. (1924). An Autobiographical Study. In *SE*, 20, pp. 1–74.

Gabbard, G.O. (1991). Technical Approaches to Transference Hate in the Analysis of Borderline Patients. *International Journal of Psychoanalysis*, 72, pp. 625–37.

Gabbard, G.O. (1994). *Psychodynamic Psychiatry in Clinical Practice* (DSM-IV edition). Arlington, VA: American Psychiatric Association.

Gabbard, G.O. (2000). *Psychodynamic Psychiatry in Clinical Practice* (3rd edition). Washington, DC: American Psychiatric Press.

Gabbard, G.O. (2001). Psychoanalytically Informed Approaches to the Treatment of Obsessive-Compulsive Disorders. *Psychoanalytic Inquiry*, 21(2).

Gabburi, E. (2005). La Caducità addomesticata. In E. mangini (ed.), *Nervosi Ossessiva*. Roma: Borla.

Grotstein, J.S. (2007). *A Beam of Intense Darkness: Wilfred Bion's Legacy to Psychoanalysis*. London: Karnac Books.

Haynal, A. (1976). Le sens du désespoir. *Revue francaise Psychanalyse*, 1977, 1–2, pp. 103–4.

Jaspers, K. (1913/1997). *General Psychopathology*. Trans. J. Hoenig, M.W. Hamilton. Baltimore and London: John Hopkins University Press.

Kancyper, L. (2005). The Confrontation Between Generations as a Dynamic Field. In *Truth, Reality and the Psychoanalyst: Latin American Contributions to Psychoanalysis*. London: International Psychoanalytical Association/Karnac Books.

Laplanche, J., and Pontalis, J.B. (1973). *The Language of Psycho-Analysis*. Trans. Donald Nicholson-Smith. The International Psycho-Analytical Library. London: The Hogarth Press and the Institute of Psycho-Analysis.

Lingiardi, V., and McWilliams, N. (eds.). (2017). *Psychodynamic Diagnostic Manual* (2nd edition). New York: The Guilford Press.

Löwenfeld, L. (1904). *Die psychischen Zwangserscheinungen: Auf klinischer Grundlage dargestellt*. Wiesbaden: Bergmann.

Lucchin, A. (1983). *La Tana degli Secchi*. Roma: Borla.

Mangini, E. (2005). *Nevrosi Ossessiva. Monografie Rivista di psicoanalisi*. Roma: Borla.

Manica, M. (2007). *La musica della psicoanalisi*. Roma: Borla.

Manica, M. (2010). *Fare psicoanalisi, vivere la clinica, sognare la teoria*. Roma: Borla.

Manica, M., and Oldoini, M.G. (2014). *Esite una cura per l'uomo dei lupi? Rottura nella clinica, rottura nella teoria*. XVII Congresso Nazionale della SPI, Milano, May 22–25, 2014.

McWilliams, N. (2011). *Psychoanalytic Diagnosis*. New York: The Guildford Press.

Modell, A.H. (1984). *Psychoanalysis in a New Context*. New York: International Universities Press.

Moreno, J.L. (1953). *Who Shall Survive? Foundations of Sociometry, Group Psychotherapy and Sociodrama*. Oxford, England: Beacon House.

Ogden, T.H. (1989). *The Primitive Edge of Experience*. Northvale, NJ: Jason Aronson.

Ogden, T.H. (2008). *Rediscovering Psychoanalysis: Thinking and Dreaming, Learning and Forgetting*. London: Routledge.

Racamier, P.C. (1992). *Le génie des origines [The spirit of the origins]*. Paris: Payot.

Rossi Monti, M. (2008). Diagnosi: una brutta parola? *Rivista di psicoanalisi*, 54, pp. 795–833.

Sanavio, E. (2014). *Ossessioni. Perché ne siamo vittime e come uscirne*. Bologna: Il Mulino.

Sassolas M. (1999). *Le groupe soignant: Des liens et des repères*, Éditions Érès. Ramonville: Saint-Agne.

Schatzman, M. (1973). *Soul Murder: Persecution in the Family*. New York: Random House.

Semi, A.A. (Ed.). (1989). *Trattato di psicoanalisi (Treatise of Psychoanalysis)*, 2 vols. Milan: R. Cortina.

Spaçal, S. (1989). La nevrosi ossessiva. In A.A. Semi (ed.), *Trattato di psicoanalisi*. Milan: Raffaello Cortina.

Speziale Bagliacca, R. (2004). *Ubi maior. Il tempo e la cura delle lacerazioni del S [Ubi maior. The time and cure of lacerations of the self]*. Rome, Astrolabio Ubaldini.

Chapter 4

Depression
Geographies and histories

Elena Molinari

'Depressed' literally means pushed out of a place where one has felt safe, and so its first association applies to birth as the primary experience of losing a place inside which one has been contained. Hence, extra-uterine space is initially a distressing void causing separation from the mother's body; a space which can be filled by means of a slow apprenticeship in inventing tools which underpin the slow development of physical and psychic capabilities for staying in equilibrium on that terrifying vortex through which the world appears to us.

There is, therefore, an existential depression, one which accompanies our being introduced into the world and which can present during life in more or less prolonged forms every time we are challenged by a situation of loss that is not necessarily concrete and associated with an object.

This is a form of pain innate to the state of being alive, which has the potential to be deadly, but also a creative and developmental force: indeed, the capacity to invent and master tools, and to escape potentially annihilating situations nourishes a sense of efficacy which fosters self-esteem (Winnicott, 1963; Kristeva, 1987; Ogden, 2001). Alongside this condition of difficulty and sadness which periodically comes over life, there exist highly heterogeneous pathological forms of depressive pain (Rossi Monti and Gosio, 2013).

In this chapter, beside the classical psychiatric nosology which defines depression as a mood disturbance and distinguishes its pathological forms into endogenous and reactive, I will use some more imaginative categories. A historical fact has played a part in my being able to imagine and describe the various aspects of depression by adopting a spatial metaphor.

The tightrope-walker Nik Wallenda recently crossed a gorge of the Colorado river on a steel cable with no safety net or harness. In the past few years, in a dizzying crescendo, he has offered the world his performances over more and more perilous drops, testing himself against a challenge which, as he openly says himself, enables him to feel he is continuing the tradition of his family of acrobats.

At the end of his feat, after experiencing the terror of annihilation, we see him kiss the ground in an impulse of affection as if she were a mother welcoming him into her arms.

There are many aspects of this news story that are helpful in visualising and reflecting on what depression can represent, starting from the spatial connotation of its etymology.

Before moving into the field of the pathological forms, I want to dwell on two conditions in which more or less serious depression finds a "natural" soil to grow in: being adolescent and being a woman. I will use the analytic histories of a teenage boy and a woman to describe the instruments that may be helpful in coping with the natural oscillation of the cable, the moves necessary for resisting unexpected gusts, and the abilities needed for keeping one's balance which I have learned to observe in relation to these two patients.

Then, following this spatial metaphor, I will describe the situations in which, rather than taking on the character of a fall into the void, depressive anxiety makes itself felt as a grip which stops one moving forwards.

Without making any claim to nosological innovation, I think it will nevertheless be helpful from a psychoanalytic viewpoint to distinguish the depressions vertically and horizontally in relation to the types of anxiety which permeate them.

By horizontal I mean those forms in which, for variable lengths of time over the course of life, one can experience a sort of cringe, a momentary suspension in the movement of thought which makes psychic life possible, and I will include in this definition those forms which classical nosology calls dysthymias.

In contrast, by vertical depression I mean that defined as major or psychotic depression. In the latter case, life seems suspended, frozen in a past which destroys the present, a vertical falling in a time and space that aren't there. The loss of contact with the present and with reality is diagnostic of psychotic breakdown.

Using clinical examples, I will also consider the main defences which cover the symptoms of depression and sometimes camouflage its pain, transforming it into a state of persistent excitation: something like the reckless performance with which Nick Wallenda seems to exorcise his anxiety about psychic death, presenting himself and the world with a temporary victory over physical death.

Lastly, I shall make a brief digression into infantile depression which I consider a "depository" for that of the parents.

4.1   Holden and Zerocalcare: transforming depression during adolescence

Being sad or having marked oscillations of mood during adolescence is a physiological fact. However, it is a disturbing statistic that in the past thirty years the number of suicides in this age group has tripled, and that suicide is the second highest cause of death during adolescence in Italy (Italian National Institute of Statistics, 2011). The first is road accidents, but here too it is impossible to rule out high speed or driving under the influence of alcohol as symptoms of psychic distress.

The symptoms of adolescent depression can be the same as those of adults: insomnia, restlessness, withdrawal. Or they can be manic defences which cover up the depressive state or alternate with it in bipolar depression: dangerous behaviour, substance abuse, an excessive or promiscuous sexuality.

I will use two literary characters to focus on some therapeutic ingredients in the treatment of depression in adolescence: young Holden (Salinger, 1951), narrator of Salinger's novel *The Catcher in the Rye*, and Zerocalcare, protagonist of a recent cartoon strip conceived by Michele Rech.[1]

4.1.1   The Catcher in the Rye

In this novel, Holden is a depressed and restless adolescent who cannot concentrate his vital energies on objectives which might sustain him and enable him to be accepted socially.

In the novel Salinger describes the week following Holden's expulsion from college, during which he wanders randomly through the city, deferring the feared moment when he will have to tell his parents that he's been expelled.

During a brief, furtive stay in the family home, readying himself for a disappearance into a future without a goal or a plan, something happens that is almost insignificant and at the same time extraordinary. His much younger sister asks him, point-blank, to tell her what he would like "*to be*", a question which wrong-foots him completely. Holden is silent for a long time, painfully transfixed by his feeling lost: that is, his inability to imagine himself in the future.

Then he starts to recount a daydream inspired by a poem by Robert Burns, "If a body meet a body coming through the rye" – though he misremembers the line "as *catch* a body". He images little children playing in a field of rye near a dangerous cliff and at risk of falling:

> I mean if they're running and they don't look where they're going I have to come out from somewhere and *catch* them. That's all I'd do all day. I'd just be the catcher in the rye and all. I know it's crazy, but that's the only thing I'd really like to be. I know it's crazy.
>
> (Salinger, 1951, pp. 179–80)

So, prompted by his little sister, Holden is able to start a transformation inside himself: he imagines the future, receives a question, and in his dream is able to split off a child self in danger from an adult self capable of passionate and responsible action.

He tells us himself in an earlier chapter that the dream is connected to a profound sadness when he describes a little boy he has seen walking in the road instead of on the pavement, singing to himself:

> He was singing that song. "If a body catch a body coming through the rye" . . . it made me feel better. It made me feel not so depressed anymore.
>
> (ibid., 121–2)[2]

Holden explicitly connects this sight to his own depression as if it were a trailer of the dream which follows. In that image there is something which concerns him deeply: the denial of danger, the propensity for challenge, and a delicate fiction which keeps pain at the right distance.

> He was walking in the street, instead of on the sidewalk, but right next to the curb. He was *making out like* he was walking a *very* straight line.
>
> (ibid., 115, My italics)

The reader intuits that "*he was making out like*" is an addition arising from a more aware mind than that of a child, and that the emphasis on the very straight line is a detail which fulfils the desire for obstacles to disappear.

It is in fact the description of an adolescent who is trying to cope with a feeling of desperate loneliness.

Besides being a truly unforgettable description of a young person's depression, these quoted extracts contain the creative intuition of a transformation and many clues about how to foster this process.

First of all, the role entrusted to the little sister, Phoebe, closely resembles that of the therapist: offering her own room as a place of temporary sanctuary, creating a shelter from an excessively severe internal parent, and above all formulating questions rich in interest, able to sustain a fragile narcissism (Bolognini, 2005).

So, if the adolescent oscillates physiologically towards depression, the adolescent analyst must counterbalance that impulse with a swing towards hope. Hope expresses that particular type of perception of reality which can be called "unsaturated" (Pellizzari, 2016) and is therefore a feeling capable of replacing the desire to walk in a straight line with an acceptance of a normal zig-zagging movement. It is developed in the tension between a trustful waiting and something that remains unknown and never fully satisfying.

There is a final point I want to emphasise, which emerges in the dialogue between Phoebe and Holden.

Phoebe corrects the quotation from which her brother's dream originates:

"If a body meet a body coming through the rye."

Holden adds, "I thought it was 'If a body catch a body'."

It is in the speed of this creative misunderstanding by the literary and also the analytic couple that there sometimes lurks the possibility of thwarting an annihilation in the abyss.

4.1.2 Zerocalcare's raft and the nightmare of non-compliance

Zerocalcare is the protagonist of a cartoon strip conceived and drawn by Michele Rech. For him, as for so many of his peers, job insecurity and the objective difficulty of finding work have prolonged his adolescence, creating a trail of uncertainty and doubt which this artist interprets very effectively.

In the cartoon, the most successful image-metaphor is that of a shipwreck: society is the ship and young people are in third class. The survivors are each clinging to planks of wood so as not to sink to the bottom. They have no alternative to keeping afloat while some of them manage to build a raft (an insecure job), someone else gets hold of a motorboat (the privileges of social class). Others are unable to keep going and sink "almost always in silence, or maybe you're just too busy staying afloat to notice."

Zerocalcare is a cartoon which tells with bitter irony about the daily lives of many young people: the computer as a modern siren which devours time, the thinned down relationships, a daily life empty of any plan for the future. Subjective features together with objective difficulties in living create what Zerocalcare calls the nightmare of non-compliance, a very apt name and effective way of describing depression (Figure 4.1).

Figure 4.1 The default demon (courtesy of BAO Publishing)

4.1.3   How to treat non-compliance?

Zeno, a fourteen-year-old boy, embarks on adolescence with a trivial theft by which he seeks to regain the capacity for scholastic success he had been so proud of when he was younger, and which has crumbled under the necessity for constant and laborious effort in intermediate school.

I become Zeno's psychotherapist from his third intermediate year until his third year of high school, where he gets by, alternating barely adequate academic results with a provincial life spent in bars and parks.

The most substantial act of rebellion in which he is able to concretise a latent desire for subjectivation is the tattoo of a star which circles his elbow. This is an enormous star which occupies about half of his upper and lower arm. I am curious about the size of the tattoo and it is the subject of many conversations which do not prove especially helpful in effecting a transformation.

I see him again aged twenty-five after two failed university courses, a semester on the Erasmus scheme which he spent barricaded indoors in the three square metres of a rented room. Back in Italy, he shuts himself away at home, doping himself with marijuana, television dramas, and, above all, music. Music becomes his coat of armour and he spends whole days downloading tracks and trying to fit them perfectly together for an imagined future compilation.

Zeno's only social relationship is with his one childhood friend; he has no romantic attachment, lives in total dependency on his parents, and has a problematic relationship with his mother. In a word, he lives crushed by the demon of non-compliance.

When I run into the following vignette (Figure 4.2), I intuit the possible meaning of the flashy, oversized star which his body has taken on the job of showing the world from an unusual place like the elbow.

I imagine that Zeno is using it as a first attempt to make visible the discontinuity which so terrifies him that he is using the bend of his elbow to try and find an oscillation between continuity and discontinuity; one that does not result in a fracture.

Focussing on the problem of fracture helps me to understand how it may be necessary to be able to stay in contact with the objects of his childhood because, for him, separation represents a tear, getting lost in a deadly interstellar space.

So, in therapy I start to point out to him more clearly when he is tugging on the cord, doing my best to avoid getting it tangled and knotted, and trying to imagine with him what life is like on nearby planets.

Zeno brings into the analysis the crucial question of traumatic discontinuity in the perception of space-time. For depressives, as for the astronomers who study the phenomena of the universe, time takes on the characteristics of a temporal chasm. For years, Zeno has lived with his eyes fixed on a distant Big Bang, blocked from living in the present and hence from imagining the future; a subjective, expanded time which denies loss and condemns him to a narcissistic solitude in a space which is narrow and immensely empty at the same time (Steiner, 1993).

Figure 4.2 Zerocalcare: getting lost in space (courtesy of BAO Publishing)

The electronic music which Zeno recorded for me on a memory stick was the means of our starting a story together, introducing a sound into the silence of cosmic space, the sketch of a rhythm, an interest. The memory stick became a key enabling me to experience more authentically how he felt by physically sharing his experience of being an outsider. I remember clearly my body's response when I started to listen to the music after a session: my hair stood on end and automatically, defensively, I pressed the off button.

I understood with my body how an excessive dissonance can eliminate the relationship with the other, and only from this type of sharing could we make our way towards the dark region of the early trauma.

4.2 Researches and researchers

Research carried out by the European Study of the Epidemiology of Mental Disorders has revealed that in Italy, over the span of their lives, women are twice as likely as men to develop a dysthymic disturbance or a major depressive disturbance (14.9% of women and 7.2% of men):[3] 10–15% of serious depressions in women manifest themselves *post partum*.

There may be multiple causes behind these figures: social marginalisation, features of the development of gender identity, invalid or insufficiently sensitive research tools.

It lies outside the scope of this chapter to understand why women are, or are shown to be by current research tools, more depressed than men, so I will confine myself to illustrating some features which may be useful for psychoanalytic research.

I am referring in particular to a possible further investigation of that theoretical clinical vertex which Winnicott (1947, pp. 146–7) brought to light in a brilliant flash of intuition: "The depressed patient requires of his analyst the understanding that the analyst's work is to some extent his effort to cope with his own (the analyst's) depression, or shall I say guilt and grief resultant from the destructive elements in his own (the analyst's) love."

With this rather cryptic sentence, Winnicott anticipates two important themes of his research and of contemporary psychoanalysis:

- The response of the analyst, which arises from his personal ability to metabolise his own feelings, has weight in relation to the therapeutic process.
- Depression has a dynamic transgenerational structure.

This intuition has been radically taken up in field theory where dreaming together becomes the hinge on which therapy turns (Ogden, 2001).

Depression cannot in fact be considered only a symptom of the patient, and once the depressive feelings are introduced into the field they belong to both the subjects of analysis and the task of transforming them is a shared one.

Using ourselves, as Winnicott suggests, also implies using ambivalent parts of ourselves, masculine and feminine. He did not intend these statements to describe aspects of gender identity, but early relational modes by which the baby puts itself into a relationship with its environment (Winnicott, 1966). These aspects become overt in both men and women to varying degrees and condition how one becomes one's personal Self. The feminine is constituted in the area of psycho-physical continuity with the mother, and in the adult is the foundation of the desire and ability to establish strongly empathic relationships with others, stamped with the desire to be at one with them.

By contrast, the mother's ability to establish a difference between herself and her son is the foundation of the subsequent masculine pole of relating, a mode which also stimulates the birth of language as a means of filling the gap between the other and oneself. The processes of development ensure that these elements remain constantly in dialogue and evolution. Nevertheless, we can speculate that individuals structure their own cognitive and relational style on the basis of the feminine and the masculine as primary experiences

I shall use a fragment of an analysis to try and expound some analytical hypotheses about how we may be able to think of depression as a two-person problem by exploring the early "feminine" phases of development.

4.2.1 Elisa

Elisa is a young researcher who loses her job at the same time as she gets married. To cope with the endless length of the days that follow, where her only activity is sending out her curriculum vitae and receiving no response, Elise decides to adopt an abandoned dog.

In therapy, through the dog's difficulties in adaptation, we can address the history of previous ill treatment, her present difficulties with her husband, and the emotional events of domestication which unfold between us.

Elisa entrusts her own feeling of abandonment to her dog, and to her husband the demand for a constant presence which is impossible to grant. For my part, Elisa inundates me with text messages which I can barely deal with, alternating more affectively engaged replies with terser ones. Like her husband, I feel under pressure, and try to push her towards a healthier ability to be alone; instead, I get a furious and vindictive response. She does not leave the house, stops looking for work, and no longer even talks the dog for walks. The build-up of excrement within the four walls of their home generates a situation of severe tension with her husband, leading them to talk about separating. She keeps coming to analysis where we concern ourselves with refuse disposal in various senses, trying to clean up a psychic container and achieve a more effective clearing away of emotional dross.

On a cold day in autumn Elisa comes to her session with the dog, sits down, keeping it close beside her on its lead, and politely declines my invitation to take the lead off.

In reality, as I give this unrequested permission, I feel that my words do not reflect what I actually feel. I am in fact worried that the dog may be attracted to the objects standing on a low table within reach of its nose and paws.

These are *my* objects, accumulated over time, affective lumps of my personal and psychoanalytic history.

It is this detail of the lead which maintains a link between Elisa and her dog, and it is the terror of having to manage without it which initiates something new. In the following session I notice that I am using "we" more often, or saying, "It happens to you, but also to me . . ." or "when we are in this state of mind . . ."

Moreover, I recall that she is a researcher, considering this not only an extra-analytic fact, and I start to be curious about the "method" she uses to recreate the sensation of connection that is indispensable for maintaining life.

Elisa finds a new job in which she is concerned with cell cultures in a multinational research project on cancer. She tells me that she loves her cells and that, in order to understand their behaviour, she really needs to feel that she is one of them. *"If you don't feel like a cell, how can you imagine the way they behave?"*

I have to admit that I thought madness was just around the corner until I speculated that there might be something original in this sentence.

Elisa does not say, "if you don't understand the way a cell behaves" but "if you don't *feel* like a cell." Like Winnicott, Elisa theorises the need to be, in some circumstances, identified, *merged*, or confused with the other (1960) before being able to discover something new.

Elisa tells me about apoptosis, which is the ability of cells to kill themselves when something alters in their functioning or when they lose their connection with neighbouring cells, a fact which does not happen in cancer cells.

Although these conversations frighten me at first, as I imagine they are hinting at suicide, I understand how Elisa wants to emphasise the critical factor in the tendency towards the formation of a tumour, the loss of contact with the regulatory mechanisms emanating from the other cells.

So, depression does not only take the form of an inability to separate oneself from the lost object but can also be a proliferation of emotions potentially capable of invading the Self, deriving from the loss of contact and mutual regulation.

For a long time, separation has been at the heart of the social value attributed to individuals in psychoanalysis too. What has started to be appreciated instead, thanks to the work of Winnicott, is that the maternal capacity for establishing a fusional bond with the newborn baby is an indispensable premise for psychic birth. Despite these theoretical attainments, the re-emergence in analysis of the requirement for a fusional relationship generates an anxiety which not infrequently provokes defensive responses. The sensation of unpleasant clinginess or of invasion which accompanies such a requirement in fact produces inadvertent emotional distancing, as in the case being reported here.

The cellular character introduced by Elisa, with its reference back to the origin of physical life was the key element for our psychic research, aimed at a deeper understanding of *how* unconscious connections are established and how they determine what we know and how we know it (Faimberg, 1987; Ferro, 2009). Through the story of her research, Elisa was trying to recreate her connections with me, studying the nascent level of the relationship and reacquiring a capacity for creativity and for dialogue between the feminine and masculine in her Self. She felt able to establish something *original* in the sense of unprecedented, but at the same time something which might contain the emotional safety of the link to her origins.

Her exploration of how cancer cells proliferate like potentially invasive emotions helps us imagine how at the origin of psychotic depression there can be this loss of contact, accompanied by defensive consequences of an autistic type (Borgna, 1972, 1995; Manica, 2016).

If separating oneself means accepting a distance between self and other, having first acquired a solid certainty about the link, we can imagine that many post-partum depressions may arise from a difficulty in rediscovering a good relationship with the internalised maternal object and with the feminine inside oneself.

Transposed onto the analytic scene, these considerations prompt a reflection on how the analyst should sometimes share a long period of gestation, stopping for a while in a fusional state. We can also wonder how difficult it may be to pass through one's own depression and one's own experience of the "feminine" which is the implicit demand of every seriously ill patient (Winnicott, 1947).

4.3   The grip and the journey: two aspects of the same problem

The beginning of a novel is concerned not so much with what the author intends to say as with the feelings she or he wants to create in the reader.

It is possible that, less consciously, a patient too begins his or her analytic story condensing into his or her first sentences the emotions which pervade him or her and in which he or she means the analyst to participate.

"*I travel a lot for work and I have to say, after a bit of time here, it doesn't just do me good to go away, it becomes a necessity.*"

A little later: "*I remember one day, when I was a little boy, I went out with my father on our bikes. He was going more quickly than me and didn't even notice he'd lost me; I took the wrong turning at a crossroads and spent hours trying to get back on the right road. When I got home I was sent to my room without supper, as if it was my fault I got left behind.*"

In this first conversation I did not imagine how deeply involved we would get in that entanglement between abandoning and being abandoned, and how that succinct "*after a bit of time here*" would also be addressed to me.

And yet, how the urgent need to go away is mixed with rage and a feeling of dark depression, and is accompanied by a need to avenge a wrong suffered, is exactly what Melville tells in the celebrated opening of *Moby Dick*.

> Whenever I find myself growing grim about the mouth; whenever it is a damp, drizzly November in my soul; whenever I find myself involuntarily pausing before coffin warehouses, and bringing up the rear of every funeral I meet; and especially whenever my hypos get such an upper hand of me, that

it requires a strong moral principle to prevent me from deliberately stepping into the street, and methodically knocking people's hats off – then, I account it high time to get to sea as soon as I can.

(Melville, 1851)

The problem which brought Mr G. to my consulting room was certainly not his travelling for work and his constantly being uprooted by it. An experienced middle-aged manager, he arrived asking for a course of analysis because he was tormented by the impossibility of achieving sexual climax.

Besides the physical suffering inflicted by this symptom, he intuited that it must be in some way related to the failure to achieve some important goals in his profession. It was as if, at a certain point, something inside him stopped him gaining the recognition he deserved and the pleasure that would go with it.

The story of being abandoned was an immediate way of expressing the difficulty of arriving at a goal together. Not ejaculating was also connected with the impossibility of letting go of painful memories, of donating something of himself without feeling defrauded.

Mr G. did not appear at all sad in a pathological way, and the only sign of classical depression was a certain propensity to be alone.

The hard kernel of his feeling pushed out of life was encapsulated in the impossibility of ejaculating, in ruminating over wrongs suffered in adolescence, and in a fear of heights. In the wave of every relational turbulence, in particular with colleagues and superiors, but also with women, the phantom of Moby Dick re-emerged powerfully.

In the illusion of being able to start his life again from the point at which his psychic difficulties had stopped him growing, Mr G. engaged in a whirlwind of relationships with women much younger than him and fled from any relational responsibility. What looked like a strong attraction to the opposite sex in fact concealed the need to be contained, the fear of not being there and hence of plunging into the void. Before a relationship could expose him to some disappointment, Mr G. took the initiative and broke it off.

In the analysis, as in Melville's novel, there were moments of transformation, in which it was able to change from a persecutory object to a good one able to accept him:

Ahab leaned over the side, and watched how his shadow in the water sank and sank to his gaze, the more and more that he strove to pierce the profundity. But the lovely aromas in that enchanted air did at last seem to dispel, for a moment, the cankerous thing in his soul . . . the stepmother world, so long cruel – forbidding – now threw affectionate arms round his stubborn neck, and did seem to joyously sob over him. . . . From beneath his slouched hat Ahab dropped a tear into the sea; nor did all the Pacific contain such wealth as that one wee drop.

(Melville, 1851, chapter CXXXII, 491)

CHAPTER I LOOMINGS

CALL ME ISHMAEL.

Figure 4.3 Moby Dick

But the image which envelopes the first letter of Melville's novel in my copy of the book became fully clear only once the analysis was over.

News of a brief transfer abroad, managed for a while by conducting sessions over Skype, became the pretext for breaking off the therapy.

Perhaps for the first time I really understood what not ejaculating meant for Mr G: that is, not being able to conclude something, both partners participating with satisfaction in a goal.

In this analysis, the descending of the black mood had followed an erratic course and, as in the novel by Melville, it was dominated by his obsession with the harm suffered and projected out of himself.

We could say, drawing on Pichon-Rivière's (1971) intuition, that depression can be related to an early disturbance of development, a "basic situation"; it would then be like a psychotic core from which all the other psychopathological structures take form, a sort of fear of falling into the billows of life and drowning. The main defence would be the paranoid projection of the evil out of or into the body, as in the case of Mr G.

4.4   Primary depression and the impossibility of moving

The term "primary depression", as first defined by Winnicott, denotes an anxiety taking the form of bodily sensations of falling forever and of annihilation (Winnicott, 1974). It arises in relation to the failure of the maternal capacity for protecting the child from the traumatic nature of space-time.

Tustin used it to describe the anxiety of autistic children, redefined by her as "anxiety of the black hole." This is therefore a very primitive anxiety related to a vertiginous existential dimension.

Bion too reflected on how the first psychosomatic nuclei are structured independently of the presence of an object in the relationship between body and space.

> These ideas (of causation + time) derive from very early experiences, just as "foot" derives from early references to the body in the exploration of what we call space. In "time" one thing is before (antecedent), the other after (subsequent); but in "space", does the infant have a left or right, before or after, or what? If it sees its foot and then its hand, does it feel its foot caused its hand?
>
> (1992, p. 121)

So we could say that psychotic depression resides in an original inability to develop the psychic movement which Bion identified in the concept of oscillation, even before the tools for thinking. The most salient characteristic of primary depression therefore lies in this psychic or, rather, psycho-physical immobility

I will discuss the clinical characteristics of this type of depression using a painting by Nicolas de Staël and some observations made during the analysis of children with symptoms of primary depression.

I shall start by expounding the suggestion I have taken from De Staël's picture, which intuitively captures the relationship I intend to trace between movement of the body and psychic immobility.

Nicolas de Staël (1914–1955) was a Russian émigré living first in Belgium and then in France. After losing his father at the age of eight and being forced to flee the October revolution, he knew the difficulties of both early abandonment and emigration. He suffered from depressive crises throughout his life.

However, it is not the events of his life which I find striking, but those of his art.

De Staël spent much of a restless youth travelling in Europe and North Africa trying to find his style as a painter. During the Nazi occupation he became noted for some very dark and distressing abstract canvases. Then on the evening of 26 March 1952 in the Parc des Princes, he and his companions attended a football match where France, who had been expected to win, were beaten by Switzerland.

We know nothing about the role played by the unexpected result and by the fascination of colours and lights, but we do know that he painted a picture of the match that same evening. Then over a very few days De Staël painted a remarkable number of small works all entitled *Footballeurs* (1952) (Figure 4.4).

Figure 4.4 Nicolas de Staël, *Footballeurs*, Aix-en-Provence

It is as if this series of paintings freed him from a sort of inhibition which had up till then held him hostage, and over the next three years he frenziedly painted an enormous number of ever larger works, luminous and richly vivid. To sum up, he found himself in an original style that is figurative and abstract at the same time, highly original in its intensity of light and colour. Then, unexpectedly, at the age of only forty-one, he killed himself by throwing himself into the void.

We can imagine that something in that football match may have triggered a fertile identification and accelerated a creative and reparative capability.

Personally, I have been struck by the relationship between the content of the paintings entitled *Footballeurs* and the regaining of a psychic capacity for movement, to some degree working through the despair which dwelt in him, recreating for himself on canvas a luminosity capable of challenging the darkness of his depression. The way a mental event can prompt a physical one and a bodily event can influence the psyche represents a mysterious interaction which has greatly interested psychoanalytic research.

The embodied mind develops through movement, sensoriality, and bodily interaction, because of which it is highly probable that in adults too there are profound exchanges between body and mind.

It is possible that a vision in movement enabled Nicolas de Staël to get in touch with deep levels of his own psychic functioning, and then to find through painting a unity and a more integrated capacity for relating. The painting reproduced here shows a violent contact, body to body, full of tension.

I imagine that in painting this series de Staël was able in some way to oscillate between a state of avoiding emotions and one in which he could represent them and thus suffer them, with bodily tension as his starting point. Perhaps the quantity of unthinkable painful emotions exceeded this artist's fragile ability to contain them.

How these transitions occur remains a mystery; nevertheless, the analytic treatment of certain children in whom a primary depression has become crystallised into a symptom enables us to formulate some hypotheses.

4.5   Children

Depression in children is not infrequent (0.5–3%) and its symptoms are manifested more in the body than in a variation in quality of mood. Restlessness, insomnia, lack of engagement in school, and bulimia can be some of the commonest symptomatic manifestations of infantile depression.

Rather than in the loss of the object, infantile depressions have their roots in a psychically absent or intrusive object; the parents of these children have difficulty in working through their own emotions, which turn back on themselves and invade the child, preventing a healthy structuring of the self (Tabanelli and Rocchetto, 2008; Bisagni, 2009).

In this section I will allude to a particular aspect of infantile depression which may be helpful in understanding the features of the relationship between the parents' mental functioning and that of their children. The symptom is not associated with feelings of sadness, but with a sort of psycho-physical block. As Winnicott writes, in primary depression parts of the subject are lost together with the object and certain aspects of the mouth disappear along with the mother and the breast (Winnicott, 1952).

Elective mutism or the refusal to chew or to swallow solid food can thus be symptoms which originate in a parent's primary depression and find their symptomatic location in the children (Williams, 2010; Williams et al. 2003). In this way the symptom can protect an authentic part of the child's Self from the violent intrusion of emotions, or sometimes of aspects not worked through in the parents. In other words, not moving the tongue to speak or to chew is not to do with oppositional aspects but with an embedding in the body of a psychotic part of the personality.

To return to the initial metaphor we could imagine these children or adults who manifest symptoms of primary depression, as people who, instead of walking on the tightrope with all the grace and flair conferred on the act by an erect posture, advance through life as if creeping along, all hunched up. Development is not blocked and so cognitive achievement and social adjustment can be preserved, but the "psychic comportment" of these subjects remains somewhat primitive.

4.5.1   Tongue, don't move

When one eats normally, the food is held firmly between the lips, broken up by the teeth, rolled around by the tongue, and, only after a certain amount of contact, pushed down into the stomach. By contrast, children who do not chew make their food disappear inside them without perceptible contact and almost without movement, apart from that of swallowing. In this way they express that deepest part of the hatred that is concerned with a radical passivity which entails the cancellation of the perception that one is getting close to psychic death.

The impossibility of using the tongue to push the food sideways under the teeth indicates an inhibition in the use of the tongue which is the first means of exploring the relationship between one's own body and external space (Bonnard, 1960).

The tongue does not, figuratively speaking, seek or find the nipple, and an experience of not being nourished takes the place of the copious flow of milk.

With these children it is necessary to find a way of communicating which does not replace that of the body but accompanies bodily experience and gives back to them the experience of being seen instead of fused with or invaded by the object.

I will try to illustrate this hypothesis through two vignettes from treatment.

Davide

Davide is a boy aged nearly five who does not chew.

At the end of the hour I tell him that it is time to say goodbye and invite him to put his shoes back on. He looks at me and becomes stiff. Then he crouches down and his body crumples in a heap. He tells me he can't do it.

I think that this request does not only contain the desire for help; in his passivity I detect a desire for fusion with me, which is legitimate since we are at the end of the session and have to separate. I too crouch down, cross my legs, and sit right in front of him. This position, an involuntary response to his prostration, brings to my mind the observations by Geneviève Haag on the importance of support for the back, a sensation embodied even before birth, that of a solid support against the uterine wall (Haag, 1991).

"Actually, to put your shoes on you need to lean against something," I say as I help him to slide a bit further back against the wall.

Davide picks up a shoe in both hands and rather doubtfully bends his right leg and slips his foot part of the way into the shoe. Then he looks at his other foot, which is further away because he has kept his left leg stretched.

I think he is simultaneously exploring the relationship between the space of his body and what is outside.

"One foot is still outside, far away," I say. "But the other one is going inside because your hands are helping it."

I smile at him and think of the shoe as being like a mouth, a black hole which Davide is exploring with his eyes, hands, and toes. I have the fantasy that a potential for autonomous movement, represented by his foot, is about to end up in a black hole.

Davide slips his foot out of the shoe again and whines, "I can't do it!"

Therapist: *Maybe the foot is scared of going into the dark, or maybe it doesn't want to feel squashed.*

He looks at me in surprise and repositions his foot at the opening of his shoe.

T: *If it slips inside we won't see it again.*

My intention is to transfer an experience of external space into internal space and also to use his body to say something about a psychic experience which is relevant to him.

After a bit of hesitation Davide pushes his foot into the shoe.

T: *Now your foot feels held and so when you stand on it you can walk.*

He puts on the other shoe in a few seconds and stands up with a little jump. I imagine that this is a motoric and spatial trial of a contact created, destroyed, and rediscovered. I imagine that this part of the therapy is a preparation for resolving the symptom. Working in parallel with his mother I have learned about her profound loneliness, the armour of a brilliant professional with which she surrounds herself, and the impossibility of weaning this child because of the difficulty in replacing food with emotional nourishment. His father has always refused to meet me.

4.5.2 Alice and the lost words

I meet Alice when she is aged ten. She will not utter a word except with her mother.

Alice lives in a family where the father is quite a violent alcoholic, while the mother is still embedded in her own family of origin.

Therapy with Alice, as in Almodóvar's film *Talk to Her*, is an adventure in search of the pleasure of speech as a weapon for escaping coma, isolation, and madness.

Among the many activities which we invented over four years of therapy, I would like here to refer to two which constituted an important transition from bodily sensations to incorporated emotions.

After about a year in which it has been very difficult even to stay together, we have been able to use plasticine.

Alice has created a seascape and after some months the furniture for a doll's house. No character, apart from mute fishes, has ever appeared in her creations (Figures 4.5a, 4.5b)

Figure 4.5a Room with plasticine furniture

Figure 4.5b Plasticine seascape

My hypothesis is that the modelling may have been able to put her back in contact with tactile sensations that have progressively been becoming vehicles for emotions; in fact, we worked in silence in the sessions and the sense of loneliness became palpable.

After this, in order to continue weaving a link between sensations and emotions, we worked on the sensory template. This work consisted of helping each other to copy our outline on a big sheet of paper and then using pieces of cloth to identify the areas of the body associated with different sensations and emotions.

What we identify as mind is not only in the head but embodied in our whole being, and so I hypothesised that Alice's sense of identity was rooted along the whole axis of her body. Step by step as she explored existence inside her skin, Alice could see others as separate beings and perhaps try to learn how to reach them through words.

One day, as she stands on the front doorstep, I see her lift her eyes from the ground and hear her exchange a brief dialogue with her mother who has come to fetch her. I have already said goodbye and do not immediately follow her into the entrance hall, so Alice probably feels she is already outside and is no longer made anxious by the presence of the other.

I realise that for some time, albeit sensitively, I have been trying to force her to look at me, so as to induce her to move beyond the defences she needs to avoid a breakdown. Alice concretely shows the world how alone she is in the hope that someone will help her to face the blockage where these defences have taken the place of whatever function has not succeeded in creating the capacity for linking.

For Alice, not speaking means concretely communicating the fact that she does not know how to fill distance symbolically, that she has no tools for facing a loss of the object which she feels as catastrophic.

I feel I am sharing her anxiety about being together in a room where she feels she cannot or will not speak, thus opposing what the whole world, including me, wants from her.

Then I think about trying to make this place disappear, playing at overturning the setting which guarantees our encounters without a real awareness of what and how this may impact on the transformative process of our unconscious emotions.

With her parents' permission, in the next session I suggest to Alice that we go out into the street to photograph her feet as she walks. This idea has arisen from the fact that Alice rarely lifts her eyes from the ground.

While I am in the street, I find myself thinking about my responsibility if anything should happen, like an accident, and I myself feel vulnerable and insecure. Varying the setting is an operation which I always oppose with considerable firmness supported by a long list of good reasons.

Deviating from the rules of the setting as they are laid down in the theory of technique so as to guarantee an analytic security for both patient and therapist is therefore a strongly inhibited and painful proceeding which initially induces in me a grave feeling of inadequacy and a fear of catastrophic accidents. For this reason, as we walk I also feel a painful compulsion which at times I find terrifying,

Figure 4.6 An arrangement of photographs

and I imagine these feelings are like those experienced by Alice when I try to pull her out of "her setting", the closed and silent room in which she lives.

When we go back inside and load the photos onto the computer, what comes out is a photographic report where I see, from her perspective, holes, disconnected cobblestones, manhole covers, stunted grass shoots looking for cracks to grow through, partial glimpses of pedestrian crossings. Urban landscapes which pop up from under her shoe and tell me more about her state of mind than words can: the desire to trample on everything and all the fragilities which derive from having to balance over that world-chasm. Alice experiences the feeling of herself as protagonist in showing me something of herself through her ability to produce photographs of a high technical standard: in other words, speaking through images. When the photos are printed, I witness the selection process, the deletion of some pictures, the timid search for an aesthetically pleasing sequence. While carrying out these operations Alice whispers almost imperceptibly "Like that". She is referring to her arrangement of the images, but I imagine she is also referring to having been able to experience a creative aspect and that at some level a communication has been established.

Movement seems to have brought Alice into an area of her mind where relating finds its roots, where touch and sight fill the distance between herself and the other, and the perception of space we have while walking relates back to the ancient experience in which space was first of all the experience of a distressing distance which separates us from our mother's arms (Milner, 1950).

A first aspect which surprises me is that the holding function of the setting was paradoxically achieved in an open space and in a variation of rhythm. This overturning of the concrete setting, which had originated in the entrance hall and the likening of this to a mental device functioning in a similar way to the *camera oscura*, helped me to wonder what up until then might have been preventing the birth of a function able to set up a process of symbolising primitive anxieties, both mine and hers.

I have asked myself how far the classical setting is a sufficient vehicle for grasping what is primitive and deep-lying.

Alice's symptom is located at a primitive level of development and my mental functioning as an adult encounters a serious difficulty in attuning itself to these early levels of development. I need a different mental set-up from the one I normally use in the consulting room, a sort of entrance hall which allows me to get closer to a part of myself of which I have no consciousness.

Something was transformed by means of this fortuitous experience. The therapy continued for two more years, and at the end of it Alice was still not talking to me or with other adults, but did communicate, albeit in a tiny voice, with her peers.

4.6   Conclusion: building a ladder

The mother's arms outline the first sketch of containment; the maternal reverie dreams the flaws, the failures of the primitive capacity for transforming the child's negative sensations and emotions. Having the experience of being physically and psychically at one with another human being is the necessary condition for the mind to be installed in the body.

The child can then face the pain of being separated and, little by little, use words to fill the void which separates him from the other. If this process does not take place, the child clings to the object, takes refuge in a position of passivity in which primitive defences predominate: the autistic retreat, splitting, projective identification. These aspects of deprivation, of painful lack, can be reactivated at certain points in life or can act like ballast weighing life down.

If the void of the missing object can instead be crossed, there can be a gradual development of the tools which enable psychic oscillation to be managed: what Bion called the apparatus for thinking thoughts.

At the start of this chapter I imagined being able to organise a discussion of depression using a spatial metaphor, and I used the experience of an acrobat walking on a rope to describe depression as the possibility of falling into the void.

In the stories of the patients I have been considering I have highlighted the therapeutic and creative aspects which they autonomously found within themselves.

In 1444 Lorenzo di Pietro painted a fresco in the Ospedale di Santa Maria in which he portrays the souls of dead children going up to heaven and being welcomed there by a Madonna who, leaning forwards, takes hold of one by the wrists and helps him to climb up. The next child is instead portrayed as if looking down at the way travelled, the distance which separates him from the earth.

It seems a good spatial image for summing up a way in which it can sometimes be possible to treat depression: building a ladder together, recreating maternal arms which reach out into the void to meet parts of the self that have suffered early damage.

Figure 4.7 Lorenzo di Pietro, also known as the Vecchietta Ospedale di Santa Maria della Scala; 1444, Florence.

Notes

1 www.zerocalcare.it/ [Translator's note: Zerocalcare is a brand of limescale remover.]
2 Holden misremembers the Scottish song he quotes, but it is precisely in the deformation, in his adding something of his own to a memory or to a prompting which comes from outside him, that we can catch the sign of an emergent creativity as a germ of self-care.
3 www.epicentro.iss.it/temi/mentale/esemed.pdf

References

Bion, W.R. (1992). *Cognitions*. London: Karnac.
Bisagni, F. (2009). *Bambini Depressi E Genitori All'inferno. Storie Di Quotidiana Psicoa-nalisi*. Torino: Antigone.
Bolognini, S. (2005). The Bar in the Desert: Symmetry and Asymmetry in the Treatment of Difficult Adolescents. *Adolescence*, 2007/1 (N.59), pp. 133–44.
Bonnard, A. (1960). The Primal Significance of the Tongue. *International Journal of Psychoanalysis*, 40, pp. 301–7.
Borgna, E. (1972). Fenomenologia Scheleriana e Psicopatologia Degli Stati Depressivi. *Rivista Sperimentale Di Frenologia*, 96.
Borgna, E. (1995). *Come Se Finisse Il Mondo. Il Senso dell'Esperienza Schizofrenica*. Milano: Fel-Trinelli.
Faimberg, H. (1987). *The Telescoping of Generations: Listening to the Narcissistic Links Between Generations*. London and New York: Routledge, 2005.
Ferro, A. (2009, April). Transformations in Dreaming and Characters in the Psychoanalytic Field. *International Journal of Psychoanalysis*, 90(2), pp. 209–30.
Haag, G. (1991). *Psychoanalytic Psychotherapy With Children, Adolescents and Families*. London: Karnac.
Kristeva, J. (1987). *Black Sun: Depression and Melancholia*. New York: Colombia University Press, 1989.
Manica, M. (2016). Dall'irrappresentabile All'intersoggettivo: Psicoanalisi e Stati Disorganizzati della Mente. In *L'arte Di Guarire*. Milano: Francoangeli.
Melville, H. (1851). *Moby Dick*. New York: Bantam Books, 1981, Chapter 1, p. 1.
Milner, M. (1950). *On Not Being Able to Paint*. London: Heinemann, 1971.
Ogden, T.H. (2001). *Conversations at the Frontier of Dreaming*. Northvale, NJ: Jason Aronson.
Pellizzari, G. (2016). Two Aspects of Therapeutic Action: Hope and Metaphor. *Italian Psychoanalytic Annual*, 10, pp. 99–110.
Pichon-Rivière, A. (1971). *Il Processo Gruppale (The Group Process)*. Loreto: Lauretana, 1985.
Rossi Monti, M., and Gosio, N. (eds.). (2013). *Depressione: Il Paradigma Errante. La Nuova Clinica fra Scienza e Cultura*. Milano: FrancoAngeli.
Salinger, J.D. (1951). *The Catcher in the Rye*. Harmondsworth: Penguin.
Steiner, J. (1993). *Psychic Retreats*. London/New York: Tavistock/Routledge.
Tabanelli, L., and Rocchetto, F. (eds.). (2008). *Buio Dentro. L'enigma Del-La Depressione Nei Bambini E Negli Adolescenti*. Milano: Francoangeli.
Williams, G. et al. (2003). *The Generosity of Acceptance: Volume I. Understanding Eating Difficulties in Children*. London: Karnac Books.
Williams, P. (2010). *The Fifth Principle*. London: Routledge.
Winnicott, D.W. (1947). Hate in the Countertransference. In D.W. Winnicott (ed.), *Through Paediatrics to Psychoanalysis*. London: Hogarth, 1975, pp. 146–7.
Winnicott, D.W. (1952). *Through Paediatrics to Psycho-Analysis*. London: Hogarth, 1975, p. 222.
Winnicott, D.W. (1960). Counter-Transference. *British Journal of Medical Psychology*, 33, pp. 17–21.
Winnicott, D.W. (1963). The Value of Depression. In *Home Is Where We Start From (1986)*. Ed. C. Winnicott, R. Shepherd, M. Davis. Harmondsworth: Penguin, p. 79.
Winnicott, D.W. (1966). The Split-off Male and Female Elements to Be Found in Men and Women. In *Playing and Reality*. London: Tavistock, 1971.
Winnicott, D.W. (1974). Fear of Breakdown. In *Psychoanalytic Explorations*. London: Karnac, 1989.

Chapter 5

Borderline

Violet Pietrantonio

5.1 Radio border: live from border camp, where dreams appear and disappear, interrupted by mysterious "intermittences"

Border Camp is a state of mind we can all go through, but one in which we may happen to remain blocked, in a restless, confused pause which seems endless and with no hope of change. It is hard to think here in Border Camp: it's strange, thoughts begin and keep getting broken off, the way dreams do. It is like trying to watch a film, when – click – the screen keeps going black after a few frames. . . . And you're left in the dark with that little fragment of story that's barely begun, in the lonely vacuum of the empty house. . . . Yes, because – in an irony of psychic fate – dreams and thoughts always seem to go dark when we're alone: relational intermittences which generate oneiric intermittences and the blackness of an anxiety that takes the breath away.

Here in Border Camp the dwellings (♀) are precarious tents: small, stuffed with combustible objects (♂♂♂) piled up any old how. We survive like refugees, crammed into a disordered heap of dangerous ♂♂♂, waiting for a real home (♀) and for the feeling that we can really exist (Bion, 1976–1979). In order not to succumb to being sucked back into despair by this waiting on the border with the hell of Psychoticland, we often take drugs: we dope ourselves so as not to feel. . . . Alcohol, cigarettes, cocaine, but also food, sport, work, sex, television, pornography, medicine. . . . The important thing is to try and sedate, just for a moment, that noisy chaos of separate dots, of proto-thoughts and proto-sensations which sometimes gets terrifyingly and intolerably stirred up. . . . The important thing is to get away: to flee from one's own unbearable feelings. . . . Knock oneself out or take refuge in visions of worlds where life seems to flow simply, easily, lightly. . . . Yes, here at Border Camp lightness is a sort of ideal-must-have: we adore and follow the model of a slimmed-down life, cut off from the unendurable heaviness of feeling. . . . The graceful colourful lightness of a butterfly's flight. . . . We loathe Neuropolis and its inhabitants: life's sweaty and mediocre labourers, struggling with the effort of conflicts and the work of weaving links. . . . The life of ants: we bordercampers aspire to the top: to rule, parade, have fun, be admired and sought after, stand out from the crowd, become somebody. . . .

We have talent and sensitivity, we are aesthetes who worship form and success. . . . But we often feel small too, terrified, hounded, nobodies in no man's land. . . . Stateless in search of Hollywood. . . . Everyone talks about our anger, but few really seem to understand that it is an anger-terror set loose by the burning of a mental pain with no end and no name.

5.2 Borderline: at the *limes* of the possible dream?

In the psychoanalytic literature, the borderline patient seems to be one of those characters who intrigues, frightens, and seduces because of his or her irreducible complexity. Portrayed and probed from the various analytic perspectives, he or she occupies whole chapters of books and manuals with descriptions of his or her psychic structure (Gabbard, 2000; Kernberg, 1989), observations about his or her mental and relational functioning (Bollas, 1996; Correale et al., 2001; Donnet, 1999; Grotstein, 1983; Ruggiero, 2012), and dissertations about the varieties of method need to treat him or her (Gabbard, 1991) and about the risks of perilous shipwrecks in the analytic navigation (Cassorla, 2012). An irresistible, flitting Arsène Lupin who has purloined all theoretical-technical certainties from psychoanalysis, while at the same time challenging psychoanalytic research to undertake empirical exploration in search of possible new understandings.

Perhaps the borderline patient presents him or herself to the analyst as kaleidoscopic and disconcerting, like Victor Mancini in the storylines of *Choke* by Chuck Palahniuk (2001).

Victor is a young American who has failed his medical studies. Alone and sex-dependent, he leads his life in a vortex of actions and experiences in which he engulfs the reader, and which follow on chaotically and desperately from each other, punctuated by flashes of black humour and fierce insights about his own existential condition. Victor makes a living by performing in a permanent show set in 1700, and in order to pay for the expensive nursing home in which he has housed his elderly mother, he goes with a friend to a restaurant every evening and half way through dinner pretends to choke, waiting in heart-stopping suspense for a repetition of the experience in which he is saved *in extremis* by a fellow-diner. These fellow-diners then continue to send him money in commemoration of having been able to save someone who needed to be saved. Is choking just a sneaky ploy to get money or a survival strategy emblematic of the atrocious nightmare which torments Victor's existence? Is it an oneiric splinter, a sample-agglomeration of pre-conceptions, proto-sensations and proto-thoughts, which Victor-director-*clochard* continues to project in the hope of meeting a DreamWorks which will offer him tools and equipment for developing and transforming them into the storyline of a dream?

The reader too feels choked, entangled in the whirlwind of actions, flashbacks, compulsive and voracious embraces, pills of βα thinking (balpha; Ferro, 1996) which chase and intertwine with each other in this first-person narration by a character who exudes the suffocating sense of an existence at the very limit of psychic and physical tolerability, catapulted from one life situation into another as he burns with the boiling magma of his lava-like feelings. We learn that Victor spent his childhood between foster carers and long periods of living with a mother in the grip of delusions and paranoid experiences of persecution, in the absence of a father who was killed at the start of his life. Sympathy, hope, and a pause in a restorative oasis of liveable emotions result from the encounter with Doctor M., who helps Victor to translate and at last read his mother's diary, written in a language which had until then been foreign and incomprehensible to the protagonist. Contact with the maternal narrative seems to re-awaken Victor's α function: particles of initially confused and scattered memories seem to coalesce back into images and sequences . . . the potential *incipit* of a story capable of giving a name, sense, and representability to the feeling of the newborn infant left stifled in the body of the young man today.

Adopting the vertex of an oneiric model of the mind (Ferro, 2009, 2017; Grotstein, 2007, 2009; Ogden, 2005) we could speculate that the tremendous experiences of chaos and annihilating precariousness which Victor the border-camper seems to suffer and convey in his acrobat's life on the edge of a volcano, arise from the impossibility of being able to dream his own emotional experience. Scraping by between attempts at intoxication, evacuative expulsions, and superegoistical pronouncements, Victor tries to stay mentally alive, to withstand his permanent besieging by the boiling fluxes of a proto-sensoriality he cannot contain and alphabetise, given the Lilliputian state of his dream-functions. If the ability to dream one's emotional experience depends on the developmental state of the dreaming ensemble (Grotstein, 2007, 2009),[1] the analytic encounter with a borderline patient often exposes the analyst to contact with the presence of a dreaming ensemble in an embryonic state: there is a container ♀, an α function, a contact barrier, albeit very flimsy and thin, and the capacity for and preconception of a ♀♂ relationship; but the developmental condition of these functions seems dramatically undersized for the needs of transformation in dream (Civitarese, 2014) which are required for existing in the world. Living in a borderline state of mind can feel like being a child in the middle of a war: you try to escape, shoot, hide, protect yourself as best you can in order to dodge the bombs of proto-sensoriality which attack you on all fronts, from inside and outside; you feel confused, you don't know who or where the enemy is, or what's going on. . . . You're always angry and terribly scared. Every now and then you find comfort in scraps of fusional relating: occasional encounters, celestial atolls destined to vanish amid the hellish flames of another inevitable abandonment . . . you will be left, or you will do the leaving, invaded by αnalphaβetised experiences of suspicion, fear of being devoured, anxiety, envy, jealousy, boredom, and disappointment. You are veteran who finds no peace, a wounded combatant, exhausted by war and hunting for opioid-βnarcoleptics capable of giving you chemical sleep in the nights of deprivationα.

ALFREDO

The doorbell rings endlessly: one ring after another, always more urgent, restless, intimidating. Five minutes early, Alfredo's Ride of the Valkyries grows in power and noise between the walls of all the consulting rooms. As I get ready to let him in, I notice that I can't find the key to a cupboard in my room. My heart starts beating crazily, and I go through a moment of pure panic. "What am I going to do? If I don't find it in a few minutes, he's sure to invade it and wreak havoc in the space where I keep documents, personal objects, and other children's toys." Tachycardia, sweat, terror: prey to a kind of deathly anxiety, the kind one only suffers when one's life is in danger, I run through the sequence of events involving my key and find it again.

"Alfredo is just a little boy," I tell myself: *"how can I be afraid of him?"* As I go to open the door to him, I wonder if it is not so much fear of Alfredo as of contact with the terrifying O of the state of mind that I am living through in unison with Alfredo and which for a moment has made me feel annihilated in an abyss of terror. Perhaps it is the same one that Alfredo has always had to try and survive: the Apocalypse Now which has been brutalising the field for months with the cruellest, blindest, most savage violence. A war I have to live in, tetanised by tedium and despair, and I've started to hate it. For months Alfredo has been arriving, arming himself with a machine gun and ammunition, and ordering me to do the same. The order comes to build a trench on the opposite side, which is all you've got in war. The machine gun firing starts. Talking is forbidden: on the battlefield all you can hear is the sinister rattling of ammunition being loaded. His expert sniping ability leads inexorably to my death from a bullet hitting my vital organs: *heart, head, stomach.* At this point, we go through the grim ritual of emptying an entire chamber of bullets into the back of the dead enemy's head. It's a death in the truculence of this ferocity. When Alfredo calls me to resume the war that has to continue, I ask him, "Soldier, why shoot dead soldiers?" Alfredo: "For safety, you never know. . . ." You can never relax, there is no peace in the hell of Border Camp . . . An unutterable Tartarus. . . . Maybe Alfred feels that if he is to be able to dream it, I must have experience E (Levine, 2014): experience of this tightrope-walking existence on a thread of sleepless vigilance, of the dizziness of emotional contact with the chasm of hatred, terror, and despair which opens appallingly under the rope. . . . Maybe Alfredo knows the law of O (Bion, 1970) and is reminding me about it: real O-neiric transformations can only arise from authentic unisons in O.

After a long crisis of rejection of the nightmare war which has exploded into the field, bleeding with the most painful and violent countertransferential hate (Winnicott, 1947), one Saturday evening I find in *American Sniper* the key character who will let me into new shared stories/dreams about the pitiless harshness of life in war which electrifies like a drug and can suck away your whole life. Metabolizationβ over a weekend and oneiric supervision from Clint Eastwood had perhaps helped me find the lost key to unison with an O against which I had mutinied.

5.3   *Border landing*: (when a bordercamper knocks on the door) proto-telluric of the analytic field. *Love story* and *crystal hell*

In my experience, it is often the panic of the abyss which opens terrifyingly after an interruption which pushes/compels a bordercamper to ask for analytic help: almost always the end of a relationship, but also giving up a drug, a lie, a planned course of study or a job, a betrayal. . . . A panic attack. A sudden blackout which leaves one exhausted by a state of intolerable terror. . . . The fear of dying of fear, knocked down by the tsunami of proto-emotions re-awakened by the experience of a separation. The electrician/analyst is called urgently in the hope that she or he will quickly be able to repair the oneiric circuits, finally bringing pictograms (Ferro, 1992, 2002a, 2007; Hayes, 2008; Barros, 2000) of dream, where darkness reigns, populated by sensations and bizarre, frightening noises. . . .

Attempting a diagnostic assessment of oneiric functioning, perhaps the borderline situation could be described as the nightmare of a micro-container ($\female$) overflowing with contents ($\male$), struggling with the impossible task of lifting the starvation-siege of other mega $\male$: in the anxiety caused by the impossibility of $\female\male$→reverie→transformation in dream, one oscillates between violent expulsions of $\male\male\male$, a search for other minds $\female$ which may help with containment, attempts at the mass extermination of $\male\male$ perceived as killjoys/enemies of an emotional-nirvana life that is yearned for as a paradise. Right from the first meeting, the analyst perceives the urgent need for a $\female$ into which to evacuate β$\male\male$ which are poisoning mental life in the absence of a wholly functioning dreaming ensemble, but she or he soon also realises that the encounter with a $\female$ stirs up a tumult of tribal $\male\male$ which are set loose in a fierce and complicated ancestral dance. An uproar of longing and terror, provoked by having smelled an original experience which exhales a *pot pourri*, a Babel of intoxicating and asphyxiating miasmas.

ARIEL

Ariel arrived in my consulting room at the suggestion of a colleague, with a demanding visiting card: precise, essential requirements about timings ($\male$) which immediately resonated in me as the need to prepare spaces ($\female$) which I was afraid I didn't have. Fears and anxieties about the impossibility of achieving $\male\female$, of an imbalance between $\female$ and $\male$ condensed onto the analytic field which had perhaps been set up from the first moments of the relationship.

THE FIRST MEETING

Standing in the hallway I am surprised: she is tall, young, and beautiful with the allure of a biracial fashion model in *Vogue*. Ariel smiles and shakes my hand: "Hi, I'm Ariel," and as she walks sinuously towards the room I have indicated, I notice that, little by little as she comes slowly nearer, it is as if – under the smoky shadow of her glamour – there is an image coming into focus, that of an undeveloped girl in high school in a black leotard and tight jeans, seeming a bit lost.

She starts talking straightaway, in a strong French accent: "The other doctor told me I've got holes in my feelings. . . . I'm the second of seven children. My parents worked a lot when I was little. I remember I sometimes thought, 'Now I'll throw myself out of the window, that'll make her angry,' – thinking of my mother."

"When you were a little girl?" I ask her as, to my dismay, I feel a bombβ of violent $\male\male$ being dropped into the field, a mine which I can only intercept and whose fundamental composition I can only intuit. On the catwalk, behind the model, the kid from *The Exorcist*[2] suddenly flickers into view: alone, in the grip of a state of such unbearable anxiety, rage, and desperation that she wants to go to the very limit of life just to exorcise the demon of this feeling, just to punish the abandoning object and send it to hell, the alleged cause of this feeling. A first reverie which tells me about the demoniac violence of the contents ($\male\male$) which were inhabiting this charming woman of the world? About experiences of abandonment perceived as demoniac presences which arouse a fury and terror with no name?

Meanwhile, Ariel is moving quickly on with the story of her adolescence *Sans toit ni loi*:[3] college, abortions, drugs, the nightlife, and dances in Nice and Cannes. Are these momentary stills of her losing herself in desperate attempts to run from the devil, only to find him in her bed? After only a few minutes we're already in the panic *pavor* of *Sleeping with the Enemy*:[4] the resumption of her studies leads her to settle in a small Berber neighbourhood in the city, where she falls into the trap of oppressive relationships with Arab men who beat and betray her, yelling with jealousy and the obsessive desire for absolute possession.

Deafened by αankylosis and the hype of all these trailers, I am not quick enough to wonder if it is this syndrome of sketching out interrupted dreams that is seeking an oneiric hospital in the analytic field, so as to be understood and cared for, because Ariel is ahead of me:

"The other doctor said I should work at it. But then I wonder, can one really change? And there are so many people who don't have analysis and keep going anyway. . . . And besides, I can't do it for two years. I couldn't pay for more than three months. . . . And that's no use, right? My cousin is studying psychiatry and has had some really bad times. I don't know. . . . What do you say? Do I need an analysis?" A dust cloud of pre-conceptions, βdoubts, fears and $\beta\alpha$memories which reacts to my affirmative reply with a real sandstorm: Ariel seems to start agitatedly arguing with herself as if she were disappearing into a whirlwind which stirs up and mixes together doubts about the effectiveness of analysis, memories of the extreme suffering she has undergone, and an urgent need to hold on to something ("Can I see you again the day after tomorrow?").

Stunned and befogged, I try to collect some cardinal points in the field so that I can provide Ariel with a small, temporary map which will enable her to feel that she can at least orient herself a little until the next consultation, given that, to my great anxiety, she seems like a frightened newborn infant in the universe. I suggest times and dates for our next two appointments and, trying to be as firm and calm as possible, I respond to her incessant pressing of questions and needs that insist on answers, confirming that I think analysis could be helpful to her because it seems to me that at this moment she is instead asking me if I truly believe that there is a way for her, a possibility, a hope of finally finding a place to be and to nurture her small oneiric apparatus that is so fragile, so gravid with O-vules which she cannot dream.

I find the leave-taking difficult and devastating: Ariel keeps on interrogating me all along the corridor until we reach the door as if she had not had enough time for our conversation, too little to fill her much greater need, and as if it were too painful and unthinkable to feel that it was time to say goodbye, as if she did not know how to be separate. . . . When she goes, after shaking hands, I find myself alone in the room in a torrent of uncertainty and trepidation: will she cope? Will she come back?

5.4   Border field: psychodynamics of an analytic field in work with a borderline patient. Morphology, physiology, and possible syndromes

From the white-water rafting among the βrapids of the first meetings to the riot of obstacles, fires, plunges and jolts between v-O-rtices and turβulences of analytic voyages that always go through rugged terrain, the unf-O-reseen always acts the hot-headed sovereign in an analytic adventure to Borderland.

Using some analytic experiences as illustrations, I will try to describe the emergence of physiological syndromes in an analytic field as it acquires a structure in analytic work with a borderline patient, adopting a field vertex, from the following premises:

a   The analytic field is that unconscious intersubjective area which comes to life in the encounter between two minds in analysis, and becomes the seat, object, and instrument of all analytic work (Ferro and Basile, 2007; Levine, 2013; Stern, 2013). The objective of analytic work is to try and dream together with the patient the dreams which he or she could not dream on his or her own (Civitarese, 2016; Ferro, 2009, 2010, 2013; Grotstein, 2007, 2009; Ogden, 2005, 2009), hypothesising that nightmares and interrupted dreams will settle into the field and pollute it, so that they can be intercepted (Manica, 2014) and dreamed.

b   Each analytic couple, in each analytic session, will generate a unique and original field, the characteristics of which will depend on those of their respective dreaming ensembles at that precise personal and analytic moment.

c   In the analyst's mind, the field can become the analytic device/vertex which permits the focalisation and psychic representability of the dream-function of the mind and of dream-work, which is animated and developed in the joint "unconsciousing" (Civitarese, 2016) of two minds in the session and in the long wave of the psych-O-analytic process[5] (Meltzer, 1967). This enables the visualisation of fluctuations along the oneiric spectrum: oscillations, transitions, and transformations between hallucinosis-reverie-transformations in dream (in the works by Ferro and Civitarese cited earlier).

5.4.1 The border and the "poisoned" setting: eggs of black widow-nightmares laid in a spiderweb? Psychosomatics of the analytic field

The black widow is considered one of the most dangerous spiders in the world. If it is pestered, it attacks, biting and injecting a very small quantity of venom which can, in rare cases, prove fatal. Its bite is not very painful, but the venom acts quickly. It begins by inducing a torpor in the bitten area, followed by muscular rigidity, sweating, headache, nausea, and intense abdominal pain accompanied by a rigidity of the upper body, breathing difficulties, dizziness, and a raised temperature. An ice cube on the bite can relieve the pain, but it is still necessary to administer the antidote.

Because it is so dangerous, the rearing of black widows is recommended for experts and specialists only. . . . They are principally reared in laboratories for producing the antidote (Wikipedia).

The strange case of the correlation between borderline pathology and problems with the setting is classic in psychoanalysis, an "evidence" of clinical practice (Bion, 1976–79) which is confronted by analysts of every theoretical school. Both the analyst's mental setting and, even more, the analytic setting's concrete frame (regularity/rhythm of the sessions, payment of the fee, breaks in the analysis, continuity of the work in the setting) become epicentres of inescapable earthquakes, detonators of threats and fears that the continuity of the analytic journey will crumble: missed sessions, lateness, failure to pay, repeated requests to change the time of sessions, bringing holidays forward from the dates agreed with the analyst, furtive or snarling threats to break off the analysis, etc.

From the outset, the borderline patient often seems to manifest an untreatable allergy to the setting. Like all pathologies of intolerance, the allergy to the setting can often emerge from a state of latency at particular, recurring points in the analytic process. There are the frequent rashes caused of the analyst's holidays and the dermatitis of weekends, but also the lichens of interpretation and the tremendous itchiness provoked by contact with the sensation of an analyst-Sphinx who seems to sit there, unmoving, on her or his analytic throne in a state of ataraxia, unperturbed by the hurricanes which constantly trouble the border condition.

If the setting can be dreamed as the body of the analytic field (Civitarese, 2013), when the setting becomes the place and seat of manifestations of βinflammations we find ourselves immersed in an area of psychosomatic suffering of the field. If we think of the psychosomatic symptom as the expression of a somato-psychosis

(Bion, 1965; Ferro, 2006; Meltzer, 1986; Rosenfeld, 1998), psychosomatic illness represents the evacuation into the body of uncontainable, unnarratable, terrifying βagglutinations/night-terrors (Ferro and Ogden, 2005). These will thus be night-mares in the pure state, the most raw and dehydrated masses of betaloma (Barale and Ferro, 1992) which embed themselves like cysts in the body of the analytic field and yet can suddenly explode like plague bubo-nightmares. With the border-line patient, the setting often seems to carry out the function of a uterus-spiderweb where the eggs of nightmares linked to devastating experiences of abandonment have been laid: aborted morulae of "black" widowhood which seem to find, in the belly of the setting, a sort of oneiric placenta able to supply that nourishment and gestation needed for their transformation from *night terror→nightmare which needs the help of another mind in order to be dreamed* (Ogden, 2005). Announced by pressures/pains that are not always acknowledged and identified, it is perhaps at this stage of newborn nightmare-dream, in search of α milk in order to be dreamed, that the baby black widow starts to walk around the field and inoculate with its bites the psycho-toxins of poisonous experience with which it has been injected.

Robbie

Robbie had landed in my consulting room like a giant ET landing on a meteorite: tall, bald, imposing, with thick-lensed glasses which made me feel I couldn't get his eyes into focus, as if they were hidden behind a dense blanket of fog. He had started by moving nervously around the room, talking disconnectedly and trying various positions: the sofa, the chair, the couch. A brief pause face to face: "I've come because of the shoving . . . I keep doing it . . .," and after fifteen minutes he's gone, leaving me in the room in the grip of a Niagara of terror and a Nile of tenderness. A second meeting; another fifteen minutes of wandering around the consulting room, and the first characters: Bob Marley, the rastas, Van Gogh, Picasso, and *Guernica*. And then, absence: a void, an appalling roar. Robbie does not attend the third meeting we have arranged, and I hear nothing more from him for months. Perhaps, in this way, the zygote of an indescribable abandonment was implanted in the uterine wall of the setting, causing nauseas of dismay and terror that I was unable to diagnose as the first symptoms of pregnancy with a nightmare.

It is Thursday, and for about a year I have been seeing Robbie once a week. My phone rings during a strange morning when I'm feeling all over the place: "Violet, there's a patient here for you. . . ." Immediately I remember Robbie, and our session, and I feel the terrifying experience of re-emerging, re-awaking from a completely befogged state, the absence of thought and mental life: the psychotic experience of being without a mind (Bion, 1962; Grotstein, 1980; Ogden, 1992; Schlesinger, 2006).

As I pedal at top speed towards the consulting room, I am invaded by fear, anxiety, and a tremendously acute pain: how could this happen to me? I've never missed an appointment in fifteen years of practice. . . . Am I in decline? Getting psychotic? And what will it be like for Robbie, how agonising will it be to experience my not being in the usual place at the usual time? A horde of concepts/theoretical interpretations assail me, stinging me all over: breaking the setting, acting out, projective counter-identification. There's no escape from the jaws of my psychoanalytic Super Ego: it seems to me that an irreparable catastrophe may have occurred. It is while I am parking my bike, eight minutes late for the session, that I find myself surprised by hosting an unexpected reverie: for the first time, with heart-breaking tenderness, I feel able to see and recognise in Robbie, waiting outside the door of my consulting room, the adopted Nigerian child, alone, lost in the catastrophic landscape of an abandonment. Robbie is a young man, adopted in early childhood by a couple who were delegates at the FAO (the UN Food and Agriculture Organisation), a piece of information which had been lodged in my mind. . . . But that morning, did I perhaps live in the viscera of my mind (Ferro, 2014) what it might mean to be adopted? To be adopted in analysis? At the end of each meeting to be suddenly scattered into the immense void of a total absence of contacts, to feel that one has no mind, to lose mental life in the absence of a mind that holds you in mind. And then the excruciating pain of being summoned, re-awoken at the start of each new meeting by this abyss of white noise. I felt that the experience I had just lived through was bringing to life in me a new, deeper understanding of the quality of the emotional experience which Robbie was carrying inside him. Perhaps the bubble of a nameless catastrophe had found a place to manifest itself in the field in the body of the setting (Civitarese, 2013, 2016) and in my hypothalamus (Bion, 1976; De Mattos and Braga, 2013). Had I hallucinated and then, coming round, started to dream the unspeakable nightmare which was devastating Robbie's mind? (Lucantoni and Pietroantonio, 2014). Was it an acute enactment (Cassorla, 2012; Grotstein, 2007, 2009) in which Robbie had assigned me a role in the nightmare nesting in the field, so that we could achieve a genuine unison and begin to dream it together? These thoughts, deriving from that first reverie, helped me to bear the profound pain which I felt as much in what had happened between us, as in imagining that the terrifying experience I had felt inflicted by for a few minutes, could be the one that was colonising Robbie's mind. The terror of mental ruin which had hounded me was transformed into a hope of oneiric possibility. Anchoring myself to the hypothesis of a projective counter-identification (K→O), perhaps I would have taken into account the fact that I was enacting the part of the mother, of the abandoning parents, probably projected into me by Robbie but, at least as I felt the experience, the halo of the idea of the analyst's insufficient capacity for containment and thought conveyed by this concept would have generated in my mind a focal point of fear, impotence, guilt, self-reproaches, and criticisms which would have choked off the possibility of hosting the pain of lived experience as the humus of analytic treatment. In me, the analyst, a super-egotistical area -K would have been activated, obstructing the possibility of accepting, living, and dreaming the emotional experience (O) which had occurred.

"Doctor! I was afraid you'd forgotten about me!!!" Robbie greets me happily, perhaps catching from the expression on my face how sorry I am for being late and, from our being together in the session, also catching the overwhelming nature of the new emotions and understandings that were running through my mind. The Joker, V in *V for Vendetta*, Rakon, the raccoon cub in search of a home, the Dodo's egg, and the frozen mammoth found by scientists were the new characters who brought into the field the possibility of feeling and talking about the violence inflicted by homicidal ♂♂, characters who can stand guard over the mind of someone who feels he or she has suffered the oppression of abandonment, but also the affects and the hope which arise again at the unfolding of pre-conceptions (♂♂) which were perhaps still alive, frozen, waiting for a home ♀ in which they could play ♂♀ and feed themselves with α milk.

If borderline, as a diagnostic definition, evokes a sort of borderland between neurosis and psychosis, a kaleidoscopic mental functioning which oscillates in brutal switches between neurotic and psychotic modalities, an archipelago in which islands of possible dreams coexist with lagoons of nightmares in search of a mind so that they can be dreamed, and Jurassic platforms of night-terrors/pavor in the wild state, perhaps it is the last of these – the so-called *psychotic nuclei* – which are holed up in the setting, probably magnetised by the concrete, pre-symbolic isomorphism immanent in this body that is the field. If I may risk a generalisation, in the ontogenesis of an analytic field which comes to life with a borderline patient, these hibernating, saurian nuclei are often condensations of violent proto-emotions, suffered but never alphabetised in moments of separation. This separation is not yet representable as the other moving away from oneself, but is perhaps perceived more on a contiguous-autistic level (Grotstein, 1983; Ogden, 1989, 2005) as a sort of geological fracture/detachment between fused masses which produces violent, frightening jolts, incomprehensible in their proto-sensory nature as much as in their relational genealogy. The αirrigation of the dream-work carried out over the long period of the analysis could re-animate the betasaurs, so that they re-waken and cry out the savage violence of their terror and hatred which pour out from the exile of oneiric abandonment: from having been treated for so long as loathsome ♂, unworthy aspirants to that αpassport which permits and legitimises mental citizenship.

5.4.2   On the borders of analysis: bordercamper strategies

A bordercamper frequently expresses the preference/demand for an analytic journey in a single-seater camper van, or at the most a two-seater mobile home. The suggestion of an analysis three or four times a week is often greeted with almost a shudder of horror: impossible! There are almost always intractable financial, work, and lifestyle problems which seem to prevent the possibility of undertaking such a journey, even where the analyst regards analysis as viable. There is a serious economic problem, so the terrified bordercamper seems to be declaring: maybe the three or four sessions are rejected as a relational situation which would entail the serious risk of passing into states of mind (Meltzer, 1973) inhabited by ♂♂ that are feared as treacherous, dirty, vile. Are they ♂♂ of the experiences of dependency, separation's conjoined twin, left in the agonising proto-mental state of the cave-dweller, which the bordercamper feels he can only marginalise and try to keep at a distance, so as to dodge the feared risk of madness and psychic death? Stigmata of a neotenic infancy which he needs to hide as shameful traces of need and sufferings which cannot be shown? Could this initial categorical rejection of a part of the analysis be dreamed as a sort of "Manhattan strategy"? Is partial acceptance of the analysis like deciding to travel to New York, but only staying in Manhattan, carefully avoiding any possible contact with the Bronx? In the analytic field, will the Bronx become a sort of no-go area surrounded by barbed wire, from which every now and then some *toxic, starving immigrant* will escape, infiltrating Central Park or Fifth Avenue? How are we to treat analytically these infiltrators, and the phantom presence of the Bronx localised in the setting on the edges of the analysis? Must they be spotted and immediately reported so that the police will intervene/interpret? Or might it be more helpful simply to try and go up to them and invite them to a table of narrative *curiositas*, trying to offer the dream-food of which they seem to have become ravenous thieves?

Maurizio

Maurizio is a young surgeon, an émigré to Bologna from a little village in Sardinia. Dark, with an olive complexion, grungy clothes, small dark eyes, the fearful and furtive gaze of a Romany refugee. He comes to my consulting room terrified by a panic attack which had stopped him from completing a surgical operation. "I'm afraid it might happen again, it's been terrible!" He tearfully begins a long and detailed account of his life. He has been engaged for some time to a chronically depressed colleague at the hospital, and has had to help his twin brother during a time of psychotic imbalance. He has always felt alone in the world, full of rage, and the fear of going mad: like his brother, but also like his mother, shut in the house for years in an impenetrable mutism, and like his father a violent alcoholic. He knows he is good at his job, but he always feels choked by the fear of making a mistake, a fatal error that could put an end to his entire career as a surgeon.

As I listen, the image of an archipelago forms in my mind: there is a flourishing island, a Manhattan in which Maurizio feels able to do and to think, but the creativity and potential for development and life on this little island are threatened by the looming presence of surrounding lands populated by impetuous madmen who could fall on the island at any moment and lay waste to it. The terror at their proximity sows panic, and there are times when Maurizio feels he can't manage to contain the fear on his own, reinforced only by a Super Ego which tries to defend the island by firing off threats of danger, collapse, and the necessity for surveillance. I think we need to make oneiric explorations of Harlem, the Bronx, Brooklyn, Ellis Island and Shutter Island: districts swarming with nightmares which take away the breath of the dream of being able to live in New York, in the possible federation of states of mind united by an affective democracy (Ferro, 2002a) which gives citizenship to all ♂♂ and an equal right to dream.

Maurizio does not accept my suggestion of three sessions a week: his hospital timetable, and, even more, his financial situation really don't permit it. Amazed by his flat refusal of an admission into analysis, which I regard as necessary in the state of anxiety which seems to be annihilating him, I end up doing some research into the salaries of hospital doctors. It is only at this point that I recall the first image/rêverie which came into my mind at the door during our first goodbyes: next to the doctor, I think, there's the Romany child who mistrusts houses, dependencies, and the dwellings that are unknown to those who are used to nomadic wandering, to a motor home which guarantees spontaneous flight and safe distances from the puppeteers, cats, foxes, and idle harpies who can be encountered in the funfair of the emotional life.[6] At the third consultation meeting Maurizio and I agree to start psychotherapy once a week: a weekly pause in which Maurizio tells me about, and makes me feel, the anguish of a gypsy's life. Drenched in the experience of a solitude which is sadness, melancholy, exclusion, appalling distance, and the slackness of personal ties perceived as inconsistent and fragile, Maurizio laments his fear of the void, the desert in which he feels swallowed up whenever he goes home and finds himself alone, while the field starts to become animated by characters who seem to incarnate the most terrifying anxieties which besiege Maurizio's mind. The young man who hanged himself but was rescued *in extremis* by the emergency services, the brother hospitalised because he has started to hallucinate, the occasional partners found on the internet. The field seems to make itself both the hostel and the diary of possible narrative transformations of the stabbing, rending proto-emotions conveyed by these ♂♂ characters in search of ♀ and reverie. There are plenty of dreams which seem to me also to portray clearly the foreclosure encrypted in the setting of a weekly session, of psychotic areas in urgent need of αdt (*alpha dream treatment*): "I dreamed I was arriving at the Star Hotel in a square nearby, but they gave me a small room. . . . And I found myself hanging my brother's clothes on the washing line out of the window." After dwelling for a long time in unison on the anxiety caused by narrow spaces, I do not restrain myself from formulating the hypothesis of a feeling that the space of one session may be too little for him. However, I realise that perhaps it is too soon. Maurizio reiterates that it is already an effort for him to keep up one session. . . . And/But the following month he leaves for a four-month journey to Oceania. I receive the announcement like a knife in the stomach, a direct hit filled with rebellious hatred for the need that causes dependency: is it payback, a retaliation against my absence from the summer holidays that have just ended? I try to absorb the blows from these violent ♂♂ and to resist the seduction of a transference interpretation: easy, clear, Lapalissian, but mightn't it turn out to be a ♂ which would simply risk hyper-saturating or fragmenting a ♀ which had already declared itself to be small and insufficient, on the eve of a long loneliness because of his departure? The disturbing oracle of a Pythoness-analyst, able only to stir up doubts, irritation, vigilance, and super-egotistical suspicions? And what if we instead tried to reconnoitre together the depths of this Ocean-Oceania that was tropicalising the field? Talking about this voyage, we discover that it is a part of the world in which it seems possible to dream about immersions that have always been desired, but also the fear of drowning that has assailed him since childhood, and the acute infections which in the past have stopped him leaving at the last minute.

When Maurizio says goodbye to me, a Rio Grande of sadness, fear, and impotence washes over me: like saying goodbye to a child who has decided to set off alone through the world, to show himself and other people that he's big enough to manage on his own. . . . But maybe in Oceania we succeeded in collecting shells/ proto-dreams and listening to their sound of immersion and togetherness, and spotted piranhas/nightmares of dependency/ separation lurking in the field . . . On his return, in *Psycho-Rapper* and *The Film Director*, two girlfriends found via the dating app Meetic, nucleoli of experiences of dependency/separation which regulate the affective genetics of a couple-relationship, seem transformed by poietic mitosis into two characters ready for new oneiric developments.

The mother-in-law

Eleonora, a university researcher in Oriental languages, is now in the sixth year of an analysis which she too has only half accepted: the dream of the two rejected sessions seems to be represented every now and again, in irregular waves. To me it seems to be there, ready in the field to be dreamed together, like a film with screenplay and actors fully prepared, ready to be shot, but if I so much as try to name it, Eleonora responds straightaway with rigidity, irritation, and persecutory anxieties. It is rather as if an area of *no-dream* had been encapsulated in these two rejected sessions (Cassorla, 2012, 2013): an impossibility/terror of being able to dream; an archaic region in which thoughts and dreams are feared and wrongly understood as concrete, burdensome presences, a region in which thoughts and dreams cannot be dreamed or shared because it is feared that the other may misunderstand them as facts or intended actions; also perhaps as a sort of minaret in the analytic field in which the ♂♂ of dependency barricade themselves in a stubborn oneiric anorexia nourished by the phobic *pavor* of oneiro-adiposity. The other half of the analysis seems to be one that makes progress, transformations, changes. Eleonora has been able to conceive two daughters after passing through the moonless straits of an initial sterility as a couple and the impulsive temptation to bypass them with a speedy intervention of artificial insemination: but also after I had wondered during the analysis if her husband's weak spermatozoa, which seemed to be the source of the difficulties with fertility, might not also represent an interpretative weakness on my part. Had I been insufficiently penetrating? And yet Eleonora had at times seemed to display clear areas suitable for exploration along Kleinian lines, and I had not held back from transference interpretations. Had a Kleinification-syndrome in the field perhaps made the ♀ inaccessible and impenetrable by β♂, despite their being potentially fecund with new dreams not yet dreamed? We began in the sessions to try dreaming together the affective vicissitudes of these spermatozoa (♂♂): did they feel weak because they could not complete the whole intrauterine journey towards the ovocyte (♀)? Did they feel disoriented, lost in the darkness of the long tunnel of the tubes? (The long separations between Fridays and Wednesdays imposed by the diet of two sessions a week?) Or, once they had arrived, did they come up against walls that were too hard and thick to be penetrated? (Autistic closures in the field?) The new oneiric treatment devoted to the spermatozoa coincided with the development of Eleonora's first natural pregnancy, which she was moved and excited to tell me about, about a month after the decision to give the couple a bit more time in sessions, and give some further opportunities to the spermatozoa, and perhaps also give our analytic couple the possibility of more creative ♀♂ encounters.

It is just before the holidays when, commenting on yet another dream about the discovery of broad spaces in which we could be more comfortable, I observe that maybe there is also the image of an analytic space of three or four sessions in which we might feel more comfortable, less hedged in. Eleonora mumbles an agreement, and then starts complaining about her mother-in-law who just doesn't get it: she keeps on intrusively insisting that she wants to see her daughters *more than twice a week*, despite repeated attempts to explain to her that this is what was agreed.

Eleonora often feels tired, oppressed, and sad because of the effort of having to look after these two little girls, but the relationship with her mother-in-law is still so infested with rage, suspicion, and anxiety about intrusion/theft (♂♂) that she cannot be used as a source of help. "It would be like Snow White asking the witch for help," I tell her. Eleonora laughs and goes on to say that all in all she would feel better with a child-minder, someone who looks after your children as a job. She could be called on *even three or four times a week*. Paying for this would make Eleonora feel freer, calmer in her role/identity as a mother. By making me present at the oneiric transformation mother-in-law→child-minder, passing through the hallucinosis→reverie of the witch, it seems to me that Eleonora has again made me rediscover (Ogden, 2009) that dream paths are much more nourishing and transformative for her than those of interpretation, which sometimes break off the possibility of an intimate and personal intercourse between ♂ and ♀: that perhaps only oneiric massages will be able step by step to dissolve the autistic thickening of the armour inside which ♂♂ are held captive, considered as being on the margins of mental legality. But on the paths of dreams, one dream is also the doorway into another, and a character is often a little Russian doll who carries another dream inside herself, one that is just starting the process of oneirification. It took several sessions for us to discover that perhaps, by dreaming of Snow White, we had opened the way for her twin, Coal-Black: the baby black widow who repeatedly failed to pay after I had been absent, thereby injecting into the setting the venom of proto-abandonments re-awakened by the loss of a session.

Maurizio and Eleonora are perhaps examples of restricted analytic dietary regimes which may be chosen by a borderline patient as a strict strategy for avoiding contact with ♂♂ that are feared as mentally toxic, deforming, disfiguring, humiliating. Orphan contents (♂♂) of ♀, which are often affected by a severe phobia of ♀ and ♀♂ (Collovà, 2013). Accepting the analytic conditions dictated by this anchoritic imperative may perhaps express an acknowledgement of the existence of and entitlement to an analytic refuge, even for that cyclopean Super Ego which bears down on them; the acknowledgement of the necessity of ♀ and of analytic listening even to the one-eyed hatred that is felt towards an emotional life perceived as hostile since it has never been seen and exploited as a primary resource of psychic life in the oneiric relationship with another mind; acknowledgement of the need for, and the possibility of, an oneiric cradle even for the ascetic gasps of the sleep-depriving Super Ego.

In the borderline structure, the micro-dimensions of the dreaming ensemble are often flanked by the suffocating presence of an obstructive maxi–Super Ego (Bion, 1962, 1992; De Mattos and Braga, 2013; Grotstein, 2007, 2009; O'Shaughnessy, 2011) which tries to distance, repress, and demonise all the emotional experiences that cannot be dreamed, issuing alarming judgements of danger, madness, prohibition. The analytic field itself can be infected by this anti-dream configuration. It is perhaps one of the most devious and pernicious "illnesses" that can infect the field: oneiric nanism accompanied by Super Ego gigantism which can make the analyst ill too, with the hope that if she or he can suffer the murderous impotence of this condition, it may re-awaken a Scheherazade function capable of rediscovering unison in the nights which must be spent together so that they can be retold. If rediscovered, this unison might also placate Shahryar's hatred, which has been exacerbated by interpretations that in certain states of mind can sound as offensive and sarcastic as Hezbollah satires.

5.4.3 Toto and Dorothy on a journey in search of brain, heart, and courage. Borderline analysis: to the Bermudas of O

If we take as indispensable and unforeseeable the subjectivation of every analytic field which can be structured with a patient in analysis, a field generated by the coupling of the subjective unconsciouses of patient and analyst, it may happen that in the experience of analysis with borderline patients we rediscover a cyclonic tendency, a climate of extreme uncertainty doped with fear, like that undergone by Dorothy and Toto during their adventures in the world of Oz.

If the rhythm of the setting may expose the bordercamper to the agonising experiences of Peter Pan in his relationship with Wendy and her brothers, which consist of lonely departures from and returns to that island of unborn child-dreams, besieged by nightmares which rend like grappling hooks and reduce everything to sponges of abominable, demoralising sensations, the life that is set up in the analytic field can, as a psycho-atmosphere, resemble that of the famous novel by

Frank Baum. The borderline patient presents a demand for immersions and unisons in the Bermudas of O, the place where natureβ is made manifest in its most disturbing, impetuous, and overbearing, confronting the human α in its smallness and impotence.

In the field of poppies: the hypnoid opiate of sleep without dreams

In search of a heart, a brain, and courage, Dorothy, Toto and their companions fall asleep in the deadly field of poppies; it is a dangerous sleep which brings with it the risk of slipping into death. The "odour" of the poppies "is so powerful that anyone who breathes it falls asleep, and if the sleeper is not carried away from the scent of the flowers, he sleeps on and on forever" (Baum, 1900). Sensations of torpor, evanescence, and mental stupefaction characterise those states of αdeprivation (Ogden, 2005) which I have often found myself passing through in the initial phases of an analysis of three or four sessions a week with borderline patients. α does not function, or respond, or transform: you wander suspended in a sort of nebulous void, as if drugged by a spiked βdrink. You feel like a robot capable only of artificial intelligence, as in the 2001 film *A.I. Artificial Intelligence*: you can see, speak, hear, and understand, but you are unable to feel, dream, or think. Heart and mind are far away in a cosmic dissociation; the sap of desire and the courage to live no longer flows.

What is happening? An αcoma caused by an overdose of βinhalations? Is this the tremendous, unbearable mental state which the borderline patient complains and shouts about as that damned lack, that emptiness that makes him or her feel annihilated? The black hole of the α's absence?

Thomas

Thomas is nearly fifty-five, works as a film distributor, and looks like a viado, small and squat, with a crown of black-dyed hair, and such bright red, fleshy lips that they seem tattooed. His clothing alternates between Seventies-style country cowboy and Eighties punk. He promotes arthouse films, but his life seems to have got stuck on the set of a seedy Christmas comedy. He had moved from Naples into a house a few metres from my consulting room at the end of a long period of consultation, but at the same time he had scotched the idea of an analysis of three sessions a week as being incompatible with his life as an independent contractor. I had found myself gasping between the overwhelming currents of Charybdis-yearning and the Scylla-*pavor* unleashed onto the field by the first attempt at an analytic relationship. Thomas had chosen to start with one session a week. A few months afterwards he came into contact with an image which made him decide to start having three sessions a week. He had just let me know that he planned to stop therapy because he was feeling better: *it wasn't raining any more in his attic*. Shaken by the βradioactivity emitted by this sudden intention to break off, I found myself telling him about the image which had appeared to me in reverie in the *hic et nunc*: *sometimes, if Spring comes and the sun is shining, we may wonder if rain might come out of holes in the plumbing, and so we would still need to make repairs*. Thomas had been touched by this, recognising in the image the dream of the *holes* he felt he had inside him, and within a week he had started to lie down on the couch three times a week.

As had been the case with Ariel, I also remember the first year of analysis with Thomas as a long wandering in a nebulous proto-sphere, in the total absence of images and thoughts. There were whole sessions in which Thomas regaled me with a logorrhoeic outpouring of wit and radical-chic comments about smoky bohemian salons where he mixed with artists, writers, film directors. Acquaintances, love affairs, and cultural debates: a blend of *La grande bellezza*[7] and the Bloomsbury Group. Lovers with whom he spent nights of passionate sex and profound intellectual intimacy. Doped by the buzz of his glamorous and inconsistent chatter, I would then find myself – even the next day – in the black depths of Nothingness: long sessions in the abysses of a blinding, breathless sensation of lack.

Thomas complained about the infected pain of absence, or the absolute loneliness which leaves one inert, with the feeling that one is drowning, the terror of dying. Lovers left him, as indeed had his wife; ties seemed to evaporate and he found himself alone again, at the edge of nothing. What with the smoke fumes and perfumes of the salons and the miasmas exhaled by the depressive decomposition of Nothingness, I started to feel painfully affected by a sort of αparalysis (αdeprivation; Ogden, 2005): unarmed, I found myself suffering the inanition of the total absence of dreams, in the witless impotence of listening without knowing what to say (Bolognini, 2010). I felt capable only of acting as a sort of absorbent filter, judged inept and stupid by Thomas, but perhaps over time βdetoxifying and capable of re-oxygenating the field's oneiric function. After months of narcoleptic highs, Thomas's first dream emerged in a session: "I feel like a pebble landing on a slab of marble. The slab is smooth, it's not a like a pond. The pebble slips off the slab, but when it falls into the pond it stays there. . . . And there's life in the pond." A wave of astonishment and relief wakes me in contact with this image/dream of the emotional experience which I feel I've been living through with him in the field. Maybe, from a field perspective, rather than interrogating oneself and trying to understand who was the pebble and who the slab of marble, it was important to acknowledge the first oneirification of the marmoreal state which had made it impossible to achieve a ♂♀ rapport because of the repeated petrifying contacts and refractions/repulsions ♂→»«←♀, resulting in the absence of reveries. This resulted in our being able to benefit from the oneiric catharsis made explicit by this first dream, a catharsis capable of pictographing the unutterable agony caused by the inaccessibility of oneiric comfort which can arise in the intimate ♀♂encounter. By trying to αlphabetise in the field the βconcreted emotions of the slab-pebble experience, we would find ourselves in the ♀ pond swarming with tadpole-dreams and clumps of βbacterial flora more compatible with mental life.

Perhaps, in order to pass through the frightful darkness of the state of α depriva-tion and to be able to comprehend how it is this condition of night without dreams that is the silent oneiro-aplasia which devours the mental life of the borderline patient, the analyst needs to be successful in maintaining a sufficient negative capability (Bion, 1970, 1992) and faith (Bion, 1970) in the analytic possibility of αre-awakening in long unisons with the gases and vapours of O (ibid.). Perhaps being able to dream together with the patient the true dreams which emerge dur-ing this gloomy αwaiting, will be the stem-cell experience capable of starting up the regeneration and/or generation of lesioned or amputated dreaming ensembles. It is hard not to fall into K→O flytraps (ibid.), attempts at artificial illumination by interpreting contents, often of transferential origin, which lend themselves to theoretical plagiarising; accidental falls from which the analyst will be able to get up again, recovering an analytic disposition unencumbered by memory and desire (Bion, 1967b), often aided by information emitted by the GPS function (Levine, 2013) performed by the field.

5.4.4 End zone

In American football, the end zone (Delillo, 1972) is the area of the field where the game is decided, where the players must be available to put themselves in play, each revealing his or her own uniqueness and personality as a subject, his or her being human. It is the area in which the player's personality, his or her being a per-son, a member of the team, an opponent, and a footballer, undergoes a sort of test. There is an end zone in every analytic field, where the analyst will also be called upon to take off his or her analytic suit and tie in order to bare his or her authentic nature and availability as a dreamer. With a borderline patient, this happens to coincide with the question of the end of the analysis, an ending which is often presentified as a shadow of the decision to start the analysis, going right back to the first conversations; an ending which is the spectre of an experience of separa-tion that one fears without the hope of passing through column 2 of dreaming (see Chapter 3). Might it give access to a feeling of oneself as a separate subject able to dream the emotional experience of the other's absence?

"I think that at a certain point it will end . . . and for me the end is the problem," Thomas had observed as soon as he had decided to start analytic work three times a week. "I'll come for ten or fifteen years and then I'll leave . . . and it will the same all over again," Janet had commented at our third consultation meeting as soon as we had agreed to start an analysis of three sessions a week. "Right now, four sessions are great, but what about when it finishes?" had been Blanko's sibyl-line question during our second conversation, and it rang out in the field with the rhythm of an alarm bell.

Sometimes the borderline patient decides to leave just at the moment when the analyst thinks that the analysis has finally reached an oneiric level, just when new dreams seem ready to be dreamed. Just when the possible transition from the Robinson Crusoe state to the post-Robinson Crusoe state (see Chapter 8) has been sketched out in the field, a recalcitrant Peter Pan wakes up and digs in his heels with desperate, terrified, furious stubbornness on an island that isn't there. Does mourning for symbiotic fusions and the limits of a link's intimacy seem to herald a change that for the moment is impossible to dream? Is it a metamorphosis which would also entail the dissolution of an autistic cocoon of idealised autonomy, which is perhaps no more than the home-made disguise of a contact barrier against exposure to emotional events and experiences which still seem intolerable?

It may occur that the breaking-off happens just when the emotional experiences linked to affective dependency start to dissolve into burdensome events which one would rather not feel: strong, violent emotions, still without a name, that one would rather not suffer, that cause fear. The long and laborious process of αlphabetisation, which would require the effort of a further analytic suffering together, is presented as hateful and maybe also dangerous. The borderline patient may communicate his or her decision to suspend the analysis as if he or she was someone deciding to discharge him or herself from hospital as soon as he or she is able to stand on his or her own two feet, rejecting suggestions and instructions about extending his or her stay in order to complete his or her convalescence. The analyst, like the physician, cannot help feeling regret and concern about what seems to be a premature departure which cuts off the potential for a consolidation of the patient's capacity for dreaming his or her own emotional experiences, and will express puzzlement, as well as pointing out that there is dream-work which could still be done: but maybe the analyst can do no more than accept that she or he has to put up with what seems like a brutal abandonment, an enforced separation which it seems could not be dreamed. Could it perhaps be that the bordercamper leaves his or her nightmare with the analyst so that she or he will continue a long-distance work of dreaming? A nightmare which the field was unable to bear and dream, yielding to the siren calls of pre-oneiric interpretations? A nightmare felt as needing access to a Skype-field dimension in order to be dreamed?

To Anzieu (1959), the works of Bion and Beckett seem to be the oneiric development in parallel to the dream-buds which sprouted in the brief analytic work they did together at the Tavistock Clinic in London, broken off by Beckett after only two years.

Meltzer used to say that there are analyses which end where others begin; maybe there are also analytic fields which continue to dream online after what seem to be premature interruptions.

Ariel left almost four years to the day after she started, attracted by what seemed a possibility she couldn't refuse of working in Tokyo, the centre of the future, just when she had started to come to sessions with her dog. Thomas suddenly announced, after only three years of analysis, that he was moving to Los Angeles, giving us a term to prepare ourselves and vaccinate his *lovebird partner*. Blanko stayed for six years until he discovered that he was capable of sexual relations, but *only with a condom*. Did further intimacies (♂♀) without protection seem unimaginable?

These were communications of abandonments which in *après-coup* it always seemed to me had not been successfully recognised and listened to in their fully challenging oneiric character: at certain moments, worried by K-fears that an analysis might be aborted, I had not been able to navigate with blind faith among the surges of the violent and frightening O which was swamping the field, or to hold firmly onto a Ulysses function when faced with the interpretative sirens which hypnotised my negative capability with songs of necessity, analytic duties, and dark predictions of danger if I went beyond the Pillars of Hercules of the already known and thought.

We can try to interpret an interruption straightaway: an ISIS attack on the analysis? Negative therapeutic reaction (see Chapter 12) and impasse between the couple in the analytic process? Limits and oneiric flaws in the analyst, corresponding to collusive/ conniving no-dream zones/clumps (Cassorla, 2012, 2013)?

Perhaps all an analyst can do is suffer the analytic responsibility for a broken off treatment: the doubts, questions, fears, pains of the emotional experience of an analytic abandonment.

An analyst will not be able to rid her or himself of the nightmare-abandonment: she or he will fulfil the function of long-range oneiric uterus which the patient has assigned her or him.

The end of a first half and the need for an interval? The advance suspension of a game because of overriding, unsustainable conditions of field and climate? Too many interpretative failures which have made it necessary to expel the analysis? The desire to leave the field, the times/rhythms of analytic life perceived as an excessively laborious emotional competition?

Every nightmare will be capable of transformation into a dream, a unique and unrepeatable conception of an analytic field. The analyst's oneiric K-expectations of the analysis as treatment can inflict pre-eclampsia on the pregnancy of the nightmare of an analytic abandonment and disturb its transformation into dream.

Maybe the end zone is the area in which the O-borderline test is brought into the field? Is this where the analyst's availability and ability to divest her or himself of her or his K baggage for close encounters of the mind-body with an O at the limits of possible dream is probed? Where the limits of the analyst's, couple's, field's ability to dream are experienced *in vivo*? Where the analyst will discover the qualities, limits, needs for development of the present state of her dreaming ensemble and her capacity for staying in humble ignorance (Bion, 1967a, chap. 3) so that she can dream the emotional truth of the O that is expanding in the field? Perhaps where one can accept walking, falling, returning repeatedly only if one can experience the oneiric creativity of the analytic apprenticeship in O?

Alfredo, Janet, Maurizio, Eleonora, and Robbie stayed in therapy: companions in analytic experience with whom I could discover and rediscover that the end zone is perhaps the area of the field where we can show ourselves that the deepest transformations in analysis arise from O→K (Bion, 1970), but also that area of the field in which faith and negative capability most tremble, vacillate, and risk succumbing to the terror of contact with an O in the bloodcurdling mood of a Gorgon.

Notes

1 The dreaming ensemble is conceptualised by Grotstein as a sort of mental chromosome for dreaming, comprising the totality of those factors/functions which participate in performing the dream-work: α function, contact barrier, ♂♀, reverie, transformations, emotional links H, L, K.
2 William Friedkin's 1973 film.
3 "With neither roof nor law". The title of Agnès Varda's 1984 film released in the English-speaking world as *Vagabond*.
4 Joseph Ruben's 1993 film.
5 *Psych'O'Analysis: Explorations in Truth*, 8th International Bion Conference (Los Angeles, 23–26 October 2014).
6 Translator's note: these are allusions to Carlo Collodi's novel *Pinocchio*.
7 Paolo Sorrentino's 2013 film, released in the English-speaking world as *The Great Beauty*.

References

Anzieu, D. (1959). *Freud's Self-Analysis*, The Hogarth Press, London, 1986.
Barale, F., and Ferro, A. (1992). Negative Therapeutic Reactions and Microfractures in Analytic Communication. In L. Nissim and A. Robutti (Eds.), *Shared Experience: The Psychoanalytic Dialogue*, Karnac Books, London, 143–65.
Barros, E.D. (2000). Affect and Pictographic Image. *The International Journal of Psychoanalysis*, 81: 1087–99.
Baum, F. (1900). *The Wonderful Wizard of Oz*, Wordsworth Editions, Hertfordshire, 2018.
Bion, W.R. (1962). *Learning From Experience*, Karnac, London, 1984.
Bion, W.R. (1965). *Transformations*, Maresfield Library, London.
Bion, W.R (1967a). Notes on the Theory of Schizophrenia. Read in the Symposium "The Psychology of Schizophrenia". In *Second Thoughts*, Karnac, London, 1984.
Bion, W.R. (1967b). The Psycho-Analytic Study of Thinking. *International Journal of Psychoanalysis*, 43: 306–10.
Bion, W.R. (1970). *Attention and Interpretation: A Scientific Approach to Insight in Psychoanalysis*, Tavistock Publication, London.
Bion, W.R. (1976–79). Emotional Turbulence, Evidence and Making the Best of a Bad Job. *Clinical Seminars and Other Works*, Karnac Books, London, 1994.
Bion, W.R. (1992). *Cogitations*, Routledge, Abingdon, 2018.
Bollas, C. (1996). Borderline Desire. *International Journal of Psychoanalysis*, 5: 5–9.
Bolognini, S. (2010). *Lo Zen e l'arte di non sapere cosa dire*, B. Boringhieri, Torino.
Cassorla, R.M.N. (2012). What Happens Before and After Acute Enactments? An Exercise in Clinical Validation and the Broadening of Hypotheses. *International Journal of Psychoanalysis*, 93: 53–80.
Cassorla, R.M.N. (2013). When the Analyst Becomes Stupid: An Attempt to Understand Enactment Using Bion's Theory of Thinking. *Psychoanalytic Quarterly*, 82: 323–60.
Civitarese, G. (2013). *Embodied Field, Somatic Reverie and Patients With Blocks to Symbolization*, Panel 92, Prague-I.PA. Congress.

Civitarese, G. (2014). *The Necessary Dream: New Theories and Technique of Interpretation in Psychoanalysis*, Routledge, London.

Civitarese, G. (2016). *Truth and the Unconscious in Psychoanalysis*, Routledge, London.

Collovà, M. (2013). The Setting as a Locus of Possible Transformations. In A. Ferro (Ed.), *Contemporary Bionian Theory and Technique in Psychoanalysis*, Routledge, London, 2017.

Correale, A. et al. (2001). *Borderline*. Borla, Roma.

Delillo, D. (1972). *End Zone*, Picador, London, 2011.

De Mattos, J.A.J., and Braga, J.C. (2013). Primitive Conscience. In H.B. Levine and L.J. Brown (Eds.), *Growth and Turbulence in the Container Contained*, Routledge, New York.

Donnet, J.-L. (1999). Patients Limites, Situations Limites. In J. André et al. (Eds.), *Les états limites*, 123–49, Puf, Paris.

Ferro, A. (1992). *The Bi-Personal Field: Experiences in Child Psychoanalysis*, Routledge, New York, 1999.

Ferro, A. (1996). *In the Analyst's Consulting Room*, Psychology Press, London and New York, 2002.

Ferro, A. (2002a). *Seeds of Illness, Seeds of Recovery: The Genesis of Suffering and the Role of Psychoanalysis*, Routledge, London, 2004.

Ferro, A. (2006). *Mind Works*, The New Library of Psychoanalysis, London, 2008.

Ferro, A. (2007). *Avoiding Emotions, Living Emotions*, Routledge, Hove, 2011.

Ferro, A. (2009). Transformations in Dreaming and Characters in the Psychoanalytic Field. *International Journal of Psychoanalysis*, 90: 209–30.

Ferro, A. (2010). *Torments of the Soul: Psychoanalytic Transformations in Dreaming and Narration*, Routledge, Hove, 2015.

Ferro, A. (2013). *Dream Model of the Mind: In Contemporary Bionian Theory and Technique in Psychoanalysis*, Routledge, New York, 2017.

Ferro, A. (2014). *Le Viscere della Mente*, Cortina, Milano.

Ferro, A. (2017). *Contemporary Bionian Theory and Technique in Psychoanalysis*, Routledge, London.

Ferro, A., and Basile, R. (2007). *The Analytic Field: A Clinical Concept*, Routledge, Abingdon, 2018.

Gabbard, G.O. (1991). Technical Approaches to Transference Hate in the Analysis of Borderline Patient. *International Journal of Psychoanalysis*, 72: 625–37.

Gabbard, G.O. (2000). *Psychodynamic Psychiatry in Clinical Practice*, American Psychiatric Association Publishing, Washington, DC.

Grotstein, J.S. (1980). Primitive Mental States. *Contemporary Psychoanalysis*, 19: 580–604.

Grotstein, J.S. (1983). A Proposed Revision of the Psychoanalytic Concept of Mental States, Part. II- The Borderline Section1: Disorders of Autistic Safety and Symbiotic Relatedness. *Contemporary Psychoanalysis*, 19: 570–604.

Grotstein, J.S. (2007). *A Beam of Intense Darkness*, Karnac, London.

Grotstein, J.S. (2009). *But at the Same Time and on Another Level*, Karnac, London.

Hayes, D. (2008). Sibling Rivalry. *Contemporary Psychoanalysis*, 44: 280–8.

Kernberg, O.F. (1989). *Psychodynamic Psychotherapy of Borderline Patients*, Basic Books, New York.

Levine, H.B. (2013). Comparing Field Theories. *Psychoanalytic Dialogues*, 23: 667–73.

Levine, H.B. (2014). Beyond Neurosis: Unrepresented States and the Construction of the Mind. *Rivista di Psicoanalisi LX*, 2: 277–94.

Lucantoni, S., and Pietroantonio, V. (2014). *Il corpo invisibile: una possibile lettura di campo*, Oral presentation at the SPI National Congress, Milan.

Manica, M. (2014). *Intercettare il sogno. Sviluppi traumatici e progressione onirica nel discorso psicoanalitica*, Borla, Roma.

Meltzer, D. (1967). *The Psycho-Analytical Process*, Karnac, London.

Meltzer, D. (1973). *Sexual States of Mind*, Karnac, London, 2008.

Meltzer, D. (1986). *Studies in Extended Metapsychology: Clinical Applications of Bion's Ideas*, Karnac, London, 2009.

Ogden, T. (1989). *The Primitive Edge of Experience*, Karnac, London.

Ogden, T. (1992). *Projective Identification and Psychotherapeutic Technique*, Karnac, London.

Ogden, T. (2005). *This Art of Psychoanalysis: Dreaming Undreamt Dreams and Interrupted Cries*, Taylor and Francis, New York.

Ogden, T. (2009). *Rediscovering Psychoanalysis*, Taylor and Francis, New York.

O'Shaughnessy, E. (2011). Relating to the Superego. In *Bion Today*, Routledge, New York.

Palahniuk, C. (2001). *Choke*. Doubleday, New York.

Rosenfeld, H. (1998). *I Seminari Italiani*, Quaderni del Centro Milanese di Psicoanalisi, Cortina, Miano.

Ruggiero, I. (2012). The Unreachable Object? Difficulties and Paradoxes in the Analytical Relationship With Borderline Patients. *Journal of Psychoanalysis*, 93: 585–606.

Schlesinger, C.A. (2006). *Adozione e oltre*. Borla, Roma.

Stern, D.B. (2013). Field Theory in Psychoanalysis, Part 2: Bionian Field Theory and Contemporary Interpersonal/Relational Psychoanalysis. *Psychoanalytic Dialogues*, 23: 630–45.

Winnicott, D.W. (1947). Hate in Counter-Transference. *International Journal of Psychoanalysis*, 30: 69–74.

Chapter 6

Paranoias

Fulvio Mazzacane

6.1 Introduction

There are three aspects to the argument that I would like to pursue in this chapter:

a   Underlining the continuity between paranoiacs' thought and affect, or the paranoid disposition which any analysand may present, albeit temporarily, and the "normal". Meissner (1978) spoke in broad terms about paranoia as a mental disposition with a broad spectrum, from pathology to adaptive states which bring no rewards, the fundamental components of which are isolation, hypersensitivity, suspicion, and the heavy use of projection. In the legacy left to us by myths and tragedies, the paranoid point of view has shown itself to oscillate in meaning between being the symptom of a delusional illness and evidence of a divine gift: a different form of consciousness, parallel to the usual kind, not necessarily mad but *other*. It is a summation of all the problems inherent in the relationship between normal and pathological, in a spectrum which runs from total delusion to – in paranoia – being just one of the levels of reason (Ferro, 2008).

   In situations that are not overtly pathological, the paranoid disposition is a mode of rapport with the world which does not rule out relationships but foregrounds the complex negotiation of emotional distance and the limits of contact. For analysts, the paranoid disposition demands that special attention be paid to our modes of interpretation, which must take into account the quality of the anxieties, defences, and necessities which the analysand needs not to be aware of. It is perhaps the clinical situation which most exposes analysts to raised levels of emotional intensity and requires them to take on difficult roles.

b   Reading the paranoid disposition as the result of a progressive accumulation of intellectual defences in response to an affective trauma. Not only imagining them as reactions to major traumas but as ways of circumscribing the emotional turbulence caused by small traumas. The patient's account is always the development of a narrative transformation of a trauma which may be a small incomprehension or an incurable wound. The couple's work of transformation requires the progressive construction of a climate of mutual trust and gifts of tact on the analyst's part as moves little by little towards the heart of the problem.

c   Speculating that, as we move towards becoming psychoanalysts, the urge to give a meaning to everything, to work by following trails, to understand the roots of unhappiness, both individual and social, leads us to adopt and expand the clue-based paradigm of psychoanalysis (Ginzburg, 1986). A drive to search for hidden meanings which, if taken to extremes, can tend to construct personality traits not unlike those which lead to the paranoid spectrum.

When difficulties arise in the session, it is only human for the analyst to let him or herself be attracted by the reassuring force of his or her theories at the risk of losing creativity. Clinging to what is already known can sometimes help to protect us from an excessive exposure to unhappiness and the systematic exercise of doubt. In this respect, the paranoid disposition could be configured as a defence against the projections which inhabit the analytic field, against thoughts that are different, other, and undermine the analyst's identity.

6.2   Normality and paranoia

6.2.1   Semantic ambiguity as paranoia's identity card

The history of the concept of paranoia contains a series of ambiguities which will accompany it as the reflections of psychopathologists are developed. These ambiguities find confirmation in the fact that few other psychiatric terms have undergone as many changes of meaning as paranoia has since it was introduced into the psychiatric lexicon (Cargnello, 1984).

The ambiguity is already present in its etymology: *para-noeo* means "understand badly, misunderstand, rave, diverge from the visual field"; but *nòos* can also mean "spirit, heart, feeling", and *para* can be "beyond", but also "beside" (Maci, 2008).

This etymological complexity testifies to the word's richness and to the progressive accumulation of meanings which have defined it over time. Indeed, it seems that in antiquity the use of the term in literature, philosophy, and medicine was not tied to a precise diagnostic configuration but was characterised by a very broad semantic range.

Traces of the word's ambiguity remain in everyday language. Outside its ever less frequent clinical use, it tends to be used as an equivalent to madness or obsession, and this shunts the word towards a usage with positive connotations, characterising for example a person in obsessive search for the truth or for a response. It describes the mental disposition of a man who explores the world, above that of relationships, with a microscope forever in front of his eyes: an individual who starts out with an uncommon sensibility amplified by the impossibility of playing with different relational distances. This is a disposition not unlike that of the researcher who makes his or her goal into a reason for living.

The hypothesis of the continuity between normality and madness depends on the concept of the *paranoid state of mind* (Meissner, 1978) which alludes to the organisation of a coherent belief system which allows the subject to interpret and organise reality in harmony with his or her needs for adaptation. The characteristics of subjects with this type of prevailing mental disposition are the inadequacy of their attitude to social relations, mistrust, suspicion, dogmatism, rigidity of thought, restricted affect, and hypersensitivity.

The prevailing disposition of the personality becomes a lifestyle, a way of entering into contact with reality through a cognitive "shock absorber" which softens the emotional impact of events. This lifestyle does not always evolve into outright delusion but can imprison important parts of life. The rigid separation between reason and feeling is useful in avoiding a mixture which is felt as explosive.

Bion, quoting Kant, often reminds us that the concepts without intuition are empty and that intuitions without a concept are blind. I detect in this a characteristic of the paranoid disposition: affectivity, kept separate and under coercion, turns concepts into pure speculation so that they become blind and can only explode.

6.2.2   Paranoid thought as a vicissitude of the human

The paranoid disposition in thought and relating appears to be one possible existential dimension which speaks of the human, representing in an exemplary and dramatic manner the continuity between the normal and the pathological, and the thin boundary which separates them.

Kretschmer used to say there is no paranoia, only paranoiacs, which I think means that what leads us to perceive something common in these patients is the atmosphere which colours their communication, and not the content of the delusion: a delusion which indeed seems indissolubly linked to their individual history. And it is inevitably of fundamental importance how the personality is constructed before a pathological picture emerges: the presence of excessive sensitivity, rigidity, mistrust, hypertrophy of the Ego, and social isolation.

Every unknown thing is reattributed to a known one, in a forced and uncritical use of the vital move of classification.[1]

In Lacan's thought, paranoia is an ontological structure of the human world. "Lived paranoid experience and the resulting conception of the world can be understood as an original syntax which contributes to maintaining, by means of characteristic bonds of comprehension, to human community" (Lacan, 1933, p. 58).

Moreover, the mirror stage speaks of the structuring of the Ego by means of the other's gaze: hence, self-knowledge is always mediated by something alien (Stein, 2010).

There is an initial kinship between passions and delusions, and this is evidence of how valuable the delusions, large and small, can be to us as they take shape in the analytic field. But if the delusion methodically constructs its own world by losing contact with reality, the passions – while altering the vision of the world, either episodically or continuously – never quite cancel reality out. The paranoiac uses small clues as the starting point for general conclusions, denies the category of the possible and accidental, and often sees what others do not but tends not to pose himself the problem of context (Bodei, 2002).

The paranoiac's aim is not the increase of his or her own knowledge, but a desperate defence against all that is complex and inevitably ambivalent. In a paragraph about the Schreber case, Canetti (1960) writes that the paranoiac's movements are not growth but a stretching out to reach a position which may enable him or her to reinforce and assert him or herself. For Canetti, a characteristic of the paranoiac is the ceaseless discovery of enemies who always show themselves to be the same when their mask is removed. He or she is the slave of anti-change: in his or her mind he or she experiences a sort of atrophy of metamorphosis, the need to see different things as identical.[2]

The paranoiac cannot yield to doubt, and other people's thoughts, which inevitably open up other horizons of meaning, cannot be allowed to live. There is no possibility of accepting, in an initially passive move, thoughts and emotions which arrive from the world.

Of course, it is not by chance that most cases of tipping over into clinical paranoia occur between the ages of 40 and 50, a period when significant balances, both existential and social, are to be reckoned. Temporal horizons suddenly seem more definite and it becomes difficult to project oneself into a future that is not closely tied to the path which has been followed up until now.

My experience as a consultant within a Medical Service working with cases of harassment has enabled me to come into contact with one of the places in which, for social and economic reasons, paranoia tends to express itself easily: the workplace. Harassment is understood as the enacting of systematic vexations with malicious intent towards a person by means of actions which aim to marginalise and damage his or her psychophysical identity.

It is obviously a situation in which we can encounter paranoid patients who "choose" work as a possible field of expression for their unhappiness. At the other end of the spectrum are people who develop persecutory experiences because of objectively extreme working conditions. The most difficult situations are those of patients who present with a paranoid outlook and internal climate, people who have built their identity on work which has often allowed them important social and personal growth. They are often highly motivated people who have found themselves taking on roles within the organisation that exceed the requirements of their job description. When an unexpected change in the way the organisation is set up suddenly dismantles their function, they have a thoroughgoing identity crisis with paranoid reactions.

6.2.3   White paranoia

Paranoid thinking can be hidden for a long time in the folds of existence, easily relying on social situations which, individually, are insidiously plausible (Ferro, 2008), which gives the delusion its social and cultural plasticity.

I would call white paranoia a paranoia "unsullied" by structured delusions in patients who have a life sufficiently integrated into the social, often more in appearance than reality, who always seem one step away from achieve a complete life. Something always happens in their life to justify flight, just when it might be possible to make a leap of responsibility in the affective field because an increase in anxiety has reached intolerable levels. The result is a continual aborting of their most human aspects.

In *Attention and Interpretation* (1970), Bion speaks about two key aspects of psychic functioning. The first is the emerging principle which perceives the world as being in constant change, and records what is mutable, singular, and distinct: it is a creative act, even though change generates anxiety. The second is the principle of continuity which seeks stability, is in constant dialogue with the rules of shared reality, acknowledges what is common and similar, and sets a limit on omnipotence and subjectivity. It is the interaction between the two principles which permits development.

In a paranoid disposition, every element is felt as emergent, the bearer of a catastrophic change: hence, it is mistrusted and microscopically investigated according to a view which admits no other perspectives. In the paranoiac's life we witness the emergence of plans, the arresting of which seems to play a part in justifying the sense of persecution. What is lost is the integration between the emergent and the continuous; that which, for Dana Amir (2015) constitutes the lyric dimension of psychic space: lyrical because it catches the most private aspect of each experience, the ineffable and inexplicable element, but also that which can communicate the most authentic part of an individual.

Dino is a professional with many interests, including the arts. The only important relationship of his life came to an end ten years ago, and he has not felt able to bear allowing the relationship to grow, and with it his responsibilities. He began a steady process of distancing, which forced his companion to leave him. In recent years he has developed a symptomatology characterised by insomnia, asthenia, the sensation of failing intellectual performance, and depression. He is receiving treatment from a public psychiatric clinic which has spent a year trying to find a suitable pharmacological therapy. Various medications have been abandoned because of sometimes inexplicable side-effects. His relationships begin with great enthusiasm but suddenly and inexplicably the climate changes and Dino starts a systematic destruction. The woman seems to be transformed into an enemy, a foreign body by which he feels invaded and threatened. He has very hesitantly started an analytic therapy. In the first six months there have been nothing but doubts and an undervaluing of the therapy. Dino is convinced that his disturbances are fundamentally organic. Initially, so as not to frighten him, I suggested "fixed term contracts" lasting a fortnight, and after two months the contract became indefinite.

Coming back after the summer break, he tells me about three women: Anna, a married woman he has never appreciated because she symbolises a relationship with no future, but who has now become interesting again; Bea, who is unattached, with whom plans could be made; and Cinzia, an attractive and enterprising woman. In this way, Dino seems to list some mental dispositions which are in his mind at the resumption of therapy, after an initial period we had spent sounding each other out: the possibility of living one day at a time without too many conflicts and investments, the possibility of being able to plan ahead, the burden of sensations that are too strong and resist being worked through.

I here report a fragment of a session.

D1: I'll tell you the news about my relationships: I'm ending it with Bea, I can't bear her, she wants to cut off my freedom. I talk every day with Anna, she's accepted that things aren't going the way she wants, I can't give her much time, and if she doesn't like it I'll finish it. Cinzia keeps trying, but what can you do with someone like her? She goes around in these miniskirts . . ., everyone envies me the attention I get from her, but she does the same with loads of other men. From an intellectual point of view, nothing's changed. If I had to try and study something new, I couldn't do it. I get away with it because I can improvise.

A1: Improvising isn't easy. You need great faith in your own ability to find a solution.

D2: It doesn't seem as if anything's changed since I've been coming to you. I'm sleeping better, but that's all. The rest hasn't changed. I feel unable to do anything. My intellect just doesn't work. I know that if I'm going to change my life I've got to leave a job that takes up all my weekends. It's not normal, never having a free weekend in ten years.

A2: It's important that you want to have more time for yourself, also because you feel haven't had an important relationship for ten years. Besides bringing prestige and money, working every weekend may have helped you shut yourself off for a long time from the possibility of affection without realising it.

D3: I don't know, unconsciously maybe, but in any case, I can't keep going like this. I'll finish with Bea, I don't want to feel responsible for her quarrels with her family because her being involved with me means she does less looking after of her old parents, it's as if she was showing me that being with me comes at a price.

A3: In today's session you've told me about unsatisfying relationships: the one with Anna because she wants more from you, the one with Bea which implies greater responsibility, and the one with Cinzia who is unreliable, although seductive. Nor do you find our relationship helpful. You have recently reduced your medication and started to build relationships, but at a certain point you've got scared. One way of being has steadily regained power and started a slow but constant retreat. You've lost interest in what you have laboriously begun and you've slowly started to call it into question. Maybe you're afraid of not being able to manage things as you would like.

D4: Well, maybe unconsciously, all I know is I can't concentrate any more, can't apply myself.

As often happens with Dino, the session is shot through with a notable aggression which attaches itself to the various characters who appear. On other occasions I have tried to emphasise that the game we were playing should make us teammates and not opponents, but Dino experiences these interventions of mine as threatening.

The field only tolerates minimal movements and most often seems blocked. Over time I have tried to create some good "carriers": words and expressions which, being mostly suggested by the patient, but sometimes by me, and accepted by Dino, may be able to become common property, circulating freely in the field and introducing novel elements, but this has not always worked. For example, the use which Dino sometimes makes of the word "relationship" might seem to be a step forward. In the beginning, when telling me about his affective experiences, the terms he used were more generic and concrete, but more often he employs it in order to destroy its meaning.

When this type of disposition predominates in the analytic field, the patient attempts by emptying words of meaning to cancel the frail relational threads which are seeking to become significant in the couple. In order to try and keep alive certain concepts and the emotional halo connected to them, he finds himself almost trying to hide them, even on a semantic level. I initially used the adverb "unconsciously" to speak about his physical symptoms and how they might be the result of conflicts inside him. Dino used it in a progressively more provocative and disparaging manner, showing his distrust of me through the use of psychoanalytic stereotypes. Alternatively, my use of the phrase "without realising it" is an attempt to revitalise the concept of the unconscious, to clear it of predefined, and therefore weakened, meanings.

My last intervention is longer than usual, and certainly the first time I have spoken at such length to Dino. This is required by the need to reconstruct the emotional experiences which have emerged out of the summer break, basing my words on the characters he is offering. I am trying to effect a kind of intensive therapy in a dangerously ill field.

6.3   Paranoia and affective trauma

6.3.1   The ambiguity of paranoia in psychopathology

As far back as the early nineteenth century, different ways of thinking about paranoia were starting to emerge. At one end of the spectrum there are those, like Kraepelin, who prefer a reading of its complex symptomatology as a disturbance of thought characterised by an orderly, clear, and coherent delusion, not one with an affective disorder behind it; chronic, without bizarre or polymorphous delusions, and with affectivity preserved.

At the other end of the spectrum are writers such as Specht and Bleuler who maintain that paranoia is a primary disturbance of affectivity, the former hypothesising that such a disturbance arises within a relationship with an affectively significant person.

Paranoia proves to be a paradigmatic example of how difficult it is to label human thought in terms of normality or pathology, and to find a precise boundary between aspects of character and the development of illness.

In this connection, Cotard's perspective is illuminating: in 1882 he spoke of delusional creation as a discovery, the attempt to solve problems connected to sensitivity, the roots of which are unconscious. In this way he opened new perspectives on paranoia, considering the construction of delusions as an attempt to explain something that has happened in the patient's life. Connecting paranoia both to delusion and to depression, Cotard made it into a form of transition.

The paranoiac always seems to be balancing between *noos* and *pathos*, constituting a challenge for the clinician: not to let her or himself be crushed by the seeming lack of meaning and not to get dragged into a guessing game about hidden meanings (Callieri and Maci, 2008).

There is a convergence here between phenomenological and psychoanalytic thinking: the search for meaning is in the relationship which exists between two individuals, Freud's intermediate realm, the field, the analytic third, intermediarity, the transition from *alius* to *alter*.

In Rossi Monti's (2009) view, where the psychoanalytic and phenomenological perspectives are wonderfully fused, paranoia is presented as a nosographic disrupter, a borderline case, in order to study the terrain on which they converge, ending with the superimposition of normality and illness, disturbances of thought processes and affective disorders, customary and consensual ways of thinking and unusual, private ways of putting facts in relation to each other and working through problems.

The paranoid state of mind becomes a style of thought, a way of living and knowing reality, an approach which co-participates in the creative and developmental activities of humankind.

It becomes a clinical event in some personalities when a crystallisation of this cognitive style occurs in an especially sensitive and vulnerable affective area. Incoming impressions are organised into a system of meaning which responds to subjective needs rather than to objective evidence or agreement reached by consensus. Affective and intellective mechanisms are not mutually exclusive, but interact.

The temporality of the paranoiac is conditioned by his or her objectives, which are fixed, by the loss of the capacity to tolerate waiting, by the dialectical and historical perspective, but also by the need to maintain his or her present state.

The first sketching out of the future delusional nucleus is pervaded by elements with a strong affective charge, composing an embryonic nucleus, an organisation rather than a structure, in which diverse fragments in a state of fluctuating instability conglomerate, forming a sort of proto-nucleus of delusion. Contact with reality "toughens" the nucleus. The goal for the patient is to mitigate the high affective charge of the proto-nucleus. The cognitive safety belt is the terrain which the paranoiac has chosen for his or her battles, where it is easiest to elaborate defensive strategies and safeguard the unhappy affective nucleus. But it is also a terrain of contact because, for the paranoiac, theories are sense organs which push themselves out to more external levels of the system in order to get close to reality.

Defensive accommodations thus become complexes which throw the system into crisis. In reality, the conspiracy which the paranoiac sees everywhere, speaks of its opposite, the fear of abandonment.

It is a constant therapeutic challenge for every clinician who is faced with a human being incapable of accepting anything that might come from the other, even something good. The challenge emerges between the inability to return affection, thereby acknowledging the dignity of the other to exist, and the desperate search for an emotional contact.

6.3.2 A case of paranoia

Carla's story seems to show the genesis of a paranoid disposition, understood as the result of a poly-traumatic family context within which rigid and intellectualised defensive strata have accumulated progressively, reaching the point where they have become delusional.

I meet Carla when she has reached the age of 50. The early affective trauma has been organised around her mother's depression. Carla remembers her being ill and spending long periods in bed, and the same thing happened to Carla herself when she started to be unwell. The family climate was impregnated by a rigid and oppressive religious culture, and by the total absence of physical contact, which has in fact made the development of her sexuality impossible.

During adolescence, Carla used the family's religious code to construct her identity. Very active in her church, an excellent student, sought after for her generosity in helping others, but actually without friendships.

Towards the age of 25, she had a psychotic breakdown after a serious road accident. She experienced the accident as a betrayal by the deity who had not protected her in spite of her absolute religious faith.

She has broken off, after many years, a tempestuous earlier analysis in which there were almost daily clashes. Carla, armed with her education and her religious faith, seemed to be conducting a personal fight with the psychoanalyst as representative of a secular culture which for the most part emphasised the importance of the emotions. After a long pause, she has resumed her analytic voyage by coming to me.

In the first session, she tells me a dream: "*I have an accident at home, I call my first analyst because I don't know what to do, even though I know I can't trust him. I ask him to teach me to draw, but he tells me to sculpt not draw. I find myself carving the Dolomites.*" For the patient, the ambivalence about analysis is expected and inevitable: this and the image of Carla trying to carve the Dolomites brings about the appearance of the character "mission impossible". Even so, despite the ambivalence of which she is fully aware, she is curious about how I work and throws herself fully into the experience. Indeed, she dreams about places never explored and isolated mountain landscapes which need to be connected.

During the early years Carla seems to keep setting up the same format for sessions as the one she imposed on her previous analyst. She furiously attacks me and the analytic method, threatening to break the work off, and my attempt to avoid conflict only earns her scorn: at least the previous analyst fought back and got angry, but I was too soft.

I gradually tried to accept her challenges which took the concrete form of violent discussions that looked like preludes to a definite breaking-off, and from which she emerged with a sudden swerve towards a good mood, leaving me a wreck at the end of the session.

She usually starts the session with one or more dreams which set the tone of the session as a whole and are a challenge to my interpretative capacity. In the flood of words and images it is as if single characters or emotions had to be isolated in order to construct small, incomplete puzzles.

A first contact with the hidden affective nucleus occurs after some years when Carla dreams about various homosexual and heterosexual encounters; in reality a sketchy, almost pre-adolescent sexuality in which she and her partner undress and touch each other: nothing more, a sign of what she feels as the limit of our intimacy. The emotions she feels are excitement, disgust, and above all guilt.

The possibility of a more intimate quality to the encounter brings her up against her *no entry signs*. Over the years, Carla has in fact matured into a more critical and distant relationship with the church, no longer feeling there is the same gap between religious thought and psychoanalysis. Her religious outlook is more tolerant and critical, unlike the fanaticism and rigidity of the past.

Every small step forward in the analysis has a rebound expressed as ferocious attacks in which she scornfully calls everything into question: "*I dreamed I was listening to a lecture about psychoanalysis, a handicapped analyst was talking about Freud, saying his thought goes in and out of the ears, mouth and eyes.*" The analyst's words are invasive and can only be rejected.

As we come closer to the affective nucleus of Carla' unhappiness, there is a fierce clash. When I let her know that there will be no session on Pavia's patron saint's day, she explodes and tells me that since I'm not religious (she had known this all along, but according to her no psychoanalyst could be) she couldn't see what reason I had for celebrating.

After a rather tense exchange in which, as always, she accuses me of being useless, Carla's tone suddenly changes and she says she has understood that keeping one's body blocked has probably been a way of avoiding sensations that would have been destructive. I tell her that her body actually finds ways of speaking, even if not directly. I tell her about my physical sensations of fear when she has her explosions of fury, and how these situations are nevertheless a way for her to try and play with her own corporeality, although in an unsatisfying way. Jokingly, she replies that it doesn't mean she won't turn this into action sooner or later.

Carla is convinced that she cannot make certain more authentic parts of herself emerge. It is painful to hear her talk about the steadily emerging awareness of the reasons for her unhappiness, about what her multiple, complex symptoms mean, about lost opportunities, the part of life that she will never live.

The image which is a snapshot of the approach to the original depressive nucleus is a dream of a girl playing with other children in the park and then leaving the group to play by herself.

For the first time a joyful character appears in her dreams, one who reminds her of her only openly affectionate relative. However, there is also the fear of losing her previous equilibrium, founded on dogmas, without finding another.

The analysis has been going on for many years, and the external links, the intellectual defensive constructions, have been confronted and seem softened. The depressive nucleus is there, we see it and know its name, treat it with respect and with a certain fear that it might reawaken.

As I comment on Carla's story, Ogden (2014) comes to mind and his re-reading of Winnicott's "The Fear of Breakdown" in which he reminds us that Winnicott speculates that the breakdown we are talking about is that of the mother-baby link. The baby cannot bear this and short-circuits its occurrence so as not to experience it, replacing it with psychotic defences. Thus, he or she lives in fear of a breakdown he or she hasn't experienced, but which has already happened. The patient has the sensation that a part of his or her life has been taken away and that he or she has been left with an unlived life. Not having experienced it, he or she lives in the constant expectation of a breakdown in the future. For Winnicott, psychosis is not the breakdown but a defensive organisation against a primitive agony. The original experience of primitive agony cannot be located in the past until the Ego is able to locate it in its present experience, in analysis, but despite this it undergoes a painful experience. Thus the patient must paradoxically live through the failure of the mother-analyst in a situation of total dependency, while at the same time feeling that the analyst is not failing, that she or he is living the experience of the present breakdown with him or her and helping him or her to understand it.

6.4 Microparanoias

6.4.1 Oedipus, paranoia, and psychoanalysis

It is well known that, in the final pages of *Constructions in Analysis* (1937), Freud outlines a process which runs from considering the possible presence of hallucinations in non-psychotic patients, to revealing the common matrix of hallucinations and delusional formations under the upward thrust of the unconscious and the return of the repressed, finally arriving at the definition of a continuity between this mechanism and that of dream-formation. The conclusion is that the ill person's delusional formations seem to be equivalent to the constructions we erect as analysts: attempts at clarification and cure.

In Drafts H and K from 1895–6, Freud identifies the mechanism of projection, a primary defence which consists of searching for the external origin of an unpleasure. The paranoiac projects his or her intolerable representations, which come back to him or her from outside in the form of reproaches. "The content and affect of the incompatible idea are retained . . . but they are projected into the external world" (1895, p. 212). In Draft H Freud reconnects paranoia to an affective disturbance which arises from intolerable events which attach themselves to a disposition with the aim of repelling a representation incompatible with the Ego.

Another characteristic of projection which Freud emphasises is that of its normality, being the basis of superstition, mythology, and animism. The paranoid delusion presents itself as the caricature of a philosophical system, while on the other hand subsequent developments of paranoid thinking link back to the paranoid-schizoid position, a mode of organising fundamental experience which lasts throughout life. Dangerous and unpleasurable thoughts and feelings are split off and projected onto others, and hence attributed to them.

In his description of the case of President Schreber (Freud, 1910), beside the diagnostic debates over whether this a case of paranoid schizophrenia or paranoia, Freud's idea is that even complex symptomatologies as unusual as those present in Schreber, originate from the commonest and most comprehensible impulses of psychic life. Freud underlines the communicative significance of paranoid delusion, identifying a link between hysteria and paranoia: paranoia dismantles, whereas hysteria condenses.

But there is another thread which connects paranoia to psychoanalysis, and this has to do with Oedipus. In *Seven Against Thebes*, Aeschylus uses the chorus to specify how Oedipus chose to "plough the furrow" of his mother Jocasta. It is no coincidence that the birth of the word "paranoia" is connected to oedipal experience, one of the pillars of Freudian thought, with its ambiguous connotations and paranoid atmosphere. Oedipus's search for a truth, which will turn out to be terrifying, will lead to the development of a paranoid delusion in an atmosphere of suspicion, denial of reality, and rage, and will thus bring about a situation typical of the paranoid disposition: reversal. Legitimate self-defence in the encounter with Laius becomes parricide; royal marriage becomes inadvertent incest; the drive to know leads to blindness (Faranda, 2008).

6.4.2   The first significant move in analysis and the paranoid rebound

Don't people often announce their descent into the analytic situation by a move in which an affective investment occurs with an almost simultaneous persecutory rebound? As if the appearance of an albeit frail beam of light caused pain and the desire to blind oneself.

Livia is a young maths teacher in the early stages of analysis. She has a social life, but also some features suggesting emotional restriction and rigidity. From the first sessions, she has been very careful to structure a ritual of engagement for entering and leaving the session. She has been through a previous analytic experience in which she felt rejected and despised, and of which she has unpleasant memories because she didn't remember her dreams and only talked about everyday life, and this seemed to annoy the therapist.

In the first six months of analysis the sessions seem repetitive: some complaints about her poorly paid and unsatisfying work, her inadequate colleagues, a routine relationship.

She tells me this dream:

L: We were at an open-air concert, and I was surprised to see you in the audi-ence. Then I was back in the consulting room, it seemed more like a house. You must have had guests, I couldn't see them, but I could tell they were there. There was the couch, and a young man was looking at me, you seemed rushed off your feet. I was annoyed that someone might be listening.

[A period of silence follows. Some promptings on my part to play with the dream have no effect]

AN: It's as if you had the sensation of a loss of intimacy. What could you connect that to?

L: When I leave after the session I don't see anyone in the waiting room. If I imag-ined that someone was there I'd be afraid that they could listen to what I say.

[I don't want to miss the opportunity of a dream and a statement in which she talks about the analytic couple, and so I resume]

AN: Through my presence in the dream it's as if you had given me access to an important part of yourself. The presence of a stranger in the session, the fear of being overheard, seems to say something about your fear of a closeness which you also fear as being dangerous.

L: No, the fear is of external presences, not the analyst, who is neutral. To get close I have to feel safe. When the relationship with my boyfriend started, I knew he liked me, I was calm, I led the way. I was the one who wasn't con-vinced, and then after spending time with him I fell in love.

[It seems that the investment in the analyst must be immediately sterilised, although Livia's observation nevertheless describes a process of increasing mutual engagement]

AN: In the dream we're listening to the same concert, and then something hap-pens which, even though it makes us stay in the same room, moves us apart, makes us lose contact. It could be absent-mindedness on my part, but it could also just be the way in which we separately straight after an intense moment, and you are thinking how even moments of closeness can bring some fear with them.

As soon as Livia starts the story of a dream in which, what is more, the analyst appears, the persecutory element is represented by intrusive presences and by the analyst's lack of interest. In the text of the session, there is also an immediate move to sterilise any emotional dimension involving the couple by evoking the analyst's neutrality.

6.4.3 The clue-based paradigm: identification of the selected fact and the paranoid analyst

Ginzburg (1981) writes that at the end of the nineteenth century a conjectural model of constructing knowledge predominated, finding its most important proponents in Giovanni Morelli, Sherlock Holmes, and Sigmund Freud. For all the differences in their fields of action, they have in common the use of obscure, improbable clues to construct an epistemological model. Furthermore, the birth of the detective novel takes place in a period shortly before the construction of psychoanalytic knowledge, and in the early days the figure of the analyst appears to share many of the constituent features of a good investigator. Freud immediately enters into this culture of suspicion: there is always something latent behind the appearance of reality and the patient's communications. The unconscious can hide any event or thought that cannot be admitted, but it is possible to reconstruct a historical truth thanks to analytic work and dream-work.

The psychoanalytic method too, like the detective novel which originates with Poe (rather than with Conan Doyle), is based on clues that are not only material but also linguistic such as omissions, lapsus, anagrams, word play. The search for a solution by an omniscient and perfect investigator is something different, as is the solution, often only possible and partial, which characterises the modern detective story (Mazzacane, 2011).

At the same time we could find similarities in the evolution of the interpretative instrument. There is a difference between the mode of intervention by means of a mutative interpretation in Strachey's sense or the "surgical" use of interpretation according to the Kleinian model, and the "weak", collaborative construction of narrative interpretations.

Indeed the method of Dupin, the investigator created by Poe, does not seem rigidly scientific, just as nobody has perhaps ever thought that interpretation, outside a background affective context, can have a function, rather than being a mere stylistic exercise.

Poe himself uses the concept of *ratiocination* to define Dupin's way of proceeding: he is referring to a mental state which makes possible a reasoning founded on hypotheses, not pure application of a rule. In Dupin's way of investigating there are inferences, attention to the non-verbal, to the perceptual, to the reading of expressions. The results of this method have the characteristics of intuition.

In the current use of weakly subjective models (Civitarese, 2014) there is a trace of new ways of investigating which, while continuing to use the similarity with the detective story, have the flavour of the "hard-boiled" revolution with its less ideal investigators who confront crime, but also their own limits.

The transition from a paradigm of deduction which presumes an ordered world dominated by relations of cause and effect to a paradigm in which the detective provokes effects rather than working back to causes (Eco, 2007), has a counterpart in the role of the analyst who tends more to immerse him or herself in the analytic situation, contributing to its instability. Giving up a strong supporting system, he or she will use a series of "showdowns", an approach to the analytic process which unfolds through successive crises.

The aim is not to find the culprit but to work back to a configuration of events, causes, and incidents which, starting from some initial elements and the more it tends towards Bion's O, will lead to the reconstruction of a truth.

The analyst/detective can quickly pass from the role of investigator to that of victim or perpetrator, in the continuous game of enactment which is played out in the session. This is an analyst conscious of his or her own potential for aggression, which can be expressed through technical errors, or a tendency to indoctrination, or by exposing the patient to an excess of truth.

The identification of a constant conjunction and hence of a selected fact, leads the analyst to highlight a certain relational configuration. This happens through the discovery of clues which nevertheless must be passed through the sieve of the reality of the session; for the discovery to become usable, there must be a gathering of threads which need to achieve a certain density and point in a common direction (Mazzacane, 2015).

Paranoia can manifest itself in what Britton and Steiner (1994) have called the *overvalued idea*, an idea which the analyst has mistakenly turned into a selected fact on which to base an interpretation. This can happen because such an idea serves to confirm the analyst's theories or stops uncomfortable things happening. The selected fact becomes a sort of delusion on the part of the analyst who tries in this way to defend him or herself against what he or she experiences as a potential attack on his or her identity.

In a field model, another sensitive point for the development of a paranoid disposition in the analyst can be in the excessive tendency to look for traces in the analysand's words which may refer to the analytic relationship or constitute a response to the analyst's intervention. In this way, a model that starts out as "weak" is transformed into an automatic decoding of the patient's text. I think it is important to emphasise that the analyst is *looking for the trace* of the relationship in the patient's words, in the level reached by the field and in the comment on his or her interventions, but the sound of these elements is not always within audible range.

6.4.4 Paranoia as a configuration in therapy: nosography of the field

There is a reason why classical diagnosis occurs in the initial phase, when the analyst must assess whether, in order to protect the analytic process, it is necessary to set up in advance some variations of the classic setting. I am talking about the need with seriously ill patients to be able to consider the possibility of a pharmacological therapy or a hospital admission or whether the use of the couch is helpful.

If we move on to consider the evolution of the analytic field, this passes through a sequence of illnesses, acute and chronic, generally benign, or potentially fatal, which the analytic couple must try to treat in an original way, in which every pathological configuration can be put into play by every analysand.

However much we imagine ourselves to be making wise use of negative capability and an immersion in the analytic field, we must expect ourselves every now and then to need to "look at the stars" and orient ourselves in accordance with the relational configuration we are experiencing.

So it is helpful to have Ferro's (2002) attempt to elaborate a nosography of the field. The facts of the session, above all its micro-transformations, can be defined (transitorily) as the fruit of the vicissitudes of the alpha function and parameters such as PS/D, $\female/\male$, Negative Capability/Selected Fact, thus thought of as an instrument for diagnosing what happens in a session.

Therefore we will find ourselves in clinical situations in which it becomes apparent that there is a deficiency in alpha function, the function which enables the mind to transform sense impressions and emotions: not only in the most serious situations, but also those holes left by traumatic events or temporary arrests of development.

However, in traumatic situations, beta elements (untransformed sense impressions and emotions) begin quantitatively and qualitatively to overwhelm the alpha function.

Then there are micro- or macro-pathologies caused by inadequate development of the ($\female/\male$) mechanism, the PS/D mechanism (paranoid-schizoid position/ depressive position), the NC/SF oscillation (negative capability/selected fact). Alpha elements are formed but the apparatuses for working with them are inadequate. Any patient can present different degrees of these three situations at varying levels.

A paranoid situation arises from a hypertrophy of what we could consider a normal function of clarification: fixing one's ideas is important, but if the ideas become rigid or the process of classifying them loses touch with its objective, there is a loss of freedom and creativity, and a paralysis of the oscillation between paranoid-schizoid and depressive positions, which acts as respiration in the field. The only way the paranoid patient can avoid the anxiety of remaining in the paranoid-schizoid position, given the impossibility of endowing one idea with meaning and tolerating the mourning of all the others, is rigidity, making the idea lose meaning, sterilising it against any new aspect.

The result is the impossibility of imagining, dreaming, and playing which leads the patient to a coerced, rigid choice, and so to a paralysis of the oscillation to and from the selected fact.

Some paranoid configurations of the analytic couple initially demand that certain fundamental principles of our work remain clandestine: for example, emphasising the primacy of feelings or adopting the language of emotions. Mistrust, the impossibility of managing feelings of dependency which an acceptance of the analytic offer would impose, makes another approach necessary. It is as if analyst and patient should initially try out the possibility of bestowing a few things on each other in the knowledge that they can be thrown away: the patient out of fear that he or she might leave dangerous traces which at the start would not be sustainable; the analyst in order not to take for granted what is in fact unstable.

If this is obvious in cases of clinical paranoia, it is equally so in transitory paranoid dispositions.

I would say that a paranoid phase occurs in a therapeutic relationship whenever movements in the field are blocked, and this is occasionally possible even in a single session or a single interaction.

In a situation where there is insufficient alpha function, we find ourselves confronting the paralysis of the three parameters which define the movements of the field (PS/D, Container/Contained, NC/SF), every psychoanalytic element is blocked in a situation which can be summarised as PS, Contained, or SF. In other words, each element of the field is presented as content: that is, with an intrusive force and no capacity for containment; in the PS position with no capacity for working through mourning and hence incapable of any transformative movement. The selected fact is obligatory and cannot be placed in the background, leaving space for other elements.

In the minefield of the relationship's paranoid configuration, the transformative action of the word must take into account the word's potential for destruction in a difficult equilibrium of forces. The construction of the analytic relationship through moments of contact brings with it the spectre of the relationship as a killer; the idea of a dynamic and multi-faceted identity is opposed to the demand that the field must be immobile; the psychoanalytic function of the mind offers itself as an alternative to delusion, suggesting that ever-growing quantities of anxiety be tolerated while they wait for a meaning to be elaborated.

From a field perspective, the persecutor is not an internal structure but a function, a thickening of psychoanalytic elements in a character which is not nourished by the patient's experience but also by the quality with which he or she is represented in the analytic situation, and of the anxieties which this tangle of elements stirs up in the analyst.

The patient, the analyst, and the field can take on persecutory qualities and become victims in the same session.

6.4.5 Paranoid phases

Using the concept of paranoia to define not only a clinical syndrome but a configuration of the couple in the session, we can have paranoid phases in every analysis, situations of impasse determined by the fear of an excess of emotions.

Ada is a young woman in the third year of analysis. The first two years had seen the laborious construction of a joint perspective, of being able to think inside a couple. There seems to have been nothing but loneliness in her life, starting in early adolescence because of her mother's serious depression.

The return from the summer break in the third year of analysis seems to have been the moment at which the perception of an emotional proximity provoked an abrupt rebound which reinforced defences of a persecutory kind. Ada tells me that she feels betrayed by her boyfriend: she was expecting the relationship to grow but he would rather go on holiday with a male friend. Her fear of sleeping on her own has returned. She dreamed she was in a choir, everyone was singing and dancing, and she was the only one who couldn't keep time with the music. She had the feeling that everything we had built up together might fall apart, she was missing our meetings. It is only at this moment that it occurs to me that these were the first long summer holidays we have had. In the first year, analysis had only been going for a few months when the time came to say goodbye for the summer holidays, and she told me, surprised, that she hadn't understood that this would be the last session. It frightened her, and so we had found a way to insert some "bridging" sessions into the summer break. In the second year she had called me in August because of the reappearance of some physical symptoms and we had brought the resumption forward by a few days. So this was the first time that the summer holidays had been complete.

This is the start of a period characterised by dreams of spiders or of menacing prehistoric reptiles. The primitive and disturbing animals are the correlative of thoughts with a strong and unelaborated emotional content set loose by the summer landslides caused by the long period of separation.

This reaches its culmination one day when Ada arrives for her session extremely distressed. She has seen a large spider outside the door of my consulting room, and in her fear she was tempted not to come in. She tells me that if I don't kill it she'll never come into my room again. The field has become so ill that it is generating physical symptoms. On Monday, the day before the first session of the week, Ada experiences a recurrence of her cystitis, while I inevitably have a cold and a blocked nose.

In the session characters with limited degrees of freedom appear, representing old relational patterns and suggesting stereotypical modes in which the session might be conducted, as if the analytic couple were frightened by the possibility of getting close to the pain of the base traumatic configuration.

The sessions become repetitive: Ada tells me a dream or an event and then refuses to play with me in constructing possible shared stories. She entrusts the material to me without taking any further responsibility for it, giving me the feeling of repeatedly going down a blind alley.

The characters in her dreams don't seem to be able to evolve or show other dimensions; they are masks which can only create predictable stories.

Trying to find solutions, to unblock a climate which has become arid and repetitive, I am surprised to find myself sometimes playing a rigid role with Ada, that of an analyst intent on tenaciously decoding the latent content of the dream, with the idea that the course of the analysis would only be changed if I made a perfect interpretation. The character "dream told to the analyst" is emptied of meaning.

In the two years when the summer holidays were shortened, my choice could certainly be considered an enactment motivated by separation anxieties which are part of Ada's story and have resonated with my sense that the analytic relationship was precarious. Furthermore, it is not the analyst's job, in my opinion, to safe-guard the integrity of the setting, so much as to be able to acknowledge and manage controlled distortions or breaks which may allow the analytic couple to get into contact with extreme but indispensable elements in order to understand how they function.

The collusion which generated the enactment was useful in not prematurely addressing the separation anxieties and seemed, as the analysis proceeded, to be an opportunity for making some paranoid nuclei emerge, defensive in nature and created as protection against the presence of the other, which had inevitably become intrusive and threatening.

6.4.6 Episodic paranoid configurations

Staying even closer to the perspective which privileges the *hic et nunc* of the session, we also observe episodic, transitory paranoid dispositions:

Luca is in the moment of moving to the couch after six months of analysis. At the start he was cautious about the number of sessions, but we have steadily arrived at an agreed three sessions a week and a move to the couch. He tells me a dream.

L: *I was living in an immigrants' district, I met a girl and I wanted to kiss her, but I don't know if she'd have liked it. Ever since I was a teenager I've had the hots for girls who didn't want me. Meanwhile the district had been taken over by Muslims who cut every resident under the chin as an initiation ritual, and I ran away.*

AN: A passion comes up and straightaway the fundamentalists turn up to ban it.

 [I detect that the increase in the intensity of the analytic relationship is stirring up opposing emotional currents: the desire to kiss and at the same time the fear of being marked for life, trapped in a rigid system, and it is this opposition that I am emphasising in my comment.]

L: *And in the past I've dreamed I was in a war, but really there was nothing bad going on* [His tone downplays his words]. *Anyway, it's all the fault of westerners who've financed dictators.*

 [The downplaying helps to reassure him that nothing is happening, and yet the message is that anyone who tries to facilitate growth of parts of the internal world risks allying himself with the wrong parts, with dictators who become stronger if the quantity of fear increases.]

 Pause.

L.: *In the surgery I saw an adopted girl whose parents said she was naughty, but they're the ones who aren't good enough. Are there really no checks after adoption?*

 [For now, we are talking about an adoption, something more complex, but for this reason more thought about. Luca is also talking about the lone-liness because of his early, abrupt abandonment by his parents, and about confirming the analyst's qualities in a moment of redefinition of the project, which is becoming more intense and engrossing.]

6.4.7   Paranoia in the psychoanalytic institution

The analytic institution is the place where, after the experience of analysis and supervision, the analytic functions should receive maintenance since they cannot be considered immune to vicissitudes.

Several writers have discussed the subject, above all Otto Kernberg (1986, 1996, 2000, 2006, 2007), who has addressed the problem many times over a period of about 30 years.

Kernberg speculates about the unconscious motivations which determine the psychopathology of psychoanalytic institutions, and identifies various factors, some linked to historical reasons at the birth of the psychoanalytic movement, which explain why the paranoid disposition had been helpful in keeping the group identity cohesive at a time when a new discipline was being born and needed to be protected from the risk of dispersion. Even today, in a period remote from the "wars of succession", a paranoid thought is always ready to express itself in disputes about the modalities for regulating training, just as we can't help touching a sensitive place in neuralgia (Mangini, 2006).

A fundamental feature for Kernberg, is the structural insecurity we find in psychoanalytic institutions, owing to the nature of the material being handled. Every psychoanalytic process releases "radioactive" by-products, originating from the phenomena of transference/countertransference which in an ordinary analysis become diluted into a range of social systems; but in training analysis, the radioactive material falls into a social setting shared by analyst and analysand.

Therefore, within the institution, phenomena of persecution and idealisation are activated, sometimes tending to conflict with a rigid hierarchical organisation. Kernberg uses the term "paranoiagenesis", which expresses the diffusion of persecutory feelings in the institution, and which fears the loss of its original heritage and translates this into exasperated forms of conservation, immobilising the original heritage which it imagines to be perfect.

As a constantly re-examined scientific theory, psychoanalysis risks becoming a given and immobile doctrine, to be defended from attack by the "others", so that a tendency to excessive respect for orthodoxy prevails over scientific exploration.

According to Kernberg, there is a tendency in seminars to ignore psychoanalytic approaches that differ from the official culture of any single institution, and there is a disproportionate amount of time dedicated to Freud at the expense of contemporary writers. There is a common phenomenon of *cross sterilisation*: the envy aroused by new ideas leads to the manifestation of appreciation for unoriginal work, with loss of creativity and of scientific productivity.

The risk is that we only show cases in which analysis has succeed, or in which temporary lack of success is used to highlight the way in which the analyst succeeds in getting out of an impasse. In this way, the idealisation of the expert analyst is reinforced, causing trainees and young analysts to try and adopt his or her style and psychoanalytic technique.

In emphasising aspects which have family life as their model, the analytic institution seems intent on valorising only the negative aspects, so that the primal scene refers only to experiences of exclusion and not also to the perception of an affectionate relationship between the parents, the transgenerational is the transmission of unresolved conflicts and not also of fertile inheritances; the sibling bond is only rivalry and not a resource.

Within the psychoanalytic association, it is taken for granted that inevitable aspects of "family life" will be repeated: intergenerational conflicts, sibling rivalries, the primal scene.

The risk is that only one model of the transference is taken into consideration, the one which refers to Oedipus, and what's more from a single perspective, one that reads the story as a parricide in which the arrogant son kills his father, takes his place, and mates with his mother.

Ferruta (2006), commenting on a work by Haynal on the relationship between Freud and Ferenczi, emphasises the need for distinct but connected containers so as to satisfy the need for belonging, for homosexual closeness, but also for distance and non-communication which are necessary for the development of new ideas. I think that the importance of homosexual transference should be imagined as a dimension in which it is not the feature linked to fecundity which predominates, but the need for mirroring, for one's own image to be reinforced with no obligation for a real coupling, a play dimension which does not entail important responsibilities.

There being no definitive solutions, it is necessary to know the advantages and disadvantages of every disposition, taking it for granted that there will be conflicts, and trying to limit their negative effects. One of the most effective methods of control both in the context of our theories and in the set-up of our institution may be a continual openness to the limits of our knowledge and to the constant comparison with those who do not think like us, thereby avoiding the risk of in-breeding.

6.5 Conclusion: paranoia as a pathology of boundaries

Erlich (2005) talks about paranoia as a pathology of boundaries, an evocative term which refers to qualities like strength, permeability, rigidity, and elasticity, which describe the way in which two people experience their encounter/clash.

Usually, when we talk about boundaries we think of a precise line of separation, placing the emphasis on their function as demarcations, but boundaries can also suggest a buffer zone, a sort of no man's land, a grey area without laws which is also thought of as a place where clashes can take place without breaking out into open warfare.

In human relations, the image of the boundary as an area suggests the idea that these mental spaces can become zones freed from all rules, areas of explorations of parts of the self that are not ordinary. The risk is that when we explore them, we may feel surrounded, with an anxiety about losing our own identity: a sort of boundary-trap which is at the bottom of those paranoid experiences that can faintly colour every opportunity for significant human encounters and becomes a useful experience on the way to defining our own personality, but one which can explode into a painful symptomatology. Being able to join the normal anxiety about meeting with a dimension of play, passing from an obscure ambiguity to an awareness of ambivalence, acknowledging in ourselves aspects we share with the world represented by the other can be a significant step in preventing the feeling that the human relationship might get transformed into a trap.

Notes

1 The categories are mental structures which we create over time, which evolve and contain organised information that can be drawn on under suitable conditions. Categorising (not to be confused with classifying) means connecting an entity or situation *provisionally and in a nuanced way* (not black and white) to a pre-existing category present in someone's mind. The idea that categorising means speaking about nuances goes against old conventions because it is disorienting and disturbing. Incessant categorisation is indispensable for initiating any piece of reasoning and having a foundation for our actions. The mechanism which performs categorisation is analogy, an art which does not aim at a correct answer, the heartbeat of thought which tries to give a meaning to what happens (Hofstadter, Sander, *Surfaces and Essences: Analogy as the Fuel and Fire of Thinking*. New York, Basic Books, 2013).
2 Because the unmasking proves the existence of the secret which he or she suspects lies behind everything, for him or her everything becomes a mask. He or she does not let him or herself be fooled: it is *he or she who penetrates with his or her gaze*; the multiple is one. With the growing rigidity of his or her system, the world becomes ever poorer in recognised figures: all that remains is what is included in the play of his or her madness (Canetti, 1960).

References

Note: S.E. = *Standard Edition of the Complete Psychological Works of Sigmund Freud*. Trans. J. Strachy. London: Hogarth Press and the Institute of Psychoanalysis.

Amir, D. (2015). La mente poetica: il Sé emergente versus il Sé continuo nella prospettiva di Bion. *Rivista Di Psicoanalisi*, LXI(1), 173–82.
Bion, W.R. (1970). *Attention and Interpretation*. Tavistock Publications, London.
Bodei, R. (2002). *Destini personali* [*Personal Destinies*]. Feltrinelli, Milano.
Britton, R., and Steiner, J. (1994). Interpretation: Selected Fact or Overvalued Idea? *International Journal of Pschoanalysis*, 75, 1069–78.
Callieri, B., and Maci, C. (2008). Il problema dell'Endon e del Reattivo nella paranoia. In Callieri, B., and Maci, C. (a cura di), *Paranoia, passione e ragione*. Anicia, Roma.
Canetti, E. (1960). *Crowds and Power*. Farrar, Straus and Giroux, New York, 1984.
Cargnello, D. (1984). *Il caso Ernst Wagner, lo sterminatore e il drammaturgo*. Feltrinelli, Milano.
Civitarese, G. (2014). *Truth and the Unconscious in Psychoanalysis*. Routledge, London, 2016.
Cotard, J. (1882). Du délire des negations. *Archives de Neurologie*, XI.

Eco, U. (2007). Prefazione. In *Elementare Wittgenstein*. Medusa, Milano.

Erlich, S.H. (2005). *Enemies Within and Without: Paranoia and Regression in Groups and Organizations*. Oral Presentation, Bologna S. Lazzaro 6–5–2005.

Faranda, L. (2008). Configurazioni mitiche della paranoia nel mondo greco. In Callieri, B., and Maci, C. (a cura di), *Paranoia. Passione e Ragione*. Anicia, Roma.

Ferro, A. (2002). *Seeds of Illness Seeds of Recovery*. New Library/Routledge, London, 2004.

Ferro, F.M. (2008). Immagini e narrazioni. Trittico mitteleuropeo. In Callieri, B., and Maci, C. (a cura di), *Paranoia. Passione e Ragione*. Anicia, Roma.

Ferruta, A. (2006). Sum\to sum. *Rivista di Psicoanalisi*, 52, 931–48.

Freud, S. (1895). Draft H. In Extracts from the Fliess Papers. In *SE* 1, 212.

Freud, S. (1910). Psycho-Analytic Notes on an Autobiographical Account of a Case of Paranoia. In *SE* 12, 9–82, 1911.

Freud, S. (1937). Constructions in analysis. In *SE* 23, 257–69.

Ginzburg, C. (1981). *Indagini su Piero. Il Battesimo. Il Ciclo di Arezzo. La Flagellazione di Urbino*. Einaudi, Torino.

Ginzburg, C. (1986). Spie. Radici di un paradigma indiziario. In Eco, U., and Sebeok, T.A. (a cura di), *Il segno dei tre*. Bompiani, Milano.

Hofstadter, D., and Sander, E. (2013). *Surfaces and Essences: Analogy as the Fuel and Fire of Thinking*. Basic Books, New York.

Kernberg, O. (1986). Institutional Problems of Psychoanalytic Education. *Journal of the American Psychiatric Nurses Association*, 34, 799–834.

Kernberg, O. (1996). Thirty Methods to Destroy the Creativity of Psychoanalytic Candidates. *IJPA*, 77, 1031–40.

Kernberg, O. (2000). A Concerned Critique of Psychoanalytic Education. *The International Journal of Psychoanalysis*, 81, 97–120.

Kernberg, O. (2006). The Coming Changes in Psychoanalytic Education, part I. *The International Journal of Psychoanalysis*, 87, 1649–73.

Kernberg, O. (2007). The Coming Changes in Psychoanalytic Education, part II. *The International Journal of Psychoanalysis*, 88, 183–202.

Lacan, J. (1933). *The Problem of Style and the Psychiatric Conception of Paranoiac Forms of Experience and Motives of Paranoiac Crime the Crime of the Papin Sisters*. Trans. Jon Anderson in Critical Texts, vol. 5, issue 3, Indiana University, 1988.

Maci, C. (2008). Lineamenti storici del concetto di paranoia. In Callieri, B., and Maci, C. (Eds.), *Paranoia. Passione e Ragione*. Anicia, Roma.

Mangini, E. (2006). The Schreber Case: The Discreet Charm of the Paranoic Solution. In *The Italian Psychoanalytic Annual*. Borla Editore, Roma, 131–49, 2007.

Mazzacane, F. (2011). L'analista sulla scena del sogno. In Ferro, A., Civitarese, G., Collovà, M., Foresti, G., Mazzacane, F., Molinari, E., and Politi, P. (Eds.), *Psicoanalisi in giallo*. Cortina, Milano.

Mazzacane, F. (2015). Le origini extra-analitiche del fatto prescelto. In Ferro, A., Mazzacane, F., and Varrani, E. (Eds.), *Nel gioco analitico, lo sviluppo della creatività in psicoanalisi da Freud a Queneau*. Mimesis, Milano.

Meissner, W.W. (1978). *The Paranoid Process*. Aronson, New York.

Ogden, T. (2014). Fear of Breakdown and the Unlived Life. *International Journal of Psychoanalysis*, 95, 205–23.

Rossi Monti, M. (2009). *Paranoia, scienza e pseudoscienza*. Fioriti, Roma.

Stein, R. (2010). Reflections on paranoia. *The Psychoanalytic Review*, 97, 231–7.

Chapter 7

Psychosis. Listening to psychosis in a state of profound ignorance

Mauro Manica

7.1 To begin a discussion

Any possible discussion of psychosis can only start from an enigma, and therefore from the need to address some doubts, questions we cannot refrain from posing, while being aware that *"La réponse est le malheur de la question"* (Blanchot).[1]

So, what is it, and from what experiences or non-experiences is the psycho-pathological circle of psychosis composed? Does it still reflect the face of the Sphinx? The "scandal of psychiatry" (Schneider, 1959) and of psychoanalysis (Freud, 1910)? The unknown of unknowns? Or are we looking out on a constellation of hyper-contents in tireless search of a container which has exploded or which never existed and, for all we know, may never be able to exist? A short-circuited journey of O that was unable to access column 2 of the Grid? Unable to be transformed into dream, play, and representation.

In attempting to formulate an entirely transitory and precarious premise, we could perhaps hazard the hypothesis that the psychotic is not simply a subject in thrall to the incandescent turbulence of the drives in an unconscious *Es*, but a subject without an unconscious (or at least without the symbolic unconscious of repression) and excluded from the possibility of making use of those functions of the *Ucs* which Freud (1915) had intuited and anticipated in his *Metapsychology*, for example, when he wrote:

> The nucleus of the *Ucs.* consists of instinctual representatives which seek to discharge their cathexis; that is to say, it consists of wishful impulses. . . . There are in this system no negation, no doubt, no degrees of certainty: all this is only introduced by the work of the censorship between the *Ucs.* and the *Pcs.* . . . . In the *Ucs.* there are only contents, cathected with greater or lesser strength.
>
> (186)

This first Freudian definition would seem to propose the foundations of a uniper-sonal unconscious, an unconscious conceived within a binary way of thinking, shot through with antinomies in a polarity which cannot be suppressed: conscious (system *P-C*)/ unconscious (system *Ucs*), primary process/secondary process, pleasure principle/reality principle, narcissism/objectuality, subject/object.

Tension, contrast, and conflict generate mental life in the same way as the presence of positive and negative poles is necessary in an electrical field for the production of energy. So 'censorship', the trauma of separation, becomes indispensable if the subject is to emerge from the object and become constituted in his or her own autonomous identity. The unconscious would thus be populated by a chaos of contents and lacking any function which might join them up and perform transformations.

But Freud's inspired imaginative speculation would seem to have led him immediately to add:

> It would nevertheless be wrong to imagine that the *Ucs.* remains at rest while the whole work of the mind is performed by the *Pcs.* – that the *Ucs.* is something finished with, a vestigial organ, a residuum from the process of development. . . . It would nevertheless be wrong to imagine that the *Ucs.* remains at rest while the whole work of the mind is performed by the *Pcs.* – that the *Ucs.* is something finished with, a vestigial organ, a residuum from the process of development. . . . Study of the derivatives of the *Ucs.* will completely disappoint our expectations of a schematically clear-cut distinction between the two psychical systems.
>
> (190)

Through the 'derivatives' of the unconscious, censorship becomes caesura, not mere interdiction, not the mere fault-line of a relational void, but also the contact barrier capable of generating development: there is a *Ucs* that is not only pre-given by phylogenesis but which is created in relation. So, as Bion will show more clearly, what is given is a semi-permeable contact barrier between conscious and unconscious, between subject and object, between mind and body. Which is why the mind needs links in order to exist, and why without links it dies, plunging into the interminable silence of innocence. The infant does not disturb the environment and the environment does not respect (and does not 'see') the infant in his or her essential need for me-ness, for being-him or herself with the consciousness that he or she exists (Manica, 2014).

And again, as Freud goes on to say,

> On the one hand we find that derivatives of the *Ucs.* become conscious as substitutive formations and symptoms – generally, it is true, after having undergone great distortion as compared with the unconscious, though often retaining many characteristics which call for repression. On the other hand, we find that many preconscious formations remain unconscious, though we should have expected that, from their nature, they might very well have become conscious. Probably in the latter case the stronger attraction of the *Ucs.* is asserting itself.
>
> (193)

In other words, the *Ucs* would not only discharge pressing needs in the form of substitutes and symptoms, but would also perform a co-operative function with the *Prec* (with the system P-C), using its derivatives to send the mind signals about the presence of urgent emotional constellations and affective scenarios which need to be acknowledged and worked through: a metabolisation by means of the mother's mind (and/or the analysts'), by means of her (their) α function and the rêverie that is derived from it and experienced via the organ of consciousness. While the *Ucs* which 'attracts' investments could carry out a protective function towards the mind, avoiding its exposure to an excessive and premature invasion of hyper-contents, and perhaps at the same time guarding the nuclei of its identity, which consist of ontogenetic functions in addition to the myths extracted from phylogenesis.

In brief (and of course reductively) we could say that not all the dimensions intuited by the Freudian conception of the unconscious can be traced in the psychotic patient, and we could even think that the psychotic mind looks onto a dizzying gulf in which there is no unconscious. It lacks that *Ucs* which Freud structured as a place, a 'psychic province', but what is missing above all is that unconscious which is definable as a process, something which gives itself and is not given once for all, which is not constituted only by subtraction, through the effect of censorship or repression, but which is continually generated in the relationship of at least two minds which participate in a primal corporeality and group nature. Thus the psychotic is alienated from the body and from the social, he or she raves in a hypochondriac body, in a transmuted body or one inhabited by extra-corporal entities (as in the extreme experience of Ekbom syndrome); in place of sociality there is a world of non-relationships controlled by the 'influencing machine' (Tausk, 1919), which comes to represent a projected or split-off and de-humanised aspect of the Self of the schizophrenic patient: a flattened, disembodied Self well portrayed in the works of Marcel Duchamp.

So, while considering how Bion always acknowledged his debt to Freud and to Melanie Klein (O'Shaughnessy, 1992), I would like to try and unfold my own discussion of the enigmas of psychosis in a Bionian dialect.

It is true that Freud's intuitions had made it possible to comprehend (in Jaspers' sense of *verstehen*) the psychoses, the role played by hate directed at reality and at the capacity for thinking (Freud, 1932), along with the role played by the loss of reality (Freud, 1924) and by the need to find, as a form of cure (for example, in delusion) some replacements for that reality which had been lost.

And Klein's discoveries (Klein, 1952) have enabled us to take into consideration how the failures of the transformation of primary psychotic anxieties, the massive recourse to defence mechanisms centred on splitting and projective identification and, again, the desperate search for an attempt at a cure, are the constitutive elements of a psychotic experience.

The early works of Bion had added to these fundamental premises the need to differentiate the functioning of the psychotic part of the personality from that of the non-psychotic part (Bion, 1957) and had proposed a model for the 'development' of the psychotic mind centred on the hypothesis that it was dominated by the principle that the evacuation of a bad breast could be experienced as obtaining support and satisfaction from a good breast.

It is pertinent to observe how, starting with the confusion about the good and bad qualities of the part-object (Rosenfeld, 1952), Bion's early intuitions had grasped how much psychotic experience occurred at the heart of a failure to develop an apparatus for thinking thoughts. The fulcrum of the psychotic enigma began to shift from contents to containers, to re-address the phenomenologists' incomplete intuition aimed at distinguishing the being-thus (*Sosein*) from the being-there (*Dasein*) of delusion and psychosis, locating psychosis in the context of an inter-subjective quality, not only in the encounter, but in the nature of the mind.

And the later Bion seemed to push himself (and take us) further, into a 'beyond' which lays down the premises for a possible expansion of the psychoanalytic understanding of the psychoses.

It is with the introduction of the empty concept of O (the noumenon, the Kantian thing-in-itself, the ultimate truth about absolute reality, β, the unknowable Real, the truth of the patient's emotional experience) that Bion introduces us to a paradigm-shift.

Table 7.1 The Bionian Grid

	Definitory Hypothesis 1	Ψ 2	Notation 3	Attention 4	Inquiry 5	Action 6	...n
A β-elements	A1	A2				A6	
B a-elements	B1	B2	B3	B4	B5	B6	...Bn
C Dreams Thoughts, Dream Myths	C1	C2	C3	C4	C5	C6	...Cn
D Pre-conception	D1	D2	D3	D4	D5	D6	...Dn
E Conception	E1	E2	E3	E4	E5	E6	...En
F Concept	F1	F2	F3	F4	F5	F6	...Fn
G Scientific Deductive System		G2					
H Algerbraic Calculus							

And so I am proposing to start from the jargon of the Grid (Bion, 1963b) as a way of exploring the magmatic enigma of psychosis. The object of psychoanalysis, its field of investigation and its field of treatment, could then become the development (or non-development) of the journey of O through the Grid, and in particular through its column 2.

As we know, the Grid is a fractal map (Civitarese, 2014a), a table which has a certain similarity to the periodic table, which correlates the elements of which matter is composed, while the Bionian Grid represents the elements of which the mind is composed and of which the analytic session could be composed. Therefore, mind and matter, an apparently unbridgeable caesura, or perhaps bridgeable given that Primo Levi, with the vatic intuition of a poet, has shown us how the periodic table can act as an emotional map of the 'business of living'.[2]

It is thus a little more legitimate for us to think that Bion's Grid may also represent a tool, a map for finding our way in that universe of emotions in evolution which compose the human mind.

And indeed, beyond the reluctance which it can certainly provoke, the Grid would seem to serve as a sort of meta-theory (Civitarese, 2014a) and could, by means of its fifty-six squares, suggest the idea of a network of 'containers' (Grotstein, 2007): a network which would foster the mind's development as it is itself composed, and a network which, if it becomes unwoven, or cannot be woven, would step by step determine its failure. Since, while the vertical axis expresses the growing of complexity of thought (from the most concrete level to the most abstract), the horizontal axis shows the 'uses' which can be made of β elements, the crudest and most sensory data of experience.

So, when the (horizontal) rows encounter the (vertical) columns, when the infant's pre-symbolic and pre-verbal mind encounters the mind of the mother-environment, the maternal/ paternal environment, either unisons can be achieved or dysphonias can occur instead. And the earlier the dysphonias (the *caco*phonies), the more disorganised are the architectures to which the infant mind with its mimicry (Ferenczi, 1932) can bring to life.

In fact, the crucial point in the mind's evolution would seem to be located at the level of column 2 of the Grid. Meltzer (1986) understood it as the line of demarcation between psychosis on the one hand, and the symbolic mind of neurosis, and any potentially harmonious psychic development, on the other; but also identified it as the place of falsification, of the Lie which poisons the mind, of borderline states and of perversity: the entry point to a negative Grid, a "– Grid", which saturates the mind with false symbols.

Grotstein (2007), however, defines it as the column of the dream and of α function: "Column 2 constitutes a container-dreamer-thinker function!", he writes (p. 284), revolutionising in a Bionian manner the psychoanalytic conception of the 'lie'. Indeed, alongside the Lie (with the upper case 'L') which poisons the mind, there could exist a nebula of small lies (lower case 'l'), fictions, dreams, which allow us to transcend the traumatic immanence of the Real. And psychosis could then become a manifestation of the inability to *pretend*, to transform hallucination into dream and to sublimate in play the apparent non-sense of life.

THE ATP TENNIS PLAYER

Adriano invades the consulting room with the grandiosity of his delusion: not living, as he really lives, in a marginal state, socially isolated, but as a famous tennis player, "one of the top hundred players in the ATP rankings". He is the husband of a well-known fashion model who is forced to live in London, far away from him, even though she has given him a son. Unfortunately, he is envied and persecuted because of his privileged condition. Even his parents, who doggedly refrain from challenging his delusion, are numbered among his persecutors.

And so, when the projective mechanisms get worn down and he re-incorporates his own hatred and envy, he has to reactivate the projections instantly in order to get rid of devastating and intolerable experiences of persecutory guilt: he is unjustly accused of drug-dealing, he is a dangerous killer, he is held responsible for the death (in fact, of natural causes) of his brother's girlfriend. He is even the target of repeated and varied murder attempts.

In the sessions, he seems to ask the analyst to be a witness and depository of the truths contained in his delusional experiences: he needs someone to believe in his tennis-playing character; it is essential that someone share his doubt that he is a terrible criminal, the "enemy of his family", "bearer of the mark of Cain" (Meltzer, 1973).

But the tennis-playing character also seems to bring with him the buried memory of an infant Self exposed to the narcissistic seduction of a mother who had tried to transform her child into a prosthesis for the inadequacies of her own identity (and for her inability to dream him in his existential truth). The "ATP tennis player" is the eruption of the drama of not being seen, even when one tries desperately to be what one cannot be in the maternal desire. The memory of a past which, if it is not relived and transformed, will never be able to find a future.

So, as an evacuation of memory, delusion tends to withdraw from the transformation of memory into memory of the future, develops like a cancerous growth, expanding the effects of the early traumatisation from which it was derived. It is not in the Real that it can be intercepted (its uncontainability resists all confutation and any criticism which may be put forward by the examination of reality [Jaspers, 1913]): at best, it is transformed into a liveable fiction by means of the oneiric progression which can be set in motion by the encounter between projective and introjective identifications that is achieved in the analytic field.

Thus, by an incessant weaving of emotional flows, Adriano will succeed in attaining the world of 'not'. "Now," he says after years and years of analysis, "I realise that I've always lived in the world of *not*-tennis, *not*-marriage, *not*-drugs." And it is certainly not a case of having definitely moved beyond delusional experience: it is the world of *not*-delusion, which is quite a different matter from being *without*-delusion. It is a delusion which coexists with the possibility of 'pretending': in his delusion, Adriano, *was* an ATP tennis player but at the same time, being an ATP tennis player – or a drug-dealer – can become a film noir or an autobiographical fantasy.

So we can speculate that it is in square A2 that the psychotic collapse comes to be experienced. In A2, the infant's proto-mental mind encounters the vortex of the object. In borderline and perverse states, just as in psychotic ones, column 2 constitutes a fjord, a deep canyon which can only be bypassed. In these areas of practice, it seems we can only move along the lines of a 2D geometry in the 'morbid geometrism' intuited by Eugene Minkowski (1953). And so the borderline patient and the perverse patient can also arrive at action (A6), but without passing through thought. They move, desperately clutching at the sides of the pre-symbolic and pre-verbal boundaries of column 2. Perhaps this is how we should understand Bion's (1963a) enigmatic and oracular statement, "I have felt that col. 2 might be replaced by a negative sense to the horizontal axis" (99). The borderline patient, and any other who is seriously ill but pre-psychotic, moves in the coplanarity of a Cartesian diagram, delimited by column 1 and row A: this may result in action (A6) but this should only be considered as acting out, and it may result in concepts (F1) which bear within them the stamp of the idiosyncratic and the bizarre.

The psychotic O instead plunges into A2 and plummets into an alienated and imaginary counter-world without ever being able to journey into dream. In this respect, I think Antonino Ferro (2014) is correct when he represents the evolution of the mind and the essence of the psychoanalytic process as "the journey of O through column 2 of the Grid."

If it is not possible for O, the ultimate truth and at the same time the subject's most intimate and radical truth, to be intercepted by α function and dream, every opportunity for subjectivation stagnates in the world of *definitory hypotheses* (Bion, 1963b), in column 1 of the Grid: the column of the proto-mental, the semiotic, the body, that which has not been divided into a group; a dimension which consigns O to an eternal waiting for evolution and confronts us with all those clinical conditions in which we perceive a traumatic scenario which, in order to be given meaning, must pass again from O, from the body, from O in the body (as much the patient's as the analyst's).

If O is unable to make the transition into a knowable world through the 'falsification' constituted by the dream, it stagnates in a sensory and emotionally chaotic dimension: it remains prey to the congenital and to unintegrated residues of phylogenesis.

> Praise the world to this angel . . .
> So show him
> something simple which, formed over generations,
> lives as our own, near our hand and within our gaze.
> (Rilke, *Ninth Elegy*)[3]

There is nothing "near our hand and within our gaze" in the psychotic world: only the "unsayable" exists, and there is no ("angelic") presence who can be shown, or who can show, "something simple". We cannot pass through the Grid of mental development in a straightforwardly evolutionary direction from left to right, and psychotic experience ends up imprisoned beyond the Pillars of Hercules of a world knowable through the senses: it is consumed beyond column 2 and reabsorbed into the unsayable world of "emerging bundles of β elements" (Civitarese, 2014a). Here there is only the possibility of -K, and transformations of K in the direction of O are not possible, nor are transformations *by* O or transformations *of* O. Thus, O remains exclusively the unknowable, the thing-in-itself, without ever becoming truth, the ultimate reality of an authentic experience of *me-ness* (Manica, 2013, 2014).

Without α, without dream, column 2 becomes a whirlpool in which one plunges into the Lie of delusion and hallucination. And then psychotic development can only unfold along the vertical axis of column 1, top-down, going to the very limit of abstraction-without-thought: an abstraction which is incapable of oneiric progress along the rows of the Grid and cannot be used to give ever more complex and sophisticated meanings to emotional experience. Perhaps this is why the psychotic lives in a world populated by "ghosts of departed quantities"[4] (Bion, 1965, p. 157) and is compelled to speak with his body and not in a shareable language; 'speaks' the silence of communication while 'emitting' emotions that are impossible to bear alone.

Although we can perhaps twist Bion's thought to make it true that, as Grotstein (2007) maintains, α precedes β – at least in the sense that maternal reverie must be present before the infant's anxieties and needs – the mother (like God) must love first, so that the infant can attain the illusion of having created himself and of creating himself independently of the mother's need and desire.

This seems to be the positive (and revolutionary) element which Bion pursues in the world of *definitory hypotheses*. It is a catastrophic principle of creativity that nothing is immoveable, nothing is pre-given. The world of definitory hypotheses should be a world which the environment preserves from the effects of the adult's narcissistic seduction of the infant, because it is the reservoir of all that may become dream and thought. It is the reservoir of the evolutions that are possible for any mind at its origin, from the raw material of proto-sensory and proto-emotional experiences to abstraction/sublimation. There must, however, be the transit through column 2, the encounter with another mind endowed with α function, reverie, and dream so that it becomes possible to make Winnicottian 'use' of the world of definitory hypotheses, enabling the movement towards actions that occur as truly transformative of the Self and of the world in which the Self can exist.

It may not be by chance that Bion (1965) clarifies the definition of *psychological turbulence* – and, I would add, of *psychotic* turbulence – meaning a state of mind whose painful quality can be expressed in terms used by St John of the Cross, as the "three nights of the soul". The first is "night to all the senses of man" and here, in a Bionian manner, arises the urgent need to deny ignorance ("the dark night of the senses"): we deny that we cannot trust our senses and are compelled to transform psychological phenomena into apparently concrete objects ("into such objects as *are*"), and this forms the basis of "transformation in hypochondriasis" (159). I would say, also in that form of -K that is hypochondriac delusion, which Freud (1914) earlier located at the heart of schizophrenic experience.

The second night is that of 'faith', of trust in the presence of the absent object (Grotstein, 2007). Faith requires intuition and not comprehension; it cannot be associated with any form of investigation and becomes a 'dark night' for K. It is the night of psychotic withdrawal, of almost absolute narcissism; and here we are shipwrecked in President Schreber's apparently impermeable narcissism in the face of any possibility of empathy (Freud, 1910).

Lastly, the *third night* is the 'night of God', "dark night to the soul in this life". And Bion associates it with transformation in O: that is, from K to O. It is a transformation which implies 'becoming' and "is felt as inseparable from becoming God, ultimate reality, the First Cause. The 'dark night' pain is fear of megalomania" (Bion, 1965, p. 159). And here we confront the delusional experience in which growth, being mature, entails *being* God, being the First Cause, the ultimate reality of an experience of grandiosity, of megalomania which is not modulated by the passage through column 2 and arrests any possibility of development.

So, put very briefly, we could think with Bion that psychosis expresses in an exaggerated form the suffering that is implicit in achieving that (Rilkean) "state of naivety inseparable from binding or definition" (ibid.): from the possibility of creating links which may generate dreams, thoughts, affects, and from the possibility of giving a name and a meaning to our emotional experience.

THE WORLD OF THE KILLJOYS

Seventeen-year-old Gaia enters the 'room' for the first time with a dreamy air, solid yet paradoxically intangible, tender yet rough, close but incredibly alienated. And immediately the question arises, what room is it whose threshold she has crossed? The consulting room? . . . the room of an unforeseeable analysis? . . . or that of my mind? Or is it that of a shared mind which, though it is impossible to tell, may or may not have existed before?

The discharge notes from the emergency clinic to which she had been admitted lists the silent symptoms of a 'panic attack':

> Patient accompanied by her parents to A & E having woken at night with anxiety, psychomotor agitation, dyspnoea, palpitations, involuntary and purposeless movements of the head, neck, and jaw. She has been treated for two years by a psychologist for panic attacks. Blood pressure 130/80, fc 130. CAT scan and ECG normal. Discharged following anxiolytic treatment, with a speculative diagnosis of Panic Attack and sent for a specialist consultation.

As I hastily scan the discharge notes which Gaia has brought with her, I am struck by the way she shudders and looks quickly around the her with frightened eyes. And when I ask her if there is something making her afraid, Gaia starts telling me about 'presences in mirrors', how they 'give her orders' and force her to hurt herself. And so she has been cutting her own body for some time, tearing her flesh, covering herself in wounds. A desperate loneliness immediately echoes in my mind.

What is more, Gaia says that she is "not allowed to talk about" the "presences" and their terrifying "voices" and so she will not even be able to talk to me about them even though I am the first and only person to whom she has been able to reveal the presence of this terrible secret world. However, alongside the 'pills' of a mild antipsychotic medication, she also accepts the 'words'[5] of future meetings.

For a long time, besides reconstructing an almost Dickensian personal novel, marked by affective and material poverty, by a significant social isolation, and by emotional and somatic turbulence (her left ovary was removed, for example, when she was eight, because of an ovarian torsion), I wonder how to intercept those aspects, those parts of Gaia's personality which seem to have toppled into a psychotic counter-world and become ever more alienated, and which have increasingly been granted only the semblance, the scraps of an authentic relational life. In fact, for all her occasional attendance at the third year at art college, she has largely withdrawn into her home and spends the days in bed, either listening to music or drawing and reading cartoon strips: she would like to become a cartoonist, although she doubts that she will have the ability.

And so, almost by chance, we find ourselves talking about her favourite singer, Gerard Way, and the "fabulous Killjoys", the comic book series she continues to re-read almost like a mantra.

So I feel impelled to search for some biographical information about Gerard Way (then unknown to me) and to buy myself a copy of the "Killjoys".

The internet is a technological monster, but it can also be a mine of hidden treasures.

And so I discover that Gerard Way is an American singer and cartoonist, born in 1977 in Summit, New Jersey, but brought up in Belleville, and founder member of the band *My Chemical Romance* for which he was lead singer from 2001 to 2013, the year when the band split up, after which he started a solo musical career.

Like Gaia, Gerard has had a troubled life and it seems that punk and metal music, as well as horror bands such as the *Misfits* and *Iron Maiden* helped him to overcome the obsession with death[6] which had accompanied his whole childhood.

Because of his extreme sensitivity, he isolated himself during his high school years and was ignored in the same way as Gaia. Then he shut himself away at home for long periods studying the guitar, drawing, and reading comics.

After overcoming a dependency on alcohol, he began a course in graphic art but, overwhelmed by the attacks of 11 September 2001, which he witnessed, he decided to abandon graphic art in order to go back to his original passion, music, founding the band *My Chemical Romance*.

So I was certainly struck by the resemblances between the lives of Gerard Way and Gaia, but I was still more surprised by the discovery of the *Killjoys*. This was a comic book written by Gerard Way himself with Shaun Simon (in a way his alter ego) and illustrated by the famous Becky Cloonan, and it inspired the concept of one of the best-known albums by *My Chemical Romance*: *Danger Days. The True Lives of the Fabulous Killjoys*.

What 'danger days' had Gaia lived through? And what 'danger days' would we have to relive together?

The comic tells of a near future when fear takes the place of freedom, a world where the Killjoys had earlier fought against the tyranny of the megacorporation *Better Living Industries* (BLI), a struggle in which they all lost their lives with the exception of The Girl. As a result, the followers of the original Killjoys lived in the desert on the margins of society while BLI systematically robbed the citizens of Battery City of their identity. The dream of freedom was vanishing, and it was up to The Girl to take on the task of doing battle with the terrible BLI and their system of power.

And so, through the 'character' of *Better Living Industries*, the 'presences' which were persecuting Gaia could find a way of entering the consulting room

Figure 7.1

and so could the parts of them which had lost their feeling that they existed and their individuality.

And The Girl, forced to live in the desert, had begun to find a travelling companion who would perhaps help her to bring life back to Battery City (Figure 7.1).

The journey undoubtedly looked uncertain and dangerous, requiring a passage through dark and alarming places in the soul (in an infantile Self which had suffered an early trauma) – primitive agonies, the hallucinatory and the delusional, the depersonalised and the de-realised – in order to reach "whatever gets you through the night":

Figure 7.2 If Satan screams out loud And violence is the only sound When the engines come squealing, Demons reeling, The dance ground Just a mask among the crowd, You need to hold tight to Whatever gets you through the night

Figure 7.2 (Continued)

Figure 7.3 Look, you've brought us here hoping to put an end to BLI, but you've stopped without even trying. we haven't fired a single shot. I haven't stopped, Val. Shooting is your way. I only had to find my way. The invisible is all around us. When you shoot, every shot can ride those waves and become perfect. I'm sorry for everything i did.

Figure 7.3 (Continued).

In particular, however, the analyst must give up the religion of his own theories in order to set up with Gaia the dreaming ensemble which, by making a "Pietà covenant"[7] (Grotstein, 2000) – agreeing to become the traumatic object by proxy and uttering that indispensable "I'm sorry" in its place – would be able to give her back an authentic experience of me-ness.

7.2 Intercepting the delusion

In considering psychosis, our conclusions can only be provisional: not so much our conclusions about the metapsychology of the psychotic process as those relating to the transformations of this process which can be achieved in the consulting room.

How do we intercept the delusion?

7.2.1 Primary psychoanalytic preoccupation

If, for Winnicott (1947), psychosis has its origin in the failed encounter between the infant's ruthless love and a mother capable of tolerating his or her hatred, what happens when a 'ruthless' mother invests her child with her own projections?

We are in fact witnessing a reversal of perspective: psychosis is not a primary, intrapsychic fact independent of any relationship with the environment; it is the environment which could establish itself as psychotising. Or rather, it is the relationship, the 'between', what could be achieved between that infant and that environment which, occurring as potentially traumatic or as essentially traumatic, upsets the organisation of the infant mind, plunging it into the abyss of psychosis. The Grid is no longer offered as that Rosetta Stone which will permit the reading of the hieroglyphs of apparently indecipherable emotional experience: here, in column 2, we plunge into the depths; here Hans Castorp, the "traveller in search of culture" would lose him or herself in the mystery of life, overthrown by illness and death in *The Magic Mountain*,[8] by the death of a breast which withdraws from enchantment and hope.

"In the beginning was the aesthetic object and the aesthetic object was the breast and the breast was the world", wrote Donald Meltzer (1986). Here, in psychosis, the beginning seems to be the void, and the void spreads terror.

Is there a possibility of redemption? And if there is, is it in the intrapsychic, in the impassable realm of the narcissistic neuroses? Or does it dwell in the interpsychic, that intersubjective which, outside the will and consciousness of the participants, has generated the evil?

There are two 'strategic' works by Winnicott which locate clinical practice in an absolutely relational perspective and introduce a renewal of psychoanalytic models, enabling psychoanalysis to pass from an intrapsychic and unipersonal paradigm to a bi-personal, intersubjective one which entails the analyst's radically emotional (and subjective) participation.

While in the first paper, 'Clinical Varieties of Transference' (1955–1956b), Winnicott is concerned with defining the demands of a new disposition in the analyst required by the transference of borderline or psychotic patients, in the second, 'Primary Maternal Preoccupation' (1955–1956a), he defines those mental states to which the analyst must 'regress' in order to intercept the disorganisation of the patient's mental states.

Addressing the earliest stages of infant development and the formation of the personality, Winnicott (1958) writes:

> it is my thesis that in the earliest phase we are dealing with a very special state of the mother, a psychological condition which deserves a name, such as *primary maternal preoccupation*. . . . A very special psychiatric condition of the mother. . . . This organized state (that would be an illness were it not for the fact of the pregnancy) could be compared with a withdrawn state, or a dissociated state, or a fugue, or even with a disturbance at a deeper level such as a schizoid episode in which some aspect of the personality takes over temporarily.
>
> (301–2, my italics)

In a similar way, I think that when faced with the most regressed patients, the analyst must also regress to states of her or his own mental functioning which may be able to recover the hallucinatory, so as to transform the patient's raw sensory and emotional experience first into hallucinosis and then into dream. This is a primary analytic preoccupation which, outside the context of an analysis, would have all the characteristics of an *illness*. And I do not believe that we can understand the function of the analyst engaged in a relationship with a psychotic patient without admitting that the therapist must be capable of achieving this state of raised sensitivity – almost a pathology – and then of curing it.

Like the maternal condition, primary analytic preoccupation also expresses the analyst's ability to adhere to the patient's needs, to become the chaotic O of his or her emotional experience and also to transform the anomic immanence of a traumatic corporeality into mental experience in the same way that a psychology can come into being as a result of an imaginative elaboration of physical experience.

Roberta

At the age of forty, Roberta comes to see me having decided to start an analysis she has wanted but run away from all her life.

In fact, during her early childhood she seems to have had to transform herself into a prosthetic, stone 'breakwater' in the face of her mother's repeated, tempestuous, and overwhelming schizophrenic episodes.

In the stretch of sea behind her, her two younger sisters have been struck by the residual turbulence of the waves, suffering a reduced impact, but outwardly they seem to bear the more obvious and troubling wounds: both of them decided in adolescence to undergo a psychotherapeutic treatment that might suture these.

In contrast, Roberta seems to have passed imperturbably through the crises of existence: separation from her nuclear family, the abandonment of her university studies, the onset of motherhood, changes in her working responsibilities, the end of her marriage, the death of her father. Conveying a sort of cast-iron and enchanted naivety which makes her seem like a 'Super-Heidi', she seems impervious to the life's blows and appears to have been able to cancel out every trace of her original suffering.

In reality, it is as if she has had to clothe herself in an exoskeleton composed of a mixture of mechanisms for maintenance and defence based on splitting and petrification, on de-realisation and emotional normativity, on negotiation and lack of insight.

To all intents and purposes, it is a prosthetic apparatus for self-containment which keeps her rigidly on her feet, but in which the infantile parts overwhelmed by unthinkable early anxieties are left enveloped in scars and wounds: a series of accidents incurring repeated broken legs has accompanied her entire life and remains the sole, barely decipherable echo from the traumatic experience, known but not thought, of her childhood.

Of course, alongside the imposing defensive structure, Roberta seems to have been able to make use of some protective factors which have enabled her to defer the return of her most psychotic anxieties or to delay dangerous regressive moves which might make her re-encounter the terror of going to pieces, falling forever, losing reality, and being invaded by her mother's delusions and hallucinations as had occurred in the first years of her life.

And by protective factors I think we can understand, for example, those opportunities for achieving good identifications with other caregiving figures present in the immediate environment of her infant experience (in Roberta's case, her father, for example), or the possibility of sealing unconscious twinship pacts, 'conjoined' or supportive, within her sibling relationships; or again the permanence of good parts of the object even though that object remains a maddening object.

From another perspective, Roberta's analytic treatment has also confirmed what has been hypothesised about early relational experiences and their possible traumatic dissolution: early traumas, occurring in a pre-symbolic and pre-verbal phase, can compromise the child's attachment system, the development of his reflective functions, and constitute an obstacle to the full formation of the Self.

So it is inevitable that such early traumatic experiences can give rise to defensive organisations which, stored up in an implicit memory, have come to form a part of an unconscious nucleus of Roberta's Self, capable of conditioning its affects, emotions, cognitive processes, and behaviour throughout the arc of her development, with the result that they have distorted the realisation and functioning of the adult parts of her personality.

The start of her psychoanalysis (four sessions a week) is indeed dramatic. The unexpected death of the analyst's father and the resulting pause in therapy after it had barely begun seem to bring back into the present the agonising anxieties experienced by Roberta's infantile parts faced with her mother's psychotic breakdown: a grieving analyst could be a mother filled with uncontainable and explosive suffering; the absence of the analyst, 'taken away' by being in mourning, becomes a complete isomorph of her mother's absences during the long hospitalisations made necessary by her psychiatric condition. Furthermore, there is no guarantee that when the therapy is resumed, the analyst will not have lost his paternal functions, just as he has lost his father, and will not be completely transformed into a maddening maternal object.

And at the climax of the drama, when the analyst returns and the analysis resumes, Roberta abruptly goes mad, seems to become delusional and suffer hallucinations like her mother, and undergoes an acute psychotic experience which gradually reveals itself as the psychosis which had been injected into her during her first relationship: to all intents and purposes an imported psychosis, but one which has brought agony and terror to the infantile parts of her Self. It has generated intolerable suffering, both in the intensity of the explosion which has struck them and in the violence of the invasion by parts of her mother's anxieties about falling apart, and because of the immediate lack of a container for her terror.

So, the context of mourning in which Roberta's analysis begins, as well as the life's unforeseeable designs, seems to offer itself as an opportunity for re-dramatising the original traumatic constellation.

In this way, Roberta was plunged into a delusional and hallucinatory world where, alongside experiences of grandiosity and expansion of her Self ("I shall save the world," "I have found the way to rescue all the children in the Third World who are victims of the plague of famine") she felt constantly persecuted by the voice of her mother threatening her with death and accusing her of killing my father, just as she had killed her own some years before.

We could consider that the psychoanalytic process got under way in an atmosphere of profound regression: primitive registers predominated in our relationship; the withdrawal of libido nurtured a grandiose and self-sufficient narcissism; and the appearance of intolerable depressive anxieties about the absence of trustworthy internal objects compelled Roberta to regress to a paranoid-schizoid position.

In the transference, the activation of primitive defence mechanisms, such as splitting and projective identifications, did indeed cause me to be perceived as her partner in her plan to 'save the world' and, at the same time, as the analyst who spoke to her with the 'same voice' as her mother, who threatened her with death and exposed her to unbearable experiences of persecutory guilt.

In my reverie, through images of a little girl, alone and desperate, ravaged by hunger caused by a radical deprivation of affects, the experiences of my mourning were reactivated, along with the sufferings and ambivalences I had worked through during my own personal, educational, and professional journey.

So I found myself offering Roberta the possibility of identifying herself with and being contained by parts of my Self and by my 'paradoxically repaired' internal objects (Meotti, 1998):[9] a mother who was able to take responsibility for her own madness; a father who, though aware of his own limitations, offered to protect her without promising manic reparations. A son who could empathise and understand the suffering of her deprived and projectively infiltrated infantile parts.

Of course, the psychoanalytic process needed to spend a long time passing through a phase in which priority was given to the 'analytic situation' (Winnicott, 1955–1956a) rather than to interpretative work: in other words, the warmth and constancy of the setting (as well as its flexibility: for example, lying down or seated, in response to Roberta's needs for contact), to attunement with her emotional experience, to the possibility of giving a name to her affective states, to the possibility of dreaming them via my reveries, and also – I would add, in relation to the acutely psychotic phase – the holding represented by the inclusion of medication.

And it was only after this long phase of support (of holding and *primary psychoanalytic preoccupation*) that Roberta began to dream, to make use of a more symbolic mind and to allow me to interpret.

She also began to be able to live and progress in her life: with her anthropologist daughter, she is currently managing an NGO, a not-for-profit organisation giving support to women and children who have been the victims of the genocide of the Tutsis by the Hutu in Rwanda.

7.2.2   "By our lady . . ."

If, as an entirely provisional hypothesis, we consider that the essence of the psychotic symptom can present as a radical loss of life, and that vitality can concretise itself in what we were before being compelled to be what we have become, then perhaps one of the fundamental aspects of the treatment of psychotic patients takes the form of withdrawing their proto-mental experience from an "abuse of consciousness" (Jankélévitch and Berowitz, 1978).[10]

Might not this be one of the possible meanings of delusion, of being delusional? Fleeing from that over-consciousness which might even have invaded foetal life and its embryos of meaning and personality? Sometimes, an excess can produce the effect of a void and this is why, as Bion suggested, the psychotic patient may find him or herself compelled to de-signify that which, by way of the innate and the ideal (Platonic) forms, could compose the foreseeable meaning of experience, even before he or she has experienced it and when he or she might never experience it.

The psychotic – observes Grotstein (2007) – deprives not only experience of its possible significance, in order to render it meaningless, but also his or her own mind which confers meaning and derives significations from the meaning it confers. The desired result is a state of pointless nullity, a concrete absence of mind (p. 322).

Long before Grotstein, Jung ('The Transcendent Function'. In *The Structure and Dynamics of the Psyche*, Collected Works, vol. 8. Princeton, 1969) had spoken of a transcendent function, meaning by this a product of the unification between 'conscious' and 'unconscious' contents, an expression of the fact that the system Ucs and the system P-C should not have a 'censor' between them, but a 'caesura',[11] a synapse with a fundamental distinction in its permeable and dialogic character, one which can be crossed in order to develop the subject's mind and entire personality.

So nullity, nothingness, absence of mind in the psychotic subject could come about essentially through the inability to achieve a transcendent function because of the invasion by an excess of the Real(too-real).

Purity, say Jankélévitch and Berowitz (1978),

> exists only in the briefest *distractions of innocence* and in the *momentary breaks of consciousness*; it is reborn when we stop thinking about it, just as Anima starts singing again when Animus is no longer looking at her: a *moment of inattention* allows it to flourish again, but the long hours of sterility and of *too conscious consciousness* once again destroy its freshness.
>
> (Jankélévitch, V., Berlowitz, 1978)

Vitality, therefore, can only exist in those 'distractions of innocence' which are achieved when we are able to withdraw from a *too conscious consciousness*. In the same way, moments of 'inattention' can allow vitality to flourish. Perhaps we can speculate that psychosis – as the death of the Anima – can also be the effect of an abuse of consciousness, a too-conscious consciousness, too exposed to the Real and therefore too much faced with O's traumatic aspect. One could in fact be faced with the vicissitudes and tragedies of a primal un-love, the black dawn of a (pre- and post-natal) life in which the infant's rudimentary consciousness, that "spark of consciousness" Bion (1954) speaks of, has not received its unconscious complement – the complement which should be made available by the unconscious of the object – as a space in which the infant can be accommodated and called into existence and to be him or herself through the maternal capacities for reverie and mirroring. Because that "spark of consciousness" needs to be protected, acknowledged, and guarded. Exposure abuses it and traumatises it with the hyper-luminous violence of a reality that it is no longer possible to *endure*, or above all, to *suffer*.[12] And so we need the cone of penumbra to create the environment, the mother-environment even before the mother-object, so that we can sleep and begin to dream.[13] It is the maternal unconscious, the function of the maternal-paternal environment, which enables the infant's unrepressed unconscious, that receptacle of unrepresentable sensory and emotional experiences, to open itself to dream and to that unconscious of the dream which, as Freud showed in an inspired intuition, can – beside the symptom (whether neurotic or psychotic) – give a new and creative meaning to the existence of every one of us, to the patient's life, but also to the analyst's.

From a complementary perspective, the form of psychotic life can also be a form of life devoured by the 'sacred', by a too-dazzling light, by that primary process which dominates primitive states of mind as much as it dominates the pre-history of humankind, and produces objects only in the form of gods and demons. Similarly, the delusional 'mystical' of psychosis can only speak about this original sacredness, cannot open itself to the transcendent 'mystical' of the secondary processes and of sublimation, remaining inexorably face to face with the numinous, the disturbing, the terrifying and incomprehensible mystery of life.

So we can understand how the Bionian 'mystical' may give representation to 'messianic' functions of the secondary process, to 'transcendent' functions which found the mind's possibility of passing from the definitory to the symbolic, from nameless dread to the hope of the word: in Freud's terminology, from the drive to the psychic representation of the drive or from thing-representation to word-representation.

Instead, in the abysses of column 2 of psychosis we plunge into the numinous and petrified unconscious of phylogenesis: in other words, into that unconscious which is compelled to remain unrepressed because of the relational failure of the process of symbolisation. In other words, if the psychotic has an unconscious, it can only be a 'sacred' unconscious, one handed over to the original and disturbing sacredness of the primary process. The psychotic lacked the possibility of developing a 'mystical' unconscious and thus of opening her or himself up to the mystical of the secondary process and the mystical of sublimation.[14]

It is here that the 'spark of consciousness', too intense, too bright and too reso-nant for a mind at its origin, has not met an unconscious that could enable it to transform into dream the impact and pressures of a still unsayable sensory and emotional experience. It has not silenced the terrifying (Rilkean) angel or the projective identification of the caregiver's anxieties, untransformed agonies (Winnicott, 1963), 'generalised seductions' (Laplanche, 2004), and narcissistic and incestuous needs (Racamier, 1995).

How can we reintroduce hope and life into this desert of terror? How can we pass through the psychotic patient's dark nights of the soul? How can we create bridges and symbolic shuttles which might allow O to cross and travel along col-umn 2 of the Grid?

Perhaps, before being a herald of life, the Angel must be silent, and so must the analyst, trusting in his or her negative capabilities, the tremulous listening of his free-floating attention, his or her possibility of being *without memory and with-out desire*. But more than this: perhaps we need a state of "profound ignorance" (Bion, 1976) – or profound innocence – in order to be able to listen/dream/bring to life the unthinkable.

At the age of almost eighty, in one of his last works, 'On a quotation from Freud', Bion challenges us to take to its ultimate conclusion, not only our thoughts and theories, but our aesthetic functions of listening and understanding:

> I want you to join me and try to achieve the same depths of ignorance I have managed to reach, to get back to a frame of mind which as nearly as pos-sible is denuded of preconceptions, theories, and so forth. What I am asking

is really something of a mental acrobatic feat. I can well appreciate that it is not easy for people well versed in anatomy, physiology, psychoanalysis and psychiatry to get back to a state of primary ignorance.

And he adds:

> I want to say something which sounds just like saying something for the sake of saying it and perhaps it is. Bloody cunt. Bloody vagina. The first phrase is, I suspect, part of a universal language. It is not sexual; it is not physiological or medical; it is something quite different. But 'bloody vagina' might be the sort of thing about which doctors talk, probably obstetricians or gynaecologists. But what about the other one? . . . As I say, 'cunt' is not an anatomical or physiological phrase. What it is I don't know. Indeed, I throw it open to you, because if you investigate this question, you may find what this very primitive and archaic language is. 'Bloody' does not have much to do with the white cells, red cells, or whatever. It is, in fact, an abbreviated way of saying, 'By Our Lady'. So it is really part and parcel of what in more sophisticated terms we think of as being sacred.
>
> (233–4)

But the 'sacred' etymologically evokes something 'separate', it is a terrifying mystery (Jung, 1961; Otto, 1917) which looks out, inevitably with terror, onto the numinous. And I think that anyone who has the experience of psychotic patients also has a sort of familiarity with those delusions that are called 'mystical'. But what does the delusional mystical want to speak about without being able to? Maybe it speaks about an immeasurable separateness which is compelled to become fragmentation in order to allow the embryonic clumps of me-ness to survive: clumps which, like the swarm of stars in a nebula or the dust ball of a comet, wander the universe waiting spasmodically for a new Big Bang that might be able to generate forms of life which can in some way be experienced and lived.

In his 'infinite' thoughts on psychosis, Bion (1970, 1963a) had considered how the psychotic patient had not always been conditioned by an absolute inability to form symbols. On the contrary, his difficulty would reside in the private and idiosyncratic character of his symbol-formation: incapable of becoming a conjunction recognised as constant by a group, in psychosis the symbol would represent a conjunction which the patient would feel as constant between him and his divinity (ibid., 89).

This is how, in psychotic non-thought, in the abysses of schizophrenic existence, 'By Our Lady' anticipates and precedes 'bloody' in a definitory manner, and drags in an empty semblance of a mind: as happened to Filippo who, in his delusional and hallucinatory state, thought he was the Archangel who had profaned the virginity of Our Lady the Madonna, making her the mother of his divinity, of his being Christ who would save the world: in reality, he was the child victim of a tragedy, one anticipated by Our Lady the Mother, a "bloody mother", wounded, bleeding, and bloodthirsty.

So it seems inevitable that the nights of the soul are too dark in psychotic experience, since they are invaded by that "black milk of daybreak" to which Paul Celan devoted unforgettable poetry.[15] They are nights inhabited by omnipotent and numinous symbols rather than by creative symbols endowed with transcendent functions, nights in which megalomania compels one to 'be God' instead of God being a vital illusion, the possibility of dreaming an urge to exist which might transcend the immanence of fundamental powerlessness, of that *Hilflosigkeit* which stands at the origin of every human being's post-natal life.

"The innocent not only sees through the darkness with a view which seems radioscopic, but is himself transparent to others: he not only sees the truth, but is himself the truth," says Jankélévitch (1978, 1966). Again, perhaps it is only in the transparency of the ignorance predicated by Bion that we can intercept the emotional truth which proclaims delusional experience without being believed. It is a truth which is certainly not the truth of the contents, but the truth of the failure and lack of containers, the Lacanian foreclosure, the tragedy of expulsion from the chain of meanings, compelled to derailment into a language which has lost or never been able to acquire any signifying function.

Innocence and ignorance seem to be what the psychotic patient asks from the analyst, a hyperbolical ability to regress to the hallucinatory and the ideographic because, like Egyptian hieroglyphics, a figure in those "signs which express an idea" often represents something different from the figure itself (for example, a 'bird' may mean not 'bird' but 'small') or as, in everyday language, 'bloody cunt' does not mean what it would mean in medical language to speak of a 'vaginal haemorrhage'.

Thus, delusion could 'speak' about a bloody, powerful or numinous experience which bears within it a vertiginous and absolute lack of containers for mental states which might have been as inaccessible for the patient's conscious as for her unconscious. These are very early (perhaps foetal) mental states which psychotic patients' minds could only get rid of, while, as a result of these experiences, they themselves could only get rid of their minds.

The void, nothingness, meaninglessness, and nameless dread which results from psychotic non-experiences: these are the 'contents' for which the analyst's reverie, indeed his or her psyche-soma, is called upon to develop mental containers. But it is necessary to go by the *way of ignorance*. He or she needs to acknowledge that there is "only a limited value/ In the knowledge derived from experience" (T.S. Eliot, 1969 .) and that, as Michael Eigen (1985) recalled, we cannot rely on K but on faith (F) in O: indeed in a total suspension of the mental faculties so that a hallucinatory mode of being can be activated. Only in this way does the psychoanalyst become able to develop a creative contact with that sphere in which the psychotic patient is lost. And while the patient finds her or himself lost or cut off in hallucinosis, we must use it as an empathetic method whose aim is always the search for new containers.

So, we cannot be containers pre-constituted by some theory or other, but containers that must be found and created *ex novo* through an emotional experience which has never travelled through column 2, which has plunged deep into the unknowable and terrifying O of that specific patient. All it takes is for the analyst to let himself be enchanted by the call of the sirens, by the soothing melody of some pre-prepared theory, by a 'bloody cunt' with traces of scientific conformism (so, a 'bleeding vagina' or a 'vaginal haemorrhage') and the patient's 'bloody cunt' remains a gaping, incurable wound of definitory hypotheses which will never be able to achieve alphabetisation (not even the primitive semiotic/semantic transition into *bloody/By-Our-Lady/cunt*).

Once again paraphrasing Jankélévitch (1978, 1966), we could say that innocence, the profound Bionian ignorance, the tool which – alongside primary psychoanalytic preoccupation – leads us to the heart of the psychotic experience because "it does not make use of intermediaries, being in direct contact with reality," is itself our intermediary with the patient, "the medium of mediation; it is therefore the spokesman for the truth and the vector of cosmic forces."

So perhaps we can hand over to the memory-without-memory of psychosis a memory of the future (Bion, 1991), passing from the terrifying to the sublime of O (Civitarese, 2014b), by means of that aesthetic intuition which brings the dream to life, restoring transcendence and the dialectic to the communication between conscious and unconscious, as Thomas Mann's Hans Castorp has shown us:

"I felt it was a dream, all along," he rambled. "A lovely and horrible dream. I knew all the time that I was making it myself – the park with the trees, the delicious moisture in the air, and all the rest, both dreadful and clear. In a way, I knew it all beforehand. But how is it a man can know all that and call it up to bring him bliss and terror both at once? Where did I get the beautiful bay with the islands, where the temple precincts, whither the eyes of that charming boy pointed me, as he stood there alone? Now I know that it is not out of our single souls we dream. We dream anonymously and communally, if each after his fashion. The great soul of which we are a part may dream through us, in our manner of dreaming, its own secret dreams, of its youth, its hope, its joy and peace – and its blood-sacrifice. . . . But he who knows the body, life, knows death. And that is not all; it is, pedagogically speaking, only the beginning. One must have the other half of the story, the other side. For all interest in disease and death is only another expression of interest in life, as is proven by the humanistic faculty of medicine, that addresses life and its ails always so politely in Latin, and is only a division of the great and pressing concern which, in all sympathy, I now name by its name: the human being, the delicate child of life, his state and standing in the universe."[16]

Bion seems to think that the meaning of the catastrophe connects aspects of the personality, that it is the cement which keeps the personality unified, a sort of primordial formative principle like water and air (Eigen, 1985). Thus, in psychosis the personality itself is a catastrophe in the process of becoming. However, the

Bionian vision goes beyond the field of the exclusively pathological. Indeed, the meaning of the catastrophe seems already to have a history when the infant emits its first cry; perhaps, indeed, it precedes life itself. Emotional life bears within it the imprint of the universe in which it grows and oscillates between the Big Bang and every possible end of the world. If this is the nature of the universe of which we are part, it seems inevitable to consider the meaning of catastrophe as our point of origin: it is the fundamental fact of our emotional life and, often, in psychosis, it is everything.

Notes

1 In *Clinical Seminars and Four Papers*, Bion (1987, p. 307) notes that "Doctor André Green" first drew his attention to this quotation from Maurice Blanchot.
2 See Levi, P. (1975).
3 Rainer Maria Rilke (1923).
4 The Bionian concept of departed quantities, as I have understood it (in fact taken from an expression used by Bishop George Berkeley [1685–1735] in his ironic critique of Isaac Newton's presumed atheistic presentation of the differential calculus), concerns the ghost of the 'infinite' possibilities of becoming what one *could have* been, instead of being suffocated by the (unique and 'finite') necessity of being what one *should have* been. In this connection, it is helpful to remember that Bion (1992) suggested replacing the terms 'conscious' and 'unconscious' with 'finite' and 'infinite'. So the ghost of departed quantities could also be the ghost of a consciousness that cannot become unconscious, the ghost of an untransformed and hard to transform β.
5 "Pills or words?" is the title of a fine book by a sensitive and astute psychoanalyst who sadly died young: Niels Peter Nielsen (1998), *Pillole o parole? Relazione verbale e rapporto psicofarmacologico*, Raffaello Cortina Editore, Milan.
6 See Gerard Way on Pearl Jam, his blonde dye job, and his regret about 'The Black Parade' on jussijames Blog – Buzznet (http://jussijames.buzznet.com/user/journal/1086-401/gerard-way-pearl-jam-his/)
7 By 'Pietà covenant' Grotstein (2000) means that original unconscious pact through which the infant tries to survive the mother's attempt to spare him unnecessary pain, suffering, and danger.
    So, every breach of the pact, each of the patient's 'abused' infantile parts, requires the analyst to take upon him or herself by proxy the guilt/responsibility for the abuse and to say that "I'm sorry" which the traumatising object has never uttered.
8 The reference is to *On Myself and Other Princeton Lectures*. Ed. James N. Bade. Frankfurt, Berlin, and Bern, Grove/Atlantic, 1997.
9 By *paradoxical reparation*, Franca Meotti (1998) means a reparation which does not eliminate wounds, but makes them the means for a new cohesion of the Self.
10 By abuse of consciousness, I would like to indicate the condition of an infantile mind compelled into a traumatic progression (Manica, 2014), to a *praeter*-maturation such as may result from exposure to an excess of the Real without adequate mediation by the symbolic.
    Civitarese (2013) observes that excessive pressure from one side or the other of the contact barrier (the slash in the formula Unc/C) coming either from the inner world or from factual reality, can traumatically prevent effective α function and thinking/dreaming. In these cases, the contact barrier is replaced by the β screen, an impermeable membrane of β elements which drastically separates the unconscious from the conscious. Then we will have various types of psychic suffering: from the entirely

(Freudian) unconscious kind that is psychosis and hallucination, to the total *reality* of people who are cut off from their own internal life and the vital sap of their own emotions, and who end up living a *more ego-syntonic but no less malign form of psychosis*.

11 It was the Bionian turn which broke the caesura/censor paradigm, revealing the intersubjective soul of psychoanalysis, that bi-personal psychological dimension which, though already present in Freudian thought, had been induced by the radioactive material it was dealing with to put on the unipersonal diving suit.

"Investigate the caesura," wrote Bion (1977) "not the analyst, not the analysand; not the unconscious; not the conscious; not sanity; not insanity. But the caesura, the link, the synapse, the (countertrans)-ference; the transitive-intransitive mood."

12 The terms *endure* and *suffer* are often used by Bion.

13 I am thinking of the cone of penumbra created by the primary object in a sense very similar to that intended by Freud in a letter to Lou Andreas Salomé. Grotstein (2009) recalls Bion translating the passage in question for him as follows: "When doing analysis, one should cast a beam of intense darkness into the interior, so that something that has hitherto been hidden in the glare of the illumination can now glow all the more in that darkness."

14 Transferring the Freudian concept of 'sublimation' into the language of Bion, I think it can be understood as an indicator of the degree and level to which the containers have developed.

15 Celan, P. (1990). 'Death Fugue' in *Selected Poems*. Harmondworth, Penguin.

16 Mann, T. (1924). *The Magic Mountain*. Trans. H.T. Lowe-Porter. London, Minerva, 1992, p. 495.

References

Note: S.E. = *The Standard Edition of the Complete Works of Sigmund Freud*. Trans. J. Strachey. London: Hogarth Press and the Institute of Psychoanalysis.

Bion, W.R. (1954). Notes on the Theory of Schizophrenia. Read in the Symposium "The Psychology of Schizophrenia" at the 18th International Psycho-Analytical Congress, London, 1953. *International Journal of Psycho-Analysis*, 35. Reprinted in Second Thoughts (1967).

Bion, W.R. (1957). The Differentiation of the Psychotic From the Non-Psychotic Personalities. *International Journal of Psycho-Analysis*, 38. Reprinted in Second Thoughts (1967).

Bion, W.R. (1963a). *Elements of Psycho-Analysis*. London: William Heinemann.

Bion, W.R. (1963b). The Grid. In *Taming Wild Thoughts*. Edited by F. Bion. London: Karnac Books, 1997.

Bion, W.R. (1965). *Transformations*. London: Heinemann.

Bion, W.R. (1970). *Attention and Interpretation*. London: Tavistock Publications.

Bion, W.R. (1976). On a Quotation From Freud. In *Clinical Seminars and Other Works*. London: Karnac Books, 2000.

Bion, W.R. (1977). *Two Papers: 'The Grid' and 'The Caesura'*. London: Karnac Books.

Bion, W.R. (1987). *Clinical Seminars and Four Papers*. Abingdon: Fleetwood Press, p. 307.

Bion, W.R. (1991). *A Memoir of the Future*. London: Karnac Books.

Bion, W.R. (1992). *Cognitions*. Edited by F. Bion. London: Karnac Books.

Celan, P. (1990). Death Fugue. In *Selected Poems*. Harmondworth: Penguin.

Civitarese, G. (2013). *The Necessary Dream: New Theories and Techniques of Interpretation in Psychoanalysis*. London: Karnac, 2014.

Civitarese, G. (2014a). *Truth and the Unconscious in Psychoanalysis*. London: Routledge, 2016.

Civitarese, G. (2014b, December). Bion and the Sublime: The Origins of an Aesthetic Paradigm. *International Journal of Psychoanalysis*, 96(6), 1059–86.

Eigen, M. (1985). Toward Bion's Starting Point: Between Catastrophe and Faith. *International Journal of Psychoanalysis*, 66, 321–30.

Eliot, T.S. (1969). Four Quartets. In *The Complete Poems and Plays of TS Eliot*. London: Faber, 1969.

Ferenczi, S. (1932). *The Clinical Diary: Sandor Ferenczi*. Edited by Judith Dupont. Translated by M. Balint and N.Z. Jackson. Cambridge, MA: Harvard University Press, 1988.

Ferro, A. (2014). *Le viscere della mente. Sillabario emotivo e narrazioni*. Torino: Cortina Raffaello.

Freud, S. (1910). Psychoanalytic Notes on an Autobiographical Account of a Case of Paranoia. In *SE* 12 (Originally published in 1911).

Freud, S. (1914). On Narcissism: An Introduction. In *SE* 14, pp. 73–103.

Freud, S. (1915). *On Metapsychology: The Theory of Psychoanalysis*. London: Penguin, 11: 1991.

Freud, S. (1924). The Loss of Reality in Neurosis and Psychosis. In *SE* 19.

Freud, S. (1932). *New Introductory Lectures on Psycho-Analysis, and Other Works* (1932–1936). London: Hogarth Press, 1986.

Grotstein, J.S. (2000). *Who Is the Dreamer Who Dreams the Dream? A Study of Psychic Presences*. Hillsdale, NJ: Analytic Press.

Grotstein, J.S. (2007). *A Beam of Intense Darkness: Wilfred Bion's Legacy to Psychoanalysis*. London: Karnac Books.

Grotstein, J.S. (2009). *But at the Same Time and on Another Level: Volume 1: Psychoanalytic Theory and Technique in the Kleinian/Bionian Mode*. London: Karnac.

Jankélévitch, V. (1966). *La Mort*. Paris: Flammarion.

Jankélévitch, V., and Berowitz, B. (1978). *Quelque Part dan l'Inchevé*. Paris: Gillimard, p. 55.

Jaspers, K. (1913). *General Psychopathology*. Baltimore, MD: Johns Hopkins University Press, 1997.

Jung, C.G. (1961). *Memories, Dreams, Reflections*. New York: Knopf Doubleday, 2011.

Jung, C.G. (1969). The Transcendent Function. In *The Structure and Dynamics of the Psyche*, Collected Works, vol. 8, Bollingen Series. Princeton: Princeton University Press.

Klein, M. (1952). Some Theoretical Conclusions Regarding the Emotional Life of the Infant. In *The Writings of Melanie Klein, Volume 8: Envy and Gratitude and Other Works*. London: Hogarth Press, pp. 61–94.

Laplanche, J. (2004). Tre accezioni del termine "inconscio" nella cornice della teoria della seduzione. *Rivista di Psicoanalisi*, 50, 11–26.

Levi, P. (1975). *The Periodic Table*. Hamondsworth: Penguin, 2000.

Manica, M. (2013). *Ogni angelo è tremendo. Esplorazioni ai confini della teoria e della clinica psicoanalitica*. Roma: Borla.

Manica, M. (2014). *Intercettare il sogno. Sviluppi traumatici e progression onirica nel discorso psicoanalitico*. Roma: Borla.

Mann, T. (1924). *The Magic Mountain*. Trans. H.T. Lowe-Porter. London: Minerva, 1992, p. 495.

Meltzer, D. (1973). *Sexual States of Mind*. Perthshire: Clunie Press.

Meltzer, D. (1986). *Studies in Extended Metapsychology*. London: Karnac Books, 2009.
Meotti, F. (1998). Un paradosso della riparazione. *Richard e Piggle*, 6, 141–51.
Minkowski, E. (1953). *La Schizophénie*. Paris: Desclée de Brouwer.
Nielsen, N.P. (1998). *Pillole o parole? Relazione verbale e rapporto psicofarmacologico.* Milan: Raffaello Cortina Editore.
O'Shaughnessy, E. (1992). Psychosis: Not Thinking in a Bizarre World. In *Clinical Lectures on Klein and Bion*. Edited by R. Anderson. New York: Routledge.
Otto, R. (1917). *The Idea of the Holy*. Translated by J.W. Harvey. New York, OUP, 1923.
Racamier, P.C. (1995). *Incesto e incestuale*, trad it. Milano: FrancoAngeli, 2003.
Rainer, M.R. (1923). *Duino, Elegies*. Translated by Stephen Mitchell. London: Picador, 1987.
Rosenfeld, H.A. (1952). Note on the Psychopathology of Confusional States in Chronic Schizophrenias. *International Journal of Psychoanalysis*, 31, 132–7.
Schneider, K. (1959). *Clinical Psychopathology*. Translated by M.W. Hamilton. New York: Grune & Stratton.
Tausk, V. (1919). Origin of the Influencing Machine in Schizophrenia. *Psychoanalytic Quarterly*, 1933, English Translated by Dorian Feigenbaum.
Winnicott, D.W. (1947). Hate in the Counter-Transference. *International Journal of Psychoanalysis*, 30, 69–74.
Winnicott, D.W. (1955–1956a). Primary Maternal Preoccupation. In *Through Pediatrics to Psychoanalysis: Collected Papers*. Edited by D.W. Winnicott. New York: Routledge, 2014.
Winnicott, D.W. (1955–1956b). Clinical Varieties of Transference. In *Through Pediatrics to Psychoanalysis: Collected Papers*. Edited by D.W. Winnicott. New York: Routledge, 2014.
Winnicott, D.W. (1958). The Capacity to Be Alone. In *The Maturational Processes and the Facilitating Environment*. Edited by D.W. Winnicott. London: Karnac Books, pp. 29–36.
Winnicott, D.W. (1963). Fear of Breakdown. In *Psycho-Analytic Explorations*. Edited by D.W. Winnicott. Cambridge, MA: Harvard University Press, 1989.

Part II

Emotions and feelings

Chapter 8

Abandonment

Antonino Ferro

One of the most painful psychic phenomena concerns abandonment. Being members of an especially fragile species (we need only think of the long period of physical, emotional, and mental care we need simply to survive), we defend ourselves against it using various mechanisms which I have previously described: from "shipwreck-survivor syndrome" to various forms of narcissistic defence based on negotiation or on manic excitation, to say nothing of the related antidepressants I have often dwelt on.

Manuela is a young woman whose point of fragility is the terror of being abandoned. She is a gynaecologist, works on the side for the secret services, and is lesbian. She is, and has always been, unable to form a stable, lasting relationship. She always chooses heterosexual women whom she seduces and has brief but intense sexual and emotionally profound affairs with, which she then breaks off. She says, "I stay in touch with all my exes. I never end an affair completely. I'm like the novels in a bookshop. You can pick them up again at any time."

Manuela's anti-abandonment strategy is as clear as it is illusory: it is as if she were putting a stamp on every woman she has a relationship with, so that they remain potentially tied to her and available. Not one tie but ten, twenty, thirty, with people who are kept on standby but could become active lifeguards if the need arises. What better way to guarantee the brevity of the affairs than to choose heterosexual women who soon go back to following their preferred inclinations? In this way she collects a great number of potential rescuers, nursemaids, babysitters, or lifeguards – call them what you will.

The mechanism of "forced goodness" or "forced gratification" is rather similar: Matteo does not behave very differently from Manuela when he freely lends things to his friends, including his holiday homes by the sea and in the mountains, even going so far as to offer a kidney to a friend with a serious illness which required a transplant. In this way, everyone owes him a debt of gratitude which will one day have to be repaid by service as a carer/lifeguard.

Some people may be administering a highly attenuated vaccine when they renew dormant friendships at Christmas or New Year with notes or greetings cards: you never know!

I think I recently identified some features which could be added to the "ship-wreck-survivor syndrome" I mentioned earlier.

There is an extremely primitive abandonment-anxiety which leads to jealousy, rage, despair, or fury as survival mechanisms against the proto-experience (not yet alphabetized) of drowning or plunging into the void without a lifebelt or para-chute. I would call this state "pre–Robinson Crusoe abandonment", meaning that the abandoned person is unconsciously convinced that he or she cannot survive the absence of the other, who is considered the only possible safeguard in an emergency.

The people have absolutely no idea that there might be a potential patch of safety where they could seek refuge, and from which they could set out again to develop new potentialities: there is only the anxiety of drowning forever.

I can't live without you! The other is oxygen: one metaphor might be that of the foetus which has not experienced the possibility of surviving once the umbilical cord has been cut. There is only asphyxia, collapse, pulmonary oedema: drowning in one's own fluids.

Respiration can only resume with a return to the foetal state in a symbiotic link. As we learn from the news, when these levels are in play there is a risk of delin-quent, sometimes criminal actions.

Then we have "Robinson Crusoe abandonment", which is desperate and tragic but contains the awareness that survival is possible because there is the pre-con-ception of a little island, and that if we can salvage something from the shipwreck, something to rely on, we may be able to survive, albeit with moments of grief and discomfort. The idea that there are alternative possibilities, other islands, and other tools that will enable the survivor not to plunge into discomfiture and panic.

Lastly, we have "post–Robinson Crusoe abandonment", in which the pain of separation and loss is experienced without threats to the cohesion of the Self and to one's own survival.

The pathologies of jealousy/possession/extreme control of the object are linked to the first model I described, and so they run through all the situations in which the continuing presence of the other is at risk. Control is then the mechanism which permits the recovery of the life-saver which the other has become.

Rage, jealousy, and possessiveness are founded on an undifferentiated unity rather like the splashing, pseudo-swimming, and chaotic, uncoordinated move-ments of someone who is about to drown.

In the second and third models, we see less dramatic signs of suffering.

What is the approach to these situations?

In the first place, it helps if we understand the positive value of rage, jealousy, and control as extreme defences which work for the time being; as do excitation, mania, stepping on the gas.

Second, we can help the patient to understand that there may be the equipment needed for survival, but it just hasn't yet been sufficiently tried out. And lastly, we can help them see how Crusoe's island may start to function and become steadily better equipped.

In the first, pre-Robinson model, the enemy is anyone who might attract the attention of the object invested with the function of "respirator". If the indispensable object has a friend, this friend becomes a terrible enemy and persecutor because he or she could potentially cause the oxygen I mentioned earlier to become unavailable. Other people might approach the object, other interests might replace old ones, other loves might come into being: a universe of total, terrifying precariousness opens up on the horizon. One's ineluctable destiny would be to drown.

The encounter with the other is not of an oedipal type, but one which takes away the lifesaving drug on which you used to rely completely.

It turns out, paradoxically, that an unreliable object helps us to cure this type of problem, which a totally symbiotic object would never have allowed to come to light.

If the person invested with the function of making you survive even sees a friend without telling you, that "not telling you" becomes a catastrophic "absence": she's not there for me! He has a piece of his own life, autonomous, independent, and therefore not attentive to my needs. I shall drown in those microseconds of absence or absent-mindedness, because I have never learned to live in the discontinuities of her presence.

In a symbiotic patient's dream, the other becomes the switchboard of the emergency services which is engaged while the fire is blazing and continuing to grow: I need, I must have, I come after Z, but meanwhile I am burning to death in the emotions which terror has ignited in me (the terror of drowning).

On Monday, a patient tells me that, while on duty over the weekend, she had to attend and hospitalize a borderline patient who had been abandoned by her boyfriend and developed a terrible vengeful rage (you abandon me, I'll destroy you), and a terrible jealousy (you're with other people and not me, so I take second place). Then she dreamed about having some injections of Risperdol which had been prescribed for her by the hospital consultant.

To abandonment (the *primum movens*), anger, and jealousy we should add the inconstancy of the object (the patient was telling me "I'm going to find another boyfriend") and the uncontainability of the emotions. It is not hard for me to interpret this to the patient in terms of the present state of the field.

What I have said so far leads me into a brief comment on some aspects of borderline patients, which is the subject of Chapter 5 of this present volume.

There is a simple and effective description of their characteristics in Gabbard (2000), who also provides a swift summary of the literature on the subject. Grinker et al. (1968) lists their rage, their relational deficiencies, the absence of an identity of the Self, and their passive depression. Gunderson (1984) underlines their intense depressive or angry affectivity, their superficial adaptation to social situations, transitory psychotic episodes, and highly unstable relational models.

Sometimes these patients wear themselves out in their attempt to establish relations with a single person with whom there is no danger of abandonment.

Moreover, on the one hand, they fear being consumed (fusion!) and experience an anxiety which borders on panic in relation to the idea of being abandoned at any moment.

They are, on the other hand, "stably unstable" and capable of making the most contradictory representations of themselves coexist.

They suffer a profound sense of emptiness, testing the object, always raising the bar, and have an impulsiveness which they frequently turn into action.

They do not consider the positive and negative qualities of others as a whole, but view others as extremes, gods or demons, and often only take the most recent event into account, cancelling out all those that preceded it.

We can add absence of anger-management, outbreaks of fury, and transitory paranoid thinking. Boredom, emptiness, and loneliness are often condensed into the term depression.

Kernberg (1975) gives a very precise description, stating that the child is worried that the mother may disappear, and shows a frantic concern about her coming and going. There is an inability to tolerate periods of solitude, and the child always fears being abandoned by significant figures. In the same way, a patient keeps her boyfriend under constant control, using the "Find my iPhone" function, having outbreaks of furious and uncontainable jealousy if he deviates by a millimetre from the previously agreed itinerary.

For these patients, being abandoned is an unconscious configuration stronger than reality itself; we could say they have entire pieces of mental territory that have not been alphabetized, dreamed, and made capable of being emotionally experienced.

Over time, a patient expressed her experience of abandonment like this: being abandoned on pack ice, in the freezing cold, while a storm blows; being abandoned in a station at night when everything is closed and a lot of no-good characters are arriving; being abandoned like the Little Match Girl or Tom Thumb; being abandoned and lost, without ever finding the road again; a labyrinth of mirrors with no way out as the Minotaur gets closer; running out of the oxygenating-empathic-warmth which keeps us alive.

In the analyst's mind there may be – sometimes silently – all the pathological potentialities which, linking with the patient's affective micro-sememes, may allow the field's illness to come to life as a predominant expression of the patient's illness. Sometimes this illness of the field can well up as an illness in the analyst if he catches too much of it: in classical terminology, we could call this a countertransference psychosis.

A patient presents with a pathology consisting of furious explosions of jealousy, explosions of rage, emotional uncontainability, and anxieties evacuated in violent acting out, the simultaneous need for the dyad and for independence, against the terror of abandonment.

The analyst takes on the field's illness, shifting it into his or her own existential reality, where he or she starts to encounter experiences of emptiness and anxieties of abandonment, and is left swamped by these experiences until a re-activation of his or her self-analysis (his or her ability to metabolize) allows him or her to digest these experiences and recognize its roots in the present field of *that* therapy with *that* patient, and not only in his or her personal history.

The silent borderline clump with its catastrophic anxieties had begun resonating, so as to enable the activation of a borderline field, but then overflowed and became a temporary illness in the analyst: we could call it a sort of necessary professional illness.

References

Gabbard, G.O. (2000). *Psychodynamic Psychiatry in Clinical Practice*, 3rd edition. American Psychiatric Press, Washington, DC.

Grinker, R.R., Werble, D., and Drye, R.C. (1968). *The Borderline Syndrome: A Behavioral Study of Ego-Functions*. Basic Books, New York.

Gunderson, J.G. (1984). *Borderline Personality Disorder*. American Psychia-Tric Press, Washington, DC.

Kernberg, O. (1975). *Borderline Conditions and Pathological Narcissism*. Jason Aronson, New York.

Chapter 9

On the feeling of exclusion

Maurizio Collovà

The aim of this chapter is to consider various ways of experiencing and representing exclusion and its different permutations; from imposed exclusion to the kind of self-exclusion that is actively desired and sought, and follows an arc of variables which can oscillate between a defensive purpose on the one hand and a search for freedom and an identity of one's own on the other. These movements can involve both the individual and the small group as well as large groups, like institutions, when they defend themselves by excluding the revolutionary (thought) which puts their founding principles in danger by not conforming to those of a dominant leadership. It may be that the subject is entirely contained inside the conflict between "socialism" and narcissism within the individual which Bion (1992) speaks of.[1] Indeed, he intends these two terms to indicate the two poles of the instincts, and claims that the individual finds him or herself faced with the problem of how to manage his own aggressive impulses, having to decide between feeling himself to be a subject and fighting for his or her own personal survival or conceiving him or herself as part of a group and fighting with and for it. Bion (ibid.) goes on to assert that in the extreme – psychotic – form of defence, the outcome of these attacks reveals an excess of narcissism which in his or her opinion should be recognised as a consequence of the fear of "socialism". I believe that good functioning should oscillate between one's own narcissistic urges and the awareness of being a social animal, not yielding to the conflictual character of opposites which would activate an excessive prevalence of one polarity, or even a destructive veering towards one or other of them, eliminating a fruitful and more mature dynamic.

9.1 We are a crossroads of emotions and feelings

I was thinking about those railway stations which require the traveller to get off a train and wait for connections in order to continue her or his journey in a new direction. These are very busy stations filled with a variety of people from all sorts of places who will only have the chance to encounter one other and leave their mark on each other at this point, possibly sharing an onward journey or going their separate ways and remaining unknown to each other. I think our mind might find itself constantly in a similar condition in relation to emotional crossroads from which we cannot withdraw except by setting up defences which make us impermeable or narcotised.

Although we name single emotions and feelings as if hypothesising that they have an independent existence, a sort of purity, I believe that actually feeling an emotion is always the result of a complex experience. The place where an emotion takes shape is always a crossroads in which, although one feeling seems to acquire a prevalent intensity, others are passing alongside it and influencing it in some way. Anger, for example, seems unequivocally and easily recognisable. But in fact we ought to speak of angers because they are connected to various other feelings. One kind of anger is coloured by hatred, another by envy, yet another by jealousy, and so on. Each of these will have its own gestural and verbal connotations and can potentially be enacted in a range of ways: for example, there can be explosive angers, blind angers, implosive and self-destructive angers, with diametrically opposed consequences.

The feeling of exclusion is also a crossroads for many other feelings and emotions. We can find a wide range in it, from anger and resentment to aggressiveness; from loneliness as negation to liberating solitude as an opportunity for gaining access to one's own capacity for imagination; from shame to guilt. I am thinking, for example, of the film *The Scarlet Letter* where the official exclusion of a women guilty of adultery is made public through additional humiliation, derision, and shame.

Sometimes our own bodies are able to tell us about exclusion by making our faces turn red and causing us to wish to disappear, a feeling expressed by our patients (and not only by them) in various ways such as "All I wanted was a hole to hide in," or "At that moment I wished I was a million miles away!" Fainting and dizziness are two other modes of expression, one an extreme search for support, the other a fear of losing it.

These reflections lead me to assert that the feeling of exclusion would mostly arise from an encounter between primary feelings and emotions. We could define it as a complex feeling which engages a person on a deep level, throwing her or him into a crisis which strikes her or him as a whole, although with predominant characteristics which makes it identifiable.

9.2 What are we being excluded from?

I have asked myself these questions in order to try and construct a representation of a space-time capable of containing before it can exclude. Indeed, only after this can the feeling of exclusion be thought about and understood. In this connection, I would endorse the definition given by Molinari in this book, in her chapter on depression (Chapter 4, p. 61): "'Depressed' literally means pushed out of a place where one has felt safe, and so its first association applies to birth as the primary experience of losing a place inside which one has been contained." But are we sure that exclusion is something which comes chronologically after containment in the mother's body? Is it possible to be uncontained even before this, even before existing physically in our own right? These questions seem to hypothesise an exclusion even before it makes itself felt in a mind, and perhaps the possibility that exclusion exists as a "thought not yet thought" and in search of a thinker (Bion, 1992). In certain clinical situations, this condition can persist and become a sense of pre-exclusion which – like all very primitive mental experiences – is hard to make evolve unless we can grasp the preverbal as it enters the session. If we consider birth, as I do, to be a strictly bi-personal matter – like analysis: that is, an event which concerns two minds in a relationship – then to be born is to have found a place in someone's mind, whether one's mother's or one's analyst's. This is the presupposition from which I shall set out to illustrate clinically the ideas I have just expounded.

9.2.1   Sara and the recovery of a retro-perspective

Sara comes to analysis because she is very worried about her five-year-old son, Alberto, with whom she has always had a difficult relationship. During the past year the problem seems to have grown worse.

"Alberto is uncontainable, I can't give him limits, he disobeys me all the time and makes me feel powerless. Sometimes I wonder if he acknowledges me as his mother, because he goes his own way like a train."

In telling me her story, Sara dwells on her the impact of her son's birth. She is young but has made great progress towards the professional goals she has dreamed of; she has an on-off relationship with a man which lacks passion; she was thrown by the unexpected news that she was expecting a baby. She did not what to do. Her extremely religious family, barely aware of Sara's emotional uncertainties, pressed her to welcome the child sent by God. The decision was quickly taken: the baby will be born and they will live together. Sara will use the time of her pregnancy to set up hasty guarantees that she will not lose any opportunities for professional growth. The university seems willing to agree to a contract, but the nine months go by quickly and there is no trace of a room for the baby. Sara's physical condition marks the passing of time, and somehow, in a final tour de force, a room is fitted out with the essentials.

Alberto's arrival is problematic from the start in relation to feeding. "Alberto did not suck, and I quickly lost patience, so I decided to bottle-feed him. My mother helped me a lot, you know, so I wouldn't lose my relationship with the university. Sometimes I'd look at him and wish he didn't exist. You know what a dreadful mother I've been, but for me it's as if since I had him my life has come to an end!"

I tell Sara that I am detecting a missing link in her story, and maybe in her life. Sara seems to try searching through her mind, but so far nothing emerges.

Then one day she tells me about a pregnant friend, and how the friend has confided in her about how much she and her partner had longed for this baby, about her thoughts and anxieties about the future, her discussions with her partner about the colour of the room, which they are already thinking about even though there are still four months to go, and also how she feels about the baby's first movements inside her. With surprise in her voice, Sara tells me, "I never thought those things, even though I had a baby inside me. It's as if they never happened. When the time came, I just did it, that's all!" We then began a long journey which arrived at a series of stories from the gossip magazines about celebrities' pregnancies, and dreams in which she herself was expecting a baby and experiencing those somatic perceptions which she had originally brought to analysis as stories about her pregnant friend. By means of these characters and their narratives, the field began to accommodate the affects linked to desire and the unknown sensorialities of a concrete waiting, a waiting which Sara had excluded from her experience of gestation beforehand, and of motherhood afterwards. What had not been granted space and time in real life had found space and time to be thought about and transformed in the form of experience in analysis.

9.2.2 From missing crib syndrome to the "ripped-off" crib

Sara's story leads me back to the "missing crib syndrome" which Ferro (2010, pp. 84–6) speaks about, and to which I would add a more widespread variation which can strike at any age and potentially appear during any analysis and in any session: "ripped-off crib syndrome". Here "ripped-off" can have a double meaning, that of tearing and that of theft; so in both cases we are dealing with a crib which originally existed. The stable, the manger, Mary and Joseph, the ox and ass are understood as necessary functions of the setting. This is the place freighted with potential narrative derivatives: that is, characters hosted by the field as it expands, developments of a growing thought, of a previously impersonal "O" (Grotstein, 2009, pp. 39–49).

Perhaps the diversity of cribs which adorn houses in some way shows how different families can have different potentialities for narrative. We can go from a hidebound narrative in which the only concession besides the manger and the infant is the presence of Mary and Joseph, to Eduardo's rich and abundant crib in *Christmas at the Cupiello's* in which every piece has its own story or perhaps stories: one linked, for example, to the role occupied by the village blacksmith, the other linked to the relationship which this figure has with his family, a story handed down from father to son: "You see this little shepherd? Your grandad bought this at a street market in Montemezzagno. It's more than a hundred years old, and grandad always put it to the right of the entrance to the stable, here, right here!" This Russian doll of stories becomes a fabric of acceptance, a matrix of identity in which it is of no importance whether the baby wants to accept and remember it, or not. What will be important, however, is that we have been able to make it come, and the care with which this story has been preserved. That will already be a great deal.

The non-permanence of these conditions represents the "ripping" which does at least allow the construction of the capacity for thinking to be pursued: that is, the birth of the "baby" understood as the birth of a thought which has something revolutionary in it.

I think of the case of a girl only a few months old who, for unavoidable circumstances, was left for a considerable time without her mother's care and entrusted to childminders. The consequences of the interruption of an affective rhythm made of contact, smells, sonorities and gazes, with modalities perhaps barely introjected, later exploded when the parents separated, coinciding with an exceptionally turbulent adolescence. Everything had in fact been kept together until that moment by effective narcissistic and obsessive defences which had constructed the classic, but in my opinion worrying, vision of the "daughter who does not give thoughts." This defence worked until the feeling of emptiness and abandonment, with powerful death anxieties, found its way through the gap opened by the imperious adolescent turbulences. The narcissistic defence collapsed under the pressure of demands, like calls to the emergency services, to stop truly psychotic anxieties which oscillated between suicidal fantasies and a terrifying feeling of abandonment requiring an urgent remedy, a sort of imminent lack of vital oxygen. The remedy concretised for a time in the girl's spasmodic search for alternative links of a sexual nature. These were experienced in a climate of total subjection and the acceptance of any demand in response to her urgent need to "save herself", with the consequent loss of any critical capacity. This occurred simultaneously with the presence of other links with a "safeguarding" function which were, so to speak, kept on the back burner in readiness for emergencies of emptiness. The analysis of three sessions a week with its regular "rhythm of safety" (Tustin, 1986), as well as the necessary flexibility of the setting, began to reconstruct the condition of the "crib", linked to the patient's adolescent condition. The oscillation of a "crib" function in the field, alternating with the recovery of split-off aspects, began very gradually to modify the quality of the links and also the aspect of subjection which had initially been deaf to all warnings. Space was created for the possibility that she could start to make choices of partner which gradually came closer to a cultural but, above all, affective and more reassuring, harmony. The sexual offer in the relationship – which had previously been the only possible way of expressing herself and her only flood barrier against the terror of abandonment, or perhaps of fragmentation – began to be accompanied by the loving dimension, until the rediscovery of a symmetrical relationship which would grant less and less space to humiliations and submission as a search for confirmation.

I think of exclusion in a uniquely bi-personal dimension where one of the parts has not taken on, or been able to take on, its responsibility for the construction or maintenance of the conditions of acceptance and care, which the sole presupposition for giving access to the development of a mind and its capacity for thinking. This stable taking of responsibility should be the constant of any analysis: without it there is the risk that the functioning of the laboriously constructed or reconstructed apparatus for thinking will be newly traumatised. Incidentally, I think this may one of the most exhausting aspects of our work: the awareness of having to be ourselves in the first person, even before we are characters whom the field asks us to play for its narrative purposes. To be clear, those of us working in public institutions are to some degree aware of fulfilling a role in which, in our absence, a certain degree of continuity is assured, especially in emergencies. This aspect is missing from the private dimension of our work, sometimes giving rise to a feeling of oppression and the risk of Tamagotchi anxiety.

9.3 At the origin of the bi-personal

The first place in which we are given the possibility of constructing our existence, the feeling of being in the world, is that mind which has reserved a place for a thought about us in advance. In general, and unlike Sara's case, this place exists before our conception and has the function of constituting a space-time-climate for our arrival. In fact, it is to be hoped that our existence can be seen as beginning in a mental gestation even before it has a physical one. The mother's womb will then give concreteness to that thought by initiating a sensory experience, the first sketch of a bi-personal relationship, imaginable first of all as a place which is neither in this world nor the next. The mental and physical processes will continue to exist together and carry out the function of standing in for an apparatus for thinking which has not yet been constructed. After the caesura of birth, the mother's womb will be transformed into the ways the baby is held in the arms, the ways he or she is fed, touched, and rocked, making him or her an object to which the first sonorities are directed, perhaps including representations of other family members.

On the theoretical level, I am referring to one of the modes of experience which Ogden (1989, pp. 31, notes 5 and 6) has called "*the autistic-contiguous mode* in order to roughly parallel the method of naming the paranoid-schizoid mode, which takes its name from both the form of psychological organisation and the form of defence associated with it." This is a preverbal mode and for this very reason it is hard to represent in words. "Rather, it is a relationship of shape to the feeling of enclosure, of beat to the feeling of rhythm, of hardness to the feeling of edgedness. . . . Early experiences of sensory contiguity define a surface (the beginnings of what will become a sense of place) on which experience is created and organised" (ibid., pp. 32–3).

Warmth, contact, the constant rhythm of a nearby sound, the mother's heartbeat, and other less constant and more distant sounds are the only things that tell us about the existence of a form we could not experience except as concrete contact with it as it emerges, or as the rhythm of its presence-absence-presence, or again as the search for a sensory perception, perhaps the beginning of a future curiosity about the world.

In order to imagine this experience of which we have no conscious traces, we can try to place ourselves physically behind a cloth onto which something is pressing: we will have the perception of a point or a roundness, and so we will experience a perceptual quality, but never the three-dimensional character which makes us experience as a whole the object on the other side of the cloth. For example, we will only experience a hand as the point at which we enter into contact with it and the related sensation.

9.4   The experience of exclusion *in vivo*

For us as psychoanalysts, environments such as narrative, film-making, music, visual art, and many other cultural environments constitute, in my opinion, an indispensable supply of images, metaphors, and modes of expression for supplying the shortcomings of a language which is sometimes incapable of coming close enough to the emotion and feeling that is asking to be expressed and to live in the field which is constituted out of the encounter between two minds. These environments also have the function of suggesting representations which are ever closer to theoretical models that have already been thought of (and yet are open to development), as well as suggesting new ones. The field model, derived from the physics of electromagnetic fields, is a current example: having entered the psychoanalytic sphere, it has steadily taken on variations which turn out to be compatible with the thinking and practice of psychoanalysis. Lastly, I think we should not rule out the possibility that these functions, which are helpful in the development of theoretical reflection, may also become a means for communicating our own thoughts in psychoanalytic writing.

These are the reasons why I am now proposing to enter *in vivo* into the experience of exclusion using some examples and situations taken for the purpose from clinical practice, narrative, and film.

9.4.1   The feeling of exclusion in a session

That morning, unlike other times, after the handshake which marked the start of our encounter, I noticed that as the patient was moving towards the couch, his attention was caught by what was on my table. I perceived a certain bad mood in the air and this became more evident during a long initial silence. Then, with some effort, the patient started talking about the book he had seen on my table, in which there was a contribution of mine. In a rather formal tone, he said how very pleased he was and launched into some further compliments: finally, right on cue, the complaining began.

> However, I have to say that while reading it, I felt something else, a feeling of stupidity; I never understand why it is that when we talk in the session I understand you and feel understood, whereas in that book everything gets complicated, it becomes difficult and remote and I feel left out, excluded from a dialogue unless I make a huge effort, wondering why I'm so stupid.

From this "accident(?)" the analysis was able to make a qualitative leap which would seize on an important nucleus of his unhappiness: the feeling of exclusion associated with an anxiety about death.

In the patient's comment there is an evident desire to think within an exclusive relationship with me, one that is considered vital for his survival. Instead, the field is populated with other characters (introduced by me?) with whom, in the patient's experience, I was conducting a conversation from which he feared being excluded because the language was inaccessible to him. But something more serious had also happened. At that moment, the patient had experienced a diminishing of the affective field, the breaking of a container which was no longer available to him, and felt that he had touched an old wound.

It was necessary to adopt an opposite vertex which might pass from the feeling of exclusion experienced as impotence, against which he opposed a barrier of stupidity or perhaps a painful shame, to the endorsement of a constructive curiosity which could be transformed into a valid desire for knowledge. This was what happened in the analysis with my patient, as I took care to make interventions which would maintain a polarity of positions, affectively oscillating between carefully measured contact with the incomprehensible unknown and the recovery of moments of exclusivity in the relationship, which the patient also needed. In these cases, the communication between patient and analyst must be able to experience moments of unison which can represent a bridge between the primitive demands to be understood by someone (the mother) without the need to speak, and developmental experiences of passing through exclusion (Gaburri, 1993).

During the course of an analysis, the excess of a communication which passes through the sensorial (a sort of telepathy) can, if it takes on a permanent character, become a pathological aspect of the field. It functions by avoiding the experience of painful distance which a language can produce, as well as through the feeling of separateness that is intrinsic to listening to the other's voice, to the detriment of the laborious search for a sufficiently communicative language.

Winnicott too (1965, p. 50), in a paragraph devoted to the examination of maternal care, warns against the prolonging beyond the period of mother-infant symbiosis of those modes which enable her to understand the infant's needs perfectly: in this period, as it were, the more the better. At a certain point, says Winnicott, with the end of the symbiosis, it is as if the mother realised that the child has acquired a new capacity, that of giving a signal that can guide her to respond to his or her needs. And this endorses the separation from the environment which has occurred. If the mother, like the analyst, were to continue giving pre-prepared responses to the infant's supposed needs, the upshot would be to deprive him or her of active experience, "The creative gesture, the cry, the protest, all the little signs that are supposed to produce what the mother does, all these things are missing, because the mother has already met the need just as if the infant were still merged with her and she with the infant" (ibid., p. 51). This paves the way for what Meltzer (Meltzer et al., 1975) called "adhesive identification in a two-dimensional world", which aims to create or defensively reconstitute a rudimentary feeling of cohesiveness in one's own surface.

Returning to our case, the Oedipal choice, thought of in Freudian terms, was ready on a plate for me to use in interpreting how the patient might have felt excluded from a privileged relationship which I had with writing, and probably with other colleagues who had shared in the composition of the book. Or worse, interpreting his curiosity about objects and whatever else he might see in my consulting room as sticking his nose into my affairs; this would only have had the effect of aggravating the guilt for the forbidden gaze and causing a feeling of infantilising humiliation.

In fact, I think that everything present in my consulting room during the session might act as a common store of goods to which the patient and I inevitably have access; access which I see more than anything else as the patient's right to be curious about my mind, and of our shared right to be curious about the field. We cannot be amazed if a child shows curiosity about what's on our table or in the drawers that we have left accessible to him.

It is important to stress that the feeling of exclusion can be seen from a multitude of vertices which also illuminate its highly diverse functions and the equally diverse ways in which it can be brought into analysis. So, I want to make clear my distance from the very restricting view, offering little scope for development, which seeks to reconstruct dynamics of this type with reference to incest and parricide (Corrao, 1991), reducing everything to the concreteness of the parents' sexual relationship from which the child would have been, and would have felt, excluded. It is certainly true that the Oedipal conceptualisation is a fundamental structure of the mind, but it is equally true that establishing it as such has occupied, and still occupies, so much space in our minds as to occlude the thinkability of any other variant, of turning our gaze towards the unknown which has been saturated by what is already known. Through Bion's widening of the field (Bion, 1963, ch. 10), the value I can give to a story which ought to describe a state of mind linked to the feeling of exclusion is solely metaphorical and would tell me about a plurality of emotions and feelings: exclusion, yes of course, but also curiosity, separateness, and inclusivity; a way of telling other stories which may use a non-oedipal dialect. I would attribute greater importance to an oscillatory function between exclusion and inclusion as a choice tending towards the search for an equilibrium between solitude and "socialism".

9.5 Opposite declensions of exclusion

I think the feeling of exclusion can have many valences which are not always as negative as the common definition seems to indicate.

In two extremely interesting films, Ingmar Bergman's *Fanny and Alexander* (1982) and Ettore Scola's *The Family* (1987), two children are the protagonists of two different ways of experiencing the feeling of exclusion. One lives his exclusion as a choice, with the pleasure of being able to observe the world and the people around him, sheltered from others' gaze; in the other film, there is a growing feeling of transparency, which becomes the dramatic perception, infused with anxiety, of not existing, of being a ghost among living people, a feeling of alienation from the world. On the one hand, the desire not to be discovered, to be able to construct one's own viewpoint on things; on the other, the desire to be found and to gain the assurance of being to/in the world. In cinematic language, we could claim that in the first child there is the hope of being a future director and in the second that of being called on to become a character among others, to be in a group with whom finally to share the scene and receive constant recognition.

9.5.1 The Family

The scene is set in the 1940s during a gathering of the whole extended family. All ages are present: grandparents, uncles, maiden aunts, young couples, and little grandchildren, of whom Paolino is one. An uncle, a minor Fascist functionary, invites Paolino to play a game of hide and seek, pretending not to be able to find him.

The uncle calls "Paolinooo! Paolinoo! Where's Paolino, have you seen him?" For a while the child stands behind him, enjoying the game, but as it goes on he starts to call out, "But, uncle, I'm here!" The game continues unremarked by everyone, with nobody telling the uncle that Paolino is behind him; besides, if it's a game shouldn't it go on? "Paolino, Paolinoo! Where's he got to?" continues the uncle in a tone of seeming anxiety. Paolino's expression starts to change into one of puzzlement. The uncle dramatically asks two aunts absorbed in conversation if they have seen the boy, but they equally dramatically say no, confirming a tragic truth in Paolino's eyes. A boundary, that of play, has given way, and a nightmare is beginning. The first uncertain, silent tear trickles down Paolino's face, and he no longer seems interested in the game. A greater anxiety is becoming clear as he looks around at the others in the room who seem not to notice him. For Paolino the drama has begun, his weeping is broken by sobs, and yet his uncle perseveres with his play-acting, asking "Have you seen Paolino? Where's he got to?" Paolino is seized by an appalling doubt which he is tearfully manage to express: "But can't you see me?" he asks this world to which he can now imagine no longer having access. In a last desperate attempt to get back in contact with that reality, he repeatedly yells, "Mamma, mamma!" until he breaks out into a crisis of despair, throwing himself face down on the floor, thrashing about convulsively as if in an epileptic fit. His parents finally hear his constant crying and run to him as his uncle looks on in astonishment. The father and mother take turns to hug him, holding him tightly against them and reassuringly saying, "I'm here Paolino, I'm here with you!", but this is not enough to contain his despair. The scene shifts to the shadows of a bedroom where the little boy, listening to a lullaby being gently sung by his mother, starts to calm down and to emerge from his nightmare, restoring those affective threads which had been damaged, of not broken beyond repair.

Paolino's experience reminds us of Winnicott's (1965) concept of "breakdown" filtered through Ogden's (2014) reflection on this work in "The Fear of Breakdown and the Unlived Life", where he states that "'breakdown' refers to the breakdown of the mother-infant tie, which leaves the infant alone and raw and on the verge of not existing." The infant in this state would be immersed in what we could call an "experience of primitive agony". I think of the images of the astronaut in *2001: A Space Odyssey*, where the cutting of the umbilical cord connecting the astronaut to the mother ship, as a result of the computer Hal's desire to kill him, leaves the astronaut beginning an infinite fall and with it an infinite agony.

Perhaps the floor, though it is hard and cold, becomes Paolino's last resort, an "autistic object",[2] Tustin (1980, 1981) would say, to prevent exactly this agony, what Winnicott calls "falling forever". In this scene from the film, the exclusion comes close to having extreme consequences through the loss of the sense of being in relation to an affective space-time, a world from which we draw constant nourishment which is offered as a generative and developmental experience.

What might have been the game bearable? Because this is what we are dealing with, in life as well as in analysis. Let's try introducing a new narrative segment at a certain point in the scene.

As the game proceeds, Paolino hears himself being called, "Paolino, Paolino!" and the boy turns towards his aunt, who makes a sign to him to come and hide in her skirts. From another vertex, Paolino is amused to intuit the new turn in the game and able to experience the alternation between existing – that is re-joining the group – and not existing; a providential alternation of roles with the uncle, which makes the game bearable. The oscillation between different ways of having an experience desired by Ogden (1989) has been achieved.

9.5.2   Fanny and Alexander

The scene sees the protagonist, a ten-year-old boy, observing the space around him and the occupants of the house while hidden under a table, staying absolutely silent even when someone is looking for him and calling him. This situation seems to be experienced as a setting for an appropriate contact with, and immersion in, the free flow of his own imagination (Civitarese, 2008), which oscillates constantly in the film between the oneiric and the hallucinatory. It is with good reason that the spectator, in tune with the equivalence which Bion (1970) proposes between hallucination and freedom, perceives Alexander as feeling freest in those moments, in the sense of being able to attain solitude. He thus creates a condition for himself in which a dream-state enables him to gain access to knowledge and to links. The scene shows how Alexander, using his imagination, animates the statues which decorate certain corners of the house, but as something absolutely natural and not disturbing. In connection with the hope of becoming a director (of one's own dreams), I think of how Fellini, with his dream-like profuseness well documented in *The Book of Dreams* (2008), could look at the space around him, animating it in his mind with characters and scenes which might become subjects of his films. Alexander's choosing to exclude himself from real relationships by making himself unreachable becomes a tool for thinkability in that it constructs and preserves an undisturbed relationship with the flow of his own imagination.

This seems to me to be the reader's prerogative, that of feeling intimately part of a story, of being emotionally involved in a scene which only exists on paper. The reader activates a personal soundproofing of her or his own hetero-perceptions, focussing her or himself on the story and not on what is happening around her or her, becoming a character among the characters.

9.6 The disappearance of the mind

We have seen how the relationship with a mind capable of making room for the other is an essential element of our growth and psychic maturation. Within this relationship we build our experience of boundaries and a capacity for relating; besides receiving what is necessary for our survival, we also receive those mental functions which enable us to live and manage the emotional events of our lives: joy, suffering, mourning a death, and thinking about our own death. But it may happen that this "other" mind leaves us in different ways and at different moments of our existence, with consequences which sometimes seem to negate the separateness and autonomy that we have gained, and which we thought were sufficient to withstand any loss.

9.6.1 Conversation with the mother

In the mental sphere we can experience a feeling of exclusion linked to the loss of a loved person, as we see well represented in Pirandello's story, "Conversations with my Mother" (1915, pp. 2687–94). In this touching account, Pirandello imagines meeting his mother shortly after her death, which occurred in the house where he was born.

Pirandello: When I ask her, "But Mamma, what's going on? Why are you here . . .?" she looks at me, nodding and saying she wanted to come and tell me what she could never say because I was far away even before she departed this life.

Mother: Besides, all of you, and you especially, you who were always far away, so far away, you think I'm still alive! Aren't I still alive for you?

Pirandello: Oh yes, Mamma – I say to her – alive, yes, alive . . . but that's not the reason! . . . I'm crying about something else, Mamma! I'm crying because you can no longer give me a reality! . . . When you used to sit over in that corner, I would say, if She is thinking about me from far away, I am alive for her." Now that you're dead, I don't say you're no longer alive for me. . . . and you'll always be alive as long as I'm alive, do you see? It's this, this: that I'm no longer alive and won't be alive for you anymore! Because you can't think about me anymore as I think about you, you can't feel me as I feel you. That's why, Mamma.

Mamma, that's why the people who think they're still alive also think they're weeping for the dead people they love, when they're really weeping for their own deaths, their own reality that's no longer there because they can't feel the ones who have gone. . . . But what am I, what am I now, for you? Nothing . . . I was a son, and I'm not that any more, I won't be that ever again. . . .

| *Mother:* | Look at things with the eyes of those who don't see them anymore! You'll grieve for them, son, in a way that makes them more sacred and more beautiful. |
| *Pirandello:* | Shadow has darkened the room. I can't see myself or feel myself any more. |

In this touching and imaginative dialogue, Pirandello expresses an exact idea of mourning and death. Indeed, he seems unconsciously to be referring to an unexpected diminution of those functions for thinking, feeling, and, I would add, dreaming, which in our experience with seriously ill patients we find ourselves having to lend, rebuild or repair, and where death anxieties often occupy an important space. It is no coincidence that when Pirandello speaks of the living who weep for the dead he says "they're really weeping for their own deaths," as if our being alive consisted of the many places which house thoughts about us, and every time one of these places is extinguished it represents a death of our own. So, every death corresponds to an exclusion from a place that is no longer there, and a sort of amputation of our mental body.

But is this loss really so irreparable? Is there no function capable of recovering objects from that corner which used to be occupied by thoughts about us?

It is Pirandello's mother who offers a possible reparation when she says, "Look at things with the eyes of those who don't see them anymore! You'll grieve for them, son, in a way that makes them more sacred and more beautiful." In recollection, in images, in the stories stored in our memory, there is still the gaze of our parents and our story-telling grandparents, who have supplied us with pasts not lived, family myths which have given our existence greater depth.

Corrao (1992, p. 27) writes about modern mankind's loss of the capacity for mythopoeia as a condition which impoverishes us and renders us helpless when faced with emotions and feelings about which our dreaming is absent or interrupted (Ogden, 2008). I see this as something which has marked a change in younger generations, a real wound in thinking, which makes them more inclined to action. The family, the nuclear family in particular, has lost this narrating function, leaving the children orphaned of family histories on which to base important elements of their identity: which makes them ill-equipped to face death, which they have no narratives, memories, stories to set against.

9.7 Ogden's napkin. Exclusion as a "collapse of the dialectic of experience"

In a fundamentally important work on the concept of the "autistic-contiguous mode", Ogden (1989) with courage and intelligence gives a memorable example of self-disclosure outside the session, which I will use as an example of an extreme form of exclusion occurring in the mind. By "collapse of the dialectic of experience" Ogden means a condition of the mind dominated by one polarity of the ways in which experience is generated. Indeed, sanity cannot do without the constant oscillation between the autistic-contiguous mode, founded essentially on sensoriality, the paranoid-schizoid, and the depressive.

Ogden tells how one evening, after dinner, as he was still sitting at the table, it came into his mind how strange it was that the object we call a "napkin" takes its name from the conjunction of the sounds "nap" and "kin". The more he thought about this, the more he fell prey to a certain anxiety linked to the fact that these sounds had lost all connection with the object that was before his eyes. He tragically thought that the link between the object and those sounds had been broken and no act of will could tie the two things together again. "I imagined that all things in the world could come to feel as disconnected as the napkin had become for me now that it had been disconnected from the word that had formerly named it" (ibid., p. 80). At that moment, Ogden felt as if he had discovered a way to go mad. He wondered if everything could undergo the same fate. The cost of this would be that he "could become utterly disconnected from the rest of the world because all other people would still share in a 'natural' (i.e., a still meaningful) system of words" (ibid.) and he would be left excluded from it.

The dictatorship of the sensory polarity, when it is the only way of generating experience at the expense of the symbolic pole, induces a regressive condition and reduces us to the condition of newborn infants who put everything into their mouths or place their cheek against the mother's breast to re-establish contact, to rebuild a skin, and to listen to her reassuring heartbeat. At the same time, it expels us from the sphere of meanings and of communicative language, turning us into illiterates of the symbolic.

In analysis, patient and analyst also try to reconstruct the "sensory base" (ibid., p. 36) of experience. This happens through, among other things, the stability of the rhythm of the sessions, the familiar sound of the voices in conversation, the regularity of the ways in which sessions are begun and ended. These hardly rigorous ways of managing the setting – leaving aside the exceptional "chance"(?) event – can function unfavourably against the addressing of these old wounds. They will be capable of manifesting themselves as scars of unlived experiences (Ogden, 2015) which, like the phenomenon of the phantom limb, will continue to make themselves painfully felt by establishing a burdensome anxiety about the disaggregation of one's own sensory surface or one's own "rhythm of safety" (Tustin, 1990; Grotstein, 1980). This anxiety will have the consequence that one feels as if one is dissolving, disappearing, or falling into a limitless, shapeless space. On the other hand, "it is not absence in itself which allows us to think, to gain access to symbolic activity, but the regular sensation of absences and presences, of the regular repeating of experiences" (Marcelli, 1991, p. 65).

The reconstitution of a distance from the object is the transition which allows us to move from the preverbal to the symbolic and will be able to reconnect the affect to the object, just as the "napkin" will be able to go back to being a "napkin". The effect will be that of re-associating the image to the sound, of recovering its function and above all the possibility of sharing all this, returning and belonging to a social group.

In the blackout of the symbolic which struck Ogden, we can imagine there being a collapse of alpha function, or a sort of pre-alpha barrier which opposes the transformation of beta into alpha. The various forms of evacuation to bring relief are replaced by their opposite, which prevents raw emotions from entering the field of representation and creates, so to speak, the mute subject who has no possibility of gaining access to a symbolic experience.

How can we reactivate symbolic weaving and regain the power of speech? We need a mind to dream something.

If Odgen, who, by the way, does not say much about the process which helped him to get out of that situation, had told me what was happening to him, I could have had a dream and told it to him like this: "You know, for some reason you've made me remember that when my son was very young, I used to get him to go to sleep by telling him that two little friends, Nap and Kin would be coming to sing him a lullaby."

What do I want to show by starting this game with the two syllables "nap" and "kin", which had become meaningless? The principle is that of recovering fragments which have lost meaning and connection, and to bring them back into circulation by articulating meanings in a different way and thereby reactivating an alpha function which had suffered a blackout at that point. So my attention would be directed not to recovering the meaning of the reunited fragments (their content) about which we could infer many things – such as wiping the mouth, absorbency, protective function; meanings which at that moment would have found no way into Ogden's mind – but to reactivating that *dreaming ensemble* (Grotstein, 2007) which allows us to begin re-dreaming those mute fragments, making them re-enter a field of familiarity to wait for their rediscovery.

9.8 Conclusions

Through the feeling of exclusion analysed by way of filmed, narrated, and clinical situations, this chapter has explored and described various modes of generating experience.

The possibility of understanding the modes of emotional experience is an important field of research which still has much room for development. In particular, the "synthesis, interpretation, and extension" of ideas introduced by Frances Tustin, Esther Bick and Donald Meltzer, aiming to configure a third way for the subject to have experiences, one which is initially located in the intrauterine condition of the foetus and continues in the preverbal dimension of experience which is present at every stage of life, is what I have the impression that I am encountering, or perhaps being able to grasp, more and more often, in my patients, in both the more and less seriously ill. I say "more and less seriously" because, as Ogden describes well in *The Primitive Edge of Experience*, it also emerges in apparently banal ways in patients who are maintaining a good psychic organisation: see the paragraph on autistic-contiguous defences (pp. 31–2). This confirms the chronological non-linearity put forward by Ogden, and not only by him, of modes of generating experience, but also of our mind's modes of functioning, as proposed earlier by Bion. So, it is no longer possible to think of our mind as constrained by developmental stages as it composes itself. In this, Ogden explicitly states his disagreement with Klein and with the theories which speak of phases. Therefore, among the three experiences cited there is a continual mediating function which reminds us about the importance of Bion's (1970) instruction to investigate the caesura, the place where things are connected. It is an area of great fragility where the lack or insufficiency of "zips" for opening up dialogue creates the risk of states of disconnection to the various modes of experience, causing pathologies of various kinds and differing degrees of severity. Our listening thus becomes more like feeling (sounds, odours) or seeing (ritualisations, repetitive behaviours, the relationship of our hands with our own bodies).

Another element I want to return to is that of the non-existence of emotions in the pure state; not only in the sense that balpha elements exist, as cited by Ferro and Odgen – that is, emotions in varying degrees of alphabetisation or betalisation – but in the sense of an emotional cocktail where it is possible at the first sip to recognise the prevalence of a component which then becomes a whole "taste".

Another feature which characterises this chapter is the hypothesis that a feeling of exclusion exists before birth, as if it were a thought in search of a thinker, or a narrative which might fill our destiny with meaning.

In this context, I would like to conclude with the legendary scene from Woody Allen's *Everything You Always Wanted to Know About Sex But Were Afraid to Ask*. A group of spermatozoa are preparing for the great leap into the unknown, wondering what fate awaits them. The sequence, already a dialogue between the three ways of having experience, seems to answer "yes" to the question of whether exclusion exists upstream of an embodied feeling of exclusion. Only one of them will be successful; the others will be excluded without ever knowing the development of their "O". But Allen, highly sensitive to the themes of difference and exclusion, accentuates the visibility of this state: among the millions of white spermatozoa, he includes one black one, and one only, who wonders "What am I doing here?" showing how aware he is of his own difference, but above all, his feeling that this is not his place, and already speculating about the existence of another place from which he sees himself being left out.

Notes

1 Bion employs the term "socialism" to indicate the group-mental aspects of the individual, and not as a political term.
2 For Tustin, "the experience of 'autistic objects' stands in marked contrast to the experience of autistic shapes. An autistic object is the experience of a hard, angular sensory surface that is created when an object is pressed hard against the infant's skin. In this form of experience, the individual experiences his surface . . . as a hard crust or armor that protects him against unspeakable dangers that only later will be given names" (Ogden, 1989, p. 56).

References

Bion, W.R. (1963). *Elements of Psycho-Analysis*. London: Heinemann.

Bion, W.R. (1970). *Attention and Interpretation*. London: Tavistock, pp. 106–24.

Bion, W.R. (1992). *Cogitations*. London: Karnac Books.

Civitarese, G. (2008). *The Intimate Room: Theory and Technique of the Analytic Field*. Abingdon: Routledge, 2010.

Corrao, F. (1991). Il Campo Edipico e I suoi Elementi. In Id., *Orme*, vol. I., Cortina Milano, 1998.

Corrao, F. (1992). Mito. In Id., *Modelli Psicoanalitici: mito, passione, memoria*. Laterza: Roma-Bari, p. 27.

Fellini, F. (2008). *The Book of Dreams*. New York: Rizzoli.

Ferro, A. (2010). *Torments of the Soul*. London: Routledge, New Library, 2014, pp. 84–6.

Gaburri, E. (1993). Il senso della interpretazione nelle aree cicatriziali psicotiche. In G. Di Chiara and C. Neri (Eds.), *Psicoanalisi futura*. Roma: Borla.

Grotstein, J.S. (1980). Primitive Mental States. *Contemporary Psychoanalysis*, 19, pp. 570–604.

Grotstein, J.S. (2007). *A Beam of Intense Darkness: Wilfred Bion's Legacy to Psychoanalysis*. London: Karnac Books.

Grotstein, J.S. (2009). *But at Same Time Another Level . . .: Psychoanalytic Theory and Technique in the Kleinian/Bionian Mode*. London: Karnac Books, pp. 39–49.

Marcelli, D. (1991). *Posizione autistic e nascita della psyche*. Roma: Armando, p. 65.

Meltzer, D. et al. (1975). *Explorations of Autism: A Psychoanalytic Study*. London: Karnac Books; Revised edition (July 21, 2008).

Ogden, T.H. (1989). *The Primitive Edge of Experience*. Northvale, NJ: Jason Aronson.

Ogden, T.H. (2008). *Rediscovering Psychoanalysis: Thinking and Dreaming, Learning and Forgetting*. London: Routledge.

Ogden, T.H. (2014). Fear of Breakdown and the Unlived Life. *International Journal of Psychoanalysis*, 95, 205–23.

Ogden, T.H. (2015). *Reclaiming Unlived Life: Experience in Psychoanalysis*. Abingdon: Routledge, 2016.

Pirandello, L. (1915). Colloqui coi personaggi, vol. III. In Id., *Novelle per un anno*. Firenze: Giunti, 1994, pp. 2687–94.

Tustin, F. (1980). Autistic Objects. *International Review of Psychoanalysis*, II, pp. 279–90.

Tustin, F. (1981). *Autistic States in Children*. Abingdon: Routledge, 2013.

Tustin, F. (1986). *Autistic Barriers in Neurotic Patients*. Abingdon: Routledge, 2018.

Tustin, F. (1990). *The Protective Shell in Children and Adults*. Abingdon: Routledge, 2018.

Winnicott, D.W. (1965). *The Maturational Process and the Facilitating Environment: Studies in the Theory of Emotional Development*. New York: International Universities Press, p. 50.

Chapter 10

Rage and shame

Giuseppe Civitarese

Rage is a primary emotion that is not derivable from others. The term comes from the Latin 'rabies', from a root which also derives from Sanskrit 'rabh-ate' (act violently, infuriating) and 'rabhas' (momentum). The same sound of the word 'rage' suggests a flaw (the 'r', as in sound 'grr' from the comics) a paroxysm (doubling of the lip) and a negative emotional state. There are cold and hot rages, rage outbreaks and chronic rage. Rage can be contained in a kind of dull irritation, it can explode, be conscious and unconscious. Rage ranges from a slightly victimized attitude from those who always complain about anything, to murderous rampage, without interruption. Confronted with an unlimited variety of concrete situations of rage, we are bound to fail at any attempt to order them into a typology.

However, we should at least separate rage from fury and hatred. In this regard, Diamond (1996; cit. in Wiener, 1998) used the power switch metaphor: rage would depend on an on/off operation and would enjoy a constant voltage. Rage could be modulated, as when one uses a dimmer switch. In that case rage passes through the ego filter; compared to a furious rage reaction which bypasses an ego filter entirely. With rage, as with all the defenses generally, the pressure on the spontaneous trigger, its automatic nature, is what renders it pathological. Therefore rage is not always an unsuitable reaction. It is not always inadequate because it can be also useful in certain situations, especially when it becomes part of a fight or flight reaction. Rage is improper when the reaction is abnormally high, relative to the stimulus. In any case, there is a continuity – even if not accepted by all authors – of the reactions to deprivations of various intensities that can be defined either physiological or frankly pathological.

We must then separate hatred, which is considered a secondary emotion, from rage. Hatred, which can also result from rage, is a more complex feeling and more enduring. Less mentalized, rage consists of an immediate and violent reaction to a frustration, or a primitive and crude sensation experienced as invasive, as a foreign element to be driven off with a gesture. The subject feels a real threat and the need to react immediately to it. In many rage reactions an outside observer would not know wherein lies the threat, so he or she recalls the intimate and idiosyncratic aspects of the danger he or she sees in front of him or her.

Rage and even more so fury often cause shame, but we cannot say the same about hatred, which generally is more compatible with a sense of self consciousness. The theme of shame in relation to rage is the central aspect that I would like to discuss here. I advance my thesis: along the spectrum from the more instinctive and 'physical' to the more 'psychic', rage comes from a sense of unconscious shame rather than felt in the clarity of consciousness. When I say shame, I mean the conscious or unconscious feeling of not being recognized, even being rejected and deprived of our dignity to exist. On the contrary, however, a rageful reaction can produce even more shame. This is the vicious circle in which the subject is caught. What is the paradoxical gain of a pathological rageful reaction? It is a temporary income, consisting in the recovery of a vain ability to decide and act, to be intended not as one among the many attributes of the ego, but as its essential essence, on the equivalent psychic plane as biological survival. In the immediate, the reaction decreases shame. (160)

The point that I suggest we consider is that even in the case of displays of rage as a short circuit or as instinctive, it is difficult, when we refer to human beings, not to place rage in a context of meaning. There is always a level at which the negative stirring that triggers the reaction of rage is seen as a 'no', or a non-recognition by an object; an object to which the subject is bound by a double dependency. I say 'double', following the teaching of Winnicott, extending the area of application of his concept to adults, because what is reactivated in rage is a state of being that belonged to the infant, such that it may recur in any moment. The more the infantile experience of impotence is called forth, which somehow we all continue to carry inside us, the more the rageful protest is sudden and violent. We understand that, for what concerns us as analysts, only humans (the inhabitants of the land of the 'no', as Rilke says) can experience this rage.

10.1   Characters who express rage

In order to identify the characteristics and psychological dynamics of rage, it can be helpful to use some figures taken from literature and cinema. The reason for this is not simply rhetorical nor purely occasional but rather because these characters are often evoked in the analytic dialog. They represent sensitive indicators of the emotional vortex of the analytic field, as well as the beginnings of their transformations or formations. These fictional characters, though sometimes taken from real life, belong to the ranks of the gods and demons of our modern mythology. Second, turning to literature can let us discover new ways to look at a well-known phenomenon, as if for the first time.

Turning again to rage, every age has felt the need to portray this emotion, which is so common and significant. It is not a coincidence – as we will see later – that the *Iliad*, the most beautiful book ever written, starts with the purpose of dealing with the 'ruinous' rage of Achilles.

Daily, in my clinical work, I use these characters, who are the 'most exemplary' among the many who can appear on a stage, evoked by the patient or myself, to give a meaning to the emotion of rage, rage which is either recounted by the patient or directly lived in the present of the session. These characters are always useful for writing the analytical 'novel', and may sometimes become part of a shared dialect. For both the analytic dyad and the patient, they promote a new ability to contain anxieties that at another time would trigger a curt answer. If, in general, in order to heal, there is nothing better to offer to the patient than a happy metaphor (Civitarese and Ferro, 2015), the character itself can be considered a metaphor, a small poetic creation or a micro-dream that we can use whenever we need to. Always different, depending on the context, and always available, a character is a mirror in which to reflect, and therefore to put a potentially explosive situation into perspective, like having pot holders to remove a hot pan from the flame without burning your fingers.

10.1.1 The lipless

The extreme point of rage is represented in the media today by the recurrent serial killer movies, from *The Silence of the Lambs* to *Red Dragon*, and to other widely distributed television series. The collective imagination is populated by people who have suffered trauma such that they are encouraged to turn it into extreme violence. Through their actions they seek to get revenge, regain a sense of self-esteem, and maintain a link with the object by identifying themselves with the aggressor.

Also in considering more cultured cinema, it is not by chance that the most acclaimed contemporary artists are all authors of cruelty: I think of Lars Von Trier, Michael Haneke, Shinya Tsukamoto, Kim Ki-Duk, etc.

In fact the figure of the greatest serial killer of all time comes to us from the first 'novel' of History, from the *Iliad*, and the myth that inspired it. In the myth, Achilles commits rape, necrophilia, cannibalism, and cruelty that go far beyond what would be justified by war. The scene in Homer's poem where Achilles drags Hector's body around Patroclus' funeral pyre for twelve days is a hyperbole of his unquenchable thirst for revenge.

According to variants of the myth, the traumas suffered by Achilles have pre-natal and perinatal origin. After Achilles' birth, having conceived Achilles as a result of a rape, his mother, Thetis, is (unfortunately) about to make him immortal by submerging him in flames. Stopped by Achilles' father, Peleus, she throws the child aside and then leaves him alone. The name Achilles, from the Greek 'achos', or from 'a' and 'kheile', means 'lipless', because he never suckled at his mother's breast. According to Delia (2004), an 'Achilles complex', a mixture of murderous impulses, both conscious and unconscious, is the hidden core of most 'visible' Oedipus complexes.

When Achilles later becomes enraged with Agamemnon, who took away his favorite slave, he uses the schizoid defense of isolation to avoid giving free rein to his destructive rage.

10.1.2 The time of the decision

Exemplary Crimes is the title of a book by Max Aub, written in 1957 but published years later. As to its literary genre, we would consider it black humor. The main characters, who are different in each of these short stories, commit the crimes which we all occasionally fantasize about in our daily lives but of course do not play out. Aub's vignettes also exemplify the dynamics of rage. They show, for example, the paroxysm (the word translates the Greek παροξυσμός, which means 'irritation, exasperation') leading to the violent act, and the feeling of frustration and humiliation that often comes first. What stands out in these very short stories is the point at which there is a 'decision' to act, the invariably lightening-fast trigger, even if sometimes preceded by a long, obsessive rumination. At one point, the measure of endurance is fulfilled and the violent impulse occurs. But this point at which the decision is made, which I shall explain later, is automatic, almost like an epileptic attack, and is the very essence of the enraged reaction. Here are some examples:

TAKING ACTION   Tab 342
Surname and name of the patient: Agrasoto Luisa. Age: 24. Place of birth: Veracruz.
Diagnosis: Skin rash of presumably polibacillare origin.
Care: Two million units of penicillin.
Result: Nothing
Observations: unique case, refractory. No precedents.

After the fifteenth day it started to bother me. The diagnosis was clear, there could be no doubt. After the failure of penicillin, I tried all sorts of medicines in vain: I did not know what to do. I squeezed my brain, for weeks and weeks, until I administered a dose of potassium cyanide. Patience, even with patients, has its limits. (73)
It was the seventh time that she made me copy that letter. I have my diploma, have a typist top degree. Once because I had not started at the top; another time because I had changed a 'then' to a 'therefore', another time a V instead of a B, another one because he added a paragraph, other times I do not know why, the fact is I had to rewrite it seven times. And when I brought it to him, he looked at me with those eyes of a hypocritical administrative director and started all over again:

– Look, Miss . . .

Do not let him finish. We should to have more respect for workers.

Seriously, I thought they would never have discovered it. Yes, he was my best friend. There's no doubt about that, and I was his best friend. But recently I could not take it anymore: he guessed what I thought. There was no way to escape. Sometimes he told me what flashed through my mind even before it had been in my thoughts. It was like living naked. I organized everything well, but evidently I left the body too close to the road.

We can see that in all three cases there is as a trigger moment, a narcissistic injury to the protagonist's feeling of self-esteem; most evidently in the cases of the doctor and the typist, but also in the third story, which has in the foreground a suspicion that his friend could read thoughts that put him in a bad light.

10.1.3   Green with rage

The Hulk, the comic book character of Stan Lee and Jack Kirby, is the alter ego of a scientist, Robert Bruce Banner, who has a doubly traumatic history. During his childhood his father murdered his mother. Then, as an adult, he was hit by a burst of gamma rays while performing an experiment in a secret military laboratory. When he becomes enraged, and that often happens, the Hulk swells and rips his clothes and gives himself over to uncontrolled violence. So he is a striking example of uncontrollable rage. The Hulk's angry color, in addition to his gigantic size and beastly expression, emphasizes in a concrete way how a crisis of rage can be achieved through a deep involvement of the body, after which the body needs a certain period to return to human features.

For years the Hulk has been the character that I use with Mario to explain his explosions of rage, often badly controlled, which affect the positive things he has built into loving relationships and work. The key aspect of the 'character' the Hulk was the simplicity and immediate utility of the 'model' as an 'as needed' device to contain the rage both in therapy and in daily life, in addition to its quality in a general aesthetic sense. I mean that these forms or metaphors not only free us from something annoying but also bear with them a sort of pleasure prize. Perhaps any aesthetic pleasure is just a kind of negative pleasure.

10.1.4   The sense of justice

With Julius, however, the happier metaphor that we found to describe his problem, in order to contain and digest his rage, was Michael Kohlhaas (K.), the character invented by Heinrich Von Kleist and that impressed Kafka so deeply ('it's a true story that I read with amazement every time,'). K. is a particular kind of enraged person; he is enraged due to his excessive sense of justice. Kleist wrote that this was due to his rigorous sense of justice, 'as the scales of a goldsmith'. This rage of K. is a glaring example of narcissistic rage. In the psychoanalytic literature he is in fact similar to Ahab, a character for whom the shortage of feeling that he exists becomes a metaphor in the amputation of a body part. Here you can see how easily rage can feed feelings of revenge, querulousness, paranoia, and, as a character trait, touchiness.

Because he has been wronged by a local squire – the kidnapping and torture of some horses – K. turns gradually into a kind of exterminating angel and then into a real demon. At the head of a rebel army, he puts fire and sword to country until the tragic outcome. In his absolute thirst for revenge, K. defines himself as free from the empire, devoted only to God, and issues delirious proclamations to the world. It is an apocalyptic time of wrath and usurpation. The increasingly numerous fires that flare up allegorize K.'s achievement for blindness of reason and the explosion of his madness. The first signs of this explosion of his rage are wisely demonstrated in the text. Like Hitchcock, in fact, Kleist demonstrates a keen ability to generate anxiety in a suspenseful PARANOID feeling. As K. begins to feel "anxiety most odious", he has "dark feelings" or "gloomy forebodings", "his heart always inclined to the more dire predictions". Several times we come close to a possible solution to his conflict, but instead we witness its most devastating resumption. The reader's attention is captivated by a narrative progression of awesome effectiveness.

10.1.5   The self-feeding effect

Similarly to Kohlhaas, we are struck by *A Cup of Rage* by Raduan Nassar (2016), a short novel published in 1978 which immediately garnered international success, and which has a compelling and swirling progression. Even more than Kleist's story, this is an illustration of an aspect that is often inherent to rage: its self-sustainment. A reaction of rage, triggered by trivial reasons, may also become progressively more intense without any apparent reason – as happens in Kohlhaas – with a sort of self-energizing effect, as with a faulty engine that gets revved without fuel injection. The increase itself in speed nurtures the sentiment of rage. It is as if the repressed rage and impulses foreign to most triggering stimuli have the opportunity to escape through an open channel.

In a long monologue, which progressively becomes a furious invective, the protagonist, a man whose name is not revealed, is talking to a woman, for whom he feels an intense erotic passion, and who appears in the first pages of the story and reappears only at the end. The narrative vertigo here is not given so much from the plot that is carried out but rather, as in certain Dostoevsky characters, by a sort of inexorable necessity of the character to get far into his own psychological depths. The reason that triggers the outburst is quite superficial:

> but my eyes were suddenly led, and when these things happen you never really know what devil's at work, and, in spite of the mist, I see this: a gap in my edge, oh misery, I press my finger into the ashtray, get burnt, uncomprehending she asked me "what is it?", but without replying I had threw myself, half tripped down the stairs (Bingo was already on the a patio, waiting for me, electrified) and she followed me, almost screaming "but what it is?", and Dona Mariana had come running from the kitchen with the commotion, her eyes wide behind her thick lenses, dumbstruck at the top of the stairs, a pot and cloth in her hands, but I didn't see anything, I left the two of them behind and hurtled over, out of my mind, and when I got close I couldn't bear what I saw "fuck leaf-cutter ants", and the I screamed even more loudly "bloody fucking leaf-cutter fucking ants", as I saw whole handbreadths of hedge had been gnawed away, saw whole handbreadths of earth covered

with little leaves, you need to have farming blood in your veins to know what this spells, I was rigid as I surveyed the damage, I was livid about the gap, and cold only think the privet shouldn't be their feast, such hard work just for the leaf-cutters to set their maws to it, and in a flash I rushed, armed, to the neighbouring plot, and straight away found the trail that would lead me to their colony, following the path concealed in the high grass, I who at this hour would surprise them in their hideaway – those who'd been so active all night with the cutting and harvesting, and without delay, trembling and foaming, I find it and already holding the bucket in my hand I pour a double dose of poison into each anthill, with a malice that only I know for what it is because only I know what I feel, livid with these wonderfully orderly ants, livid with their model of efficiency, livid with how fucking organized they are.

(pp. 17–8)

she was waiting for me With this look, just unbelievable, that made me want to give her a slap, and as that weren't enough she also said, "it's not a big deal, especially for a rational little boy like you", and I have to admit that "little boy" was a kick in the shins, that was tough, even more so because of how she said it, for it contained that posed casualness she put in everything, which in this case was something like distancing herself, as if this must necessarily establish how sensible she her comment was, and this only served to make me even more angry, "right" I said to myself as if I were saying "now's the time", and I getting hung up on that "boy" could perfectly well have said to her, "time had taken more of a toll in me" (although she wouldn't have understood what advantage I drew from this), and could also have given her an earful for essentially boring use of a nasty irony, not that I nurture a boiling hunger for harsh words, a bent towards the tragic, it was neither that nor the opposite, but it would do her good, she who saw in her irony the exercise of high intelligence, if I were to sensibly remind her that irony and a solid character don't mix, and I could have said many other things in reply to the comment, because it was easy to see, half-revealed, half-hidden, multiple accusations and plants, or the perhaps even stronger accusation that I didn't act at the same temperature in bed (that is, with the same ardour that I had in exterminating the ants).

(pp. 20–1)

In a sense the psychological knot of the novel can be generalized: rage always has to do with an 'erotic love'; and sometimes with an expression of sadism as an erotic form of hatred. The energy shift used in the extermination of the ants that have created a gap in the hedge (in the ego? In the sense of self-esteem?) of its opposite, that is, insufficient loving energy, shows how a source of rage can be the seductive power of the object, as well as the desperate need to escape from his overpowering power.

10.1.6 Full moon

Sonia gets to my office fifteen minutes late. Until now I have always thought of her as a bit of a 'boring' patient. It seemed to me that emotions did not circulate here with her. It was all flat. She tells me today that she spent a really bad weekend and that soon she will get her period and that there is a full moon. The full moon affects so much here. She marked every full moon on her calendar. She then talked about her husband. Moments of rage and quarreling alternate with times when they look good together and they are very close. But he often gets drunk or smokes weed. She points it out to him and then the screaming and fighting begin again. But then he has kind thoughts, offers flowers, gives her fragrances, helps her in the house. Soon after, though, Sonia remarked again that when she hugs him, in general she does not feel anything for him, that she does not smile and does not care about the housework. Her husband sees her as unhappy, that she is always playing with her cell phone. She turns the observation against him. It is unclear which of the two is most unhappy. In the background there is a conflict: whether or not to have a child. If a child came (the new/Messianic idea?), Sonia is afraid that he might leave, but her husband is also concerned that once the baby's born, she may leave him.

Listening to them I think they are a couple who are stuck and unable to make sense of what is happening. I can feel a lot of rage in the air, but also a lot of attraction. They are caught in a relation that has sadomasochistic overtones. Each is dangerous for the other, but they cannot leave. They would like to change, but they're terrified that something new can bring them to destruction. Meanwhile I think, with some surprise, that I was wrong when I said that there were not many emotions. After the stage entrance of the wolf-woman I started to get interested in Sonia in a new way. 'When there's a full moon' the frustrated wife turns unexpectedly into a dangerous animal who 'bites into' the session by coming in late; and that portrays me as a husband who seems only to be able to run after her and suggest as the solution a more or less toxic dependence and immobility (boredom?). After all, I thought, I come from the only Italian region where wolves and bears still live in the mountains, and there is a certain wildness in its inhabitants, that is mine. But overall, I think, I have some familiarity with these places and with the famous sheepdogs that are not afraid of wolves.

The point is this: how to transform the wolf into a sheep dog? How to preserve the fragile aspects of the patient's psyche and even the analysis from the destructiveness of wolf-emotion? The full moon, the association with rage and aggression by the she-wolf and then with my homeland (here, the analysis) helps me to return to the dream of the session that had until then been treated as real and due to outside reality (her husband, etc.). From this comes a new ability to contain Sonia's rage as an emotion that concerns us too. The full moon then becomes the figure of the analyst's receptivity, as someone who can understand unconscious speech. Like that special ability, it fascinates and lightens. Precisely because it is weak, also it highlights things we would rather not see, things that we could not see if we projected on it the glare of a rationality without insight.

The next session Sonia is late again and she arrives at the office with coffee. She tells me about one of her students whose mother forgot to pick her up (again, I retreat into my 'bored' detachment and loneliness), and says that they waited together, and that's why she's late. She added that she had a terrible headache. I connect the two and I tell myself that perhaps what blocks the thinking is the fear of separation and the fact of not being in tune. Sonia continues to speak to me of her husband and of her rage. She mentions an episode in which he slammed down his phone, which to me represents an allegory of a violent action as meaning both the impossibility of thinking and also a way to discharge tension, vomiting words in the session. Then followed, as always, a quarrel, tears, and then reconciliation. Significantly, Sonia said: "On the other hand, if I did not quarrel with him, I would lose myself and my life."

For this, I think, then, there is need for 'coffee' rage, something that excites and revives. What you see, in short, is that rage is both a symptom of the disease and the glue for the symptom itself. After every crisis, for a little time, rage works both as an insulator or a partner or another substitute. I now understand how hidden by or coincident with 'boredom' rage is both for her and for me – isn't boredom a form of minor depression? and doesn't depression look like an unconscious hatred directed at the object? But it blocks any possibility for the analysis to progress. But now a new idea – this very idea or interpretation – has managed to overcome the emotional barrier of boredom-symptom. The ability to dream the session was awakened by a resonance of the images offered by Sonia with something more mine, more private.

In the vignette I tried to portray the psychic transformation processes through which the creation of meaning is done in analysis. I mean a real emotional 'work' which for the analyst implies almost literally a 'pain' felt in his own flesh (and I use this term in the same way in which Bion writes 'suffer pain' or 'suffer pleasure': as synonymous with emotional experiencing, but also inevitably 'negative', namely, tied to a work of mourning). To listen, as Bion asks us to do, without memory, desire, or understanding, means that memory, desire and understanding are 'suffered' or, you could say, 'become'. It means getting involved in some way in the other, in the most intimate sphere of their loved ones.

10.1.7 Impotence

In *Rage and Helplessness*, one of his youthful stories, Gustave Flaubert attaches to rage the concept of powerlessness, implicitly suggesting a relationship of cause and effect between one and the other. Written in 1836, the short text anticipates the horror stories that Poe will publish a few years later. A man is buried alive. Waking after ecstatic dreams he is forced to realize his desperate condition and reacts angrily.

– Dying! Dying like this, without help, without mercy! Oh! No! I will exit this hell, I will get out of this grave. I've never seen this, I'm going crazy before dying from despair . . . Yeah, I'm about to die . . . Oh! Die! I will not see anything of what is happening in the world; the nature, the fields, the sky, the mountains, all that I am about to leave, I left it for ever! – He was twisting in his grave like a serpent in the clutches of a tiger.

He wept with rage, tore his hair, cursing life, so full of strength and health.

How many tears fell onto his hands! How many screams were thrown onto his grave! How many wrathful impulses struck the coffin! He took the napkin, tore it with his fingernails, tore it to pieces with his teeth; he needed something to break, to destroy with his own hands, he felt so crushed and without mercy, in the hands of fate.[. . .]

So he tore his hair, scratching his own face with his nails: – Do you think I'll get to pray to you in my last hour? Oh! I am too proud and too unfortunate, I'll not beg you, I hate you! Eternity? I deny it! Your paradise? Illusion! Your heavenly bliss? Illusion! Your hell? I challenge you! Eternity? You will find a skull here in my place in a few months.

Laughter was altering his face and tears choked his voice: – Bless me, o hand that crushes me! Embrace the executioner! Oh! If you can take human shape, come to the grave with me, you can bring the eternity that one day will devour you, that you can deliver to that anything in your same name. Come! Come! I can crush you, crush you between my grave and me, and eat your flesh! Do something tangible, so that, snickering, I'll break you to pieces!

His teeth chattered like the devil when it was won by Christ; He was furious, shook and rolled into the grave, cursing God with the screaming mouth and soul upset: – Where are you? Sky God, if you exist, come! Why do not you release me? If you exist, why this misfortune? What a pleasure to try to see me suffer? If I did not believe in you, it is because I was a wretch. Make me live, I will love you . . . if that's not up to you, well, do it, for you are all-powerful; do it, give me faith! . . . Why do you want me not to believe in you? Do you want me to suffer, to cry; shorten my sufferings, dry my tears!

(pp. 41–4)

It is hard to think of an image that gives a better idea of impotence. Obvious, but no less true, is that we can see the invective addressed to God (father, mother . . .) as a metaphor of the object relationship that produces this catastrophe. The rage is, according to what Flaubert suggests, like a snake writhing in the claws of the tiger – the tiger understood to be the animal whose tail, according to Bion, psychoanalysis sometimes succeeds in catching –. But what we can take from the tale? That at the bottom of the rage and its older sister, fury, there's a sense of death; and that the effective expression of rage implies an unbearable life of claustrophobia and choking.

10.1.8 Shame

In previous examples, shame has always been left in the background or recalled by other feelings. In Sophocles' *Ajax*, a character with whom one of my patients (Anna) used to identify, shame is emphasized. In Sophocles' tragedy, Ajax is the most heroic among the Greeks who took part in the Trojan war. After Achilles' death, it was Ajax who was to receive his weapons, with pride. Instead, they went to Ulysses. Ajax's rage, 'cholos', a rage due to failure, is so strong as to make him crazy. Then, with his mind confused by Athena, he butchers the livestock as a revenge upon the companion who betrayed him, and then commits suicide.

The rage of the Greek hero is so important as to have inspired one of the most famous scenes of world literature, a scene defined by Longinus, one of the most fulfilled examples of the sublime (the highest and greatest expression of every question). In the XIth poem of the Odyssey, when Ulysses visits Ajax in Hades, Ajax does not reply to him and retreats. His silence has so many meanings. Such a silence represents yet another figure, as with the one by Flaubert about claustrophobia. This silence represents the infantile impotence which is the core of rage: the silence of the lipless (referring to the myth of Achilles), beyond language itself, focusing on its uselessness.

The Human Torch

I went to play volleyball, which is something I used to be terrified of when I was a girl. *Every Saturday was a real trauma*, having to play matches against *strangers*. There was a time when I would have said no. But now . . . I feel changed. When I am with other people I am relaxed, different from usual, even extroverted. It was nice to tell my elder sister what I'm learning here, really satisfying . . . especially when I think of the relationship we have always had. A breach has opened, a space; to put it in legal terms, 'a precedent'. We talked about our parents' lack of affection for us and how we both tried to fill the *gaps*.

It seems that this is another game one can now play . . . without too much fear of strangers [one can leave the other without feeling bad] . . .

I felt appreciated for what I really am. . . . When I got a little upset because of my state of health, my mum told me about some episodes from my childhood. When I was small I used to fall ill easily, *my immune defenses were low*, so I was never taken outdoors. I remember the feeling of being a bit of a recluse at home, unable to do the things that others were doing . . . I had been given a Human Torch as a present, one of the Fantastic Four. One evening I began saying: 'Voio Omo-To'ciaa!' ('Wanna Human Torch'). I just started talking. My mum did not understand me and I got more and more angry. Then she would despair. When I was a child, and she had to go somewhere, she always did so in secret. I don't remember this. When she told me about it, the feeling of anguish I felt then came back. . . . This very probably had an influence on my *fear of loved ones going away*. That's why I become obsessive! She told me something else. I was always hungry and *she* didn't realize. She told me that I was always hungry as a child. I don't know, but when you're little, affection can also be interpreted in terms of food.

This story of the Human Torch has aroused my curiosity . . .

It's what I told you . . . when I got something new I had to take it to bed with me . . . I clearly remember the feeling of helplessness and my mother not understanding.

. . . And what did the Human Torch do?

One of the Fantastic Four was a woman, then there was another character, who was strong and whose flesh was made of stone (just between the two of us, that was my friend S.), then, the intellectual of the group, who was able to stretch his body, and this was my other friend A.; and me, the smallest, I was the Human Torch, the one who could generate flames. *His body caught fire and he could fly and became a superhero.* I was very fond of this character.

The woman?

She wasn't assigned to anybody. *There were no women among us.* Women were also somewhat looked down upon.

I try to reformulate the situation to myself. We have become a little alien to each other after the weekend. . . . The gap of separation. . . . It doesn't take much to make her feel bad . . . The mother who goes away in secret. . . . The female member of the Fantastic Four (the sessions?) is missing, and, as in the comic, has the power to become invisible. . . . She was back to being a little girl, lacking the words (*in-fans*) to ask for food/affection after two weeks of starvation over the Christmas holidays . . . the Human Torch . . . the fire that burns, consumes, suffocates with smoke (passions?) . . . but perhaps also light and heat.

A KILLER

"I am a potential killer! I took the scrubbing brush, covered it with toilet paper and attacked the spider on the wall. Bastard! He had to put himself right next to the switch of all places! I'm bad. And to think that I always keep the shutters closed. But where the f . . . did the spider come from?!? I thought it had popped out of the sewers. GOODNESS ME . . . ! What if in the next life I came back as a spider? I could have killed one of my ancestors! So, basically, this morning I wasted twenty minutes dealing with this spider, and I arrived late for work."

In other words: the risks of (symbolic) patricide or the pain of guilt. But the real killer in analysis is the negative reverie of the analyst (Civitarese, 2014).

I would like to mention a small but significant effect of *après-coup*. Rereading the last two lines I could not help but remove the brackets (oops!) from the bibliographic self-reference, and then suddenly, to my surprise, I found myself in the shoes of an analyst in a state of negative reverie: from 'the analyst (Civitarese, 2014)' to '*the analyst Civitarese*'. A small epiphany, with the unconscious speaking with the unmistakable ring of truth. It's a kind of *lived* confirmation – perhaps, as in this case, something that we already know, albeit only in the abstract – that enhances the analysis. It's the excitement, the unexpected spark that makes that something convincing. Naturally, this would be only the starting point of a process of interpretation that would then widen to take in progressively broader contexts.

COHIBA CIGARS

Stefano has accomplished something important in his life. He thanks me symbolically by giving me a cigar (I do not smoke) as we stand at the door about to say goodbye at the end of the session. (He must have read somewhere that Freud lit up a cigar when he felt he had made progress with a patient.) He tells me it's top of the range: "Apparently it's the brand of cigar Fidel Castro smokes." At that moment I'm very pleased. I accept the gift. Now that I am on my own alone, I read the label on the box containing the precious cigar: "Smoking clogs the arteries and causes heart attacks and strokes." My goodness! A shiver runs down my spine. I immediately realize the ambivalence of the gift. Yet it is only months later, finding myself holding the cigar again (which for some time I avoided smoking), that I grasp the reference to the castration suffered by Stefano as a result of his father's dictatorial education.

Stefano's gift could be quite rightfully interpreted as the expression of an intense transference. But it could also signify the automatic and *mutual* hatred we feel when the session ends, the stroke the field suffers each time: FIDEL(ITY), in other words a setting one can have faith in, that is stable and consistent, but that also involves separations and is therefore inevitably also CASTR(O)ATING!

10.1.9 Slow rage and the art of exaggeration

The flower of my anger grows wild.

Thomas Bernhard

No one better than Bernhard explained the effects of slow rage, rage that gnaws at the liver or consumes one excruciatingly. His characters hate Austria, hate each other, and hate themselves, which is expressed in the vivid and sarcastic style, "focused on provoking . . . and following a prose similar to a spiral, with continuous and obsessive repetition, like a rope tightening around the neck of the victim, sometimes very close to the taste of hyperbole" (Latin, 2007, pp. 36–7); from this "art of exaggeration (Übertreibungskunst)" you need to tolerate the existence, to make it possible. Have we not said many times that there is always something exaggerated in pathological rage? And isn't the rope tightening around the neck another image of the rage that smothers, like that of the Flaubert's man buried alive? 'We hear' the voice of Bernhard in a famous passage of the Ancient Masters, where he becomes furious and ungenerous with Heidegger:

Heidegger, like Stifter, is a reading pudding, tasteless but easy to digest, for the average German soul. With his philosophical spirit, Heidegger has as little to do as Stifter with literature – in relation to philosophy and literature Heidegger and Stifter are worth virtually nothing, even if I place Stiffer a little higher than Heidegger, whom I have always found repellent, because everything in Heidegger has always disgusted me, not just the night-cap on his head or the hand-made winter bloomers hung out on the stove that he used to fire up in Todtnauenberg, not just his homemade walking stick from the Black Forest, but also his homemade philosophy of the Black Forest, everything in this tragicomic man has always disgusted me, every thought of him has always profoundly repelled me; it was enough to know a line of Heidegger to be disgusted, but only when I read it I realized what Reger said; I always had the feeling that Heidegger was a charlatan, who all his life has done nothing but take advantage of all that was around him, and exploiting everything taking a sunbath in Todtnauenberg. If I think that even very smart people have become duped by Heidegger and even one of my best friends has written a doctoral thesis on Heidegger and that it has also been written seriously, I feel sick.

Heidegger – in whose footsteps war and post-war generations have moved, overwhelming him with stupid and disgusting doctoral theses when he was still alive – I see him still sitting on the bench in front of his house in the Black Forest next to his wife, who, in her perverse enthusiasm for knitting, working continuously to make winter socks with wool that she sheared from their Heidegger sheep. Heidegger, I can not see him but sitting on the bench in front of his house in the Black Forest, and beside him I see his wife who was completely subjugated all life long, and she worked all the time at socks, and crocheted all his caps, making bread, sheets, and even sandals.

(Kindle, pos. 780–92)

Getting angry is always an exaggeration. Etymologically inherent in it is the idea of 'amassing, making bank', 'a grammar of the defense', but in exaggeration, as a caricature for facial expression, identifies some truth and some sense. The same Bernhard gives an explanation through his protagonist's mouth: to make things more comprehensible, he explained, you have to overdo it, "only the exaggeration gives visible form to things." "[T]he art of exaggeration, is more than anything, the secret of the spirit."

10.2   Shame as the photo-like negative of rage

Until now we have developed these fundamental characteristics of the emotion of rage: the proximity to hatred and fury, the massive psychophysical mobilization (muscle tension, gastrointestinal reactions, increased heart rate and blood pressure), the contraction of time, the effect of self-supply, the experience of helplessness, the sense of shame that follows the uncontrolled reaction of rage. But let us now see if we can relate these diffuse elements, focusing on what we can consider the opposite of rage, that is, the unconscious shame linked to the threat to narcissism or an opened narcissistic wound.

Putting together the pieces of our discussion, we see that at the origin of rage there is never a purely material frustration, as might be suggested by the distinction between primary or pre-cultural emotions and cultural emotions. In such a case it would be an almost instinctive reaction. But looking at it in another way is not always immediate. We are used to taking psychic reality into account and yet the less 'psychic' appearance of rage tends at times to let us overlook it. Just look, as we have seen, at how when someone becomes enraged, the reason is often absolutely futile. People take offense over nothing, and on a completely disproportionate scale relative to the offense. The fact is that others do not see the threat that whoever gets angry sees quite clearly, and which is real, even if only in the mind of the subject. This aspect well captures the touchiness (and paranoia, with all its malignant implication), a form of chronic rage, inherent in which is the futility of the reasons for the rage.

So the game must be different: it must be that even seemingly insignificant events jeopardize the conscious and unconscious social image – but mostly unconscious, if we want to explain the disproportion of the rage response in certain situations – the subject, and his or her being or not being part of the social forum. After all, what triggers rage if not a radical signal from the other: "You're not like me, you are different, the two of us – we have nothing in common." The common ground of co-feeling that lays the foundations for the pre-reflective and pre-logical horizon of humanity is denied (deleted).

In this sense rage seeks to change a negative situation in different ways, either by removing it (concretely, or even in the sense of the specifically psychoanalytic Italian term 'rimuovere', i.e. 'to repress') or by sending out a signal and asking for help. As Freud says in the *Project*, it is the mother who carries out the function of removing harmful stimuli, a feature which comes before removal. But later, every obstacle the subject meets will always be as if there were still someone – and sometimes there also has to be – to put away the pain, as if the preconception or memory of this object's function should never cease.

But then again, what is at stake? To a highly variable degree, what is at stake is the sense of being of the subject. This interpretation, that rage and the shame connected to it, which is certainly the most social of all emotions – that which, as Freud said in his *Interpretation of Dreams*, was born at the expulsion from Eden; or, at the passage from animal to human – is based on a conception of human beings not as isolated subjects with a locked consciousness, and establishes the essence of what it means to be human, in what such a philosopher as Heidegger calls being-there, or what Bion's formulates as the 'proto' system. Ultimately it is based on language as what is made possible by a co-feeling and communication, unconscious in nature, both pre-verbal and verbal, which in turn perpetuates this opportunity creatively. Language is founded a horizon of meaning that precedes us, and in which we are all inevitably immersed, and it is an emanation. However, sharing this horizon is still not enough. To be human, or rather subjects, we have strong roots in this common ground, and also must reclaim our unfathomable uniqueness, our destiny of separate individuals. Shame is the most sensitive thermometer that measures the degree of rootedness in this common ground. Anyone can react angrily to a given stimulus if he or she perceives that the roots of his or her humanity are in danger. However, if he or she reacts too easily with rage, he or she demonstrates the fragility of these roots. There are indeed people who are the 'poorest in existence', in the sense that they have never been allowed the feeling that they could exist for someone simply for what they are. Instead, they often received the message that they could not exist, or would only be allowed to exist if they confirmed the expectations of others and gave up being themselves.

If we wanted to sum it up all in a formula, we could say that *rage is directly proportional to shame, and that shame is sensitive and a negative index of existence.* From the psychological point of view, a poverty of a world or existence can only result from deficient ego-building in parental relationships.

To grasp the essence of rage, a key point to consider is temporality: time contracts in an infinitesimal fraction of a second. Suddenly you cannot wait, cannot be patient. Time persecutes. The decision, as we said, is only apparent. In fact, the reaction is automatic. But what is the sense of time, and in a similar way, space (and in fact we could agree to combine them into a notion of 'spacing'), if not the introjection of the quality of the encounter with the object? Time and human space are never the time and 'pure' space of animals, but rather are born from the shock that imprint stimuli upon the senses, an imagined dream space that is a product of words.

Now, it is true that sometimes we use the expression 'dying of boredom', which is equivalent to having internalized the 'depressive' object; the temporality that triggers the rage reaction is far more threatening. Becoming enraged means to decide, in the sense of 'cutting off'. No less than boredom, rage reveals the relationship we have with temporality and in particular with the temporality of meeting with the other (the primary object). In boredom, time expands so unbearably; in rage it shrinks, equally intolerably. In the case of boredom, the subject tries to 'kill' time, in the case of rage, to revitalize it, to return to a state of 'patience'.

Therefore it can be said that shame is the negative of rage. A reaction of rage has the sense to avoid or stanch a narcissistic bleeding that is perceived as a vital danger. In extreme cases, sometimes with extreme bursts of violence, a rage reaction to a situation means stanching the hemorrhaging. As they again become able to decide and act, subjects regain to their own eyes (in fact to those of the Other), a minimal feeling of being beloved. They momentarily exit the helplessness of being 'buried alive'. As Fonagy (2004) writes, "the sign of a self starved of love is shame".

Unmentalised shame is not an 'as if' experience. It is tantamount to the destruction of the self. It would not be an exaggeration to label this emotion 'ego destructive shame'. The coherence of the self representation, identity itself, is under attack. . . . The shame concerns being treated as a physical object in the very context where special personal recognition is expected. Unbearable shame is generated through the incongruity of having one's humanity negated, exactly when one is legitimately expecting to be cherished. Violence or the threat of violence to the body is literally soul-destroying because it is the ultimate way of communicating the absence of love by the person inflicting the violence, from whom understanding is expected. As Freud (1914) taught us, the self is sustained by the love of the object so that it can become self-love; the sign of a self starved of love is shame, just as cold is an indication of an absence of heat (Gilligan, 1997). And just like cold, shame, while painful as an acute experience, when intense and severe is experienced as a feeling of numbness or deadness.

In certain contexts, Fonagy suggests, an act of extreme violence could make sense of re-establishing, perversely, a rudimentary function of mentalizing (mentalizing function). The violent act is not at all blind to that effect. Rather it represents a desperate attempt to defend a fragile self from an 'onslaught' of shame. "In this sense violence is a gesture of hope, a wish for a new beginning, even if in reality it is usually just a tragic end" (2004, p. 42).

What is the difference between conscious shame and rage? Why does an event arouse in one a feeling of shame, while in another it may have triggered rage? Rage is shame that we do not know we are experiencing or that we cannot bear. And whoever killed himself for shame? After all, the moment when you take away life is an expression of rage, unconsciously returning the violence of the group or object which has shaken you back to its sender: "You do not want me to exist" becomes "I do not want you to exist."

10.3 Curing rage

Rage is ubiquitous in our lives and in clinical work. Patients get upset and make us angry. There is no therapy in which, sooner or later, one fails speak of about angry reactions, from minimal to severe. In each clinical vignette, at some point, there is a description or reference to motions or expressions of rage. However, in certain psychopathological quarters, rage is the main character; in particular, this is a constant in borderline disorder.

In the clinical consideration of a personality such as the character of Achilles and the myth in which he is featured, it may help us to understand a patient who is dominated by violent impulses toward self and others, and, in the transference, the analyst. In such cases the patient feels he or she has had a sadistic mother or a father, and projects this attitude onto the analyst. Even the slightest failure seems to be confirmation of the inadequacy and negligence of the object and revives a narcissistic rage. There may be an active attitude of subtle provocation. The patient attempts to put his or her overwhelming rage onto the analyst, in hopes that he or she will be able to transform it into something more manageable. The unquenchable thirst for existence renders other demands impossible, which therefore fuels the frustration. The analyst, in turn, lives in response to these very intense negative emotions. He or she may be tempted by the rejection because he cannot contain his hatred for the patient, possibly aborting the analysis; or, he or she can be tempted by the solution of reassuring the patient (and himself) and giving him (and himself) an appreciation that has a short-circuiting quality. Both roads have proven inconclusive and sometimes even harmful. The first for obvious reasons, the latter because it's just a defensive maneuver devoid of authenticity: denying hate, the analyst also denies love and in so doing may encourage a "malignant form of dependence" (Ornstein, 1998, p. 58, n.).

In everyday life, a similar patient could live quite isolated and may occasionally give vent to his or her limited tension with rage or thrusting him or herself into ephemeral, sadomasochistic relationships. If serial killers are rare it is because most of these borderline patients still reach the oedipal phase of development and are able more or less efficiently to use guilt as a brake for their impulses. The fact remains that the patient-Achilles has imprinted in his flesh the belief that someone has actually tried to kill him, along with a lust for revenge.

With these people it is important always to keep in mind that the most extreme rage is real agony that signals an emergency. However, you should also keep in mind that you don't have to let yourself get too involved, otherwise you will find yourself in a negative relationship for both patient and analyst, in a perverse relationship wherein you are either the abuser or the abused. Nor should you think that, at least in the most severe cases, you can consider analysis alone as enough.

In a wider context than that of the consulting room, we might say that our society encourages this kind of suffering. If it is true that we live in a culture of narcissism, then it is also true that we live in a culture of rage (Bonime, 1976). A more fragile narcissism is more easily inclined towards reactions of rage. Privations that may not have seemed so initially are more easily perceived as frustrating. In combination with this fragility, a loss in society of stable models for identification, the now-volatile nature of our identities, and the drive to be consumers, lead to a feeling of self-worth that depends on the amount of goods the individual may acquire and the consumption of which the individual is capable.

For those who feel an outcast compared to this new hierarchy of values, rage itself can take on a paradoxical sense of identity, as in some of John Fante's likable characters. The total commitment to the principles of modern society, to its one-dimensional nature, is reversed into the opposite. The reversal may be embodied in a character and play shades in intimacy, or it may push them to join social or ideological proposals that challenge the current system. Sometimes the results can also be very creative politically or artistically. For example, so it was in the 1950s and 1960s for the generation of young novelists and playwrights who called themselves 'angry', including John Osborne, Kingsley Amis, and Harold Pinter.

Again, it is important to catch the function of adaptation and strengthening of self-esteem that can hold a personality together by a chronic feeling of rage. This makes us realize the fixity of these structures of personality. There are patients who will say that they only really feel themselves when they are angry, or will have a superficially self-exculpatory attitude, or even be smug about their sadistic impulses, even when fatally acted upon against others, especially those to whom they are linked by bonds of affection. The reason is that they feel they have a right to some form of compensation from others. Such personalities can be very successful, but do not realize that their triumphal march takes place in the ruins of affective failures. The side effect of an identity founded on rage is that it can easily fade into paranoia. It is in the paranoia that we can now see that the fear of being completely annihilated reveals itself.

Finally, the issue of rage is interwoven with the nature of aggression, which, as we know, marks an important theoretical bifurcation in psychoanalysis: between those who argue that aggression is primary and inborn, maybe bringing it back to the death drive, and those who believe that it is always the response to frustration.

The first is the position of the classical Freudian psychoanalysis, the second is proper, among others, to the theorists of self psychology from Kohut onwards (which, however, distinguish between an aggressiveness in the service of self-affirmation, and destructive aggression, which arises from narcissistic rage). Ego psychology, object relations theory, self psychology, and Bion's theory of the analytical field would offer different visions and argue consequently different analytical techniques.

According to the classical approach, instinctual aggression serves to achieve the goal of pleasure, but in certain cases is not justified.

For Kohut, narcissistic rage it is quite different from the rage that arises from frustration and the subject's need to be assertive. The first would be the result of very early trauma and a fragmented self or a self threatened with fragmentation. From here arises the persistent need for revenge. According to self psychology, all forms of destructive aggression come from narcissistic rage. This rage may take the form of sadistic attacks, masochistic behaviors, and paranoid attitudes: "haughty withdrawal, writing people off, holding grudges, collecting injustices as well as self-recriminations, depression, self-cutting, and suicidal threats" (Ornstein, 1998, p. 56).

The first case (instinctual aggression) deals with letting patient understand the unconscious meaning of his or her aggressive reactions (Jones, 1999), in the second (rage as stemming from a narcissistic injury) re-equilibrating the narcissistic balance and sense of self-cohesion, and raising the ability for the subject to withstand empathic failures (according to the key words of Kohut: "to stay within the patient's subjective world"; E. & M. Shane, 1998, p. 129).

It is so important to differentiate when a rage reaction is the right answer to an unjustified deprivation, when it can be part of an ability to assert oneself and to impose oneself, and when it arises from the 'injured Achilles'. In certain cases, an expression of rage by a patient is only a sign that he or she is becoming capable of entering into contact with unconscious rage, or that he or she is starting to know how to be assertive, and then corresponds to psychic growth. In managing the therapy, it is important to be permeable to the projective identifications of patients; to 'empower' them to experience the entire range of possible emotions and feelings, neither excluding nor counteracting hatred; to be firm with respect to the more subtle manipulations; and to avoid superficial attitudes and unnecessary reassurance.

An issue on which Waiess focused (1998) is not to confront the patient too much with the meaning of his or her rage in relationships. This may result from his or her intolerance of the patient's rage in the transference. By doing so, the analyst would not realize that the patient needs not to divest him or herself of his rage too soon, which assures a constraint object and supports, however precariously, the self. If premature, the confrontation to which the analyst exposes the patient to has the effect of depleting the sense of self and forcing him or her to suffer what unconsciously is lived as a new separation from the object. For a long time, however, he or she might need to feed 'the illusion of a non-traumatic relationship with the object' (ibid., p. 294). The same thing will also happen if the analyst's intentions are to push him or her to feel rage toward those who make him or her suffer or made him or her suffer in the past. In a field perspective it would also mean not seeing the 'appropriate' meanings, that may exist in the relationship with the analyst, who arouses the rage. If it becomes chronic, the unconscious shame can lead to mental states that last for some time and that are dominated by a thirst for revenge (Lansky, 2007).

References

Bonime, W. (1976). Rage as a Basis for a Sense of Self. *J. Amer. Acad. Psychoanal.*, 4:7–12.
Civitarese, G. (2014). *Truth and the Unconscious in Psychoanalysis*. London: Routledge, 2016.
Civitarese, G. and Ferro, A. (2015). *The Analytic Field and Its Transformation*. London: Klarnac Books.
Delia, D. (2004). The Achilles Complex: Preoedipal Trauma, Rage, and Repetition. *Psychoanal. Rev.*, 91:179–99.
Fonagy, P. (2004). The Developmental Roots of Violence in the Failure of Mentalization. In F. Pfäfflin and G. Adshead (Eds.), *A Matter of Security: The Application of Attachment Theory to Forensic Psychiatry and Psychotherapy*. London: Jessica Kingsley Publishers, pp. 13–56.
Freud, S. (1914). On Narcissism: An Introduction. In J. Strachey et al. (Trans.), *The Standard Edition of the Complete Psychological Works of Sigmund Freud*. London: Hogarth Press.
Gilligan, J. (1997). *Violence: Reflections on a National Epidemic*. New York: Vintage Books.
Jones, A. (1999). Ornstein, Anna. 'The Fate of Narcissistic Rage in Psychotherapy'. *Psychoanal. Inq.*, 1998, 18, 1:59–70. *J. Anal. Psychol.*, 44:423–5.
Lansky, M.R. (2007). Unbearable Shame, Splitting, and Forgiveness in the Resolution of Vengefulness. *J. Amer. Psychoanal. Assn.*, 55:571–93.
Latini, M. (2007). Estinzione e violenza. Il carattere distruttivo nell'opera di Thomas Bernhard. In V. Rasini (a cura di), *Aggressività. Un'indagine polifonica*. Milano: Mimesis, pp. 35–47.
Nassar, R. (2016). *A Cup of Rage*. London: Penguin.
Ornstein, A. (1998). Response to the Discussants: The Fate of Narcissistic Rage in Psychotherapy. *Psychoanal. Inq.*, 18:107–19.
Shane, E. and Shane, M. (1998). The Fate of Narcissistic Rage in Psychotherapy: A Commentary on Discussions by Stephen Mitchell, James Fosshage, Adrienne Harris, and David Raphling on the Theory and Clinical Application of Aggression Based on a Case Presentation by Anna Ornstein. *Psychoanal. Inq.*, 18:120–36.
Waiess, E.A. (1998). A Clinical Note on Traumatic Experiences and the Patient's Rage. *Psychoanal. Psychol.*, 15:294–6.
Wiener, J. (1998). Under the Volcano: Varieties of Rage and Their Transformation. *J. Anal. Psychol.*, 43:493–508.

Chapter 11

Jealousy

The treachery of a forgotten sister

Violet Pietrantonio

I used to be famous. William[1] really understood me, making me famous in the tragedy of the Moor. The great Sigmund placed me at the heart of his disconcerting oedipal discovery. . . . Then along came that bitch, Melanie Klein, and all the psychoanalytic spotlights started shining on my poisonous sister, envy, always off having fun with my brother, hatred, and our cousin, destructiveness . . . and it was as if everyone had suddenly forgotten me. Have a look in the IJP:[2] until the Fifties there was there was lot of noise and discussion about me . . . dozens of articles . . . just think, they even ended up thinking it possible that someone could become homosexual just to avoid me (Lagache, 1952). Such honour paid to my power, such acknowledgements of my importance, and what an inexplicable fall into the obscurity of empty words and bland chitchat!

In the great family of the emotions, I am perhaps the one with the least Aryan features: a strange intersection of LHK (Bion, 1962, 1965, 1970; Sandler, 2005) makes me a unique, fierce mixture of fear, love, hate, offence, betrayal, suspicion, envy, humiliation, shame, and hunger for revenge. My bite is savage and can turn even the mildest, kindest soul into a crazed killer. I am petrol, with the lethal potential to burn up every monogamous couple, but also fraternities, sisterhoods, and family ties. . . . And yet there is a widespread tendency to deny my presence, or to intellectualise me (Freud, 1961) as an obsolete warrior queen of distant psychic lands and epochs, to which it seems pointless and old-fashioned to devote those treatments of α-oneirisation that are capable of giving aesthetic viability to an emotion (Ferro and Civitarese, 2015). Because we know that, after an α-treatment, even the ugliest toad of an emotion feels a bit transformed (Bion, 1965; Grotstein, 2007; Ferro, 2007), if not beautiful and desirable, at least passably human, tolerable to look at and think about.

In the ranks of the emotions, jealousy seems to correspond to a sort of grainy polychrome, a blinding jumble of acrylic envy, vinyl hatred, oils of humiliation, offence, shame, betrayal, anger, fear, abandonment, all-consuming love, and voracious possessiveness, mixed in various proportions and intensities: an unmistakable mixture of primary emotions which the arrival of a third can transform into a murderous cocktail capable of killing the jealous subject, the other suspected or guilty of betrayal, and the loathed intruding third party who drops like a bomb from the dyadic Olympus of absolute love causing a plunge into the precipice of

Hades, where Cerberean triangulations devour human souls with their torments (Ferro, 2010).

If envy is hatefully and intolerably seeing in the other (*invideo* in Latin) a treasure which we feel we lack and are condemned to be miserably deprived of, jealousy is β-fire which breaks out in contact with the discovery (K) of affective or mental links which the other has or could be interested in without us. Such relationships, from which we feel excluded, seem like threats, danger signals, or even unequivocal proofs of the atrocious usurpation of our place in the mind of the other; a place imagined as unique, in an atavistic architectonic vision of the mind, as if it were a hut or bedsit.

But who is this irritating spectral third who arrives without warning and unleashes such an apocalyptic storm capable of transfiguring in seconds the tried and tested pictograms (Barros, 2000; Ferro, 2002) of a couple, and of established emotional constellations? Who drops acid capable of rendering toxic the sweetest nectar of love? Is it a man? A woman? A couple? A thought disguised as a doubt? A ghost masked by suspicion?

Described in hundreds of articles and texts as a crucial element for the psycho-sexual constitution of the individual and the development of mental health, this famous third, this nebuliser spreading the experience of thirdness (Green and Weller, 2005), has been able to create openings for contact and metapsychological unisons even in autistic barriers which, for over a century, have enveloped French and British psychoanalysis in swathes of elective mutism and hermit-like retreat. In the complicity of an unprecedented warmth, the two ladies are agreed: the mental capacity to bear and pass through the transition from the fusional couple to the oedipal triangulation (for example, Britton and Laufer and Aulagnier and Racamier) – in other words, to contain and digest the experiences provoked by the presence of the third – is a fundamental necessity if we are to gain access to the adult ability to love and procreate, and to be able to live with affective relation-ships; if, in short, we are not to go mad.

Adopting an oneiric model of the mind, it can be deduced that the possibility of dreaming the emotional experience of jealousy must be a dream-undertaking which is not easy to achieve, but is nonetheless indispensable. Jealousy must also belong to one of those violent groups of purulent $\male\beta$ which require the endow-ment of a mature and well-equipped dreaming ensemble (Grotstein, 2007) in order to be metabolised and dreamt. Or the presence, especially at the start of psychic life, of another mind capable of slow, lengthy work with a crochet hook, in repeated $\female\rightarrow\female\male\rightarrow rêverie$.

11.1   Oedipal jealousy: cryptograms of psychoanalytic riddling

In the psychoanalytic fable, there is a riddle waiting on standby: but was Oedipus jealous? Or, having been abandoned as a newborn on Cithaeron, with his feet bound and pierced, had he been impregnated with those tremendous experiences of rejection and exclusion which are always present in the proto-emotional cluster of jealousy? Well then, where does it originate, this official/officious definition of jealousy as oedipal?

We might wonder if the choice of the Oedipus myth as a collective transitional object (Green, 1992; De Simone, 2002) capable of narrating, among others, the ideo-affective experience of jealousy, might not be the literary daughter of a remarkable coincidence. One which young Sigmund came across during his self-analysis. In other words, if through jealousy as well as through incest phantasies and family conflicts (Bergmann, 2010; Bernstein, 2001), the story of Oedipus might have performed a Rorschach function for Freud through the projection of disturbing personal phenomena catalysed by the probe of his self-analysis.

Because, in the end, who would Oedipus be jealous of? Oedipus seems to have been adopted, inhabited by the nameless darkness of a neonatal experience of murderous rejection by his father, and finding himself suddenly bombarded by ♂♂K of intense, radioactive luminosity. Riddles, prophecies, prognostications, a lunar park (Ellis, 2005) of lights and reflectors which dazzle thought and deafen the sense of hearing: a real chaos of βα seems to be convulsing in the mind of the dazed young Oedipus, as he goes on his way through life, running into a succession of messages and accidents which involve him in unexpected and unthinkable actions.

Or is it in precisely this respect that Oedipus' experience is an emblematic myth of jealousy? Because it irradiates the ideogram of the KO drama at the origins of this emotional disturbance (Bion, 1963; De Simone, 2002). Because at bottom it is the story of the tragic misfortunes of an avid K which, tantalised by the flutings of prophetic truths, finds itself without oneiric equipment on the threshold of an O which is an abyss of horror, pain, and unspeakable nightmares. In other words, Oedipus would be a character-parabola of jealousy as tremendous β-devastation, provoked by a knowledge K which conveys swarms of feeling (O) for which there seem not to be sufficient ♀ and α function. And so, could the third be the oracle? The Sphinx? Or that malignant Pythoness? (Dürrenmatt, 1976). An element of K-ancestry which cast the existence of Oedipus down into hell? I wonder if the possible tragedy of jealousy could not also be dreamed as the outcome of a K-ὕβρις (Bion, 1967) which clouds the awareness of the emotional body of every knowledge and of the human mind's neoteny in relation to the possibilities of tolerance and O-neiric digestion of mental pain. The epic of a bulimic K which, ignorant of its stomach's limits (♀), leads to the edge of a β-occlusion.

11.2 Othello, Oedipus, and Cain at the mouths of the Nile. Field, jealousy, and plagues in Egypt. When K trembles at the encounter with O

ALFREDO

It had all started with the feeling of a new game, brought into the room in Alfredo's hands: a little cardboard box illustrated with pyramids and pharaohs' heads. Surprised by this unusual gust of creativity, I had listened as Alfredo excitedly invited me to collaborate with him in the archaeological undertaking which seemed to be encapsulated in that little container: to the sound of a scalpel and a brush we would have to look for two animals hidden in the block of chalk.

After a few minutes, a dusty cat and dog appear in Alfredo's hands.

Alfredo: "We must wash them, they're covered in poo!"
Analyst: "Oh, were there two animals buried in the hard poo?"
Alfredo: "Yes, now I'll go and get some water so we can wash them and get them out."

In a flash he goes out and comes back with a little bag full of water which he tips onto the floor, slipping his hands into the paste of chalk and water like a gynaecologist in the womb of a pregnant woman: "Let's see if we can find something else. . . . So much poo!" Before I can take in the amazement stirred up in me by this obstetricising of the field, Alfredo is standing on the little piles of mud and squashing them, spattering the walls, the furniture, and the couch. An image from the film *Slumdog Millionaire*[3] flashes into my mind. I tell him about Indian children who feel abandoned, and sometimes find themselves only having rubbish and poo to play in. Then, as the mess gets worse and worse, I suggest that it's time to stop: "When we're so dirty with poo, like when we have an upset tummy and make a lot of diarrhoea, there comes a time when we have to clean ourselves up!" To my astonishment, Alfredo silently lies down on the couch: "All right, but you clean it up. Now I want to see what the other children will find afterwards!" he sneers. Eureka, Violet! This infernal upheaval of history and geography, pharaonic omnipotence, Biblical plagues, and wretchedness in Calcutta, is perhaps nothing but a sticky coating of jealousy!

As soon as Alfred leaves the room, the sight of all that muck scattered everywhere makes me despair of being able to put my mind and my room back together again in the half hour which, over the years, I have learned to keep free after every session with him. I'm afraid I won't manage to get the room ready in time to receive the girl who comes next. In the field, it is incredible how Cain-Alfredo's experience is being reanimated, the firstborn injected with fratricidal hatred for a usurping little sister who seems to have taken away all space, time, attention, and love from the minds of parents hypnotised by enchantment of her grace and cleverness. How the snaky blood of that damned βgroup, jealousy's proto-mental synonym, is running through the veins of the field. Snarling rage, blind hatred, mortifying impotence, stinging fire of revenge, uneatable prey, and betrayal, the feeling of a devastation with no reparation on the horizon: as I wipe, squeeze out brownish water into the bucket, and fill bags with scraps of cloth and bits of chalk, I think that Alfredo is making me feel and rediscover (Ogden, 2009) the terrifying and agonising quality of the experience of jealousy in the pure βstate. But also the murderous tangle of experiences and phantasies which c-O-agulate in that emotional experience which the name, jealousy, is sometimes no longer able to evoke, given the domesticated harmony of the word's sound, which seems to have lost familiarity with the semantic reality of the wild beast it names.

A matchless Pollock in "action painting" the violence of emotions (Civitarese, 2011), in a few minutes Alfredo has succeeded in setting up such a pandemonium of LHK in the field that it may explode and pull apart a mind affected by that emotional state called jealousy. With the skill of an archaeo-Bionian, he has tracked the primary routes of a K in search of secrets and mysteries which drowns in the unexpected floods of the em-O-tional storm that erupts from the unveiling of the arcanum. Is it an epistemophilic impulse annihilated in the experience of a knowing which also brings with it an unforeseen, unbearable, uncontainable feeling? What had happened when the cat and dog were found? And in the mission of obstetric immersion in search of hidden $\male\male$ inside a $\female$? Why had the sight of, and contact with, Bast and Anubis[4] suddenly turned the field into a shantytown? Had the emotional experience of a knowledge as blinding as the sun or as annihilating as death appeared in Rosetta Stone code? The desperate, hostile resistance of a K which goes into reverse when faced with the immanence of an O demanding the undertaking of transformations that are impossible to dream? (Bion, 1963; Grotstein, 2007). Perhaps in the same way as we might imagine the resistance of a child who, in the heat of his excited curiosity, triumphantly discovers the existence of a little sister in his mother's tummy, but also in her mind, and after a few nanoseconds of scientific ecstasy finds herself flooded with proto-feelings of shit: proto-fecaloids of hate, rage, fear, pain; fetid lumps of proto-thoughts which infest very corner of a mind that is still micro $\female$, not equipped with the development of α function and oneiric processes necessary for the containment-metabolization-transformation in dream of such an invasion by ultraβ. The $\male$ sister/brother, like the more famous primal scene, is perhaps one of those $\male$K with O-hypervalence: a Copernican $\male$ which suddenly opens up the immensity of an unknown O and sucks the subject back into the vortex of a bloody mental revolution. The discovery (K) of the existence of a little brother/sister ($\male$) abruptly dismantles the known set-up of a mental and relational geography, revealing an unkn-O-wn which arouses bewilderment, hatred, and nameless dread. It is a proto-oneiric $\male$-magma bomb, which at the same time fertilises and floods the $\female$ with a silt in an extreme state of proto-mental hypercondensation, and which can cause a temporary shock to the α function and requires a long time for the absorption, filtering, alphabetisation of proto-emotions, and thinkability of proto-thoughts: a $\male$ which will be able to transform the $\female$ (Brown, 2013) or paralyse it in a state of developmental breakdown.

If it took perhaps centuries to mourn the death of geocentrism, we may conclude that it certainly takes years, sometimes decades, and good oneiric help in order for the emotional experience of jeal-O-usy, which manifests itself in the recognition/revelation of affective polygamy, to become dreamable.

11.3   Looking for Iago: jealousy as clashes between βα noumena? Sherlock K and O

With the lack of precision inherent in any generalisation, it seems to me that in the emotional experience of jealousy we can highlight three fundamental moments/ stages/ sequences.

11.3.1   Phase K

Prompted by the scent of proto-feelings boiling up from the contact between em-O-tional life and two preconceptions of relational geometry, the couple and the triangle, the subject finds him or herself in the grip of a raging investigative fever: a bloodhound invaded by an unstoppable hunt for truth, a truth that is sought and imagined as a content ($\male$) of pure knowledge (K); an Aladdin's lamp (K), idealised as a beacon capable of allaying the fear of the shad-O-ws flickering in the mists of doubt. A truth that is believed to be K-information with an instantaneous tranquillising effect:

> if we succeed in discovering the truth, if we can finally be sure about the existence and nature of a relationship between him and her, or between her and her, or him and him, whether they be companions, lovers, parents, siblings, or friends, if we can understand whether or not we are the only one, or at least the first in line, in the other's mind, this whole racket of presentiments, premonitions, (see Bion, 1963) anger and panic will surely be silenced.

It is a truth presumed to be a K-unity with an absolute value, capable of guaranteeing a feeling of potency and lucid, clear vision, a real Valium for surges of LHK. A K-truth with a fantasy of being a mathematical clairvoyant able to re-establish order and criteria of validity, values, domains, and the trustworthiness of ideal noumena which, every time they are touched in the em-O-tional experience of the other, seem to enter into a collision with a β-detonating effect. Because there, in the realm of the noumena (Grotstein, 2007; Ferro and Civitarese, 2015; Manica, 2014), two preconceptions of how relationships may be achieved seem to cohabit (Bion, 1962; Sandler, 2005): there is the preconception of a relationship with the other as a nourishing and ameliorating hieroglyph of a symbiotic couple and of fusional enchantments; and there is the more Pythagorean one of the Δ, precursor of all polygons, the oedipal ideogram which can emerge from the experience of commensal relations between $\female\male$ (Bion, 1970), opening up visions of angular spaces ∠ of love between the couple within triangular areas created by links with a third. From the beginnings of psychic life there is the risk that the dream of realising these two preconceptions may become obstructed by the setting up of a parasitic relationship between $\female\male$ (ibid.), hysterectomising the symbiotic couple in a closed and sterile link, and condemning both these preconceptions to the state of distant, mistrustful strangers.

11.3.2 Phase KO

K-investigation (Bion, 1963, 1965) leads inexorably to the revelation of the poly-meric constitution of the other's affective life. At the start, and for a long time afterwards, it is a discovery which leads to the edge of an O which is the ocean and night of a still nameless emotional experience. The subject's availability/capacity/possibility for venturing into the abysses of this O, which bears within it the experience of a catastrophic change (Bion, 1974), will depend on the state of development of its dreaming ensemble ($\female$-$\male\female$-LHK-contact barrier) and on the presence or absence of one or more other minds which may be able to perform the functions of a dreaming team. The digestion of the proto-emotional bolus of jealousy distils into dream the sunset of monogamous czarism and the advent of an affective cosmopolis where, in the game of multi-ethnic cohabitation between a couple's intimacies, one can feel that triangular affections can exist and that one can belong to polygonal groups. This is a matter of large-scale dream-work, slow action by α-protease, which can result in subsequent micro-transformations in dreams, in repeated encounters and unisons in O. The αlphization of the emo-tional experience of jealousy may be a process of such enormous oneiric com-plexity that, in order to develop, it also requires the activation of a γ function (Corrao, 1981) in the relevant affective group.

11.4 Possible outcomes of jealousy

What happens to us when we finally know (K) that someone apart from us exists in the other's mind? Is this another internal (Searles, 1986) or external object? In other words, what happens when we find ourselves face to face with the need to suffer the emotional experience conveyed by this knowledge? – the experience of becoming the O we have known (Bion, 1970; Civitarese, 2014), so that K→O can evolve in the realisation of that experience O→K which will be able to give us the feeling of new understandings and transformations which can come into being only as a result of being able to suffer the pain of an emotional experience (Bion, 1970; Grot-stein, 2007; Civitarese, 2014). In the case of the emotional suffering of jealousy, the affirmation of K⇄O is a condition for the realisation of that oedipal preconception (Bion, 1962; De Simone, 2002) which causes our existence to look out onto pan-oramas of dream and affective navigation which are unthinkable and unliveable in the fusional-symbiotic cell. An oneiric opportunity which can nevertheless come to grief and be derailed in hallucinosis (Bion, 1965; Civitarese, 2014) if the emotional experience in O is too violent for the dreaming ensemble's capacities for contain-ment ($\female$) and transformation in dream: if the preconception of a fusional rapport with another mind is still waiting to be realised or is in the process of realisation and the emotional experience of separation is still an incubus which cannot be dreamed; that is, when the absence of the other is not yet *no-thing* (Bion, 1965, 1970), a frame of absence in which thought can arise, but *nothing* (Bion, 1965), a vortex which swallows one into a state of agonising inability to go on existing.

Between the necessary dream (Civitarese, 2013) and a nightmare which enchains the psyche (Ogden, 2005), jealousy seems to carve out a place for itself in the landscape of the emotions as a crucial nucleus-crux-interchange for mental growth and the development of that feeling of subjectivation which arises from the ability to dream one's own emotional experience. Decisive elements for the dreamability of the emotional experience of jealousy could be the ability to enjoy the presence of oneiric closeness and reverie, having previously embarked on the process of oneirization of the emotional experience of separation.

11.4.1   K retreats before O

K→ O→ Devel-O-pmental Break-Down.
Othello, Cain, Alfredo, Sylvia Plath and Drama of Jealousy[5]

If we are still completely engaged in trying to realise the preconception of a fusional couple, because of our chronological age or a history of deprivation of primary experiences, the presentification of the third in our own mind or the other's hurls us into a show which may seem horrifying, gruesome, a blasphemy against all the myths encapsulated in this preconception; a revolting Sodom and Gomorrah blazing with phantoms and passions which violate the idyllic sacredness of dyadic love, shamefully desecrating the ninth commandment which seems to be the standard-bearer and defender of this preconception. Confronted with the emotional experience (O) of this scenario, our small human mind may repeatedly draw back in terror, resorting to the most varied defensive strategies used by the psyche to try and neutralise the betalomic charge of nightmares that cannot be dreamed. Autistic isolations/encapsulations, evacuations into the body (hibernations in psychosomatic symptoms) or chain-reactions of revenge and betrayal are some examples of anti-O behaviours which can manifest themselves when K resists O (Bion, 1965); when we find ourselves knowing something that entails an emotional experience which we are afraid we will not be able to dream; when we have wanted at all costs to *know* (K) something that we do not want/are unable to *feel* (O), because to experience/become O seems to be a portent of nameless catastrophe instead of a catastrophic change which would herald creative transformations. Perhaps, using Manica's pendulum (see Chapter 15), these are the cases in which the oscillation of the emotional experience of jealousy is blocked in PS: the violence of the emotions felt in advance in O activates a defensive reaction H, with an effect like an autoimmune response. The atrocious disappointment about the absolute value of the breast-preconception, the terror of the deadly Nothing which looms over the dismantling of the symbiotic illusion, and ignorance of the potential L for more complex emotional geometries generate a well of mental pain so scalding that it unleashes a pitiless hatred (H) of emotional life and the other. Hostage to a transformation in hallucinosis from which it is unable to reawaken, the other is perceived and attacked as a deceitful enemy, an ignoble promise breaker and dirty forger of love. Killing oneself, the other, and the link as a means of setting oneself free from an unbearable emotional experience can become the only escape route for a mind that feels it has no resources and oneiric links for bearing tribulations, sufferings, and the pangs of jealousy.

Sylvia, Othello, and Cain seem to embody the insane devastation which can irrupt into the human mind when it is assailed by jealousy in its most tempestuous state; the ruinous calamity into which the drama of jealousy can slide when it is ♂ that does not find a dreaming ensemble endowed with maturity and sufficient means to dream it; when it invades a mind orphaned of those experiences of unison and reverie that are necessary for the development of dream-functions: faith (F; Bion, 1970) in the nutritive value of em-O-tional life and in the α-oneirogenic value of ♀♂encounters and relationships, the negative capability (Bion, 1970, 1992) for keeping in contact with the unkn-O-wn until it can be dreamt.

Having entered psychiatric diagnostic practice as the "Othello syndrome" (Todd and Dewhurst, 1955) to indicate a state of morbid possession by obsessive jealousy, Othello's emotional drama has also been frequently used in the psycho-analytic literature as a myth/map for reading and interpreting the possible causes and psychic configurations which lie at the origin of what makes jealousy impossible to contain and work through. In the search for the primary object-virus or -worm, the pathognomonic source of the sudden explosion of the whole system of psychic mentalisation under the shocks of the emotion called jealousy, an entire tropical garden of diagnostic hypotheses has grown up. Among descriptions of the devastating effects of latent homosexuality – taken for granted as the cause of a failure to mentalise jealousy – (Feldman, 1952; Wangh, 1950), portrayals of psycho-deconstruction by the reawakening of split-off bad-mother spectres (Carloni and Nobili, 1975) in the couple relationship (Faber, 1974), reports of a complex intrigue between splits and projections of the Self between the intrapsychic and the group (West, 1968), we find ourselves in a hothouse of exotic psychodynamic diagnoses in which all the clinical evidence seems to converge on the *Iago nucleus* as the active ingredient/principle of the identificatory tragedy.

All agree that the *lupus in tragedia* was none other than the malign and unctuous Iago.

Fundamentally they are all trying to answer the same question: why did Othello trust Iago and not his wife Desdemona? Why did he prefer to drink the lying hemlock of his subaltern's jealous envy, instead of the truthful cordial of his young wife's faithful love?

Fundamentally, they all think that in this mystery there are encrypted traces of the Moor's psychic history, a child soldier at the age of just seven, brutally severed from any real childhood and adolescence.

Attempting a panoramic view by means of Bion Field Theory (Stern, 2013), in this storyline Shakespeare has perhaps succeeded in pictographing the palingenesis of the mental contagion into a transformation in hallucinosis which may be activated and start propagating itself as a result of K withdrawing from O, from the impossibility of containing/suffering/dreaming the emotional experience of jealousy. Othello seems to be the portrayal of the ischaemic Brobdingnagism[6] of the emotional ♂♂ of jealousy, when instead of finding ♀♂, they roam around in an emotional field characterised by a ♂♂ functioning (psychic homosexuality; Ferro, 2007). The incubator and spreader of the jealousy-nucleus seems to be Iago. Iago knows (K) that Cassio has been promoted to the rank of lieutenant by Othello, K-news which sets loose the O of an emotional experience from which Iago seems to want to escape, being inflamed by resentment and murderous rage against Othello, who has betrayed him, and Cassio who has usurped him. He has no confidence (faith; Bion, 1970) that he will be able to endure the pain of jealousy towards this pair who seem united in a bond from which he feels excluded, or that he will be able to confide in Othello or Cassio in a unison which might be the prelude to a dream capable of giving a name, form, and meaning to the emotional experience of jealousy that he is living through. Drunk, perhaps, with terror, Iago tries to expel instead of αlphabetising the flaming βrands of a fearful burning jealousy which is turning his mind to charcoal. He runs as fast as he can from O and finds himself in the abyss of -K (Sandler, 2005), in thrall to a proliferating process of transformation in hallucinosis. Instead of suffering the pain of envy, exclusion, disappointment, and the fear of no longer being loved, being betrayed and permanently displaced, he finds himself completely dissociated and rendered autistic by O, in a state of hallucinotic excitation, perpetrator of a vengeance which is the injection into Othello of hallucinoses of betrayal.

Because he is probably homozygous with Iago in α-malnutrition and the hypotrophy of his dreaming ensemble, Othello is unable to recognise in reverie the sound of the jeal-O-usy which vibrates among the strings of the malign insinuation which his ensign is firing at him. That is, he cannot perform those operations of ♀, ♀♂, and reverie which might perhaps have reactivated the oscillatory-transformative functioning of the oneiric spectrum, among TH (transformations in hallucinosis)-reverie-TD (transformations in dream) (Civitarese, 2014). Child soldier, premature orphan of oneiric relationships, Othello likewise seems not to have matured a faith (F) in mental relating as an opportunity for restoration and oneiric procreation. He does not speak to Desdemona: he does not try to ask her or tell her what he is feeling and thinking, in search of that at-one-ment (Bion, 1970) which might be an oasis of a surprising ability to dream together the nightmares clutching at our minds. Ripened by Iago, Othello seems to make himself the host for feverish replication of a hallucinotic virus which inflames him with resentment, hatred, disappointment, and murderous despair; a virus which seems to turn into androids of H, and is unable to find a hospital (♀) and oneiric medicine (♀♂-reverie) in the other, stirring up only fear, distance, and defences (♂➡️⬅️♀). To begin with, Desdemona seems deaf and impermeable to Othello's unhappiness. Othello is tense, suspicious, and aggressive, but Desdemona never seems to get close to him with a genuine intention to listen emotionally. She does not dare to explore the disturbances which are making him cold and moody, and seems to be sealed in an emotional hypo-acousis with a phobic quality, making her a detached and alien presence. Mistaking (-K) signs of friendship for unequivocal proof of that obscene affair between the lovers Desdemona and Cassio, with which the corrosive promptings of Iago have TH-infused his mind, Othello smothers Desdemona on the marriage bed, perhaps trying in this way to stifle atrocious proto-feelings.

After long periods of exile and ♂♂ battles, it will perhaps be in the dialogue with Iago's wife, Emilia, Desdemona's maid, that Othello has his first experience of a ♂♀ encounter and wakes from his hallucinosis: in a dream-state he acknowledges the delusional nature of the nightmare which has poisoned his mind, but he cannot contain, suffer, and dream the mental pain which streams from the sight of the crazed uxoricide he has just committed. Othello stabs himself to death with a sword, becoming our living exemplar of the perilous torments which can tear open the human psyche affected by jealousy.

Like Othello, Sylvia was also unable to survive the blaze of jealousy. Ted's[7] unfaithfulness and their separation exposed the young poet to unbearably hot tongues of em-O-tional flame. She tried to get away from this scorching O; maybe she hallucinated that by losing weight and burning calories she could reduce its heat. She tried to find refuge from -K in the song of poems which were not lamentations about emotional oppression, but a hosanna to a lyrical entelechy, exalted as a self-made triumph over mental pain. In the last poems which Sylvia wrote before her suicide, mute lumps of a nameless pain and desperation seem deep frozen. Her words, her verses seem to be *axes* (Plath, 1963a), stalactites of frozen tears which sting, penetrate, and wound like nails, perhaps seeking outlets in the mind of a reader who might be able to act as a container to dissolve all that frozen pain in dream. In *The Bell Jar* (Plath, 1963b) she had perhaps tried to dream the glow of such a dramatic impossibility to suffer and αlphabetise the violence of emotions which may come to life and demonically possess existence in a couple relationship. Perhaps also the dream of being able to find a uterus/bell jar in the couple relationship, where she could hide away quietly in the symbiotic safety of an umbilical link/cord, had been smashed to pieces under the disruptive pressure of an incandescent jealousy towards a husband who had suddenly shown unexpected sides to him: an intense sibling rival in poetic competition and a faithless breaker of the marriage vows. Sylvia's mind was not ready to dream the ontogenesis of an oedipal conception she had tried to achieve by marrying and becoming a mother. Not even the bond with her children is able to stop her drowning in the swamp of β-detritus which has now drowned her young mind: young Sylvia dies of consumption caused by serious oneiric deprivation which makes her feel less a mother than a newborn infant lost in the Nothingness of a dystopian universe where she glimpses no hope of a dream. Nor was Sylvia able to unearth an oneiric shelter or oneiric-receptive sensitivity: contact with her only seemed to provoke an astonished, petrifying stupor (Alvarez, 1971, 1989, 2000), as if she were asking for help in a β-alphabet which the other was too dyslexic to read and understand.

After her ode to death, *The Edge* (Plath, 1963a), a piercing fresco with a suicidal atmosphere, Plath opened her children's bedroom window, left bread and milk for their breakfast by their beds, and killed herself with gas after sealing the kitchen.

The same deadly sniper was behind the primal jealousy of Cain. As the first person to experience life as a child and a brother in the oldest Biblical family, Cain is emblematic of the often scotomised virulence of the arsenal of proto-emotions which boil up in sibling relations: the bestial savagery of experiences of envy, exclusion, humiliation, shame, hatred, and of being robbed which can get mixed up together into a fratricidal jealousy if they do not find ♀, ♀♂, and reverie in the parental figures. This experience at the beginning of the world/family leads to our being ill-prepared novices, often bewildered and overwhelmed by the powerful and dismaying floods of proto-emotions which flow around inside family rela-tionships; and especially on our α-illiterate debut, as we take our first steps in the world of emotional lava-flows which erupt in the branching and intertwining links at when the realisation of the oedipal preconception is at its dawn; when we start to taste the apple of the third and have to leave the paradise of bipersonal love. For Adam and Eve, Cain is their first child; for Cain, Abel is his first brother: and there are also those who say that Abel and Cain were rivals in love for their own sister. Forerunners of emotional experiences of thirdness which make us terrified, or simply irritated, hosts of the most horrible nightmares, of feeling more ungrateful that we would desperately try to disavow and to confine to our prehistory of cave-dwelling brutality. Could there be a collective repudiation of jealousy because it reminds us of the pygmy constitution of our ♀ mind and the venomous jungle of ♂ which can inhabit it? Of a jealousy which is still perhaps one of the emotional experiences most easily subjected to denial, negation, sugaring over, and transfor-mation into a symptom.

11.4.2 K⇄O. Jealousy: grieving mother of unexpected oneiric conceptions. Being able to dream jealousy. When K succeeds in pausing on the riverbanks or swimming in the numinous[8]

If we can dream being betrayed and betraying, recognising in the future of the dream the cleansing and healing of a jealousy which is no longer a nightmare that annihilates the psyche, but a Vesuvian dream-comedy of the emotional Scampia[9] endlessly raging at the periphery of the encounter with the other, it may be one of those dreaming benefits which can best be enjoyed *in senectute*;[10] a bonus of our dream-apprenticeship and the maturity of the dreaming ensemble, which can perhaps also help us to dream the livid jealousy that may oppress us at the thought of the game of life going on even after our death/expulsion; the thought that those dear to us will carry on the game without us when we are no longer there (S. Bier, *After the Wedding*, 2006). Will we perhaps be able to dream the karstic river of a sad, bitter jealousy which might start flowing when we are pensioned off? Or in the mind of an analyst saying goodbye to his or her practice and leaving the field to younger colleagues? Or in an analytic field when there is a parting, when an analysis comes to an end, or a pause, or is broken off? Jealousy in the anguish of separation when we feel we are being left on our own, leaving the other to hover in another life, another world, other relationships. A jealousy which lights up bereavements, differences, and asymmetries which it may also be painful to confront.

To paraphrase Jovanotti (the singer Lorenzo Cherubini) "no great love can exist without a betrayal", we could perhaps claim that in order to dream jealousy we need to be able to suffer the pain of mourning the other's love for us and us only. But a funeral lament is also indispensable if we are to transform the clumps of this pain into a narrated dream, and the narratability of our emotional experience presupposes faith (F) in the presence of one or more minds ready to engage in shared oneiric listening. In rhapsodic verses set to music and statements made in interviews, Lorenzo has been able to recount the pains and rebirth of a new feeling of love in his experience as a betrayed lover, describing the possible birth of a feeling of forgiveness in taking emotional responsibility for one's own LHK complex in relation to the other's LHK. This narrative tension, which is itself a trace of previous and possible dream-relationships, α-solvents of a mental pain which might otherwise send β-projectiles raining down, fired at us in such caustic projective identifications that they turn $\female$, $\female\male$, and reverie into a Mission-almost-Impossible.

The field and ultrasonic howls of jealousy. Itard and "*l'enfant sauvage*".[11]
Analytic phases of oneiric embryology

Ottavia

Built like a lumberjack, wearing a metalworker's overall, but in fact an electronic engineer in a multinational company, Ottavia came into my consulting room with shining eyes. She wept big tears as she told me about her fear that she might kill her daughter while in the grip of the infanticidal *furor* which had blazed up in her since she had given birth. A long face to face consultation stamped the sensation of a black shadow on the field, perhaps the shadow of a puppet representing the murky proto-mental whole to be jointly "unconscioused" (Civitarese, 2014) with this blue-collar Medea. Not without some trepidation I suggested that Ottavia begin an analysis of three sessions a week and Ottavia agreed, not without considerable resistance and hesitation, though she never missed a session. The walk to the couch seemed to coincide with the arrival of an obtuse, deafening, fanatical jihadi who, for a long time, paralysed the field with a sort of anti-dreaming embargo. The other face of Medea? Her black shadow? Her secret lover? In terms of analytic material, the consulting room seemed to become a sort of Taleban cell for more than a year, an incessant scream of fundamentalist hatred against her stepfather, whom she insulted and lynched with ignominious verbal stones, claiming he was the enemy who caused all her misfortunes and deserved nothing but the most shameful death.

Ottavia yelled and spat out the entrails of memories and accusations about this acquired father who was guilty of repeated adultery, absences, swindles, suspected abuse, total violation of every affective ethic. The basic assumption of the enemy stepfather, the cause of all her pain, was interspersed with screams of metallic contempt for the inadequacies of her daughter (the desperate proclamation of a grave insufficiency of ♀?).

Time passed, but the dream-functioning of the field seemed to be chained in a sort of furtive, tenacious Itard syndrome. What proto-mental link was this dreamscarer-homunculus made of? At the same time, the sound of Ottavia's injuries, complaints, and resentment was so shrill, strident, and relentless, with such a bitter stink of putrefaction, that it generated an emotional acoustic like ultrasound for the human ear: I felt it but couldn't hear it. I tried to give a name to the experiences bottled up between the lines of her totemic manifestations, and Ottavia listened but seemed deaf to the vibrations of her emotions. We seemed to be groping after useless attempts at emotional contact like two zombies in the most stupefying possible din of hardcore β-heavy-metal. However, I managed to stay in unison with this clam-O-ur of proto-decibels, resulting in some unexpected oneiric effects. Ottavia began to put down her machine-gun of slogans from time to time and allowed herself some intimate confidences (♀♂), enabling me to peer through the burqa of her autistic barrier and glimpse the dried-up garden of dreams that had never been α-watered.

After two years, just before the summer break, as the re-mujahidinisation of the field was getting going again, I started to dream about her at night, a slalom of countertransferential dreams which, from a field perspective, could perhaps be thought of as extra time that was needed for the oneiric carrying out of high-intensity analytic encounters full of proto-mental violence. They were dreams which left me astonished and disturbed but, above all, relieved because I perceived them as the first oneiric photograms of the *pavor nocturnus* (Ogden, 2005) which had been paralysing the analytic field for two years in a sort of *delirium tremens*. *I dreamed that she was jumping at me, grabbing my throat to throttle me, after she had silently watched my husband entering and leaving our consulting room before going into a dimly lit cubby hole. I dreamed about her being in my sitting room busy breaking a little Lego house my son had just built.* Dreams about the first naked pictographic contact with the mute, savage violence of primitive jealousy unleashed by the presentification of the third, which fully sh-O-wed itself to me in its tremendous, titanic, uncontainable proto-mental essence in a third dream, again on the eve of a break in the analysis. *I dreamed that my sister arrived and I found myself giving her a resounding slap on the cheek, then feeling annihilated by horror at my own bullying aggression which seemed to be flooding up from the most secret depths of my mind's viscera.* On waking, I immediately thought of Ottavia: the oneiric encounter with my *enfant sauvage* enabled me to recognise in the deafening volume of the baying which had been echoing around the field for three years now, the suppurating howl of a jeal-O-usy which continued to cause an acute infection of wildly roaming proto-emotions. Throughout my childhood my sister had been the source and object of a tremendous, bloodthirsty fury. Envy, jealousy, rage, hatred, experiences of usurpation and abandonment which were often uncontainable because they were still nameless and unthinkable, were often evacuated by me in violent attacks. Ottavia's violence which had for so long seemed so overwhelming, incomprehensible, almost alien, suddenly became clear to me as part of the family v-O-cabulary of an eldest child's uncontainable and desperate fury. It had been a long journey O→K, filled with accidents, drenched in fear, secret defences and stubborn resistances for a jealousy which, as I had nevertheless deduced (K→O), was an emotional nucleus present in the words of protest being insistently shouted in the session.

The analytic experience with Ottavia was an extraordinary *magistra* for me, as much in tuning my ear to the atonal sound with which the proto-mental music of jealousy can express itself, as in the surprising and unpredictable phenomenology of fertilisation and oneiric conception in an analytic treatment. But also in an oneiric generativity of the analytic field which sometimes requires protracted, breathless pauses by the shores of Acheron, on the threshold of an O which is the tumult and uproar of nameless β-damnation. A long wait in the dark which can permit access to a numinous area where the aurora of dreams may arise in first possible contacts between rediscovered preconceptions and proto-emotional βarbarities suffered (Manica, 2014).

Housewifeliness and thirst of Jeal-O-usy at-one-ment (Bion, 1970)

"I am talking about jealousy which empties your veins of the idea that your beloved might penetrate another person's body, the jealousy which makes your legs buckle, stops you sleeping, consumes your liver, torments your thoughts; jealousy which poisons your intelligence with ever-questioning suspicions and fears, and mortifies your self-esteem with investigations, complaints, and deceptions, making you feel robbed and ridiculous, turning you into a detective, inquisitor, and jailer of your beloved" (Fallaci, 1979. p. 31).

Maddalena

A thirty-five-year-old Calabrian, married to a rich businessman from Modena, isolated in the greyness of a dull domestic routine, Maddalena has been in therapy for some years when she starts to tell me about the torture of suspicions and fantasies of betrayal which assail her all day long, blazing through her as she sits on an electric chair of hatred, impotence, rage, shame, and experiences of exclusion in which she feels she is dying. In vain she becomes a private investigator in ploys of K-espionage: tailing her husband, making veiled interrogations, checking his messages and emails on his phone and computer. The result is always the same: ambiguous traces which could either be glaring evidence of her husband committing unpunished adultery with his omnipresent secretary or signs of a liaison motivated by the legitimate requirements of work. For months, the rebus identified by Maddalena as the cause and starting point of all her jeal-O-us dyspepsia is a wooden Sphinx which handcuffs the field in a K tribunal. How can she know the truth? The husband who tries to calm her down by denying any betrayal is either sincere or a wretched liar, but which? With Maddalena I find I am suffering the anxiety of not knowing, the fear of not understanding and of not knowing what to say, the demoralising, infuriating disappointment of an analysis and analyst who cannot give definitive K answers. Until one day:

Maddalena: I kept phoning Mario yesterday evening. He didn't answer at first: he sent me a message saying he was in a meeting. Then he rang at 8.30 to tell me he had to stay on in the office with Lina to finish some urgent business. As usual . . . I know what his work is like, but even so. . . . Then at 9.30 he called me again to say he was staying to have something to eat with Lina and then they'd go on working till late because they had to get something delivered today. I was waiting for him, I'd made dinner. . . . And maybe I'm crazy, but I had all kinds of thoughts going through my head. . . . The two of them are always on their own together in the office till late. . . . And then Mario's told me that next week they have to go to Romania and they'll be staying in the same hotel. . . . He says it's just a working relationship and friendship, that I'm paranoid . . . But I don't trust him. . . .

Analyst: [*Savaged by the ferocious fangs of a m-O-nstrous jealousy, I find myself hallucinating, tormented in vivid unison by an emotional experience of such violence that it seems to go beyond the limits of the psycho-bearable*] Well, who wouldn't go mad with jealousy, all alone in the house, dinner ready, waiting for one's husband, thinking of him by himself with his secretary at work? . . . You'd find yourself imagining all kinds of things. . . . Your mind filled with all kinds of fantasies of betrayal . . . and the feeling of being burnt up in a blaze of fear, sadness, anger, powerlessness.

Maddalena [*A long silence, like a deep oxygenating breath after the exhaustion of panting and gasping in asthmatic anxiety*] You know what . . .? I should talk to Mario about it. Constantly trying to check up on him like a detective is no use. The problem is it's hard for me, staying at home on my own, with him being so far away. Now I understand what you've been telling me about experiences of abandonment.

It was an experience of unison in the terrifying madness of jealousy which stirred us both. Above all, perhaps, because it was an experience of the elementary and primal simplicity of at-one-ment as a fundamental, founding moment for the start of a possible dream about one's own emotional experience. Conferring on jealousy the dignity of a terrifying nightmare by means of a hypothalamic sharing (Bion, 1976–79; De Mattos and Braga, 2013), had reconnected the field to the trajectory O→K. The stinging experiences of lacerating abandonment now seemed more profoundly comprehensible, and could be brought into focus as an apodictic aetiology of the Othello-malaria. The oneiric chloroquine allowed the taking of emotional responsibility for these experiences. The experience of separation as annihilating *nothingness* was gradually transformed into a space of *no-thing*: a state in which one is able to be, and to feel, alone in a less terrifying intimate contact with one's own mental ♂♂, a state which revealed itself as a forge of new and unexpected images, thoughts, and dreams. In her free time, Maddalena decided to enrol in a painting course where she discovered an inspired and passionate expressionist in herself. After a few years, pregnancy too – having been abhorred as a chamber of bovine horrors – was transformed into an oneiric Boterian[12] object of desire. Jealousy became a dreamable mental emotional experience and a more tolerable mental pain with the opening up of new triangular affective scenarios perceived as desirable and practicable.

Jealousy in the protozoic state with Ottavia, and with its more familiar Othello stamp in Maddalena. The oneiric transformation happened at different speeds, but the same experience of unison was the key moment of access that was necessary for the transformation in dream of the emotional experience of jealousy to become possible.

Being able to suffer at-one-ment (Bion, 1970), the emotional experience which is circulating in the field performs multiple preliminary dream-functions: it extends the capacity for containment (♀), preparing the container to accommodate proto-mental contents (♂♂) which were previously uncontainable; it permits a process of αlphabetisation of the most pregnant emotions because it arises from an O-experience in communion; it legitimates and expiates (Grotstein, 2007) the guilt and shame of mental pain.

Unison which in the case of jealousy can be strongly obstructed by the magnetic force of a K which tends to attract and orient the analytic field towards a -K functioning clothed in the judicial-forensic robes of the superego, in the strenuous attempt to eclipse the suffering of an O which seems to be a cloaca of disgusting proto-emotional ♂♂ unworthy of a place in the mind.

In the treachery of jealousy, is there perhaps the trembling, rebellious rancour of an emotion which raves in exasperated longing to be dreamed, rejecting the condition of β-pariah to which it has until now been relegated by that strange tribe of *homines* who still think they can become *sapientes* without learning from the experience of what they feel (Bion, 1962)?

Notes

1 William Shakespeare.
2 *The International Journal of Psychoanalysis.*
3 Danny Boyle's film of 2008.
4 The Egyptian deities, Bast the cat, goddess of the sun, and Anubis the dog, god of the dead.
5 Ettore Scola's 1970 film *Dramma della gelosia*, also released in English as *The Pizza Triangle*.
6 An allusion to the giant people in *Gulliver's Travels*.
7 Ted Hughes, Plath's husband and fellow-poet.
8 The numinous (Grotstein, 2007; Manica, 2014) "seems to present itself as an intermediate area of O, a space for a possible encounter between preconceptions and the β elements of nameless proto-emotional experience" (Manica, ibid.).

9   Scampia is a district in Naples which has given its name to a prolonged and bloody feud between rival factions of the Camorra.
10 Cicero (44 BCE), *Cato Maior de senectute*.
11 The 1970 film starring and directed by François Truffaut; the book *Victor de l'Aveyron* by Jean Itard; Paris, Éditions Allia, 1994.
12 The artist Fernando Botero is noted for his enormously inflated portraits.

References

Alvarez, A. (1971). *The Savage God*. Weidenfeld and Nicholson, London.
Alvarez, A. (1989). A Poet and Her Myth, *The New York Review*.
Alvarez, A. (2000). I Failed Her: I Was Thirty and Stupid. *The Guardian*.
Barros, E.D. (2000). Affect and Pictographic Image: The Constitution of Meaning in Mental Life. *The International Journal of Psychoanalysis*, 81: 1087–99.
Bergmann, M.S. (2010). The Oedipus Complex and Psychoanalytic technique. *Psychoanalytic Inquiry*, 30: 535–40.
Bernstein, A. (2001). Freud and Oedipus: A New Look at the Oedipus Complex in the Light of Freud's Life. *Mod Psychoanalysis*, 26: 269–82.
Bion, W.R. (1962). *Learning From Experience*. Heinemann, London.
Bion, W.R. (1963). *Elements of Psychoanalysis*. Heimann, London.
Bion, W.R. (1965). *Transformations*. Maresfield Library, London, 1991.
Bion, W.R. (1967). *Second Thoughts*. Basic Books, New York.
Bion, W.R. (1970). *Attention and Interpretation: A Scientific Approach to Insight in Psychoanalysis*. Tavistock Publication, London.
Bion, W.R. (1974). *Bion in New York and Sao Paulo*. Karnac Books, London, 1980.
Bion, W.R. (1976). *Clinical Seminars and Other Works*. Karnac Books, London, 1994.
Bion, W.R. (1992). *Cogitations*. Karnac Books, London.
Brown, L.J. (2013). The Development of Bion's Concept of Container and Contained. In H.B. Levine and L.J. Brown (Eds.), *Growth and Turbulence in the Container/Contained*. Routledge, New York.
Carloni, G. and Nobili, D. (1975). *La mamma cattiva*. Guaraldi, Rimini.
Civitarese, G. (2011). *The Violence of Emotions*. Routledge, London, 2013.
Civitarese, G. (2013). *The Necessary Dream: New Theories and Technique of Interpretation in Psychoanalysis*. Karnac Books, London.
Civitarese, G. (2014). *Truth and the Unconscious in Psychoanalysis*. Routledge, London, 2016.
Corrao, F. (1981). Struttura poliadica e funzione Gamma. *Gruppo e Funzione Analitica*, II(2).
De Simone, G. (2002). *Le famiglie di Edipo*. Borla, Roma.
De Mattos, J.A.J. and Braga, J.C. (2013). Primitive Conscience. In H.B. Levine and L.J. Brown (Eds.), *Growth and Turbulence in the Container Contained*. Routledge, New York.
Dürrenmatt, F. (1976). The Dying of the Pythia. In *Friedrich Dürrenmatt: Selected Writings*. University of Chicago Press, Chicago, 2006.
Ellis, B.E. (2005). *Lunar Park*. Einaudi, Torino.
Faber, M.D. (1974). Othello: Symbolic Action, Ritual and Myth. *American Imago*, 31: 159–205.
Fallaci, O. (1979). *A Man: A Novel*. RSC Libri/Rizzoli, Milan, 2013.
Ferro, A. (2002). *Seeds of Illness, Seeds of Recovery*. Brunner-Routledge, New York.

Ferro, A. (2007). *Avoiding Emotions, Living Emotions*. Routledge, London, 2011.

Ferro, A. (2010). *Torments of the Soul: Psychoanalytic Transformations in Dreaming and Narration*. Routledge, London and New York, 2015.

Ferro, A. and Civitarese, G. (2015). *The Analytic Field and Its Transformations*. Karnac Books, London.

Feldman, A.B. (1952). Othello's Obsession. *The International Journal of Psychoanalysis*, 147–64.

Freud, A. (1961). *The Ego and the Mechanism of Defence*. The Hogarth Press, London.

Green, A. (1992). *Slegare*. Borla, Roma, 1994.

Green, A. and Weller, A. (2005). *Key Ideas for a Contemporary Psychoanalysis*. Routledge, London.

Grotstein, J. (2007). *Un raggio d'intensa oscurità*. R. Cortina, Milano.

Lagache, D. (1952). From Homosexuality to Jealousy. *Psychoanal Q.*, 21: 592.

Manica, M. (2014). Memoir of the Future, Memoir of the Numinous. In *Bion and Contemporary Psychoanalysis*. Routledge, London, 2018.

Manica, M. (2015). *Intercettare il sogno*. Roma, Borla, 2015.

Ogden, T. (2005). *This Art of Psychoanalysis: Dreaming Undreamt Dreams and Interrupted Cries*. Taylor and Francis, New York.

Ogden, T. (2009). *Rediscovering Psychoanalysis*. Taylor and Francis, New York.

Plath, S. (1963a). *Collected Poems of Sylvia Plath*. Turtleback School and Library Binding Edition, Logan, IA, 2008.

Plath, S. (1963b). *The Bell Jar*. Faber & Faber, London, 2008.

Sandler, P.C. (2005). *The Language of Bion*. Karnac Books, London.

Searles, H. (1986). *My Work With Borderline Patients*. Rowman and Littlefield Publishing Groups, Northvale, NJ.

Stern, D.B. (2013). Field Theory in Psychoanalysis, Part 2: Bionian Field Theory and Contemporary Interpersonal/Relational Psychoanalysis. *Psychoanalytic Dialogues*, 23: 630–45.

Todd, J. and Dewhurst, K. (1955). The Othello Syndrome: A Study in the Psychopathology of Sexual Jealousy. *The Journal of Nervous and Mental Disease*, 122: 367–74.

Wangh, M. (1950). Orthello: The Tragedy of Iago. *Psychoanalytic Quarterly*, 19: 202–12.

West, L.J. (1968). The Othello Syndrome. *Contemporary Psychoanalysis*, 4: 103–10.

Chapter 12

Betrayals. Psychoanalytic pathways in the works of James Joyce

Fulvio Mazzacane

12.1 Introduction

Joyce's works often emphasise the contradictions between all that belongs to the natural and instinctual dimension, and the evolutions of human thought. In the transformation of emotions into feelings and instincts into affects, there are the traces of the complex daily challenge which we face in dealing with those who trust us.

Etymologically, the verb "betray" comes from the Latin *tradere*, composed of *trans* (beyond) and *dare* (give): the Latin verb combines the two meanings of "to transmit something to someone" (an inheritance, a doctrine, etc.) and "to hand someone or something over to the enemy", "to make an attempt on someone's life." These meanings have been subjected to a long Christian tradition founded on Judas's betrayal of Christ, with the result that the ambivalence of the word has been lost.

In this chapter, I will address the various forms of betrayal which can present themselves in the analytic relationship and, more generally, in the human relationship.

The analytic device creates links of a high emotional intensity and allows us to experience *in vivo* what happens in the relational life of us all. We find ourselves facing an inevitable sequence of betrayals, large and small. The ability to make sense of the experience of betrayal is indispensable if we do not want to miss out on what the human relationship can offer us.

My starting point could be what Badoni (2015) calls "original betrayal": the inevitable work which the subject does on the traces left by the other, a process which serves to maintain his or her own originality. The betrayal becomes a bridge, the result of a state of mind in which the two parties try to live together in fidelity to their origins and to project themselves into a future.

We do not resign ourselves easily and without suffering to the imperfection of our love objects and the impossibility of possessing them completely. We delegate to our significant links our need for affective stability in a complex balancing act where stability itself has to find a point of equilibrium, balanced against the drive to explore in the spheres of relationships, self-knowledge, and work.

I will consider some features linked to the betrayals which can occur between analyst and analysand and which are concerned with the "normal" vicissitudes of any analytic journey. Some of these themes touch on topics that are the subject of debate between different analytic perspectives: the relationship between psychic reality and factual reality, the analyst's subjectivity as it intrudes into the session, the internal institutional aspect (the relationship which each of us has with his or her own models) and the external one (moments of institutional transition, supervisions, and publications).

The extra-analytic guiding thread will be provided by the works of James Joyce, of which I am no more than a passionate reader. In his private life, Joyce was an expert in betrayals both real and imagined, so much so that he made it a theme which runs through his entire output. It is no coincidence that some of his works (especially *Ulysses* and *Finnegans Wake*) are impossible to translate and, according to many critics, are re-written by his translators.

Paradoxically, Joyce, the master of "stream of consciousness", called his style "new realism", using this definition in a completely different sense from the one it has taken on in recent philosophical debate. By realism he means concerning oneself not with external things, but with the subterranean, with what governs humankind but is not visible: "those poisonous subtleties which envelop the soul, the ascending fumes of sex": very Freudian themes, even though Joyce was never much in sympathy with psychoanalysis. "My imagination grows when I read Vico as it doesn't when I read Freud or Jung" (Ellmann, 1982, p. 693).

Bion speculated that the mind expands under pressure, reacting to new stimuli which oblige a man to equip himself with new functions. In a similar way, Joyce understands writing as a creative process which continually expands its dimensions and directions, the possible levels on which it can be read.

Like a patient who is demanding but eager to communicate, or an analyst intensely experiencing the dream-quality of the relationship, Joyce is an author capable of entering into and moving out of profound regressive states (Jacobs, 2002) and cannot fail to have influenced the thinking of many analysts with his dreamlike atmospheres, including Bion, as we can see when we read his trilogy, *Memoir of the Future*.

There is another character always present in this chapter, and that is the concept of paradox with its function of posing questions, not so much in order that a conclusion can be reached but so that the search for a meaning never comes to an end.

There are several reasons for associating Joyce's works with paradox. Giordano Bruno's thesis of the coincidence of opposites and the dialectic of contraries had a strong impact on his intellectual development: holding together apparently irreconcilable concepts with the aim of suggesting the infinite complexity of the world and of human thought.

A paradox which is constantly present in Joyce's work is the central place he gives to the importance of ties with one's homeland, family, the other, but also the inevitable pain which arises from any relationship. This is an experience which we live through daily in analytic practice, if only because we remain convinced about the importance of establishing links and investing in them affectively, aware of the risks and disappointments which this may entail for our patients.

12.2   16 June 1904

This is Bloomsday, the day Joyce chose for Leopold Bloom's ordinarily crazy day described in *Ulysses*.

There are constant autobiographical references in Joyce's work and the theme of betrayal always looms over it: 16 June 1904 is the day on which Joyce first went out with Nora Barnacle, the woman from a social class below his own who would be his lifelong companion. It is an important day because in fact the first betrayal, real or supposed, in his relationship with Nora was already happening. Returning to Dublin in 1921, Joyce met up with a childhood friend who told him that while the writer was seeing Nora, the friend, unknown to Joyce, was seeing her too. This was probably a mere boast, but it had a powerful impact on Joyce (D'Amico, 1982).

In a letter, Joyce speaks about the emotion on hearing his partner's voice at a moment when his suspicion about her betrayal was strong, saying "I will never hear that music again because I can never believe again." Mere suspicion decisively shuts off any possibility of resuming an emotionally serene relationship. It will be this experience on which he later builds the plot of *Exiles*.

One of the betrayals present in Joyce's work concerns the father-son relationship. The stories woven through *Ulysses* include that of the relationship between Leopold and Stephen Dedalus, a son pursued through many of the book's chapters but never really met. In *Exiles* Joyce makes his alter ego Richard say, "There is a faith still stranger than the faith of the disciple in his master. . . . The faith of a master in the disciple who will betray him".[1] There is already plenty of material to support the claim that Joyce's work is filled with the theme of betrayal in the most important relationships. To this we can add the theme of exile, which is another form of betrayal: the homeland's betrayal of the exile who is forced to distance himself from his own origins, and the voluntary exile's betrayal of the homeland and what it represents.

In *Ulysses*, Leopold Bloom's day is the space-time of everyday life which contains birth, the passions, dream, betrayal, and death, the drama which arises from every human being's need to assert his or her own uniqueness: to deceive him or herself into believing that, in every significant relationship, he or she is the first and the last; not the last in a series or the first in a succession.

The contrast which is created between the need for "permanence" and uniqueness, and the reality of life which tends not to allow these, is one of the aspects which Bion (1991, vol. 1) grasps when he talks about every individual's attempts to manipulate feelings and ideas so that nothing can disturb his need for permanence, for continuity.

The analytic scenario, like the day described in *Ulysses*, is the place where the engine of transference reactivates the betrayals of the past and permits the re-playing of games involving fantasies about, and the need for, exclusiveness and the resulting material of exclusion.

12.3   Betrayals great and small: language as a source of betrayal

Betrayal is inherent in the act of translation. When he had to translate Queneau's *Exercises in Style*, ninety-nine brilliant variations on a brief text, Umberto Eco played with rhetorical figures and styles, and said that fidelity in translating comes about by understanding the rules of the game, respecting them, and then playing a new match.

"Tradurre è tradire" (To translate is to betray) is a saying which can also apply to small betrayals which, though they are an everyday occurrence, can often have significant consequences. These are the small linguistic incomprehensions caused by the inadequacy of language to express mental events completely. For Bion, our language inevitably depends on sensory experiences, making it inadequate to describe psychic reality, which is not perceptible with the senses. This is one of the reasons why analysts express themselves in jargon. Bion decided to use neutral terms (β, α, $\female$, $\male$) to describe certain elements or psychoanalytic functions so that he could eliminate the penumbra of meanings which have accumulated over time and have added to the difficulty of speaking about that ultimate reality which is unknowable.

Words have a variety of semantic haloes. In the minds of two people who are trying to get to know each other, they bring with them the nuances of different meanings which echo in a different way according to the legacy or scars which each single experience has produced, in the absolutely unique way in which every human being has lived it.

The session, the moment of the encounter between the analytic couple, is the place where various levels converge: the inevitable transferential components which inhabit every human relationship, and the responses which such components activate in the partner, who brings his or her own sensibility and the scars of past relationships; the trans-generational component, understood as the progressive accumulation of a code of relational functioning in which are stored the inevitably traumatic aspects of the encounter with the other, him or herself the bearer of different codes. The linguistic nuances are not random, but contain elements which speak of the individual's style and psychological profile, and impinge on the dialogic exchange, not only as an attempt at mutual understanding but also as a place for reducing emotional distance.

Sessions are therefore shot through with unstable, provisional, reversible micro-transformations which are the gymnasium where the analytic couple can start a continuous training programme by bringing potentially conflictual aspects into play: moves which may arise from the intrinsically destabilising potential of some feelings and thoughts, but also from the simple difficulty of facing the world which every other human being offers and counter-offers us.

It is a level on which the small events which constitute the fabric of interaction become important: the language of the body, gesture, imitation, tone of voice; a meta-communicative level, often also transmitted verbally by means of nuances in the choice of words, in turn-taking (the rhythm of the dialogic exchange), and in the prosody of language.

One part of this level of interaction is implicit, does not pass through consciousness, and is associated with procedural memory, as theorised by Stern's group. Implicit relational knowledge, as distinct from the symbolic sphere, comes into play in intersubjective moments which can lead to new dispositions, or reorganise not only the therapeutic relationship but, above all, the patient's implicit knowledge, his way of being with others (Boston Change Process Study Group, 2010)

The linguistic level of the interaction therefore requires a sequence of small communicative incidents which activate a series of more or less effective responses which the couple tries to construct. From a bi-personal perspective, these incidents become the authentic engine of the analytic relationship, being an opportunity for linguistic games in Wittgenstein's sense of the term: the creation of new forms of life inside a social and cultural dimension made of rules and, I would add, "regular" violations of these rules.

I think this may be what Ogden (2013) means when he claims that the objective of an analytic couple is the construction of their own language: a language which progressively becomes the field's language, the analytic couple's original production which is adopted as a code on the most intimate levels of their interaction.

12.4   *The Dead*: history as a source of betrayals

The first hints at the theme of betrayal arrive in *The Dead*, the last story of the collection published by Joyce with the title *Dubliners* between 1902 and 1906. The collection as a whole is populated by a series of ordinary characters who run into small, everyday dramas. Joyce seems to present the idea that one's own personal story and one's environment are a legacy, for the most part uncomfortable, which will always accompany us and inevitably colour every new event.

This is the plot of *The Dead*: a young man named Gabriel is attending a Christmas party where he dances with a friend from university days who rebukes him for writing for an English newspaper and thus betraying his country, Ireland. The woman teases him humorously, calling him a "West-Briton", an expression used for an Irishman who sides with the English. She also scolds him for planning a trip abroad to study a foreign language when he ought to be staying in his native land and cultivating the national language. Cut to the quick, Gabriel replies that he is fed up with his native land. This introduces one of the central themes of Joyce's work, which has an obvious autobiographical reference and will be developed in other works: the betrayal of one's native land and language, exile as an inevitable life choice.

At the end of the evening, Gabriel comes upon his wife as she is listening, spell-bound, to the singing of a tenor. Gabriel is seized by a strong feeling of passion for his wife, and waits anxiously for the moment when they will go back to the hotel. But when he tries to come close to her, Gretta bursts into tears. That music had reminded her of a boy from her village with whom she used to go out before mov-ing to Dublin. Gabriel feels intensely jealous, and asks her if she had been in love with him. Gretta replies that the boy is dead. He was ill at the time but, despite this, he had gone to say goodbye to her on the evening before she left for Dublin, only to die a week later. The contrast between the physical desire Gabriel had felt for his wife during the evening and the strength of that boy's love leaves him with a wretched image of himself. He has never felt such feelings for a woman, and is surprised by the discovery that feelings of love can be so strong as to exceed self-love and love of one's own life. But now he starts to doubt: could Gretta have had another man? Perhaps she hasn't told him the whole story. His jealousy arises from the impossibility of possessing the other completely, not only in the present and the future, but also in the past.

Dubliners enabled Joyce to come to terms with his homeland and his origins. In *The Dead*, the protagonist's morbid curiosity about his wife's past recalls the persecutory insistence with which Joyce asked Nora to tell him the details of her experiences, both sentimental and sexual, before they met.

In many senses, history is the main protagonist of *The Dead*: the weight of one's own history is present, as is that of the place and the family in which we are born, as a network of bonds to be broken free of in some way: a heritage of expe-riences which do not permit us to come close to the other in a completely virgin state, but in some way "soiled" by every relationship.

History plays a central role in the history and technique of analysis: history and its repetition (a theme very dear to Joyce) are fundamental to the Freudian idea of transference. The inevitable reappearance of traumatic events and unresolved features of important relationships is the basis on which Freud builds his therapy.

Different analytic models arise from different views of what history is: it can be material which must be re-narrated in work that has no definitive conclusion, or something with an ultimate meaning to be objectively discovered. History can be understood as one level of the analytic relationship or as a looming presence, a product of the strongest resistance that the patient can make to the analysis: history-memory to be actively opposed, to be obscured so that something may be left to emerge which we would otherwise not see (O) and which, for Bion, constitutes the analytic experience against which we defend ourselves by means of various technical ruses such as transformation in dream (Ferro, 2006), or which we obscure by means of negative hallucination (Civitarese, 2016).

As I imagine it in the analytic session, history understood as a sequence of facts which have occurred stands as an opposite pole to the oneiric in a continual confrontation-clash where reality constitutes a potential obstacle to the expansion of the analytic couple's ability to dream, but also an appropriate limit which stops the development of the oneiric from turning into delusion.

12.5   *Dedalus*: betrayals by the artist/analyst

Joyce always kept in mind the Dublin where he spent the first twenty years of his life. Putting a decisive spatial distance between him and it did not mitigate the intensity of the relationship but helped him to bring into mental focus the various elements which composed the place of his roots.

A Portrait of the Artist as a Young Man (which I will call by the briefer *Dedalus*) is the work through which Joyce comes to terms with his adolescence. I want to take two moments from this book which recount experiences of betrayal as necessary events in the construction of identity, as well as through painful distancing or even more traumatic but inevitable breaks.

> I will try to express myself in some mode of life or art as freely as I can and as wholly as I can, using for my defence the only arms I allow myself to use – silence, exile, and cunning.
>
> (Joyce, 1917 p. 247)

The three weapons which Joyce believes he can allow himself to use are highly suggestive as a stimulus to analytic reflection: *silence* is a strange weapon for a writer, however fertile it might be, and we could consider it an analogue of negative capability in analysis. Giving priority to listening, resisting the temptation to saturate the dialogue with our thoughts, allows the analytic space to be filled with new thoughts. In another context, Joyce's idea concerns the silence of the past, of its heaviest and most burdensome features, whereby new voices may assert themselves and tell stories that are not (excessively) conditioned by undigested residues of experiences which have already been lived.

The second weapon is exile, understood as the disposition of the mind which renounces the certainties and comfortable sensations of familiarity. The objective is to experience new ways of living which can only come into being at times when the usual points of reference are lost: times, in other words, of confusion.

Exile from safe havens suggests Ulysses who, after his return to Ithaca, feels the need to set off again, abandoning his homeland and his family to end his life at the Pillars of Hercules, a symbol of the limit of human knowledge. The constant search for new ways forward in an analyst's training not only aids his research but is the antidote to a lethal tendency to remain anchored to his own ideas. I am thinking of what Bion writes about the need, especially with psychotic patients or when the psychotic part emerges, to accept the loss of our theories so as to allow our interventions to acquire uniqueness, even if this involves an experience of alienation, and to work with the psychotic patient in a way he will be able to perceive and accept (Bion, 2013).

The third weapon Joyce speaks about is cunning, *mêtis* in Greek which, in the adventures of Ulysses (already present in Joyce's mind), reflects the role which made him famous among the Greeks. Ulysses is tasked with inventing ad hoc solutions, and unmasks deceptions because he himself thought of them first. For example, he discovers Achilles, who wants to stay out of the war by dressing as a woman, because he himself had tried to avoid leaving for Troy by pretending to be mad. He finds solutions because he has experienced the weight of every emotion on himself and he knows their structure; he understands others because he has reflected on himself.

What emerges is the way Joyce conceives the work of the artist as the creation of something which becomes progressively independent of the artist himself and animates its own life.

> The artist, like the God of the creation, remains within or behind or beyond or above his handiwork, refined out of existence, indifferent, paring his fingernails.
>
> (Joyce, 1917, p. 215)

This seems an extremely effective, bitterly ironic image for an analyst-artist who, at the end of the creative process, such as the work of the couple in analysis, detaches himself so as to leave this joint production to one person who (we hope) will now resume her life with better prospects.

This happens in an ideal analytic process: the reality of the analytic encounter is instead, and above all, a matter of small and large betrayals. There is much analytic writing about errors and misunderstandings, but not so much about lies, secrets, and silent withholdings which occur in the analytic context: betrayals which come about when we hide ourselves behind our role and avoid detecting certain negative feelings which the patient has about us, thus amputating parts of the other if this implies danger or effort for us, or contact with unknown or highly conflictual aspects of ourselves. Or when we do not consider the effort the patient makes or the pain he or she suffers in being with us, letting ourselves be taken over by the search for truth, or forcing parts of the patient into moves towards integration; when we are blind to our inevitable errors and do not take responsibility for them. We betray if we only listen to the content of what the patient tells us and not its emotional aspect; if we refer everything that happens in the session to the past and not to the present, taking ourselves in some way out of the relationship; if we do not tolerate being simultaneously traitors and betrayed, in the inevitable game of enactment which the analytic relationship offers (Charles, 1997).

But there are also betrayals which relate to that dimension, emphasised by Freud, of analysis as an impossible task.

a   One paradoxical feature of the analytic situation is obvious, and derives from the contrast between what starts out as a working relationship marked out by defined times (if only by the frequency of the meetings), an agreement which entails an economic component, with the depth of the emotions that are being put into play. This feature, present in the clinical experiences which Freud passed on to us, seems even more evident today. The bi-personal perspective makes the couple, not the patient, the object of attention in the session, and this accentuates the paradox.

Presenting the analytic situation as fiction does not seem to diminish its power but reinforces it. In the literary sphere, Umberto Eco reveals that there is no character more real than those in fiction, because we know all of Raskolnikov's intimate thoughts, but are not sure what is going on inside one of our own relatives.[2] In the same way, the possibility of catching *in vivo* and knowing the smallest details about a character from the session, of observing the ongoing composition of a relationship with its components, both those that are transferential and those that are original to the analytic encounter, sweeps away any fictional aspect, if by this we mean the sense of being an artefact (a term which should have no negative connotations since, etymologically speaking, it only underlines how man has intervened in a certain process). What happens is real and provokes changes, crises, pleasure, pain.

b   Included in this picture are the analyst's periods of solitude which characterise certain complex moments of every therapy and the need to confirm his own identity. Much has been written about the risk that some analytic tools, such as the interpretation of the transference, may become the analyst's way of recognising himself as an analyst, and may do more to reinforce his own identity than to serve the needs of the patient. More macroscopic cases concern an analyst in difficulty, or one who is no longer taking care to develop, and these can lead to very serious infringements of the patient-analyst relationship. An analyst who is functioning well enough does work which in some way leads him or her to spend a lot of time exposed to what Kernberg (1986) called radioactive fallout: that is, to be exposed for several hours a day to elevated levels of human suffering. A necessary complement to add to this is active study and training in contact with colleagues. Furthermore, so as not to fall into an obvious contradiction with what we are trying to communicate to our patients, there are those moments we keep for ourselves within a way of life which does not neglect a good balance between work and our own affects and interests. All this in a day which continues to have only twenty-four hours.

c   An aspect which makes analytic work ever more alive and perhaps also more dangerous is the constant experimentation which takes place in the consulting room. Especially with psychotic patients, but in fact every time we move off onto psychotic paths in any relationship, we are engaging in research. Bion (2013) wrote that there are certain patients and certain situations we should have nothing to do with, but in a spirit of research or by accident we end up being involved with them and have to try and do something. A paradox is created in that the analytic relationship is configured as an intimate affective relationship whose objective is the achievement of greater emotional stability and greater freedom on the part of the analysand, but it contains a degree of experimentation and risk since, however well trained we are and however much we act in good faith, it is inconceivable that we will be able to deal with every analytic event.

The problem of research is also posed when we try to extend ourselves and enrich our understanding of a clinical experience through contact with colleagues. While we take the greatest care to preserve anonymity, there is inevitably a betrayal of intimacy which is often detected by the patient and marked by the arrival in dreams of intrusive or over-numerous characters derived from a perceived loss of privacy in the consulting room.

12.6 *Exiles*: betrayal as a shadow of the relationship

Exiles is Joyce's only work for the theatre, composed after *Dubliners*, in which he had spoken about his city, and *Dedalus*, in which he had spoken about his education, and before *Ulysses* and *Finnegans Wake*. In this play, Joyce concludes his rethinking of important autobiographical elements.

A critic at the time of its first performances wrote that the characters seemed to have had all vital energy taken from them and were entirely in the sway of emotions they were unable to direct or control.

The play makes constant reference to autobiographical situations. It tells of Richard, an Irish writer who has come home after a stay in Italy, as Joyce himself had done, and like the author he is accompanied by a woman he has never married, of a lower class, with a son born abroad. Richard's companion, Bertha, is courted by Robert, her husband's best friend. She seems to accept Robert's advances, urged on by her husband himself, who denies that he is jealous, but obliges her to tell him all the details of her seduction by Robert.

This refers to two real episodes from Joyce's life in which the writer had doubted Nora's faithfulness. The second of these episodes occurred in Trieste, when a Triestine journalist courted Nora, who told Joyce about it. The journalist's name, Roberto, is the name he gives the man who tries to seduce Bertha in *Exiles*.

When the moment draws near for the betrayal to take concrete form, Bertha asks Richard whether or not she should go. In a terse dialogue, Richard leaves the decision entirely to Bertha, apparently respecting her freedom, but in reality placing her in an impossible situation. Indeed, Richard leaves us to understand that the possibility of a physical betrayal does not change the inevitability of the mental betrayal which has already happened and is irreparable: "You didn't do it, but you regret it." The soul, says Joyce, has its virginity, just as the body does. Love, understood as desire for the other's wellbeing, is such an unnatural phenomenon that it is hard to repeat since the soul is incapable of recovering its virginity or of regaining enough energy to be "united" with another "in body and soul" (1918, p. 154).

Richard/Joyce plays cat and mouse with his wife, and the name of "Woman-killer" which Nora/Bertha gives him signals the dramatic nature of the emotions in play.

in the very core of my ignoble heart I longed to be betrayed by you and by her – in the dark and the night – secretly, meanly, craftily. By you, my best

friend, and by her. I longed for that passionately and ignobly, to be dishon-
oured for ever in love and in lust. . . . To be for ever a shameful creature and
to build up my soul again out of the ruins of its shame.

(ibid., p. 88)

So, being betrayed is effective in confirming a persecutory disposition and in
some way justifying one's own mistrust of human relations, and it helps to defend
one from the risk of a total involvement.

The play offers a radical perspective on the mental betrayal which seems to
occur when, if only for a moment, we come across so much as a single thought
in a person's mind about someone other than his partner; and overcoming this
betrayal is impossible.

If we are analysts naturally inclined to immersion in the field, we are making
ourselves available to raised emotional temperatures. The fantasies of exclusiveness in the relationship cannot fail to come into the picture. When elements of
reality intrude into the analytic situation, we are faced with the problem of the
"field's virginity". The risk is that the analytic temperature abruptly drops, causing the collapse of that aspect of the analysis which is concerned with the limits
and paradoxes of the relationship itself; that is, with the difficult co-presence of
intense affective experiences and certain concrete features: for example, paying a
professional for his or her work or the exclusion of physical contact.

12.7   *Ulysses*: a day-long analytic session

"When one can have the cooked flesh, why have the raw?" is one of Virginia
Woolf's disparaging comments as she tried to read *Ulysses*. But it is precisely this
raw quality which incites the reader's collaboration, an invitation to cook together.
Ulysses is a work in which the most usual, banal acts of daily life become opportunities for narrative; a work which has brought about a break with tradition, just
as psychoanalytic thinking did at its birth.

The fundamental characteristic of *Ulysses* is that each episode creates its own
technique. Beckett said that Joyce's writing is not *about* something, but *is* something: the complexity which derives from this mirrors the human condition. Similarly, every analyst experiences with surprise (and weariness) the way in which
every analytic journey, if it is working well, steadily acquires its own unique language, rhythm, and structure. The difference between interior monologue, which
characterises a line of novels written during the turn of the nineteenth and twenti-
eth centuries, and the stream of consciousness in *Ulysses* is Joyce's continual evo-
cation of non-verbal characteristics, the musicality of words, and the request for
the reader's collaboration, calling on him to re-live and interpret the word itself.
All these characteristics are echoed in the attention paid in every single analytic
dialogue to the preverbal and to features of style.

Continuarration is the term used by Joyce to define how different levels of
consciousness and the unconscious can be superimposed in determining the

construction of the narrative. In this process, memory is the basis of imagination, which becomes the more or less conscious reworking of what is remembered (Sabatini, 2011).

Although this view could seem remote from Bion's invitation to work without memory and desire, in fact the use of memory in Joyce does not obstruct the emergence of the new but testifies to the continuous evolution of memory itself and of the narratives in a potentially endless game. It is this memory which does not obstruct the emergence of the new, which is the basis of creativity: "the experience where some idea or pictorial impression floats into the mind unbidden and as a whole" (Bion, 1992, p. 383).

The idea of *continuarration* suggests a vision of human communication in which many levels are simultaneously present, each continuing in another, leaving everyone with the possibility of attuning him or herself on one or other of the levels. This is what happens in analysis too if we imagine a slash in the Conscious/Unconscious variable which unites instead of separating, so that there is a binocular view of every analytic object (Civitarese, 2016). Likewise, the various levels of interaction and temporality should be thought of as being in continuous mutual tension.

The omniscient and judging narrator disappears and we have an opening onto a multi-layered narrative universe with varied and complementary meanings (Eco, 1962). Indeed, the variety of styles and characters in the novel gradually gives way to an extra-terrestrial figure, the arranger, the orchestrator, who does the organising, commenting, sometimes addressing the reader directly, and keeping the various pieces of the mosaic together (Terrinoni, 2012).

In the analytic arrangement, which privileges a joint construction of the text of the session, a sort of voice of the field progressively emerges and takes on responsibility for ensuring the continuity of the journey. We can understand it as a function which the analyst performs in the name of the field. When we try to define it we also have to resort to metaphor (second sight, emergence of the field). Stylistically speaking, it is perhaps the sum of all that is expressed by the couple's original language, including the non-verbal language which finds expression in the small acts that constitute any couple's particular way of encountering each other. It is a difficult feature to define and is concerned with the artistic quality of analytic work, both as an attribute of the analyst's subjectivity and as a function of the analyst as a medium between the level of the field and the couple.

Returning to the theme of betrayal, having been a fundamental ingredient of Joyce's previous works, it does not disappear in *Ulysses* but is obvious in the first chapter when Stephen Dedalus is betrayed by his friend Buck Mulligan who invites a British intruder, Haines, to their tower. However, a quality of reconciliation becomes predominant as the book progresses; the strength of feelings overcomes the pain of betrayal as a shadow over relationships.

Stephen, terrified by the ghost of his mother, with whom he did not want and has not sought a reconciliation, asks her "Tell me the word, mother, if you know now. The word known to all men" (Harmondsworth, Penguin, 1968, p. 516).

There are various hypotheses about the word known to all men: one is that it is *love*, especially if we take into account an earlier sentence (Ellmann, 1988): "Do you know what you are talking about? Love, yes. Word known to all men".[3]

The word known to all men takes us back to the pervasive and indispensable force of feelings. Again, in the last chapter, the monologue which has what we could call Molly's waking dream-thought as its protagonist (forty pages with scarcely any punctuation), starts with the memory of a recent marital betrayal: but then we see the steady emergence of feeling and a painful but complete acceptance of the dramatic human condition.

In Joyce the deepest and most vital affects are given to female characters: Molly's noisy finale is not a happy ending but a reconciliation, as if Molly were wondering "Is it worthwhile going through the pain of loving, of making ties?" and the answer is her final "Yes".

12.8   Negative therapeutic reaction: from betrayal to the perception of the boundary

The constant alternation in Joyce's work between moments of extreme intimacy and abrupt remoteness, and the impossibility of finding an ideal distance in one's relationship with one's own history, homeland, family, and with women, make us think of the paradoxical phenomenon *par excellence* of psychoanalysis: the negative therapeutic reaction (NTR), a clinical event which presents itself in fertile periods of work and can lead to the therapy being abruptly broken off.

NTR was initially thought of only as a disturbance in the relationship caused by the patient's pathology or by technical errors on the part of the analyst, and over time has become something more varied.

This clinical phenomenon was brought to light by Freud (1909, 1914, 1923), who described clinical situations in which the patient cannot tolerate the progress of the treatment or certain stimuli which he or she is receiving in therapy, and reacts in a paradoxically negative way.

As often happens in psychoanalytic practice when we try to give meaning to features which are obstructing the work, writers who have subsequently addressed the phenomenon show an oscillation between privileging the vertex which leads them to read it as resistance, a sort of betrayal by the analysand, and a different perspective in which the temporary or definitive withdrawal from the analytic relationship is taken as a legitimate defence adopted by the analysand to protect himself from an excess of intimacy or truth (in the Bionian sense). Such defensive configurations have the aim of denying dependency in order to avoid catastrophic reactions and of maintaining the torpor of the analysand's most suffering aspects.

A fundamental step forward has been the consideration of NTR as a tool which shows up the dysfunction of the analytic dialogue and the need to retune it (Barale and Ferro, 1992). NTR points to functions of the analytic field that are not yet sufficiently active, and so it can be an opportunity to express important emotional areas that have not yet had access to thinkability, or it can indicate the presence of defensive walls: a defensive resource of the analysand in moments of intolerable suffering, but also a sign of life enacted in the transference which speaks about anxieties of separation and individuation. A sort of paranoid reaction which the patient adopts in order to deny the need not to feel threatened by the perception of dependency (Zapparoli, 1992).

For some authors, NTR is inevitable in any valid analytic process, a particular form of enactment which must occur if an analysis is to be carried out success-fully. It is as if the patient needed to re-live certain experiences of the past in order to regain control over them. NTR could also signal the dissolution of a fictitious agreement which has brought a "false Self" to analysis and with which the analyst has been colluding.

A further evolution of the concept of NTR could be to think about it as an inevi-table central event in any analytic journey, one which is manifested in different ways depending on the analyst's theoretical model, and signals the most important collateral effects of the model itself: the paradox effect.

In a field model, the central factors are a great involvement of the analyst and patient with each other, with lower degrees of asymmetry than in more classical models, and the reading of every communication from the patient as potentially concerning the analytic relationship. The result is an extreme closeness which inevitably undergoes a traumatic moment when the field is entered by aspects that are too real, or when the analyst uses her or his "second gaze" to detect the move-ments of the couple, thereby breaking the illusion of an absolute rapport.

NTR therefore presents itself as a phenomenon arising from the end of the illusion of a pure, virginal analytic field in which external reality has no weight and in which the relationship is absolute. It tells of mourning for the analyst's feelings of omnipotence, her or his idealisation of analysis and its transforma-tive abilities.

The psychotic phases which every analysand may pass through are caused by the perception of need as something tyrannical. Betrayal becomes a sort of rebel-lion and often assumes the configuration of NTR, which thus becomes a "neces-sary betrayal".

12.9   *Memoir of the Future:* Joyce and Bion

It is no surprise that, in the epilogue to his trilogy *Memoir of the Future*, which contains Joycean echoes in its structure and use of characters, Bion wrote

All my life I have been imprisoned, frustrated, dogged by common-sense, reason, memories, desires and – greatest bug-bear of all – understanding and being understood. This is my attempt to express my rebellion, to say "Good-bye" to all that. It is my wish, I now realize doomed to failure, to write a book unspoiled by any tincture of common-sense, reason, etc.

(Bion, 1991, p. 13)

This is how Bion explains a work with, besides its literary richness, contains his most original thoughts, dismantled and reassembled in various ways.

But what impact does the trilogy have on a reader who loves the works of Joyce?

> I can't stand this damned noise. It is like being bombarded with chunks of feeble puns, bits of Shakespeare, imitations of James Joyce, vulgarizations of Ezra Pound, phoney mathematics, visions of boyhood, second childhood and visions of old age
>
> (ibid., *The Dream*)

This sentence comes from the first novel in the trilogy and could be a perfect description of the sensations I had on a first reading, when I felt it was a stylistic exercise which was not always entirely effective.

In his Introduction, Bion says that the key to reading the book is not in its changes of meaning but in its changes of rhythm which are difficult to identify, as it would be hard to identify the key of a musical composition written with no modulations indicated.

The tonic or home key could be the one which Foresti (2014) called an always unstable dialectical tension, creating a virtuous circle between order and disorder, and between complexity and simplicity, which, in my opinion, has the sole limitation that it repeats itself over and over in an alternation between passion and disenchantment.

It is, however, a structure more like a Platonic dialogue in which the play of characters and dialogue has a maieutic function. The concepts are dismantled and seen from a variety of perspectives, but the sensation is that that this may bring to light truths already present in the author's mind and that the aim may not be unlike Freud's when he imagined himself having to address an interlocutor hostile to psychoanalytic thought, anticipating his objections and arguing against them.

A second reading has led me to concentrate only on the book's conceptual aspects, which are numerous. Bion is aware that his thinking is different from that of the psychoanalytic tradition. He refers to the invention of non-Euclidean geometries (he calls them "mad") which turn out to be useful in a non-Euclidean, infinite space. This is a question of a new type of mental space (the analysis of psychotic parts, the bi-personal perspective), and so it is necessary to invent a new system which will work for it. If the environment which Freud found adequate is unable to contain a psychoanalytic discussion, then it will need to be enlarged as he himself enlarged it when he discovered that not all his patients had been sexually assaulted.

When the paradigm changes (and it is in this sense that I see an affinity between Bion and Joyce), we have to find a field on which to play the new game and, in fact, the trilogy seemed to me to be Bion's opportunity to benefit from a literary and therefore "psychoanalytically neutral" field to put his thoughts into play, freely disseminating them, hiding them, as it were, in the folds of the narrative, free from the obligations of scientific communication.

12.10 Psychoanalytic experiences: betrayal or translation of the method?

Ulysses has been considered a betrayal of the idea of the novel, its death-sentence. Fortunately, this hasn't happened but it has certainly brought about an irreversible turn in the history of literature.

In the psychoanalytic field, the problem of new ideas which bring about changes of paradigm is not only posed by the emergence of new meta-psychologies, but also by new ways of using the analytic instrument.

The debate about extensions of the psychoanalytic method could have para-doxical features, and like all paradoxes, these are there to stimulate thought and to challenge, rather than to be resolved.

The Sorites paradox sets us the problem of what we can take away from some-thing (which for us is psychoanalysis) without the thing being changed so sub-stantially that it has to be called something else.[4]

The growth and even the survival of psychoanalysis depend on the possibility of constantly calling into question certain components which, until a few decades ago, would have been considered sacred, adapting them to our patients, to their requests, and to the context in which we are acting.

I am thinking, for example, about the use of the couch, which is no longer indispensable, at least in the phases when the relationship is being built up, and which is counter-indicated in the treatment of seriously ill patients, according to some writers.

Or the frequency of the sessions, with the search for the highest number pos-sible, while on the whole abandoning the canonical four sessions a week, except in the case of training analyses.

In the private practice of most analysts, the alternation of more classically ana-lytic therapies with therapies involving external support or with therapies that are less intensive in terms of the number of sessions, changes the character of the working day and cannot help having an impact on the analyst's mental disposition (which is obviously always the same).

The exploration of other contexts – institutional, for example (psychiatric facili-ties, hospitals, schools, prisons), or couples therapy (obviously I am not including the psychoanalysis of children and groups because they have a well-established tradition, although it should make us think of the evolution which is already part of the common heritage) – makes us think that something analytic can also occur in contexts other than the classical.

The increasing use of Skype for therapy, dispensing with all physical contact, seems to require a chapter of its own.[5]

All of this has repercussions for the identity of the analyst, who must find the way to manage his or her everyday life without feeling that his or her identity is being called too much into question. There is a risk of our finding ourselves constantly faced with an impossible choice: betray the institution and its super-egoistical aspects, or betray ourselves and our own original individual journey.

Having run through all these varied scenarios, I would like to make some observations about psychiatric consultation. I have found myself wondering if a consultation in a hospital setting, which very often entails a single contact with the patient (though behind it there is a history created between the consultant and the medical and surgical team), has a different quality when it is made by a psychiatrist-psychoanalyst.

In the encounter between patient and care team in an institutional setting there are certain concepts and tools originating in our consulting rooms which act as a bridge between the analytic experience in the strict sense and encounters in other settings which may be able to preserve an analytic quality.

I start from the presupposition that in every significant human relationship there is a level of implicit, unconscious communication in which the elements which appear in the conversation and their correlated emotions are not the sum total of the thoughts and emotions of the couple, and cannot be attributed to one or the other, but are configured as a third element with independent qualities and dynamics. It is a level which finds its greatest expression in the classical analytic scenario, but operates in any emotionally significant encounter.

In any relationship within an institution, various levels are activated which derive from the transference-countertransference (between patient and doctor, care team, institution), from the trans-generational, from the uniqueness of the experience of illness and the encounter with the different caring figures, and from the perspective of human finiteness. The quality of the analytic intervention lies in thinking that these levels are all present all of the time with differing degrees of intensity. Extra-verbal communications have great importance as the language of the body, a body obviously all the more eloquent in the hospital setting.

As happens in an analytic journey, when the therapeutic encounter takes place in an institution, elements can intrude which threaten to put the relationship into crisis. These can originate in the patient's suffering, in the therapist's fear for his or her own psychic suffering correlated to his or her sensation of impotence, in the impact of the patient and her or his pathology on the medical and surgical team and their internal codes, in the relationship with the institution. In the institutional situation it can also be helpful to imagine enactment as an inevitable phenomenon, dangerous but potentially fertile.

In analysis, the possibility of using interventions with varying degrees of saturation (interpretations that are weak, or narrative, or presented using the patient's own words) alerts the analyst to the need to gauge the sustainability of his or her intervention according to the patient's capacity. In this way, the analyst reduces the degree of variation between the various interventions he or she makes in the different contexts where he or she works.

The narrative style, functioning as a bridge towards what is foreign and as a mitigating instrument, can colour the analyst's interventions, facilitating a dilution of the mass of emotions generated by physical illness.

In the work of psychiatric consultancy, contact with bodily illness creates an impact with some very strong elements of reality. Inevitably this poses the problem of how to reconcile these with the oneiric, which constitutes a fundamental feature of the analytic stance.

It can be helpful to imagine that the development of the oneiric does not arise from the negation of reality, but from the continual play of forces between the specific weight of reality and the negative capability of the analyst who tries to maintain a free space in his mind for producing images, fantasies, and emotions.

The first important change in the attempt to offer a psychoanalytic model in the institution has been to stop thinking about a psychoanalysis in the institution but about a psychoanalyst in the institution:[6] in other words, stressing the importance of the *internal* setting, understood as the therapist's readiness to accept the patient's projections and those of the care team, while offering her or his own psychoanalytic perspective. Not forgetting that what I have described is a two-directional process: we too acquire new skills from these experiences.

The distinctiveness in an institutional setting of the encounter with a psychiatrist-psychoanalyst could be formulated in this way: first and most fundamental is the continuous training which is made possible by belonging to our society, not only through the instruments of personal analysis and supervision, but also by means of the various groups in which we compare ourselves with our peers on clinical and theoretical matters. As for the specific quality of the encounter, the analyst has a mental disposition which leads him or her to listen on different levels, and hence also to a capacity for reading what happens on different levels which are present simultaneously and colour the various moments of the encounter in a more or less significant way.

12.11   *Finnegans Wake*: the play of characters in a dream environment

> I might easily have written this story in the traditional manner. . . . But I, after all, am trying to tell the story of this Chapelizod family in a new way. Time and the river and the mountain are the real heroes of my book. . . . Yet the elements are exactly what every novelist might use: man and woman, birth, childhood, night, sleep, marriage, prayer, death. . . . There is nothing paradoxical about this . . . only I am trying to tell my story on many planes of narrative with a single aesthetic purpose.
>
> (Ellmann, 1982)

This is indeed what surprises us when we read *Finnegans Wake*: the extreme complexity of a story whose *fabula* is the one which constitutes the plot of many stories, including analytic ones. The distinctive feature which has interested psychoanalysts has been the continuous mutation of the characters' identities as they take on different identities in different contexts, to such an extent that someone has tried to make a count of the characters and their roles, defining "who is who when everyone is someone else".[7]

A paradigmatic situation is that of H.C.E., the innkeeper protagonist whose initials, depending on the context, can mean the innkeeper's name, Humphrey Chimpden Earwicker, but also suggest God (Haveth Childers Everywhere) or Everyman (Here Comes Everybody) across time, from Adam to Finnegan.

The play of the characters in the book is fascinating and effectively describes the role which the concept of character has taken on in the field model, the vertex of which in the analytic scene is to read the continual mise-en-scène of the couple's highly varied configurations. Eco (1962) calls this play a movement which disentangles and re-embodies: in psychoanalytic terms we could say that the couple tries to strip each word of rusty meanings that are the product of defensive moves so as to leave space for new and surprising meanings.

After *Ulysses*, the reconciliation of mankind with his condition continues in the dream environment of *Finnegans Wake*, a dream not only because it is set at night, a night in which the protagonist H.C.E. re-evokes the story of humanity in his dream, but because dream-logic colours the characters. The narrative levels cut across each other, and the text is made up of linguistic games, allegories, allusions, ambiguities, metamorphoses: a representation of the chaos of human life using portmanteau words which require the reader to make choices and to pay great attention to the harmonies (thinking of words as if they were musical chords).

The notions of time, identity, and causal connection are called into question. The meanings of words change depending on the observer's position in a universe dominated by isotropia, where no perspective is privileged *a priori* (Eco, 1962).

Every story in an analysis should be thought of in an oneiric manner which permits the possibility of reading the text of the session, accepting the story's incoherence, the dismantling of the narrator's responsibility, and the artistic component which gives the story its dramatic colour.

The privileging of narrative aspects related to the oneiric is one of the characteristic features of post-Bionian psychoanalytic thought: from Bion's waking dream-thought and reverie to Ferro's transformation in dream and Ogden's talking as dreaming. The analyst's dream, or rather the field's, is the way we can gain access to the most complex levels of interaction.

But going back to the fundamental play between characters and context which is distinctive of *Finnegans Wake*, this leads to subjects which are first literary and then psychoanalytic. One of the cruxes of character as a literary concept is its relationship to the action, the storyline, which is evoked in an extreme form in *Finnegans Wake*. In order to know who the character is, I must read the context, the point we have reached in his or her history.

Over time, in the literary sphere, the relationship between plot and characters has changed. From Aristotle to the Russian formalists, plot understood as the totality of actions was considered the most important part of tragedy. The characters become who they are as parts of the action, playing a role and performing actions, linking and connecting a series of motives, subordinate to the way these interweave.

Todorov re-evaluated the role of the character as an encounter with a new face which enables the adoption of a different viewpoint. For some authors, what happens is a sort of revolt by the characters who no longer want to be treated as physical phenomena but lay claim to a psychological dimension and to autonomy, the right to have dark, not immediately evident features (De Benedetti, 1977).

In psychoanalysis, the character revolution has concretised into the concept of functional aggregate (Bezorari and Ferro, 1992). This has privileged its emergence from the field, its function as a way of describing the state of the emerging affective configuration. The relationship between character and plot has been placed in parenthesis because, as in *Finnegans Wake*, plot colours and co-defines that very configuration.

We could say that the plot gives time and tonality to the movements of the characters in the narrative. A variety of literary genres can be chosen by the patient, or rather by the relational field which is set up and to which the patient gives a voice (Ferro, 2014). There are many ways to dramatise a certain configuration, but it makes a difference whether the literary genre is a detective novel or an erotic one, a film or a dream. The parameters in play could be the story's greater or lesser intimacy, its greater or lesser degree of freedom.

12.12 A brief conclusion

It seemed possible to highlight an evolution in Joyce's works which shows pathways common to every human being, pathways which we find in our analytic experience. The protagonists of the Dublin which Joyce tells us about, human beings coping with everyday events, have evolved into characters who come into contact with the fulness of the human condition in the drama of detachment from homeland and family, as occurs in *Dedalus*. In *Exiles* we are made aware of the extreme danger in feelings, from a psychological perspective which places the inevitability of betrayal at the centre of everything. In *Ulysses* character manifests itself through narrative style and begins to interact with the reader in adventures which can be read on different levels, and in which the reader finds herself making a choice about which meanings to highlight.

Molly's Yes, the final word in *Ulysses*, is the acceptance of the human condition through the exaltation of moments of emotional intensity scattered throughout everyday life, an acceptance which in *Finnegans Wake* is extended into a context which concerns man's relationship with his condition, no longer circumscribed by the everyday, but extended throughout his history.

Notes

1 Joyce J. (1918 [2011]). *Exiles*. Redditch, Read Books Ltd, p. 47.
2 Bion, on the same wavelength: "Falstaff, a known artefact, is more 'real' in Shakespeare's verbal formulation than countless millions of people who are dim, invisible, lifeless, unreal, whose birth, deaths – alas, even marriages – we are called upon to

believe in, though certification of their existence is vouched for by the said official certification." (Bion, 1991, p. 4).

3 Ibid., p. 195.

4 The sorites is a paradox, an argument which assumes predicates that seem indisputably true and yet, by using rules of reference recognised as valid, it allows the inference of a conclusion which appears unacceptable. Sorites derives from *soròs*, which means "heap" in Greek. Indeed, the sorites is the paradox of the heap: if a heap of sand is reduced by one grain at a time, at what point does it cease to be a heap? As a further illustration, let's take the (vague) predicate "being bald". If we have 100,001 people described as bald, and there is only a single hair's difference between each one and the next, where is the point at which a person can no longer be described as bald? (Paganini, 2008).

5 Andrea Marzi has written just such an article: "The analyst's identity and the digital world: a new frontier in psychoanalysis" (The Italian Psychoanalytic Annual XI. Milan, Raffaello Cortina, 2018).

6 Many works have been written on this subject by the Pavia school of psychiatry, including De Martis, Petrella, and Ambrosi (1987).

7 *A Passion for Joyce: The Letters of Hugh Kenner and Adaline Glasheen*, edited by Edward M. Burns. Dublin, University College Dublin Press, 2008.

References

Badoni, M. (2015). *Tradimenti originali*. Lecture given at CPdP, 14 April 2015.

Barale, F. and Ferro, A. (1992). Negative therapeutic reactions and microfractures in analytic communication. In L. Nissim and A. Robutti (eds.), *Shared Experience: The Psychoanalytic Dialogue*. London, Karnac Books, pp. 143–65.

Bezorari, M. and Ferro, A. (1992). Percorsi bipersonali dell'analisi. Dal giocho delle parti alle trasformzioni di coppia. In L. Nissim and A. Robutti (eds.), *L'esperienza condivisa*. Milano, Raffaello Cortina.

Bion, W. R. (1991). *A Memoir of the Future*. Abingdon, Routledge.

Bion, W. R. (1992). *Cogitations* (edited by F. Bion). London: Karnac Books.

Bion, W. R. (2013). *Los Angeles Seminars and Supervision* (edited by J. Aguayo and B. Malin). London, Routledge.

Boston Change Process Study Group. (2010). *Change in Psychotherapy: A Unifying Paradigm*. New York, Norton.

Charles, M. (1997). Betrayal. *Contemporary Psychoanalysis*, 33, pp. 109–22.

Civitarese, G. (2016). *Truth and the Unconscious in Psychoanalysis*. Routledge, London and New York.

D'Amico, M. (1982). Introduzione. In *Exiles*. Pordenone, Edizioni Studio Tesi.

De Benedetti, G. (1977). *Personaggi e destino. La metamorfosi del romanzo contemporaneo*. Milano, Il Saggiatore.

De Martis, D., Petrella, F. and Ambrosi, P. (a cura di). (1987). *Fare e pensare in psichiatria*. Milano, Cortina.

Eco, U. (1962). The aesthetics of chaosmos: The middle ages of Joyce. In *The Open Work*, Vol. 1. Cambridge, Havard University Press, 1989.

Ellmann, R. (1982). *James Joyce*. Oxford Press University.

Ellmann, R. (1988). Prefazione. In J. Joyce (ed.), *Ulisse*. Milano, Mondadori.

Ferro, A. (2006). Da una psicoanalisi dei contenuti e delle memorie a una psicoanalisi per gli apparati per sognare, pensare: transfert, transfer, trasferimenti. *Rivista di Psicoanalisi*, 52(2), pp. 401–78.

Ferro, A. (2014). *Dreams and Psychoanalysis*. Abingdon, Routledge (2018) in press.

Foresti, G. (2014). Il rasoio di Wilfred. Leggendo Memoria del futuro di W.R.Bion. In Memoria del futuro, a cura di Civitarese G., Hinshelwood R.D., Marinelli S. *Funzione Gamma*, 33.

Freud, S. (1909). Notes upon a case of obsessional neurosis. In *SE* 10, pp. 151–318.

Freud, S. (1914). From the history of an infantile neurosis (Wolf Man case). In *SE* 17, pp. 1–122.

Freud, S. (1923). The Ego and the Id. In *SE* 19, pp. 1–66.

Jacobs, T. J. (2002). James Joyce and Molly Bloom: Reflections on their relationship. *Journal of the American Psychoanalytic Association*, 50, pp. 1271–82.

Joyce, J. (1914). *Dubliners*. Novara, De Agostini (1985).

Joyce, J. (1917). *Portrait of the Artist as a Young Man*. Milano, Adelphi (1976).

Joyce, J. (1918). *Exiles*. Rome, Edizioni Studio Tesi (1982).

Joyce, J. (1922). *Ulysses*. Harmondsworth, Penguin (1968).

Joyce, J. (1939). *Finnegans Wake HCE*. Milano, Mondadori (1982).

Joyce, J. (1939). *Finnegans Wake*. Libro secondo. Milano, Mondadori (2004).

Kernberg, O. (1986). Institutional problems of psychoanalytic education. *Journal of the American Psychoanalytic Association*, 34, pp. 799–834.

Ogden, T. H. (2013). Thomas H. Ogden in conversation with Luca Di Donna. *Rivista di Psicoanalisi*, LIX(3), pp. 625–41.

Paganini, E. (2008). *La vaghezza*. Roma, Carocci.

Sabatini, F. (a cura di). (2011). *James Joyce. Scrivere pericolosamente. Riflessioni su vita, arte, letteratura*. Roma, Minimum fax.

Terrinoni, E. (2012). Introduzione. In J. Joyce (ed.), *Ulisse*. Roma, Newton Compton.

Zapparoli, G. C. (1992). *Paranoia e tradimento*. Torino, Bollati Boringhieri.

Chapter 13

Surprise

Elena Molinari

Translation by Gina Atkinson

13.1 The experience of surprise: to surprise or be surprised?

The Bionian recommendation to begin every session without memory or desire, like Freud's dictum to listen with evenly hovering attention, forms the basis for a mental state that predisposes to the eruption of the unpredictable. To be surprised, then, is not only to be able to temporarily abandon the theoretical or method-ological constructs that support analytic practice, but also to approach the birth of something new.

Winnicott (1970, 1971) was the first to more explicitly use the term *surprise*, emphasizing that it was not the analyst's interpretation that was the engine of transformation, but rather his capacity to lead the child or adult patient to surprise himself. Lore Schacht (2001), clarifying the Winnicottian concept, specifies that the "capacity to surprise one's self" is both an intersubjective phenomenon and an intrasubjective one (Bolognini, 2001). In the former, one can be surprised in using the presence of the other to allow something new to emerge; in the latter, one marvels at the discovery of an aspect of the self that until then has remained unknown and inexpressible. The capacities to surprise the other, to be surprised, and to surprise the self are thus three situations intrinsic to the analytic process and to the capacity to play that underlies it. Winnicott's sense of the capacity to surprise one's self, whether applied to analyst or patient, has an essentially posi-tive and creative connotation.

Not infrequently, however, surprise can involve not only a feeling of marveling, but also a sense of whirling destabilization and a more or less explicit conflict – or even a feeling of pain, as in the case of an unexpected interruption in the therapy, see, for example Smith (1995). The reaction to an excessive degree of surprise challenges the mind with an emotional flood that is then violently projected. This fact leads us to consider that surprise must be adjusted, like any other emotion, to the transformative capacity of the subject who experiences it.

Bromberg (1998–2002) created a very apt expression to describe the moments in which, in the analytic process, microtraumatic flashes of discontinuity in understanding the other occur without producing fractures or breaks. Bromberg described and emphasized the capacity of the two subjects in analysis to transform enactments that continually punctuate the analytic process in "safe surprises". The moments in which feelings of fear and shame are activated actually generate primarily projective defensive movements that risk reenacting "tsunamis" of past traumatic situations in session. However, the inevitable collision between the subjectivities of the subjects involved in the analysis can become a relational event that generates an occasion for increased self-cohesion. With its ability to govern the intensity and degree of destabilization, surprise is a feeling that can create a new reality, a new space between spontaneity and security.

Certainly, in addition to the way in which it enters the analytic space, surprise in its various forms retains the characteristic of rapidly revealing itself. Such a characteristic locates surprise among the feelings that accompany creative processes; these feelings, in general, involve the work of slow and steady preparation, but the movement toward a solution, the satisfying form, the new idea takes shape in the mind in only a few seconds.

In this nearness to creative processes, surprise can be likened to what we have called psychoanalytic insight. An interesting definition, according to this perspective, is that given by Di Benedetto (2000): "Insight is the introspective act that results in a creation in itself, in a generative psychic event, by virtue of which new thoughts and emotions are born" (p. 33).[1]

The slow time course of the preparatory phase, very quick to reveal itself, besides aligning surprise with artistic and cognitive processes, calls to mind the originary aspect of birth. In considering this incarnate root of surprise, I would like to emphasize that the surprise accompanying every birth and every appearance of the new cannot be other than a relational experience, like a sort of play located midway between body and intellect. For these reasons, it finds a natural home in children and in parents who are able to surprise themselves yet again at the appearance of any apparently banal new knowledge gained by their child.

In trying to learn from this capacity to promote a life that is both so instinctual and yet sophisticated, when the analyst protects his o her ability to surprise him or herself and takes pleasure in the discoveries the patient makes about him or herself – in the relationship and in the possibility that new patterns of behavior may appear in his life – is a powerful curative factor in and of itself.

Through some examples, I will try to demonstrate how surprise supports the analytic process, indicating the various subtleties through which it appears.

13.2 I'm home!

When listening to events in the patient's life, it isn't always easy for the analyst to maintain an awareness of how much the constitution of reality, which also exists, may be the particular distinction of analytic listening. Every narration that occurs in the analytic office has the primary aim of communicating something about the emotion that analyst and patient together are living and trying to transform. In a certain sense, analytic listening is very close to what is activated when we listen to a book on tape: that is, though immersed in the narrated events, we are still aware that the story, as much as it draws on the author's personal and intimate life events, does not exactly mirror them. In an interview in which he was asked rather insistently about the relationship between a novel of his and real autobiographical events, the Israeli author Amos Oz answered: "Every story . . . is an autobiography, none is a confession" (p. 42).[2] With this pithy reply, Oz intended to emphasize that the obsessive search for historical, autobiographical truth transforms the reader of a novel into a voyeur. The impossibility of abandoning curiosity about the roots of a lived experience from which a novel takes its inspiration results in not only a loss of the author's creative experience, but also a distancing of one's own creative experience that arises from the reading encounter. Something similar can also happen in analysis when analytic listening lets itself be seduced by the real: surprising and often tragic developments hide in the shadow of the familiar and can destroy the analytic play.

Barbara came to her first session with her eyes filled with tears. After some months, she told me that the sadness dwelling within her was so intense that she felt she needed medication in addition to analysis. I agreed with her about the possible utility of an antidepressant, and Barbara consulted a colleague for this particular aspect of her care. In the meantime, the reasons for her immense pain became clear to me: her boyfriend had abandoned her at the beginning of her pregnancy, and shortly afterward she had lost the baby. In the background of the relationship difficulties with this man, there also seemed to be physical and psychological abuse that had gone on for a long time before she became pregnant. After losing the baby, Barbara had decided to file a legal complaint against her boyfriend because of this mistreatment, and she had even brought to her session evidence to document these tragic events.

About a year after analytic treatment began, my psychiatrist colleague called me to check in about the effectiveness of Barbara's medication treatment. During the phone call, almost casually, I learned that her legal complaint against this man, her ex-boyfriend – whom Barbara said had been violent toward her, and whose judicial course I had followed with trepidation in her accounts that had filled many sessions – had actually been withdrawn a few days after having been made. I clearly remember the surprise I felt that constricted my stomach and was then transformed into bewilderment when a question crossed my mind: why had Barbara felt the need to tell me in minute detail the steps leading up to a trial that was never held?

In the moments that followed, my colleague had continued to speak, and now that I was again tuned in, I heard that he had been telling me of Barbara's habit of recounting different stories to different interlocutors. "And the baby?" I asked, almost instinctively. "Excuse me – what baby?" asked my colleague.

The memory of how I had secretly cried inside while listening to accounts of the baby's burial and the torment of daily visits to the cemetery (even though I had sometimes briefly questioned myself about the strangeness of burying a fetus in a cemetery) came back to me as a sort of dizziness. I knew I had considered more than once that, in telling me about her dead baby, Barbara was also telling me about a part of herself that could not grow, that was indeed dead almost without having been born, but I had never thought that her torment did not have a basis in historical truth.

Had Barbara lied to me about everything, then? Maybe that wasn't even her real name, she didn't live where she claimed to, and she didn't do the work that she described to me the development of! Everything, I thought – she had lied to me about everything! My fantasy galloped toward stories of spies, to crime news, to a rapid succession of dark conspiracies.

"Doctor, are you hearing me?" The voice of my colleague came to me as though from another planet. I swallowed and for "solidarity" I, too, lied: "Yes, I'm hearing you but sometimes I lose the thread." That I had lost the thread was at any rate an undeniable truth, though on a different level.

If I had remembered a fragment of the novel *A Story of Love and Darkness* – which was, furthermore, a perfect title for this analysis (and perhaps for any analysis) – it would really have been helpful to me. The sense of that fragment was that we should not search for the heart of any story in the small space between its creation and author; the place to look is not in the space between writing and writer, but in the field between writer and reader (Oz, 2002).[3]

Certainly, the dead baby could stand in for a destroyed part of the patient, but also for a part not recognized by me and so mistreated. The man incapable of being close to her or of supporting the baby's development could also surely be me. The accusations and disappointing events of a long judicial course could represent an attempt to seek witnesses to the wrongs she had suffered.

These thoughts were painfully surprising, but to once again be in my analytic house restored a sense of hope and faith to me. Nonetheless, scratched all over and half destroyed like Calvin, I remained in doubt as to whether it is better to surprise or to be surprised.

13.3 A lie to tell the truth

Giacomo, a nine-year-old boy, had purposefully thrown his breakfast, consisting of hot chocolate, out the window. The liquid had landed on the neighbor's white deck chair and valuable wooden table on the balcony underneath. The neighbor's violent reaction in turn produced another disaster: Giacomo's father argued with him and then with Giacomo.

Feeling himself to be at the limits of his tolerance of the provocations that Giacomo came up with on a daily basis, the father decided to bring him to therapy.

At the first meeting at his father's initiative, Giacomo decides to give me his version of the event: "I was near the window and I tripped. The hot chocolate flew downward and Mr. Tiziano got very mad." After a brief hesitation, he adds: "But luckily I rescued the cup!"

Being familiar with the paternal version of this matter, I am unable to suppress an outbreak of laughter. Giacomo looks at me, surprised, and then laughs with me, perhaps somewhat struck by the fact that he has not made me angry, as often happens to him with adults. Surprise comes to life within each of us and connects us in an enjoyable emotional unison.

This child has lived through the separation of his parents with difficulty and cannot accept his father's new girlfriend. With his throwing the hot chocolate out the window, his contrariness reached the point of finally expressing to the world that certain things, even though they nourish him and he likes them, are at the same time things he would like to eliminate.

What really amuses me is his capacity to transform reality, because I think that, in this apparently manipulative act, the seed of a special creativity is hidden, a creativity that can be used to renew his capacity to cope with a difficult environmental situation. Giacomo is telling a story in which the character of a cup represents his capacity to contain intolerable emotions that he overturns in actuality in the environment around him.

In his manipulation of the story of what really happened – that is, with the addition of his having fortuitously prevented the cup from breaking – there is obviously a desire to mitigate his own responsibility with respect to the event, but also a desire to protect a container: the relationship with his father who is indispensable to his life.

In this context, what I would like to emphasize is Giacomo's capacity to surprise me with his inventiveness, and then to surprise himself at having found a way to establish a good relationship in analysis through a particular lie. Falsification of the event had the intent of getting adults to keep in mind that something barely manageable taxes a child's mind – but also to consider his capacity to bring into play emotional events disguised as provocations.

The inventiveness of which Giacomo is capable introduces a certain style into our analytic relationship, one in which I am called upon to be equally capable of imagination in order to stay close to him, inventing stories that can emotionally help him.

13.4 The surprise that crouches hidden in the session

The setting is a more stable methodological aspect of the analytic arrangement, set up to guarantee the possibility of observing the process. We are thus less prepared for an upheaval of it through which marginalization and surprise can lead to possible creative developments.

"Pardon me, doctor, do you by any chance have a diaper?"

This question is addressed to me from the door at the end of an initial consultation meeting. The problem for which this woman and her husband have consulted me concerns their eldest child, a son, but since she is breastfeeding and they have come from relatively far away, they arrived at the consultation together with their second child, a little girl who is just a few months old.

At first it takes a few seconds for me to get my bearings; then the mother gestures toward the baby in the stroller. I understand and politely reply that unfortunately I do not have any diapers.

When I decide the next day to take some notes on the consultation, the surprise I had felt in the anteroom on the previous evening begins to take on a wider significance. First, I am more aware of the way in which the couple arrived: "My husband dropped us off and went to park the car; he'll be here in a moment," the wife had begun in explanation of her husband's momentary absence. Although it is not at all difficult to park near my office at that hour, the husband did not join us until about a half hour later. In the meantime, the wife had described the behavioral and linguistic difficulties of their elder child to me. According to her account, these difficulties were bound up with the twofold trauma that had afflicted him when he started school: separation from the grandmother who had cared for him until then, and separation from his diapers. Since the child, according to the mother, had not yet mastered sphincter control, this drastic demand had in her view given rise to humiliation on a number of occasions. The father, who had meanwhile joined us, told me that a previous therapy had been broken off because the boy did not like being observed.

Since the family's provisional explanations of their child's difficulties in terms of direct causality had seemed to me, even while I listened to them, somewhat simplistic, the little appendix to the dialogue in the anteroom played a fundamental part in helping me put certain things together and assign at least a provisional meaning to them.

It seemed to me that the protagonists had in various ways invited me to understand that there was both an overflowing and a void that they found difficult to handle. I had experienced this in the first part of the consultation, when the constant interruptions due to the mother's caring for her crying infant and the account of the elder child's difficulties made me feel that so many demands were being made on me that I was quite unable to think. Thereafter, every so often I found myself looking at the empty chair, expecting the father and wondering where he might have ended up. The theory they had thought up to explain their child's problem once again suggested an unexpected deficiency of caring and the absence of a diaper to absorb evacuations.

At the door, they had given me the key to how the therapy could begin without being immediately evacuated, given that the father had *dropped off* his wife and daughter, and then explained to me that he absolutely did not want to be seen. Surprise was graphically portrayed in my mental image of the coyote in an animated cartoon about Wile E. Coyote and the Road Runner – in which, after a few moments of perilous suspension over an abyss, the adventure concluded with an inevitable flight in the crevice of a canyon.

To propose a form of observation/therapy to the father would have immediately provoked an interruption; to receive the mother and child would mean a collusion with the nonlistening of an infantile part of the father. To decide to see the child a few times either together with the mother or by himself, proposing a participatory consultation, might have been taken as a copout that immediately imposed unacceptable rules.

The solution grew out of my entering with greater awareness into the roles suggested to me, orienting my choice about the setting by proposing an approach pervaded by a relative passivity. I began by trying to be a diaper to receive and absorb the toxic fluids disseminated in the form of various kinds of action, which in the older child ended by becoming a disturbance of language and behavior. I told the parents that we could establish a schedule of when to meet and that they could take turns coming together, with or without the children, according to what seemed most useful to them.

Sometimes a selected fact, as Bion taught us, can succeed in pulling together a common feeling, a gathering up of scattered sensations, emotional perceptions flooded by projective identifications flowing through the analytic field.

13.5   Ellipsis points

Carla regularly comes to her sessions at a time other than the agreed-upon one. Having both worked outside the city and used public transportation for some time, we talked about this, sharing our mutual dismay at the trains' lack of punctuality.

Carla is a very conscientious person and when she is late, her arrival is always preceded by a text message: "Doctor, at this moment I'm in Rogoredo . . . I will get to your office at about 6:15"; "Again today . . . I will be a little late."

Only a small typographical error allowed me one evening to take note of the many ellipses that always filled her messages. I decided to play a little that evening, and I said to her: "Carla, in your texts there are always ellipses, and I was thinking that in weekly puzzle magazines, they stand for a missing word. How about if we play a game and take turns trying to add the missing word – one set of ellipsis points for me and one for you? For example, this evening's text said, 'Still late . . . I don't even know if I'll make it.' I would put in, 'I'm dead tired.'"

Carla: "As a matter of fact . . ."

I continue: "I could go get an aperitif and to hell with my session."

Carla, for whom even the smallest transgression had to be wiped clean, embraced the game and ironically entitled it "Round Trip," the name of a television series set on commuter trains. Filling in the ellipses with "suspended" words became a game that was truly surprising and transformative.

13.6   A touching surprise hidden in an ordinary session

Sandro had instigated his analysis with a request to be able to use the familiar form of speech in our meetings and had then reacted to my reluctance with anger. His request included a legitimate wish for closeness, which I imagined could not be so easily satisfied simply on a linguistic level, however. The decision to remain close without excluding the need to tolerate distance as well became an iceberg on which – like the *Titanic* – the analysis risked sinking shortly after being launched. My taking the time to understand, in fact, came to be felt by the patient as an act of intolerably presumptuous superiority.

For some time, he conveyed the extent of this experience to me through political stories of dictatorship and examples of sociological abuses of power, with which he was concerned in relation to his job in historical research. The "revolution" we would have to carry out in order to liberate his dissociated oppressed self from a pain that had matured during his developmental years, and that was reactivated in the analysis, would need to have the resolute and rapid nature of all liberation movements.

The desire for greater equality that hid his wish for deeper understanding kept alive in Sandro the violence of vengeful demands. In order to preserve this, it was also necessary for him to frequently emphasize the difference and distance in our dialogical exchanges: "You say this, while I, on the other hand . . .," "No, it isn't easy to put this together with that; they are two completely different things."

In many sessions over some years of our work together, we had to create temporary democracies, to see them overturned by furious rage, and to refine the art of emotional diplomacy. The experience of a humanly shared relationship as a goal with which to combat the anxiety of being emotionally overcome arrived stealthily, like a gentle surprise – one that was very far from a sudden and violent overthrowing. But like the experience of surprise, it had the character of a joyous birth.

Sandro: "What we said yesterday evening . . ."
Analyst: "We said?!"
Sandro: "Did I really talk like that?"
Analyst: "Yes, you did."
Sandro: "Well, what we said yesterday evening seemed to me to open a window in a closed room . . ."

13.7   A surprise enclosed within a shell

Gaia alternates moments of fullness with moments of emptiness. After periods of vivacious vitality, she is again sucked in by serious apathy, dense and tenacious, which keeps her in bed for weeks. Every choice, every place seems a prison to her after a time, one from which she must escape, but as soon as she is outside and has the liberty she craved, she finds it as empty as it is anxiety-provoking.

We begin to get acquainted, and I notice that, in an unexpected way, we feel very reciprocally engaged. As soon as this happens, Gaia skips a session, and in the next one she lets it drop that she will be abroad for six months.

On the threshold at her last session, she tells me she has to give me an object, and she slips a shell into my hand. It is a fossil shell with two very different sides: a smooth, colored one, and a white and chalky one that traces a spiral in relief. Since I am not at all sure whether the patient will return, I am surprised, moved, and stirred up by doubt about whether the gift represents a permanent goodbye or her entrustment of a part of herself to me until she comes back.

I immediately look for a place, even a temporary one, where I can put the shell before my next patient arrives. Without thinking much about it, I put it into a bowl that contains black sand from the Dead Sea, which sits together with other types of sand on a piece of furniture next to my armchair. The idea that determined my choice is both aesthetic and emotional: in the black sand, the light color of the shell creates a very pretty contrast, and the fact that this object is within my gaze cures me of the painful break with Gaia.

Then, in subsequent hours, I think further and notice the layers of meaning condensed in the little shell, as though in a dream. Its two-sidedness is a visible and concrete rendition of the double track on which Gaia seems able to live, and other elements – the sandy return to a "dead" sea, the color contrast that seems to address the idea of a relationship between vital aspects and lethal ones, the grains of sand as the multitude of thoughts not yet thought – seem to form a dream of mine and of Gaia's, a concrete dream still not dreamt.

13.8 Surprise as an antidote

To begin a session without memory or desire sets the stage for the possibility that the mind may embrace the new, allowing the emotion of surprise to invade it. Bion was evidently well acquainted with the human tendency to defend against the unknown, to organize inside what has already been experienced, forming a sense of reassuring security. To surprise and to be surprised is what the patient requires and what the analyst continually needs in order to stay alive. As both analysts and patients, we are always afraid of being born and of dying in our own eyes, of abandoning thoughts that have already been thought, and so allowing ourselves the experience of surprise can be one of the antidotes to psychic death, to an enclosure within theory. To surprise and be surprised can be the emotional path to a productive encounter.

Notes

1 Translation by Gina Atkinson.
2 Translation by Gina Atkinson.
3 Translation (of an Italian translation) by Gina Atkinson.

References

Bolognini, S. (2001). È Solo Accaduto. . .: Un Breve Commento A "La Capacità Di Sor-prendersi" Di Lore Schacht. *Richard E Piggle*, 2(9), pp. 131–6.
Bromberg, P. M. (1998–2001). *Standing in the Spaces: Essays on Clinical Processes, Trauma, and Dissociation.* The Analytic Press Inc., New York.
Di Benedetto, A. (2000). *Before Words.* Free Association Books, London, 2005.
Oz, A. (2002). *A Tale of Love and Darkness.* Mariner Books, New York, 2005.
Schacht, L. (2001). The Capacity to Be Surprised. *Richard e Piggle*, 9, pp. 117–30.
Smith, H. F. (1995). Analytic Listening and The Experience of Surprise. *International Journal of Psychoanalysis*, 76, pp. 67–78.
Winnicott, D. W. (1970). Living Creatively. In C. Winnicott, R. Shepherd and M. Davis (Eds.), *Home Is Where We Start From: Essays by a Psychoanalyst* (pp. 39–54). Harmondsworth: Penguin, 1986.
Winnicott, D. W. (1971). *Therapeutic Consultations in Child Psychiatry.* London: Hogarth.

Chapter 14

Contempt in clinical practice

Luca Nicoli

14.1 Introduction

I don't remember the exact reasons why that young man had consulted me so many years ago. He must have been coping with a chronic illness, he was very nervous.

He insisted that we address each other informally as "tu", and I replied that he could do so, but I preferred the formal "lei".

One day he was talking to me and I closed my eyes for a few moments to try and dream what he was explaining to me in laboriously concrete detail.

"If I'm worthless to you, there's no point staying here and talking!" he shouted, rushing out and slamming the door.

I never saw him again.

By closing my eyes, I had literally cancelled him from my world, denying him any value: he felt he was a victim of my contempt.

Contempt (Latin, *contemnere*, to despise), complete disdain for the other, is undoubtedly a matter of the gaze. Looking down from above, turning one's back, looking askance: the eyes of the contemptuous do not accept the figure of the interlocutor, his or her story, his or her identity, as something to approach with interest or curiosity, but reject – or even worse – ignore him or her.

The human animal, communal by nature, makes use of contempt as a social regulator: he or she denies interest and companionship – his or her gaze – to what he or she considers morally or socially unacceptable. By means of contempt, the individual reinforces his or her own membership of the group he or she belongs to, keeping his or her distance from betrayal, falsehood, moral weakness, and temptations, or whatever else his or her own cultural order may regard as abject.

If we take away the aura of cruel superiority with which we have clothed the term, we will be able to notice that much of children's upbringing and the transgenerational transmission of family values occurs by means of contempt for thinking and behaviour that are judged, consciously or otherwise, to be unsuitable or unacceptable. Adults may feel angry about something a child has done wrong, and the impulse may be to inflict a sharp dressing-down or a spanking. In this way there will be an approach, even if an aggressive one.

Alternatively, certain conduct may provoke contempt when it is experienced as being so remote from someone's own morality as to make her or him wish to keep her or his distance. In certain situations, for example when women are being abused, the development of contempt is decidedly helpful because detachment from the abusive and violent behaviour of one's partner represents a first step in freeing oneself from these lethal ties (Stein, 2011).

However, there are excesses, above all when parents, family members, and friends make an action, gesture or thought so wholly expressive of themselves that they become wholly unacceptable. I recall an adolescent boy, still very child-ish in the way he managed his emotions, whom I saw for a consultation some years ago. One evening, while he was staying with his mother's family in another town, he felt confused and frightened by a sudden pubertal excitation which he experienced guiltily as something completely foreign to him; he asked his young cousin to stroke his penis and make the nasty feeling go away. Both of them were immediately left troubled by this attempt, prematurely broken off.

The contempt with which the fourteen-year-old was treated by his mother's family was such that, having become "the paedophile", he was sent home the next day, and all contact was broken off with no possibility of an apology or amends.

We have all heard stories of fathers reacting to their adolescent children's mis-takes with similar contempt, going so far as not to speak to them for a month or even a year. "I would never have expected that from you!" is the terse sentence which seems to shut affection away in a tomb of irreparable disappointment. That cigarette or drunken episode, that escapade with a boyfriend, may not represent a mere misdemeanour that can be expiated, but a shame which covers the young person's whole identity, causing a "loss of face" now and forever. The conse-quences of such acts can also interfere seriously with narcissistic development and the integration of one's own impulses. The sense of modesty which should regulate the distance between the Ego and Ego Ideal ("take care of your image, honour, dignity, and beauty") can be violated and degraded by shame, a psychic state which makes us cover our faces with our hands, censor our own desires and feelings, disappear from the sight of the world, take our own lives.

As far as the relationship between guilt and shame is concerned, I refer the reader to Chapter 10 and will confine myself to recalling that the history of psy-choanalysis has focussed its attention on the first more than the second. Today, however, psychoanalysis recognises shame as a central problem in emotional suf-fering, even more so because of the enormous importance which image is assum-ing in our culture.

Beside these more extreme examples, children's everyday lives are regulated by constant observation of adults' faces, which express more or less consciously their approval or disapproval. Contempt is shown by "dirty looks", indifference, and physical or emotional distancing.

When the emotional turbulences of whoever is performing the maternal func-tion do not interfere too much with the mirroring process, the child sees benev-olence in the mother's gaze (Winnicott, 1967), or at the very least a moderate contempt for the various parts of him or her according to the moral and cultural context of which the parent is the bearer ("Don't steal!", "I can't believe you'd tell such a lie!"). Depending on how the infant identifies with the maternal gaze, the demands of his or her own superego will impinge in a similar way on his or her own self and his or her own desires. Their expression may be inclined more to an angry reaction which can lead to self-punishment in order to try and expiate a fault ("How can I ever forgive myself for what I did?") or a withdrawal into a self-disparagement tending towards exclusion and shame ("I know, I took that envelope, it's like stealing: I'm disgusted at myself!", "I don't deserve your love after lying to you like that!").

I will let the English analyst Paul Williams describe the consequences of seriously compromised maternal mirroring in his autobiographical account *The Fifth Principle*, which tells with merciless clarity about the first infantile reactions to the mother's contempt (2010, p. 23).

> My sister and I made demands on her that she felt were outrageous, unreasonable, impossible to meet and potentially highly damaging to her. We soon got the message that we were not wanted. . . . By the time I was four, I knew never to make any further demands on her and, wherever possible, to make myself invisible. The responsibility for this disastrous state of affairs with my mother I always felt was mine. Although forced to become grimly independent, I felt deeply ashamed at being a failure as a son.

14.2   The myth of the good (and blind) analyst

In my clinical experience I have found evident traces of contempt in many patients who otherwise have had very little in common. In this chapter I will try to give an account of my way of working with these features. Field theory helps me pay attention to the emergence of such themes as signals that, on some level of the analytic relationship, something is being rejected by somebody. I often choose not to make the matter overt, letting my mind wander among the multiplicity of possible levels: historical-reconstructive, transferential, concerned with the internal objects, or the here and now (Ferro, 1996). It is as if, counting on that quantum of negative capability (Bion, 1970) which the oedipal engineer in me permits, I may be present at the sudden emergence of unexpected scenes and characters.

I am thinking of a particular event in the brief therapy of Manolo, a pleasant university student from the south, studying away from home, who introduced himself to me for the first time by means of this brief email: "I need a consultation because of anxiety attacks. Any day will do, I'm always available." Manolo was tall and thin, and very generous: in his free time, he went home to look after his ill parents or helped friends with bar work here and there around Italy, saving a bit of money. Having a free hour that I generally didn't use, I decided to try and see "what might come up", charging him a "student rate" below my usual minimum.

After a very few months, the traffic on the motorway and my still not being used to the time of this new session caused me to cancel two upcoming sessions.

To be honest, that was the "official" version; in fact, in the second case, I had completely forgotten about the session and was going calmly on with my usual timetable when Manolo rang me from outside the front door of my consulting room. I cursed my nomadic life and the changes of setting, and promised to give this some thought.

At the next session I immediately apologised to Manolo for the inconvenience, and he was extremely considerate about what had happened. Instead he was very angry with a friend in Bologna who had rung to ask him for help in a bar, in return for an agreed sum of money. At the end of the evening, the friend had thanked him profusely and saw him off at the station with a vigorous handshake, but no payment. Noting that, apart from anything else, the number of euros owed to him was the same amount that he was paying me per session, I interpreted that he had surely also been quite angry with me about the previous session when he had rung the doorbell and not found me waiting for him.

Manolo firmly denied this: the two situations were very different because I acted in good faith and could be excused, whereas his friend had exploited him: it was a simple as that.

And having said this, he continued his imprecations against his friend!

Today I would reconsider that direct interpretative line as being obviously incapable of shedding light on our relationship, and I would rather interpret in the transference (Gibeault, 1991) or develop the character in the field (Ferro, 1996, 2009) taking a more tangential approach.

Then, having listened a little more to his reflections on trust, his having been let down, and the ingratitude of modern society, I said to him that if it took twenty minutes to get to the session, the previous, missed session had cost about forty-five minutes of his time.

"So," I added to a puzzled Manolo, "I was thinking you shouldn't pay for today's session. Seeing that your time is worth the same as mine, today it's my turn to spend time without being paid for it."

Manolo's face took on an amazed expression, and he briefly admitted how angry he got with apologies which "cost nothing, and so people use them for their own gain. . . . Someone says sorry and feels everything's fine!" He added that he was afraid of being a patient of little importance, second-rate, since he paid so little.

Here I want to highlight the surprise (see Chapter 13) with which I became aware of the deep unconscious contempt in which I held Manolo's therapy. From the start, my paternalistic, benign condescension concealed the idea that he would never become a "real", first-rate patient, but that in my great kindness I could do something with him "for a bit of small change". The action by which I set up a certain symmetry between us, which began with a cloying scene played out between a desperate migrant and a charitable organisation, allowed me to get to grips with the analyst's inadmissible feeling of contempt for his patient. Winnicott

(1947) wrote the masterly essay on hate in the countertransference, but I am afraid it may be yet more mortifying for the analyst's human and professional identity to discover that she or he can feel contempt for one of her or his patients, a feeling of detachment due to a presumed superiority of status. One's first reaction might be to wonder if it wouldn't be a good idea to have some more analysis oneself.

I take reassurance from a warning given by an old analyst from Bologna, who said that, when all is said and done, we just might not like the patient very much; all you can do is find a little bit that you do like and pitch your tent there while you wait for the terrain to be cleared.

14.3   Transformations: the eternal problem of the Roma

> They say man loves himself. Alas, how great this self-love needs to be.
> How much contempt it has to overcome!
>
> Friedrich Wilhelm Nietzsche, *Aphorisms*

The exculpation of contempt helps the analyst not to scotomise important points to be observed in the analytic field: in this way, and on the analyst's side too, characters can take the stage who are snobs, omnipotent, sadistic, or pernickety. The analyst's partial identification with these characters, in so far as it is experienced in a painful and ego-dystonic way, will compel him to take personal responsibility for it by living through these painful emotions, which Racker would call the complementary countertransference (Etchegoyen, 1986), instead of observing them only from the patient's viewpoint, in a state of unison.

In a panel discussion of this topic, Joseph Lichtenberg explains how, in every dyadic relationship, the persistence of a feeling of shame in one party tends to give rise to contempt in the other (Reed, 2001). Therefore, the analyst should acknowledge the presence of this type of relationship, so that she or he can work through it rather than acting it out unawares.

I will try to give the flavour of this kind of work, using an example as embarrassing to put into writing as it was to go through it.

Often, when Zevran came into the consulting room, I would feel disgusted by this scruffy, fuzzy-haired man with his faint stink of sweat and urine, who greeted me with a half-smile like a beaten dog and the handshake of a frightened sissy.

In reality (but what reality?), the young manager was always well dressed and agreeably scented, meticulously groomed and shyly well bred: it was just that I didn't perceive him like that.

One day, well dressed as usual, but just as "smelly", he is looking forward to telling me a dream in which a traveller's camp near his home is being cleared and, by the roadside, he finds a crying, filthy Roma child whom he picks up in his car to save him from the nationalists.

I decide not to interpret the child as his small, ill-treated part because my mood is still too clouded by the irritation I feel towards him to say anything authentic, and – strangely – I find the dream itself frankly "banal".[1] I set aside the dream and wait until I feel calm enough to work on it with due respect.

The session continues with passing references to the present situation, until a window opens on the distant past.

Zevran was very young and, as usual, was being sent by his parents to pay the grocer's bill. It often happened that his mother didn't give him enough money and asked him to tell the grocer that they would "settle up" the following week.

This time, the grocer protested more than usual and the child replied that he needed a lot of milk so that his little brother could grow.

Zevran: The grocer retorted, "He can drink tap water if he's thirsty!" with such scorn that I was furious and gave him a kick! At home, my big brother yelled at me and told my granny, and she yelled at me too.

When my father heard about it the next day, he yelled at me and punished me by shutting me in the broom cupboard in the dark, and I was so scared that I pissed myself.

Analyst: They all had a proper go at you! Didn't anyone give a thought to the little boy who was standing up for his younger brother?
Zevran: But you don't kick people! (He says this in the tone of a child repeating a parental injunction.)
Analyst: And this little boy, dirty with fear and guilt, who looks after him?
Zevran: I don't know . . . (His low, muffled, thoughtful tone of voice brings the session to a close.)

During the session, experiencing the violence with which the patient's infantile needs had been treated enabled me to attune myself to that little boy sent "begging" and left alone, by himself too, in a darkness of fear, guilt, shame, and urine.

The strongest aspect of my almost uncontainable "nationalist" contempt was the violence with which this sensation presented itself again and again, session after session, always the same, in spite of the narrative that was being constructed.

In fact, I felt like an adoptive father struggling with a dirty and repellent child who needed to be cleaned up time after time in order to rediscover the harmless beauty concealed beneath. We might conclude that the "dirty" patient's projective identification performs a therapeutic function, preventing the analyst from paying mere lip service to him and accepting him superficially as a do-gooder would, instead forcing her to cleanse the Roma camp inside herself before she works on the one outside. More precisely, I think she takes part in the creation of an intersubjective character, whose existence in the analytic field is even more real than that of the well-ordered professional: a dirty, smelly little child who nags her for acceptance and transformation.

14.4   Apology for the banal, the abnormal, the infantile, and for *me-tooism*

My consulting room is almost always full of idiots, weirdos, snivelling kids, and egoists.

They are the guests who find their way in every time I hear certain key words spoken, always more or less the same ones, often repeated now by one patient, now by another:

> . . . I know my life is *banal* . . .
>
> . . . I'd ask you if I'd done the right thing, but I don't want to be *childish* as usual . . .
>
> . . . But it seems *normal* to you, Doctor . . .
>
> . . . I feel so *egoistical* thinking that I'm better!

If we wanted to make a game of it, I think that with these four adjectives and their combinations (the disabled child who is infantile and abnormal; the middle-class hypocrite who is banal and egoistical, and so on) we would come up with most of the self-reproaches people use to ruin their existence. Health is creative and original, whereas only pathology is forced to repeat itself endlessly.

Adopting the perspective of the two minds in contact, we can imagine that all people in a state of growth need constant confirmation that they are adults. If the fertilisation happens fruitfully, the individual will gain acknowledgement of his or her rights as an interesting, developing being enriched by his or her own difference from others, concerned with him or herself. Interest, development, difference, and healthy narcissism are the indispensable ingredients for creativity, originality, courage, and all the other human capacities which enable us to generate authentic and vital stories and experiences.

Conversely, it often happens that adults are unable, for the most varied reasons, to accept these requests from children. If such demands are frustrated in the long term, they start to be despised by the children themselves and considered banal, anomalous, infantile, or egoistical. And this is not necessarily because adults despise children, who therefore make contempt their own by identification, but because their projective, communicative, and physiological identifications are not accepted, acknowledged, and transformed, but rejected or misunderstood.

I am thinking of Stadéra, for example, a man whose affections, interests, and self-esteem have prematurely dried up, who describes his parents as fine people, but keen to have a child "who wouldn't cause them trouble." The old couple still look forward to entertaining him as far as they can, but he knows he can't tell them anything about himself because it would cause them such anxiety that they would simply shut the conversation down ("Well don't make things so difficult for yourself, sort them out!", "Don't tell things like that, you'll make me ill!", "But what will you be doing all the way down there?"). This historical account, whether we take it literally or as a communication in the analytic field, seems in either case to inform us about a chronic inadequacy of the mental container.

It may seem "banal" at first to consider contempt for oneself as not necessarily an identification with an old contempt that has been suffered, but for me it has been rich in consequences: first, in the way I work, I have largely lost interest in the historical reconstruction of parental figures, and am now more careful to recognise the quality of affective contacts, both within the patient's narrative and in the here and now of the session, between the two of us.

In the second place, considering self-deprecation as the child of the mental coupling that is lacked, rather than as the result of an identification with a contemptuous parent, prompts me to keep a close eye on my capacity for containment in addition to the analytic good will that we all aim for.

Well then, what do we do with all this?

One of the greatest freedoms offered by psychoanalysis is the democracy of the affects, the freedom of speech as a fundamental rule.

In the initial phases of therapy, I find it very helpful to prioritise the word-signals I indicated just now: "banal", "infantile", "normal", "egoistic". I believe they allow us to begin casting characters who would otherwise perform in the shadows, those sadistic primary school teachers, bigoted parents, and so on. I think it appropriate to highlight these figures as soon as possible, before they can silently sabotage the analytic work and stifle it at birth. Most of the early failures in therapeutic endeavours originate in reprisals on the part of the superego. In these cases, we are often faced not with a furious aggression against the parts considered infantile, weak, and banal, with verbal or physical self-directed attacks within the setting (which would, in theory, be containable and interpretable), but with a contempt that wants to make the "stupid snivelling egoists" shut up, a need for censorship capable of inflicting sudden, fatal attacks on the analytic process.

There are therapeutic situations, and I remember several, in which an inhibited patient feels a complete *coup de foudre* for the analysis as a place of possible freedom. The flight of the slave – the wounded, needy, split-off part of the patient– from the superego prison is sometimes so quick that the analyst is often able to meet him or her in mutual idealisation. The analytic journey can be the relationship which finally replaces and repairs the fallible relationships of the past and offers compensation for the sufferings undergone.

However, there are also jailers, and if these are not helped to make themselves visible in the analytic field, and hence to persecute the slave openly, they will move into action.

Ariel comes to mind, a fragile thirty-one-year old woman who seemed lost and wanted desperately to escape the emotional and social isolation she was living in with her parents. Her pleasure in being listened to was so great that only a couple of sessions were enough to bring to life a very powerful and equally unacceptable infatuation. Her contempt for this "abnormal" feeling was total, and the only remedy was the immediate breaking off of our meetings.

I could tell many such stories, mostly from the start of my career when I was more vulnerable to idealised encounters which tremulously infest confused young therapists' "dreams" of glory.

In other cases, the constant suffering of the patient because of attacks from her or his own superego's demands makes the analysis so painful and grievous as to put the continuation of the analytic journey in doubt.

MADDALENA

I am thinking about Maddalena, a middle-aged lady who had experienced several extreme depressive episodes following a seriously deprived childhood. This woman, whose loneliness was palpable, saved herself from complete despair thanks to a continual inner conversation with Padre Pio, a sort of silent prayer/ mantra. When she came to analysis, she was shaken by the possibility of freely expressing her own thoughts because she found such a concession miraculous. Very soon her jailer caught up with her and she started feeling egoistical simply for having the analyst all to herself. For some weeks, the meaning of the sessions was "Everyone should have analysis, I don't deserve it!"

In these situations, I find it helpful to point out that someone is violently silencing or mortifying the patient, so that the characters can come to life.

In the situation just described, there was a danger that the rigidly Catholic masochist-pauper vocation which was mortifying Maddalena would take her out of analysis, which would have delighted quite a few external and internal saboteurs, and so I challenged her "inner preacher" on the teleological level. The woman had just revealed to me that she had felt better from the start of her analysis, but that there was something greatly tormenting her, as she confided to me in her faint little voice:

Maddalena: Doctor, this thing about thinking freely is really lovely, but isn't it egoistical?
Analyst: Maddalena, you know the teaching that says, "Love thy neighbour as thyself"?
Maddalena: Of course, it's the commandment about love.
Analyst: What does it mean, in your opinion?
Maddalena: That I must love my neighbour. I must think of him.
Analyst: You see, you're leaving out the last bit without noticing. "As thyself."
Maddalena: So the commandment means I must love myself?

There was a silence of quite intense reflection, after which Maddalena added, surprised:

Maddalena: I'd never thought of that. I'd never seen it that way. My father told me it was egoism to think of oneself. So, if I think about myself too, it's not egoism . . .
Anst: Is it me-tooism?

And since then, me-tooism has become the name I give to the need for the consulting room to guarantee a minimum living space for the despised parts, whether it be an orphanage, a leper colony, or a mental hospital. Otherwise the risk is the advance of Nothingness.

14.5   Nothingness

In the imaginary realm of Fantasia, described by Michael Ende in his novel *The Neverending Story*, the Nothing is a fluid entity in a state of continual growth, a non-place which devours living things, landscapes, cities. Approaching its edges, the inhabitants of Fantasia lose hope, finally being sucked into the Nothing: "The Nothing has a terrible force of attraction, and none of you will be able to resist it for long" (Ende, 1979). Once they are drawn into the Nothing, the characters of fantasy become lies and go on to fill the human world.

I find this an extraordinary way of describing the collapse of the oneiric and poetic capacity that deprives the individual of truth which, according to Bion, is food for the mind.

It seems similar to what the Barangers describe when they say it is essential for progress in analysis that every thing or event in the field is simultaneously something else. In fact, if this ambiguity is lost, analysis stops being analysis (Baranger and Baranger, 1961–62).

When the field is devoured by contempt for the childish, for uncertainty, for the apparent uniformity of the everyday and of narrative, there is a danger that the concreteness of the real will cause a collapse of the intermediate dimension, the seat of creativity (Winnicott, 1967; Civitarese, 2014). These situations, which seem to me to be linked more to the affective analyst-patient relationship than to the patient's pathology, are those in which the field is stripped of any vital and affective new growth because of depressive, obsessional, and psychotic poisoning.

"That's the way things are: end of story."

We are in a highly risky area where the analyst despises the patient, who nevertheless represents a possible way around the impasse of Nothingness. It is the area of the analyst's boredom (Bergstein, 2009), of the attack on thinking and of envious aggression against hope. These are situations which can be highly diverse from both theoretical and clinical viewpoints, so I only put them together, perhaps inappropriately, because they both create an obstacle to the growth of the creative capacity in the analytic couple.

Analyses which are functioning well on the level of symbolisation can also reveal points where the symbolic area has been put under strain, as happens in this brief exchange.

VALENTINA

Coming from a family marked by depression, Valentina is rediscovering the pleasure of having a mind and interests. A trainee in child-care, she is passionate about her work. She is fond of little Marco, a newborn she said goodbye to after a brief internship, but still visits from time to time.

She comes to the session in a cheerful mood. She says that perhaps she could put more faith in the stories she composes.

Valentina: I've started writing letters to Marco. I've opened an email account, marcovalentina@ – no one knows about it – I put my thoughts about Marco and me in it. It's like a secret diary. Maybe when Marco grows up I'll give him access to it, so that if he wants to he'll be able to read it.

Then for a moment Valentina comes close to the edge of the Nothing.

Valentina: But when I think, "I'm writing to a one year old child who doesn't understand anything, and I don't really even know him," I start wondering what's the point of it?

[Her expression goes blank.]

Analyst: Well, maybe Marco doesn't know much about it, but Marcovalentina does. It's there between you, in between, the place where its poetry comes from.

[There is a brief reflective pause.]

Valentina: I found a CD that my mother would like. I listen to it all the time. I'd like to send it to her, but there wouldn't be much of a response. A "thank you" at most, nothing more. But I like thinking about how pleased Mamma Valentina would be.

[A hint of a self-satisfied smile.]

The clinical experience with Valentina is useful for observing the micro-movements in the session as they approach the Nothing: in this case, it happens when contempt, which in Valentina is expressed by depressed internal objects, risks sabotaging the maintenance of an intermediate area of experience (Civitarese, 2014). In this case, the presence in the analytic field of a sufficient transformative capacity enables Valentina to have faith in her own oneiric and narrative work. The analytic field can stay alive, grow, and develop only if one believes in its existence (Bion, 1970) and nourish it with narrative dream-work, refraining from interpretative enquiries into its structure.

I think that Nothingness represents the progressive dismantling of this faith, and therefore the reduction of the transformative capacity, of the dream shared by the analytic pair, the progressive emptying out of the three-dimensionality of emotional experience.

And so, the fabric of an emotional storyline gets chopped up, soiled, worn out, as in Morfeo's analysis.

MORFEO

Morfeo is a shy, awkward man. He studies the sciences, and appears lost in the attempt to give meaning to his own experience, the affective foundations of which seem to elude him. He reminds me of the little Wisteria I have just planted on my terrace, which has thrown two long tendrils out into the void in search for something to support it.

The first shoot is stretched out towards nothing and about to flop, while the second is now a few centimetres from the branches of a robust holly bush which would provide a solid vantage point for a prolific arboreal collaboration. Will it get there?

Morfeo struggles to throw his tendrils towards me from the couch. Slowly and monotonously he tells me about the inhibitions in his professional life, his fear of being judged and despised, and about his physical discomforts. I don't see his face, only glimpse the pearls of sweat which cover his nose, and hear the creaking of his joints as he anxiously moves his legs.

"How can I ever find myself if my work suffocates me? I'm not a slave. . . . A man shouldn't use himself up in his work . . . he should have room for inner growth, something to develop his creative potential . . . give him a feeling of his place in the world, because our soul has . . . Our spirit . . . I've lost my self." Silence.

Morfeo has lost himself, but so have I. However hard I try, I find no scene I can get close to, I am unable to help him give form to some credible characters with whom to compare himself. Perhaps he doesn't interest me. Fundamentally, his life doesn't interest me. Working with him doesn't interest me. And yet Morfeo never misses a session. If he is three minutes late, I almost start hoping he's stuck in traffic – at least I could read something interesting – and immediately the doorbell rings. He tells me about the disappointment in his new piece of research, that it isn't stimulating, and I'm afraid he wants to give up analysis. Well, I sort of am . . . Maybe I wish he would.

I don't fall asleep, but I doze. I have some oneiric images, but even those aren't the beautiful reveries you read about in articles. They are "half-dreams". As a compensation, the session is now half way through, and I don't have the faintest idea what Morfeo has said. Nothing.

I feel ashamed. He's haemorrhaging money, I'm robbing him. I can perhaps only redeem myself with the thought that you sometimes have to cross a desert with your patients, and blah blah blah.

I'd rather stop here, right in the middle of the Nothing, in a meaningless, endless present, risking censure from more capable and expert colleagues than myself, rather than recount what followed. We live in the present with our patients, we live through this kind of emotion, even if we don't often attempt to write them down, unless it is to reveal how we overcame them.

For my part, I am learning not to expect the little tendril to reach my branches, but I try to construct a decently comfortable environment, and to get close to him.

I make the kind of interpretations which help keep me alive rather than Morfeo, though in the awareness that this helps him as well as me, because you can't do analysis without an analyst who survives (Winnicott, 1969). The analytic field helps me to keep in mind that all my little plays on words, every question I ask to try to arouse my own curiosity is a way in which the shared narrative fabric is trying to put itself into action so as not to dry up.

I am confident that next Spring I will find the Wisteria and the holly wrapped up in each other.

14.6 Friday self-analysis

Anyone who has lived and thought, cannot fail to despise men in his soul.
Aleksandr Sergeevich Pushkin, *Evgeny Onegin*

It has been anything but easy to display "the dirt between my toes" in public, as the rock band *Elio e le storie tese*[2] sang in *Silos*. There is a certain grey area of privacy in all of us, analysts included, which we protect from other people's gaze. And, as we have seen, the gaze is the first conveyor of contempt and can paralyse through the feeling of shame it induces.

It is certainly less hard to bear if we scotomise our contempt for the patient and our embarrassment about our not always clear way of working, and instead confine ourselves to observing the discontinuity of the patient's movements. The patient alternates between the roles of shamed child and contemptuous adult, and we deceive ourselves into thinking that we stand outside the mixture, catching only "the spray", maybe a projective identification. However, if we are honest enough with ourselves, we realise instead that we are up to our eyes in the situation and must do something. But what?

The classical mono-personal paradigm, at least in my superego-inspired interpretation, would prescribe the cleansing of the analytic instrument, even with a further spell of analysis or a supervision. In my opinion, this is not enough. Indeed, such a solution implicitly seems to add a further load of severity: "Be a better analyst, clear the field of your neurotic encrustations!"

Having spent decades de-idealising analysis, we know very well that we still have many swampy areas inside us which resist draining. For example, I know that my narcissistic traits are not and never will be those of the analyst with a depressive and "naturally" welcoming structure (McWilliams, 1994). An obsessional or anxious colleague could make similar observations. I think we should learn to come to terms with our own imperfect, not always efficient instrument, accepting it as not always ideal but reasonably smooth-running and regularly serviced.

I have found it liberating to consider the cycle of contempt and shame in analytic work as a natural and intersubjective phenomenon which pervades the field and makes it ill (Ferro, 2008). Furthermore, I experience the occasional derailing of my usual mental disposition, which is reasonably curious and respectful, as the irritating need to interpret, however unwillingly, an unpleasant character. Nevertheless, it turns out to be emotionally less burdensome if, beyond the emotions experienced in the session, I can adopt a professional stance – shared and renewed by means of the necessary association with colleagues – of profound respect for each patient, who is the co-author and protagonist of the text we are dramatising, but also another individual, unique and complex, safe from the presumption of all our enquiries and judgements.

Notes

1 As I will explain shortly, I am very alert to the perception of somebody as "banal". For this reason, the feeling I have always felt seems to me to deserve particular attention.
2 Translator's note: literally "Elio and the Uptight Stories".

References

Baranger, W. and Baranger, M. (1961–62). The Analytic Situation as a Dynamic Field. *International Journal of Psychoanalysis*, 89(4) (2008), pp. 795–826.
Bergstein, A. (2009). On Boredom: A Close Encounter With Encapsulated Parts of the Psyche. *International Journal of Psychoanalysis*, 90, pp. 613–31.
Bion, W. R. (1970). *Attention and Interpretation*. London, Tavistock Publications.
Civitarese, G. (2014). *Truth and the Unconscious in Psychoanalysis*. London, Routledge, 2016.
Ende, M. (1979). *The Neverending Story*. New York, Puffin Books, Penguin Random House LLC, 2008.
Etchegoyen, H. (1986). *The Fundamentals of Psychoanalytic Technique*. London, Karnac Books.
Ferro, A. (1996). *In the Analyst's Consulting Room*. London, Routledge, 2002.
Ferro, A. (2008). The Patient as the Analyst's Best Colleague: Transformation into a Dream and Narrative Transformations. *Italian Psychoanalytic Annual*, pp. 199–205.
Ferro, A. (2009). Transformations in Dreaming and Characters in the Psychoanalytic Field. *International Journal of Psychoanalysis*, 90(2), pp. 209–30.
Gibeault, A. (1991). Interpretation et transfert. *Psychanalyse en Europe, Bulletin de la FEP*, 36, pp. 49–63.
McWilliams, N. (1994). *Psychoanalytic Diagnosis: Understanding Personality Structure in the Clinical Process*. New York, Guilford Press.
Pushkin, A. S. (1833). *Evgene Onegin*. New York, Basic Books; New edition (1 July 1999).
Reed, G. S. (2001). Shame/Contempt Interchanges. *Journal of American Psychoanalytic Association*, 49, pp. 269–75.
Stein, A. (2011). The Utility of Contempt. *Contemporary Psychoanalysis*, 47, pp. 80–100.
Williams, P. (2010). *The Fifth Principle*. London, Karnac Books.
Winnicott, D. W. (1947). Hate in the Counter-Transference. *International Journal of Psychoanalysis*, 30, pp. 69–74.
Winnicott, D. W. (1967). The Location of Cultural Experience. *International journal of Psychoanalysis*, 48, pp. 368–72.
Winnicott, D. W. (1969). The Use of an Object. *International Journal of Psychoanalysis*, 50, pp. 711–6.

Chapter 15

Sadness. Sadness between phenomenology and psychoanalysis

From *nameless* sadness to sadness in *O*

Mauro Manica

15.1 A phenomenological premise

We do not know, and still cannot say, if mourning is the most intimate and radical element in sadness, but we have come to know how psychoanalysis has made mourning the leitmotiv, the guiding thread, the dominant theme, of every melancholy crevice in the human spirit.

Freud's thesis was taken to be axiomatic: at the core of all melancholy, all sadness, there is mourning, a loss, whether real or fantasied. There is a loss and there is the distress which accompanies it. However, in its succinctness the Freudian thesis may have prevented (or perhaps only limited the possibility of) our penetrating the layers of emotional life and the complex forms which sadness can adopt in the depths of the soul of each one of us. Because sadness may be a state of mind, a *Stimmung*, resonance with something that moves us, and it may be an "illness". It may be a melancholy (with which sadness maintains endless semantic relations) which has reasons, intentional echoes, or which becomes an agonizing illness of the soul.

A dialectical and well-informed psychiatry (like that in the tradition of Schneider) then distinguished the various forms and figures of this suffering, which is full of tears, all the tears we can weep and also all those tears we have never been able to weep. It thus acknowledged the existence of sadness as the dominant affective theme of a *motivated* depression, an *existential* depression, and a *psychotic* depression. And it attributed these semantic permutations, these clinical pictures, to the Schelerian phenomenology of affective life.

By profound and rigorous reflection, Max Scheler (1916) had deciphered at the heart of our affective life a stratifying of experiences that can be distinguished by the depth (which is not intensity) with which feelings are lived (and re-lived). In relation to intentionality – that is, to the possibility of states of mind, of being open to the world, to the encounter with objects and with others, to intersubjectivity, and to their "closeness" to the Ego – he distinguished the *sensory* feelings from those that are *vital*, those that are of the *psyche*, and those that are of the *spirit* (or the personality).

Sensory feelings (the "sensible feeling"[1] exist "here and now in the living body" and are situated in specific parts of it, although in pain, for example, they can expand and be extended to other parts of the body. They do not make use of any intentionality and cannot be consented to or the subject of presentiments, just as they cannot be remembered or understood by introspection. They are the feelings most altered by attention and most submissive to the will: for this reason, every sensory pain grows when attention is paid to it but, equally, always lets itself be drugged (Scheler significantly places sensory "pleasure" alongside "pain"). So, while the sensible feelings are alterable by exercises and efforts of will, the vital feelings are less modifiable, and the psychic feelings are even less so, while the feelings of the personality are not at all (ecstasy, and still more, the heroin high, are in fact a pure and artificial sensory pleasure and certainly not a state of bliss).

The *vital* feelings present with different characteristics from the sensible feelings and cannot be simply reduced to pleasure and unpleasure. The vital sense participates in the global extension of the living-body (the lived-body, the *Leib*-body), without elective localization and without constituting itself as a sum of sensations. It is an extension which derives from the *unitary* perception of corporeality. Indeed, we cannot feel ourselves to be at ease or not, well or ill, tired or fit, by reference to a specific organ or precise location of the experience, since these emotional states are expressly feelings of our body understood as a whole.

Nevertheless, the vital feelings always have a functional and intentional character. Whereas the sensory affects can be objectively represented as "clues" to certain states and processes taking place in the organs and tissues, as far as the vital feelings are concerned, we feel our actual life, its "rise" and "fall", its health and sickness, its "danger" and "realization" (Borgna, 1972, 1992, 1999, 2013).

Lastly, the ultimate significance of the vital feelings (anxiety, nervousness, or fear, nausea, shame, appetite, aversion, vital sympathy, vital disgust in the presence of animals and people, dizziness, [and Kurt Scheider also added sadness])[2] consists in an anticipation: they announce the value of something that *is coming*, not the value of something that *is* present.

The *psychic* feelings ("*pure feelings of the Ego*"[3] are clearly separated from the level of the vital senses. They are in themselves "qualities of the Ego". And a feeling of profound "psychic" sadness does not participate at all in the body's extension, which always characterizes a vital feeling. We nevertheless understand that, even within this stratum of emotional life, feeling may still variously express a proximity to or distance from the Ego. In the linguistic expressions "I feel sad", "I am experiencing sadness", "I am sad" (the first expression is already at the limit of what is linguistically possible), there is a progressive closeness to the Ego. And insofar as the feelings of the Ego can be, as it were, influenced and coloured by the body's feelings, they preserve a substantial specificity, obeying the necessity of being "motivated".

Finally, in the *spiritual* feelings (the "feelings of the personality"[4] – in "bliss" and "despair" as much as in "serenity" and "peace of mind" (these are the spiritual feelings mentioned by Scheler) – every state of the Ego is, as it were, extinguished.

We cannot simply "be" blissful or despairing, and we cannot "feel" bliss or despair, and still less can we say that "we" feel despairing or blissful. If there is still something *for* which we are despairing, then we are not in fact despairing: it is the *being* and *value in oneself* of the person which constitute the "foundation" of bliss and despair. Thus, despair is manifested when any possibility of withdrawing from the negative is "cut off at birth" and every action, every move, all conduct which might be able to modify the metaphysical nature of this feeling seems unthinkable.

Thus, if there are *reactive* (motivated) depressions characterized by a *psychic* sadness, if there are *existential* depressions whose keynote is despair, and, finally, if there are *endogenous*, psychotic, melancholic depressions which are pervaded by a *vital* (somatic and unmotivated) sadness,[5] we cannot say that sadness is (only) depression or (only) melancholy. Similarly, we cannot say that loss and mourning are the only affective architectures and roof beams of every human sadness. There is, in fact, a sadness or sadnesses which run through the affective life of all of us and have done so since its origin because they are "dissolved in the water that makes the seed light",[6] because they are connected to the limit, to transience, and to the finitude of all that belongs to existence.

This is something which Freud (1916, p. 303) had prefigured in his almost poetic description which opens the pages of *On Transience*:

> Not long ago I went on a summer walk through a smiling countryside in the company of a taciturn friend and of a young but already famous poet. The poet admired the beauty of the scene around us but felt no joy in it. He was disturbed by the thought that all this beauty was fated to extinction, that it would vanish when winter came, like all human beauty and all the beauty and splendour that men have created or may create. All that he would otherwise have loved and admired seemed to him to be shorn of its worth by the transience which was its doom.

And, as Elena Molinari observes with crystalline clarity in Chapter 4 of this book (p. 61):

> 'Depressed' literally means pushed out of a place where one has felt safe, and so its first association applies to birth as the primary experience of losing a place inside which one has been content. Hence, extra-uterine space is initially a distressing void causing separation from the mother's body; a space which can be filled by means of a slow apprenticeship in inventing tools which underpin the slow development of physical and psychic capabilities for staying in equilibrium on that terrifying vortex through which the world appears to us.

There might therefore be a primary sadness – with Leopardian melancholy as its emblem – which shares a nature with being-cast-out-into-the-world and may make itself known during a life when we feel confronted by the task and necessity of giving life a meaning.

And in the letter to Pietro Giordani of 30 April 1817, Giacomo Leopardi grasps in all its most intimate and profound resonance the link between a creative, almost luminous melancholy and a melancholy which looks out on the darkness of existence:

> Add to all this the stubborn, black, horrendous, barbarous melancholy that eats into me and devours me, and feeds on studying, and increases if I do not study. I do know (and I have felt, but now no longer feel) what that sweet melancholy is that brings forth beautiful things, sweeter than cheerfulness; it is, if I may be permitted to put it this way, like twilight, whereas this is the thickest horrible night, it is a poison, as you say, which destroys strength of body and of spirit.[7]

And so, in the Winnicottian manner suggested by Elena Molinari, can we regard this as the "thickest horrible night" of being faced once again with that void which originally separated us from our mother's body? And yet, can we really think of an "extra-uterine-non-place"? Or rather, can a foetus "think" of the uterus as a place? And can a newborn's bundle of proto-sensations and proto-emotions allow him or her to think or feel that, at birth, a transition has been made from a place to a non-place? Will it not rather be the case that some sensory affects or vital senses will be those proto-experiences by which the foetus is led into an apparently endless emotional turbulence?

And so only a pain or pains which torture the body, an orgasmic prostration, feeling weighed down by the effect of gravity on one's life, feeling plunged into the infinite, and all the other primitive (Winnicottian) agonies could constitute a *nameless* sadness, an original sadness, a sadness which cannot make use of any mentalization, and since it cannot be transformed into a psychic or personal feeling, remains an emotion suspended between the non-value of what there was before and the non-sense, void, cold, dark of what lies before it.

Because there, at the origin, there is nothing but emotion, and the emotion is a *geyser*, unlike feeling, which is an essentially relational creature.

Indeed, I would say that feeling is an emotion with traces x, quanta n of alphabetization, an emotion which, starting from primary intersubjectivity (conscious and unconscious), becomes ever more alphabetized.

15.2 A psychoanalytic perspective

And so, if there is a nameless sadness which inhabits our origins like a *geyser*, sadness cannot by any means be attributed solely to D: it cannot only be emotion which connotes the approach to, arrival at, or passage beyond the threshold of the depressive position (Klein, 1935, 1940).

In relation to the depressive position (D), Melanie Klein has taught us how the confluence of hate and love in integrating the fragmented ("good" and "bad") perceptions of the mother may early on arouse a sadness of particular intensity in the infant, one that takes on the contours of a depressive anxiety (*pining*). This is where the earliest and most anxiety-inducing sense of guilt caused by the ambivalence of the feelings towards a primary object would be expressed. Because when part-objects and their qualities ("good" and "bad") are united into a whole object, there appears the threat of forming a whole object that is contaminated, damaged, or dead (Hinshelwood, 1989). Depressive "sadness" (anxiety) thus becomes the crucial element in more mature relationships, the source of generous and altruistic feelings which aim at the object's well-being. And so the infant exerts her or himself in the attempt to make the loving aspects prevail in the relationship with the "whole" object, which must now be repaired.

Alongside the reparative aspects, the crucial point is that the reactivation of the anxiety (however "depressive" it may be) can provoke the return of paranoid-schizoid (PS) defences in the infant or bring manic defences into play.

And while Klein described the movement from D to PS solely as a paranoid defence against depressive anxiety, Bion, starting from his conception of normal (and pathological) projective identification, was able to think in terms of a non-pathological movement towards PS. Indeed, for him, tolerating a certain degree of persecution and disintegration without recourse to primitive defence mechanisms would be an essential step in the development of creative thinking.

This is a catastrophic reversal of perspective: creativity would take its first step in disintegration and not integration, in the diabolical (*dia-ballein*) and not in the symbolic (*sym-ballein*). The birth of new thinking entails the dismantling and mourning of previous views and theories in order to achieve the development of unprecedented points of view. When we change our way of thinking, it is necessary for the container to dissolve before being formed anew. Bion seemed to believe that the effects of such a dissolution constituted a small psychic catastrophe. In his view, this was a movement towards PS, whereas the forming of a new system of opinions and theories would entail an integrative movement, entirely in terms of D. Hinshelwood (1989) writes

> Creative effort can therefore be viewed as a process, on a small scale, of movements to and fro between the paranoid-schizoid and depressive positions. Bion represented this *to-and-fro* process by the symbol Ps-D.

So, like any other feeling, like any other liveable and creative emotion, sadness is also perhaps achieved in PS↔D: it is an oscillation of the soul, of the soul in every one of us; and the two-directional arrow could in fact represent emotion, the link, the emotion which creates the link.

Taking the Kleinian viewpoint to its extreme conclusion (Klein, 1923, 1931), whereby cognitive development depends to a large extent on emotional development, Bion (1963) formulated a theory of thinking based on the coupling that could be created between thoughts: a theory which, for the subject, comes to stand for the link between the parents and between their genital organs in the primal scene, the *Ur-szene*. This *Ur*, which comes before *szene* (Manica and

Oldoini, 2014), may acquire the sense of an undifferentiation of emotional experience which needs a net, a grid, an affective fabric to function as a container in order to be dreamed/thought.

From a phenomenological perspective, as we have seen, Max Scheler has given us the concept of a layering of emotional life which allows us to see its permutations in relation to proximity to the Ego (and distance from the body) in a sequence which moves from somatic feelings to vital ones, to the psychic and, finally, the spiritual.

From a psychoanalytic perspective, this layering could signify a progression from β to α, from raw emotions to liveable ones, from an emotional experience which cannot be tolerated – and which is expelled into the individual or social body, or by means of delusion and transformation in hallucinosis – to an emotional experience which, through the filter of column 2 of the Grid, can be dreamed and thought, can be used for living.

To quote again from Elena Molinari (chapter 4):

> The term primary depression, as first defined by Winnicott (1963), denotes an anxiety taking the form of bodily sensations of falling forever and of annihilation. It arises in relation to the failure of the maternal capacity for protecting the child from the traumatic nature of space-time. . . . So we could say that psychotic depression resides in an original inability to develop the psychic movement which Bion identified in the concept of oscillation, even before the tools for thinking. The most salient characteristic of primary depression therefore lies in this psychic or, rather, psychophysical immobility.

So, we could say that the sadness of our origins, a *nameless* sadness,[8] may reside in the inability to develop this initial oscillating psychic movement, making psychic, or rather psycho-physical immobility the load-bearing emotional structure of primary depression.

15.3 Sadness is not (only) D

When sadness can be regarded as a form of PS↔D, an oscillation is also made between the sayable and the unsayable, between the "shadow" and "grace" which Simone Weil (1947) spoke of in her *Notebooks*,[9] referring to a "dignity" which, when wounded, constitutes a large part of the shadow (of melancholy) and, when redeemed, starts to become part of life's grace. Similarly, in his letters to a young poet, Rainer Maria Rilke spoke of sadness as an initiation and a process of profound transformation:

> You have had many great sorrows, which have passed away. And you say that even this passing was difficult and jarring for you. but please consider whether these great sorrows have not rather passed through the midst of

yourself? Whether much in you has not altered, whether you have not somehow changed in some part of your being, while you were sorrowful? . . . If it
were possible for us to see further than our knowledge extends and out a little
over the outworks of our surmising, perhaps we should then bear our sorrows
with greater confidence than our joys. For they are the moments when something new, something unknown, has entered into us.[10]

Perhaps, then, we can give a different extension to this fundamental dynamic
oscillation, to PS↔D, an extension which crosses and passes through both the
paranoid-schizoid position, in a regressive direction, and Kleinian pining, in
an evolutionary direction, integrating the most recent developments in psychoanalytic research. Indeed, we must not ignore Ogden's (1989) hypothesis of an
autistic-contiguous position (AC) and Grotstein (2007) pointing us towards a
transcendent position (TP), enabling us to think psychoanalytically outside the
confines of PS as much as of D.

In fact, Ogden held that the concept of a dialectic of experience founded
exclusively on the paranoid-schizoid and depressive modes was incomplete, and
supposed that beyond PS it was possible to recognize a still more primitive, pre-
symbolic and predominantly sensory mode, which he referred to as the *autistic-
contiguous* mode.

> The rudiments of the sensory experience of the self in an autistic-contiguous
> mode have nothing to do with the representation of one's affective states,
> either ideographically or fully symbolically. The sensory experience *is* the
> infant In this mode, and the abrupt disruption of shape, symmetry, rhythm,
> skin moldedness, and so on, marks the end of the infant. . . . More specific to
> the autistic-contiguous mode of experience is countertransference experience
> in which bodily sensations dominate.
>
> (Ogden, 1989, 35 and 44)[11]

Implicitly following Ogden's intuition, Grotstein (2007) also considers that the
paranoid-schizoid is not primary, but is in fact transcended, preceded, and sur-
passed by the presence, transformations, immanence of O. And, once we introduce the concept of O, all existing psychoanalytic theories could be considered
as out-and-out manic defences against the unknown, unknowable, ineffable, and
inscrutable ontological experience of ultimate being, the experience Bion calls
absolute Truth about ultimate Reality: O, which is located in eternally inaccessible dimensions even though it completely permeates our conscious and unconscious existence and the objects with which we interact.

So, psychoanalytic transcendence could be explained by the intrinsic purpose of analysis, and would therefore consist in helping the subject to transcend the veils of illusion which stand between the subject and the Other and
between the subject and her or him being her or himself, her or his own O, her
or his own *Dasein*.

When the analyst succeeds in becoming the truth, the O of the patient's emotional experience, and when the patient succeeds in becoming her or his own emotional experience, rendering the impersonal O into an O of her or his own, then subjectivity (the patient's and the analyst's) evolves.

> Becoming O represents the achievement, albeit transitory, of what I propose is the "transcendent position" – the individual's gradually developing capacity, from infancy (or perhaps even fetaldom) onward, to tolerate (suffer) and therefore to resonate with O, the ultimate reality of anything and everything. This capacity, therefore, exists before, during, and after, hovers over, surrounds, embraces, and is beyond (in every dimension and perspective) the paranoid-schizoid and depressive positions, both of which constitute, I believe, an emotional and epistemic "ozone layer" or protective lens or filter against the blinding illumination of the Absolute, O's *nom de plume*.
>
> (Grotstein, 2007, 127–8).

So, by adopting the concept of the *transcendent position* (TP), we can think in terms of a positioning which exists with, before, during, and after the other positions, interpenetrating them and conveying the supreme theme of transcending the impersonal O, chaos, the thing-in-itself, the β element, passing through AC, PS, D to attain the personal, subjective O. Taking this back to the theme of sadness, we can refer to a "self-positioning" which articulates the sensory and emotional experience of it, beginning with a nameless sadness in AC, a sadness which precedes speech and can only occur through the Schelerian concepts of "sensory affection" or "vital sense", until a sadness is achieved (in TP) as a "spiritual feeling", a sadness which resonates in the radicalness of "being sad or despairing" and can finally be fulfilled in O.

So we could have the formula:

$$AC \leftrightarrow PS \leftrightarrow D \leftrightarrow TP$$

where PS↔D is contained by AC↔TP and there are progressive micro-oscillations of PS↔D which allow raw O to be transformed into a subjective O, a personal version of O: a nameless sadness into a persecutory sadness, into a depressive sadness, and finally into a sadness in O, with every possibility of a return and inversion of the emotional flow.

15.4   AC↔PS

Patrizio is a seriously borderline patient who seems only to be surviving thanks to analysis. He had come after endless suicide attempts, a persistent search for a voluntary death, which had led him to seal his own apartment and turn it into a gas chamber, and at the same time into a time-bomb which could have destroyed the entire building in which he lived. A survivor of life's shipwreck, he had reached the final shore of analysis. He had not begun to live, but only managed to survive. And from survival, he had moved on to brief glints of life, always oscillating between a desperate, angry sadness and the illusion of existing again.

In one of his most recent sessions, he tells me again about the absurdity of life and the fact that he has no fear of death. Thus, in a state of "profound ignorance", I surprise myself by commenting on the "remarkable fact that you aren't afraid of dying, and yet you are filled with crippling anxiety when you want to go into a bar." Unexpectedly, Patrizio smiles: "It's true . . . it's unbelievable!" And it is still more surprising that I find myself saying, "A man goes into a café: and . . . splash!" At this point, Patrizio starts laughing with real amusement.

What has turned pining into a smile? What has inserted a metaphorizing function into the traumatic concreteness of his proto-emotional experience?

We could conclude that it is unison, the analyst's becoming part of the patient's emotional experience, the possibility of intuiting (Bion's *intuit*) that his anxiety is not an anxiety about dying but an anxiety about living, something that comes about on this side, not the other side, of the pleasure principle.

15.5 PS↔D

Over the sixteen years of her life, Stella had plunged into a psychotic world which seemed well organized in terms of apparently adequate relationships and social intercourse (she carried on attending school and her dance lessons, but had largely withdrawn from more intimate and personal contacts).

From our first conversation, she had invaded the consulting room with her delusions and hallucinations: a parallel reality pervaded by "voices" and "visions".

The voices, which she said were "bad", had begun at some unspecifiable time in the past and become ever more insistent, resisting every previous attempt at psycho(therapeutic) intervention: they had driven her, and continued to drive her, to self-harm, to cutting herself and trying to take her own life.

The visions, however, were "good". Only a few months before, she had gone out onto the balcony of her home, impelled by "voices" which would have made her throw herself off. However, a figure "in a black tunic . . . with red hair . . . flaming hair . . ." had materialized in a "vision", and this figure had "pulled her off" the balcony, saving her life. I had sketched out a question, asking her if it had been a male or female presence who saved her life, to which Stella had replied that "it might have been an Angel . . . and you can't tell what sex they are."

And with the figure of the Angel, we had decided to start a psychotherapeutic journey together.

Several weeks had passed since the start of the treatment, and Stella (who had readily and surprisingly stopped "cutting herself"), in a still unreal atmosphere, had started to tell me about having been a "strange child", so strange that her primary schoolteacher had asked her parents to come in: "I don't know . . . maybe because I used to draw the corpses of girls . . . or dead girls . . . with crosses or coffins . . . but my favourite drawing was one of a girl dressed like a punk." And she went on to recall how the "punk girl" had an extraordinary and terrible power: "as she went by, everything died around her . . . plants, grass, and flowers too . . . in fact, life died."

There we are – life died! I had found myself saying to her that perhaps the strange-girl-Stella had in fact been a terribly sad girl, and that the death of the plants, grass, and flowers had not been caused by the extraordinary destructive power of the "little punk". That punk-girl-Stella was not an Exterminating Angel, but perhaps just a girl who had lacked the necessary protections (her father had been struck by a post-poliomyelitic tetraplegia, and her mother was emotionally impoverished and low in affect) and, as she grew, had been exposed to the risk of life being extinguished inside her.

Stella had smiled at that with her usual slightly vacant expression and slightly sad smile: "I think if I hadn't come here, I would never even have got through high school . . . now I'm 'crazy' but at least I'm alive."

So it seems that, faced with a D which confronted her like a black hole, a bottomless vortex of anxiety, an infinite void of existence, Stella had been compelled to activate PS, the train of paranoid-schizoid defences (D→PS), to the maximum extent; but in the dreaming ensemble (of patient and analyst) realized around the character of the "punk girl" (PS↔D), she seemed to have been re-animated and could also re-vive that "sad girl" (PS→D) who had been forced to go mad in order not to die.

15.6   D↔TP

Even psychoanalysts weep, and weep, are moved in the session: but they also weep in life and outside their consulting rooms.

And so, Gino Zucchini (2002, p. 509), pupil of Egon Molinari (one of the first Italian psychoanalysts), entrusts to the pages of the *Rivista di Psicoanalisi* his intimate, profound, and heartfelt grief for the loss of his teacher and friend:

> Dear old noble Egon, if my voice breaks as I say this last goodbye, I know you'll smile and forgive me, like the time years ago on your couch when I found myself sobbing with rage and resentment, and you said, "Have you ever considered that Homer's heroes wept too?" How much more, then, may we weep who are not heroes, and who, by means of this healthy pain, will not give up the only compensation for losing you: the treasure of memory in the garden of good experiences.

And in poetic, almost sacramental words consigned to the pages of a profound and beautiful book, another psychoanalyst, Tonia Cancrini (2002), offers us the testimony of her own sadness at the prospective loss of an ill friend:

> I'm told that a friend of mine is ill, that he will not be with us for much longer, and my eyes fill with tears again. My little sparrow has also passed away; it fell gently asleep on my hand. And it seems as if I'm missing a part of myself,

something that has gone from my life and my body. I don't know how to free myself from this pain. It seems as life's only problem is death, even though death itself, which has now taken away so many creatures that were dear to me, sometimes seems a more comfortable place since it is home to so many of the creatures I have loved.

And so in my fantasy, death is nothing but a fine full-blooded gallop in a lovely green meadow with my beloved grey Glandoran. And all the others running behind him, Flash, Turno and Dune; and Cirillo, Bella, Yoghi, Duchessa, Bubi, Macchietta, and Benvenuto will be running together, and the two beautiful Siamese cats, dear animals, obvious symbols of love and affection, and with them all the creatures I have loved and who have loved me. And I think they are there now, in the pastures of heaven, waiting for me, and I will soon run to them.

Delicate, touching images, strong heart-melting feelings, a lament which manages to express torment and joy, nostalgia and beauty, almost an aesthetic of dying: the possibility of feeling and "becoming" the emotional experience of a loved person who is dying; and at the same time, the possibility of remaining oneself in the sadness of farewell; and also the possibility of perceiving that all the creatures who have loved us and whom we have loved may never in fact have died.

Is all this what Gino Zucchini and Tonia Cancrini have told us in their intimate, private, affectionate, but also universal *moïroloi*?[12]

Is it the ability to fantasize a "lovely green meadow" where it may be possible to ride with someone who has gone? Or is it the impassioned search in "the garden of good experiences", of inexhaustible "treasures of memory"? Or is it perhaps the extraordinary transformation of memories of the past into "memories of the future"?

I have the feeling that these catastrophic transitions (K→O) are the product of a symbolic labour which demands the support of a profound work of reverie until the pain of a sadness, of a lack which immediately presents itself as inexorable, can be made into dream and memory, and until those recollections and dreams can render thinkable and tolerable the fracture created in our souls, a fracture which echoes another that takes us back into the distress of our origins.

15.7   AC↔TP

When, halfway through her analysis, Federica seems to regress to a level of infantile, intolerable greed and jealousy, she inveighs against analysis and her analyst because of an unavoidably long separation and having just met the patient who had the session before hers, the analyst finds himself having to sublimate/contain the implicit sexual aims in Federica's communications.

Suddenly noises and the sound of voices enter the consulting room from the analyst's home. I recognize my son's voice, angry with the housekeeper because, according to him, she had forgotten to get ready the clothes he needed. I notice, paradoxically, how unpleasant and intrusive my son's voice seems. My perception is that he is disturbing and invading the intimacy which Federica's infantile Self seems absolutely to need at that moment. So I point out to her the disturbance caused by the voices coming from outside the room. She seems accommodating about this, and says she only feels disturbed by interferences which directly involve the analysis: "I felt a profound jealousy when I met the patient who came before me. . . . I thought she was younger and prettier than me and that you would prefer her. . . . Instead, the noises from your house and your son's voice don't disturb me, they make me feel part of your life and your family."

I reply that I, on the other hand, felt deeply disturbed by my son's voice: "And, however absurd and surprising it may seem, I almost found myself hating him because he was invading a space that your very little Federica desperately needed."

She remains quiet for a long time and then, her voice breaking with emotion, whispers: "I hadn't noticed that I was also disturbed by your son's voice . . . I could never have said, as you did, that I hated him. . . . I would never have dared! . . . Now I realise how desperate I was as a child . . . I must have ended up hating what I loved. . . . It's as if you had become me. . . . Now it seems as if that desperate child I used to be can start hoping again . . . I remember how my father, who used to travel by sea, always said that sailors on the eve of a long voyage should be wished 'a fair wind and gentle waves' . . . I little while ago, I was full of anxiety and anger . . . now I think that when I leave here I'll go back to my life and maybe the waves will be smaller and the wind lighter. . . . Until the next gale, of course . . . but I'm less scared about it because I know you'll still be there."

I say nothing – I'm moved too – until the usual goodbye which ends the session. The atmosphere is charged with emotions, but there is something underneath which contains them as a tender, melancholy, peaceful whole.

In the next day's session, Federica starts straight off by saying, "Last night I dreamed I was swimming inside you, like in a sea . . . with a profound feeling of relaxation and peace. . . . I thought that old knots get untied in dreams and that the dusty attics of time are emptied of their deposits of hate and anxiety."

"A fair wind and gentle waves": it is when things go well and the analyst is able to become the patient's O, when he or she succeeds in grasping that minimum of truth about the ultimate essence of the patient's emotional experience, that an unspeakable (*nameless*) sadness finds the possibility of being told without too much fiction and distortion, but can above all be experienced, beyond words and symbols, as the sadness that is itself: sadness in O, the sadness, as Grotstein (2007, p. 128) would say, of "the mystic or genius" who is "that aspect of us which is potentially able to be at one with transcendence as O – but only after we have 'cleared' with PS and D."

Notes

1 Scheler (1916).
2 Kurt Schneider (1955) always breaks down sadness into its psychic and vital expressions, distinguishing himself from Scheler who speaks instead of sadness as merely a feeling of the psychic stratum of emotional life.

3 (Scheler, 1916). M. S. Frings and R. L. Funk (eds.), *Formalism in Ethics and Non-Formal Ethics of Values*. Evanston, Northwestern University Press, 1973.
4 Scheler (1916).
5 In reality, there are also intermediate, transitional experiences which belong to the psychopathological territory of the depressions and configure the clinical scenarios of the endoreactive dysthymias in the sense used by Weitbrecht (1963). These are marked by the fact that, in these cases, sadness *first* involves the stratum of the psychic feelings and *then* becomes extended to include also the stratum of the vital senses (Manica, 1999).
6 Rilke (1923).
7 Leopardi (2017).
8 Perhaps we can say that some forms of psychotic depression are substantiated by a *nameless* sadness.
9 Weil (1947).
10 Rilke (1875–1926).
11 With Grotstein (2007), we can understand Bion's concept of O, the absolute Truth about ultimate Reality, as analogous to "dark matter", that amorphous mass which is hidden in our universe and completely permeates it (Tucker and Tucker, 1988); or we can think of O as including within it the Heideggerian concept of *Dasein* (1927), as being the pure ontology of psychoanalysis, a particular idea of *ananké* ("necessity" in Greek, or "fate" [Ricoeur, 1970]) and the Lacanian concept of the register of the "Real" (1966).
12 The *moïroloi*, chanted by the *korifee* in Greek lamentations, are ritualized choral manifestations of the grief of mourning for a loved or admired person.

References

Bion, W. R. (1963). *Elements of Psycho-Analysis*. Heinemann, London.
Borgna, E. (1972). Fenomenologia Scheleriana E Psicopatologia Degli Stati Depressivi. *Rivista Sperimentale Di Frenologia*, 96.
Borgna, E. (1992). *Malinconia*. Feltrinelli, Milano.
Borgna, E. (1999). *Noi Siamo Un Colloquio*. Feltrinelli, Milano.
Borgna, E. (2013). *La Dignità Ferita*. Feltrinelli, Milano.
Cancrini, T. (2002). *Un Tempo Per Il Dolore. Eros, Dolore E Colpa*. Bollati Bo-Ringhieri, Torino.
Freud, S. (1916). On Transience. In *The Standard Edition of the Complete Psychological Works of Sigmund Freud*, Vol. 14, translated by J. Strachey. London, Hogarth Press and the Institute of Psychoanalysis, pp. 303–7.
Grotstein, J. S. (2007). *A Beam of Intense Darkness: Wilfred Bion's Legacy to Psychoanalysis*. London: Karnac Books, p. 128.
Hinshelwood, R. D. (1989). *A Dictionary of Kleinian Thought*. London: Free Association Books.
Klein, M. (1923). The Role of the School in the Libidinal Development of the Child. In *The Collected Works of Melanie Klein, Volume I – "Love, Guilt and Reparation" and Other Works 1921–1945*. London, Karnac Books, 2017.
Klein, M. (1931). A Contribution to the Theory of Intellectual Inhibition. In *The Collected Works of Melanie Klein, Volume I – "Love, Guilt and Reparation" and Other Works 1921–1945*. London, Karnac Books, 2017.
Klein, M. (1935). A Contribution to the Psychogenesis of Manic-Depressive States. In *The Collected Works of Melanie Klein, Volume I – "Love, Guilt and Reparation" and Other Works 1921–1945*. London, Karnac Books, 2017.

Klein, M. (1940). Mourning and Its Relation to Manic-Depressive States. In *The Collected Works of Melanie Klein, Volume I – "Love, Guilt and Reparation" and Other Works 1921–1945*. London, Karnac Books, 2017.

Leopardi, G. (2017). *Letters of Giacomo Leopardi 1817–1837*, selected and translated by Prue Shaw. Abingdo, Routledge.

Manica, M. (1999). *Guardare nell'ombra. Saggi per una psichiatria psicoanalitica*. Roma, Borla.

Manica, M. and Oldoini, M. G. (2014). *Esiste Una Cura Per L'uomo Dei Lupi? Rot-Ture Nella Clinica, Rotture Nella Teoria*. Xvii Congresso Nazionale Della Spi, Milano, 22–25 Maggio.

Ogden, T. H. (1989). *The Primitive Edge of Experience*. Northvale, Jason Aronson.

Ricoeur, P. (1970). *Freud and Philosophy: An Essay on Interpretation* (translated by Denis Savage). New Haven, Yale University Press.

Rilke, R. M. (1923). *Duino Elegies*. Manchester, Carcanet Press Ltd; New edition (1 July 1989).

Rilke, R. M. (1875–1926). *Letters to a Young Poet*, translated by R. Snell. New York, Dover, 2012.

Scheler, M. (1916). *Formalism in Ethics and Non-Formal Ethics of Values*, edited by M. S. Frings and R. L. Funk. Evanston, Northwestern University Press, 1973.

Schneider, K. (1955). Zur Differentialdiagnose Der Depressionszustände. *Fortschritte Der Neurologie-Psychiatrie*, 23, pp. 1–6.Weil, S. (1947). *The Notebooks of Simone Weil*. Abingdon, Routledge, 2004.

Tucker, W., Tucker, K. (1988). *The Dark Matter: Contemporary Science's Quest for Hidden Mass in our Universe*. New York, William Morrow.

Weitbrecht, H. J. (1963). *Psychiarie im Grundriss*. Berlin, Springer.

Winnicott, D. W. (1963). Fear of breakdown. In *Psychoanalytic Explorations*. London: Karnac Books (1989).

Index

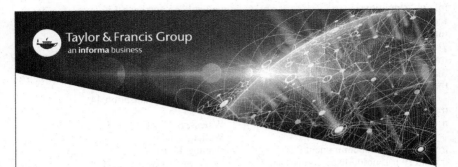